Disclaimer

Please be advised, while every effort was made to provide the best in quality and accuracy, all comments and narratives are opinion and do not necessarily reflect the correct methods of construction, real time field assessment of the material item or structure or have complete or full interpretation of any specific code referenced.

All the information contained in this book/documentation is published in good faith and is intended for inspectors, contractors, related entities and for general information purposes only. Though every effort was exhausted to ensure the most accuracy, we do not make any warranties for the completeness and accuracy and as stated above, pertaining to any content within this book.

By using this book/documentation, you acknowledge any use of the information within this book/documentation is completely at your own risk and Paradygm Forms Software LLC, the author and any affiliates are held harmless. Paradygm Forms Software LLC, the author or any of their affiliates and associates hold no liability for any losses and/or damages in connection with the use or misuse of any information contained in this book/document; have no relation to the governmental agencies, private laboratories, businesses, products or any entities named or links provided to these entities within this book. We have no control over the contents and nature of these sites and/or the links to other websites we have indicated in the book and do not imply a recommendation for all the content found on these sites.

The purchaser, herein named "the purchaser", having in their possession, proof of purchase, may use all comments and narratives within this book/documentation, for their personal use, for inspections and/or reports personally performed by the purchaser for individual clients. Comments or material reprinted in physical or digital platforms for the purchasers' individual clients, must be for and within the body of a larger report structure, where the report is intended to report on the present conditions of the structure or specific system. Reprints of this book in paper, any digital media, in any format for anyone else but the purchaser, or for any more than one PC, iOS, android or apple device is strictly prohibited.

The purchaser may make one back up copy solely for back up purposes. The original and the one copy must reside on the device the purchase has originally been made on or is the sole device that is used in conjunction with the book or its content and no other copies are on any other device OR one copy may be stored on an external media storage item that is a flash drive, SD or Micro SD card, CD, DVD or any other storage device that is not a hard drive or related device.

The contents of all material available in this book/documentation are copyrighted unless otherwise indicated. All rights are reserved and content may not be reproduced, downloaded, disseminated, published, or transferred in any form or by any means for any other reason other than what's stated herein. All content is subject to copyright and may not be reproduced in any form without express written consent of the author.

This book/documentation is designed to provide information on Home/Building Inspection only. This information is provided and sold with the knowledge that the publisher and author do not offer any legal or other professional advice. In the case of a need for any such expertise, consult with the appropriate professional. This book/documentation does not contain all information available on any single subject matter. This book/documentation has not been created to be specific to any individual's or organizations' situation or needs. Every effort has been made to make this book/documentation as accurate as possible. However, there may be typographical and or content errors. Therefore, this book/documentation should serve only as a general guide and not as the ultimate source of subject information. This book/documentation contains information that might be dated. If you are in possession of an outdated or older version, because codes and material methods change from time to time, the contents should be intended only to educate and entertain. The author and publisher shall have no liability or responsibility to any person or entity regarding any loss or damage incurred, or alleged to have incurred, directly or indirectly, by the information contained in this book/documentation. By using and/or reading this book in any way and to any degree, acknowledges that you agree to the terms in the aforementioned disclaimer and hereby agree to be bound by this disclaimer in its entirety.

This page is intentionally left blank.

Introduction

Before I started in the inspection field, I was well on my way into the carpentry and handyman fields. I remember when I was just 6 years old, I kicked a wall. To my surprise, my foot didn't stop at the wall, it had other plans. When my father returned home that evening, he gave me an offer I couldn't refuse, I can either fix the wall, or he would fix me. I did the best papier Mache a 6 year old could do. I think he realized my very low chance for success. While I think he was trying to teach me not to make the same mistake, I can't help but remember my father repairing the holes he frequently created. I also remembered my 1st grade "project" using papier Mache. After some coordinating and lots of hard work shoving newspaper in the wall soaked in joint compound, and then layering the surface with sheets of paper, in hopes to make a plush surface, it was repaired! No more hole!

Looking back now, I can only imagine how uneven and cracked my patch job was, when it started peeling off in layers to when my father re-repaired it. I was however; left with the impression I repaired it. From that day on I was hooked. I knew no problem came without a solution. As a kid, I had a sort of OCD (obsessive compulsive disorder) to disassemble and reassemble all my electronics. I had to know the inner workings. Most of the time, to my dismay, I was unsuccessful in the re-assembly process.

I believe with knowledge comes great responsibility and in the field of inspections, that is to communicate effectively and efficiently. Unfortunately, sometimes it takes much more time in writing one simple narrative, even a simple comment. Over the years of constant educational courses and in my field experience, having seen over a 1000 buildings a year, I developed basic narrative templates. It was to help my own customers and agents in explaining the most common of problems on a building. As all of us quality obsessed inspectors know, the write up is the most exhausting time. There are what seem to be endless narratives and comments to be written. Many home and commercial building clients are first time buyers or know little in regards to materials, their defects and resulting present and future damage that can progress. Some years back I took a look at all the comments and narratives relating to so many building inspections, I knew I had to get this out to my fellow inspectors. It took so many hours and countless days and nights to accumulate the knowledge and to provide it in each narrative so as to explain the details of the deficiency while in many cases, providing full recommendations.

Throughout the last 18 years, I have been inspecting commercial and residential structures. The endless hours of studying and the constant testing, most assume will subside over the years. With constant new developments in technology and building materials, there is simply no end. It is great to have at our disposal, thousands and thousands of pages of code and hours in the field attaining the knowledge of how thousands of different possible ways products degrade. While it sure is nice to attain all the knowledge and collect all the costly books, then relay all that in a way that can relay the defect to the lay person for them to understand it, there has to be a more efficient way to narrow the process down, saving countless hours of time. So over the last ten years I have been documenting the most common and some not so common defects, seen in homes throughout the country. As you will see, there is no shortage of code references, recommendations or descriptions of materials and how they degrade.

In 2008, I became a member of the International Association of Home Inspectors. I have performed 6 home renovations before, during and after the market crash of 2008, personally feeling the ups and sudden downs of the market and industry. In 2010, when state licensing in Florida was established, I became state licensed as a home inspector and in 2013, I became an all lines insurance adjuster in the State of Florida.

I was always fiddling with basic dynamic form creation and sought to create an innovative form and program system to really make a single inspector or small firm compete with the big boys and in 2014, I founded Paradygm Forms Software LLC, a software startup company. I have worked in construction on residential commercial buildings for other companies, from installing the pilasters and crown moldings throughout the Trump Ballroom on the Kellogg Estate in Florida, a meticulous task of sculpting the hemp meshed plaster casted crown molding designs and angels before paint and gold leafing was applied to hotel and bar renovations. From small residential home renovations to complete rehabilitations on prior investments. The most experience an inspector can have is actual field experience, first in construction to provide an installer's perspective and then a seasoned length of experience in inspecting the systems as they degrade. Like most inspector, when I first came on the scene, I knew very little of how much my life would be entrenched in the books.

New to the industry? This book can be your saving grace, giving you virtually everything you need to diagnose, explain and even recommend what to do to remediate the general defect. With this book, new and seasoned inspectors alike may be able to reduce their work load by hours a day. No more referencing several different codes to assess a single area or to comprise a single comment. All the narratives were pain stakingly thought out so as to reflect on both residential and commercial/residential buildings, in both terminology and the legal aspects in the framing of the narratives, while still providing a lengthy detail to express the issues. Many comments are also included to provide building owners with a general understanding of the materials in the structure, such as pipe materials, siding, roofing, drainage, fencing, driveways, sidewalks, foundations and various other systems material types and descriptions. This is especially useful with a newer home that may have little to no defects. With little to reference in the report, the client may feel cheated or short changed, even though you provided everything you should have. However, when some references to materials and there common benefits and attributes/defects are added to a report, it provides the "beef" to help your client feel they left with something informative, as they expected and more. As I have seen countless times through the years in my business, referrals increased substantially as I perfected my style of integrating these descriptions into the report. I have spent years of my life compiling these narratives in the hopes that others do not have to.

"Life is worth living." **With this book you can start living life, not working.** All you have to do is point and click or "copy and paste", that simple.

Daniel Zevetchin

Acknowledgements

In the course of compiling the book this last year, it has been a constant roller coaster. Between performing inspections full time to running and developing our websites, creating a startup, learning and developing code for software, referencing and constantly studying code for this book, writing and compiling the book, editing etcetera. None of it could have been possible without my team, whom were the driving force responsible for getting this book completed.

First, I would like to thank my editor, Nancy J. Berghammer. She is an outstanding team member and was absolutely crucial with her help in making this happen. I simply cannot thank her enough.

To my wife, my very patient beautiful wife, Ashley who has endured so many late nights dealing with my incessant studying. She is one to whom I can't thank enough for her determined, continued patience with me and her true worth as a partner both in life as well as in all our mutual business aspirations. She has been the pinnacle of my life and temperance, to stay the course.

To my father, Terry Bleistein who gave me the disciplines, determination, and work ethics that were needed to keep me going. We have worked side by side for nearly 2 decades in this field. I would not have even heard of the inspection industry if it wasn't for him. He is a true hero and mentor in my life.

And to all those who have helped in the course of my career, in construction, business and life, thank you so much. Your efforts were not in vein.

This page is intentionally left blank.

Table of Contents

FENCES; TYPES 1
PVC Fence 1
Wood Privacy Fence 1
Tips for Making your Wooden Fence Last Longer 1
Stock Fencing 2
Various Burrows Observed at Various Fencing Sections at Grade 2
Loose Post Observed 2
No Post Concrete Footers Observed; Posts Enter Grade 2
PVC Post Caps Broken/Missing at Posts 2
Neighboring Tree Heaving Fence Section/Post 2
Foliage Encumbers Fencing Sections 2
Gate Obstructed by Walkway 2
Gate Obstructed by Grading/Vegetation 2
Gate Latches Do Not Engage; Door is not Aligned/Sags uneven from Latching Properly when Closing 2
Gate Hardware Missing 2
Gate Hardware Appeared Loose 3
Gate Hardware Appeared Loose; Wood Appeared Rotted at the Fasteners Locations 3
Wood Members Suspected to be Rotting 3
Iron Stains Observed on Fencing 3
Excessive Wood Warping Observed 3
Wood Warping 3
Top Railing to Chain Link Fence is Damaged 4
Various Boards are Broken, Several Posts are Leaning/Warped and Fence Shows Excessive Algae
    Accumulation 4
Oxidation Visible on Fittings and Hinges to the Gate/Fence Sections 4
Oxidation Visible on Fittings and Aluminum Fence Sections 4
Fencing: Potential Termite Damage Observed. No live Termites Observed 4
Potential Termite Damage Observed. Suspected Live Formosan Subterranean Termites Observed ... 5
Potential Termite Damage Observed. Suspected Live Drywood Termites Observed 5

RETAINING WALLS 6
Reinforced Retaining Wall 6
Masonry and Concrete: Residential Construction 6
Mechanically Stabilized Earth Retaining Walls 6
Gravity Retaining Walls 6
Basic Comments Overview/Degradation Process: Retaining Walls 7
Preemptions and Maintenance Comments for Sea Walls 7
Treated Wood and Retaining Walls 7
Vinyl Composite Sea Wall 7
Heavy Surface Oxidation to Exposed Thread Bar, Bolt and Plates that Fasten the Deadman/Tie Backs 7
Foliage Overgrowth Encumbers the Retaining Wall. Cannot Fully Inspect 8
Expansion Cracks Observed. Suspect Steel Oxidation Expansion from Rebar 8
No Expansion Joint Sealant Observed at the Expansion Joints 8
Repairing/Replacing Wood Retaining Wall 8
Retaining Wall is Overturning (eccentricity) and/or the Bearing Capacity is Insufficient 8
Retaining Wall is Sliding 9
Small Retaining Wall is overturning (eccentricity) and/or the Bearing Exceeds its Structural Capacity 9
Small Retaining Wall at the Parking Area is overturning (eccentricity) and/or the
    Bearing Exceeds its Structural Capacity 9
Suspect Improper Swale at the Retaining Wall Back Face Top 9
Excessive Wood Rotting Observed 9
Tree Roots from Neighboring Tree(s) are Causing Significant Heaving to the Retaining Wall 10

Potential Termite Damage Observed. Suspected Live Formosan Subterranean Termites Observed 10
Concrete Retaining Wall Horizontal Cracking Observed 10
Retaining Wall Vertical/Diagonal Cracks Observed 10
Gravity Retaining Wall is in Disrepair, Sliding/Displaced Sections Throughout 10
Sliding/Displaced Sections Throughout 11

SIDEWALKS 12
Exposed Aggregate 12
Concrete 12
Concrete Pavers 13
Brick 13
Treated Wood 13
Fiberglass/Composite Decking 13
Trip Hazard. Uneven Pavers Observed 13
Vegetation Growth through Brick/Paver Joints and Excess Algae found at the Time of Inspection 14
Concrete Walkways; Moisture Cracking from Weathering Observed 14
Small Stone Gravity Retaining Wall at the Sidewalk is Overturning and/or Bearing
      Exceeds Structural Capacity 14
Center Crack in Sectioned/Jointed Poured Concrete 14
Slight Algae Growth on Walkway 14
Excessive Suspected Algae Growth on Walkway 14
No Expansion Joint Sealant Observed at the Expansion Joints 14
Tree Roots from Neighboring Tree and Significant Heaving to the Sidewalk(s) Midsection 15
Tree Roots from Neighboring Tree and Significant Settlement to the Sidewalk(s) Midsections 15
Paver Joint Sand Appears Insufficiently Applied Between the Pavers/Joints 15
Iron Stains Observed on Sidewalks 15
Foliage Obstructs the Path of the Walkway 15
Trip Hazard; Concrete Sidewalk was observed Dilapidated with Cubicle Cracking and Spalling 15

DRIVEWAYS 16
Concrete 16
Concrete Pavers 16
Exposed Aggregate 16
Brick 16
Treated Wood 17
Asphalt 17
Fiberglass/Composite Decking 17
Iron Stains Observed on Driveways 17
No Expansion Joint Sealant Observed at the Expansion Joints 17
Gravel is Displaced Throughout 18
Center Crack in Sectioned/Jointed Poured Concrete 18
Pavers Appeared Installed Improperly Over Sand 18
Adhesive Sand Appears Liberally Applied Between the Pavers/Joints 18
Tree(s) Heaving Grading at the Driveway 18
Excessive Oil Spots Observed 18
Vehicle Loading Cracks Observed on the Driveway 18
Progressive Vehicle Loading Cracks on Driveway 19
Parking Markings Faded/Missing 19
Vegetation Growth through Cracks/Joints and Excess Algae Found at the Time of Inspection 19
Algae Growth on Driveway 19
Subsidence Suspected; Significant Settlement and Cracks Observed 19
Concrete Driveways; Moisture Cracking from Weathering Observed 19
Asphalt Fatigue (Alligator) Cracking Observed 19
Block Cracking Observed on the Asphalt 19
Edge Cracks to Asphalt Observed 20
Settlement/Grade Depression(s) Observed in the Asphalt 20

PATIOS 21
Exposed Aggregate 21
Concrete 21
Fiberglass/Composite Decking 21
Concrete Pavers 21

Door Closer Inoperable on Screened/Storm Door to the Patio Enclosure ... 22
Door Closer Missing on Screened/Storm Door to Patio ... 22
Treated Wood ... 22
Leaf Debris Observed Covering the Patio ... 22
Tree Roots Heaving/Subsidence Suspected ... 22
Concrete Pool Deck; Moisture and Basic Settlement Cracks Observed ... 22
Trip Hazard. Uneven Pavers Observed ... 23
Pool Wall Inlet(s) Apparatus Observed Damaged/Missing ... 23
Pool Marcite/Plaster Coating was Observed Etching at the Time of the Inspection ... 23
Iron Stains Observed on Patio ... 23
No Expansion Joint Sealant Observed at the Expansion Joints ... 23
Algae Growth on the Patio Observed ... 23
Tree(s) Heaving Grading at the Patio ... 24
Pavers Appeared Installed Improperly Over Sand ... 24
Adhesive Sand Appears Liberally Applied Between the Pavers/Joints ... 24
Vegetation Growth through Cracks/Joints and Slight Algae found at the Time of Inspection ... 24
Erosion Observed at the Patio from Lack of Gutters/Downspouts at the Location ... 24
Concrete Moisture Cracks Observed ... 24
Brick Mortar Deterioration Observed ... 24
Deterioration of Brick Observed ... 25
Uneven Settlement Observed at the Patio/Building Abutment ... 25
Salt Spalling Observed ... 25
Basic Cracks in the Concrete Floor ... 25
Settlement Crack Observed ... 25
Erosion Observed at the Patio from Gutter Downspouts Terminating at the Location ... 25
Trip Hazard. Uneven Pavers Observed ... 26
Loose/Leaning Rail Observed ... 26
Exposed Rebar Observed at the Patio Concrete Slab ... 26
Concrete Patios; Cubicle/Moisture Cracking from Weathering Observed ... 26
Wood Deck Plank Boards are Warping/Loose and Can Pose a Trip Hazard ... 26
No Railing Observed at the Time of the Inspection ... 26
Loose Railing Observed ... 27

PATIO COVERS ... 28
Thermoplastic Polyolefin (TPO) Membrane ... 28
Modified Bitumen Roll Roofing ... 28
Bitumen Rolled Roofing ... 28
Spray Polyurethane Foam Roofing with Elastomeric ... 28
Galvanized Metal Panel Roof Upkeep Comments ... 29
Aluminum Panel Screws Need Maintenance ... 29
Aluminum Raised Seam Metal Roof ... 29
UV Exposure Appears to have Caused Significant Wear to the Skylight Dome, causing Cracking/Damage ... 29
Rusted Galvanized Drip Edge Flashing Observed ... 29
Basic Shingle Maintenance Comments (Architectural) ... 29
Popped Nail(s) Observed at the Roof Cover ... 30
Missing/Damaged Crown Shingle(s) Observed ... 30
Basic Shingle Maintenance Comments (3 Tab) ... 30
Basic Tile Algae/Fungi Maintenance Comments ... 30
End Cap Crown Shingle(s) Nail Fasteners Need Sealant ... 30
Missing/Damaged Shingle(s) Observed ... 30
Compromise along the Seam/Flashing, where the Patio Roof meets the Fascia ... 30
Posts/Columns Span is Too Far Spaced and can be Structurally Compromised ... 30
Aluminum Panel Seam and Screws Need Maintenance ... 31
Excess Debris Buildup/Screw Oxidation Observed ... 31
Modified Bitumen Roll Roof has "Bubbles" Observed ... 31
End Caps to Ridge Vent Missing ... 31
Compromise to the Aluminum Ridge Vent Flashing Viewed from Exterior/Interior ... 31
Ridge Vent(s) Fasteners Observed Loose with Insufficient Sealants ... 31
Kick out Flashing Not Observed ... 31
Lanai Fastener/Mounting Screws Oxidation Observed ... 31

Modified Bitumen Roll Roof has "Ponding" Observed 32
Fractured Plank Board Decking Observed in the Attic System at the Time of the Inspection 32
Visible Compromise to the Drip Edge Flashing to the Soffit/Eave Viewed from Exterior 32
Compromises/Lifting along the Seams 32
Potential Termite Damage Observed. Suspected Formosan Termites Observed 32
Post 2000 Installed Membrane; Crescent Fractures Observed to the Roof Surface 32
Post 2000 Installed Membrane; Star Fractures Observed to the Roof Surface 33
Compromises/Lifting along the Seams – PRE 2001 Roof Covers 33
Wood Fascia Paint is Peeling/Chipping is and Appears Unsealed at Sections with Surface Fungi 34
Various Areas of the Lanai were Observed Cut/Ripped or Worn 34
Tree Limbs Observed Touching the Roof Surface 34
Composition Asphalt Roof Cover Observed On a Slight Slope/Flat Roof 34
Seals at Vents/Stacks and Roof Transitions are Insufficient/Antiquated 34
Compromise Suspected at the Apron/Counter Flashing/Exterior Wall Abutment. Visible Water Stains ...34
Metal Roof Panel Is Rusted/Corroded. Galvanized Fasteners Observed Rusting/Corroded 34

DECKS/PORCHES 35
Exposed Aggregate 35
Aluminum Siding 35
Stone 35
Galvanized Steel Siding 35
Hardboard 35
Masonry Block Recladding 36
Brick Veneer 36
Asphalt Shingle Siding 36
Manufactured Stone 36
Cement Fiber (Hardi) Siding 36
Stucco 37
Asbestos Cement-Based Siding 37
Clay and Slate Siding General Comments 37
Slab on Grade, Exposed Aggregate Finish 37
Fiberglass/Composite Decking 38
Concrete 38
Concrete Pavers 38
Treated Wood 38
Paint/Primer Seal Insufficient at the Base of the Wall 38
Significant Settlement/Spalling Cracks 38
Stucco Cladding on Frame Structure Abuts Grading; Inhibited from Expelling Moisture 39
Loose Posts Suspected at the Wood Dock 39
Vinyl Siding Abuts Grading; Moisture is inhibited from Expelling Moisture at the Siding Base 39
Iron Stains Observed on Porches 39
Iron Stains Observed on Decking 39
Suspected Excessive Wood Rotting Observed 40
Pool Marcite/Plaster Coating was Observed Etching at the Time of the Inspection 40
Ceramic Tile Flooring Exposed to the Elements and could Pose a Trip Hazard 40
Trip Hazard. Uneven Pavers Observed 40
Algae Growth on the Porch Observed 40
Erosion Observed at the Porch from Gutter Downspouts Terminating at the Location 40
Tree Roots Heaving/Subsidence Suspected 41
Posts/Columns Span is too far spaced and can be Structurally Compromised 41
Tree(s) Heaving Grading at the Porch 41
Adhesive Sand Appears Liberally Applied Between the Pavers/Joints 41
Door Closer Missing on Screened/Storm Door to Porch 41
Moisture and Basic Settlement Cracks Observed on the Concrete Pool Deck 41
Concrete Moisture Cracks Observed 41
Brick Mortar Deterioration Observed 42
Deterioration of Brick Observed 42
Deterioration of Brick Foundation Piers Observed 42
Uneven Settlement Observed at the Porch/Building Abutment 42
Salt Spalling Observed 42

Basic Cracks in the Concrete Floor 42
Tree Roots from Neighboring Tree; Significant Settlement to the Porch/Deck Slab Midsection(s) 43
Balustrade; Various Loose Balusters Observed 43
Loose Hand Rail Mounts/Fasteners Observed 43
Bannister/Rail to Stairs Dilapidated 43
Corroded Screws Observed. Various Plank Boards Loose Throughout 43
Concrete Porch; Cubicle/Moisture Cracking from Weathering Observed 43
Ballasts Are Spread Too Far Apart, Exceeding 3 ½ inches Width 43
Chalking Observed to the Exterior Vinyl Siding 43
Wood Deck Plank Boards are Warping/Loose and can Pose a Trip Hazard 44
Hardi-Siding Lap Board Fasteners Missing at Various Joints/Areas 44
Suspected Rot Observed at the Base of the Column 44
Loose Railing Observed 44

PORCH ROOF COVERS 45

Raised Seam Metal Roof 45
Popped Nail(s) Observed at the Roof Cover 45
Missing/Damaged Crown Shingle(s) Observed 45
End Cap Crown Shingle(s) Nail Fasteners Need Sealant 45
Missing/Damaged Shingle(s) Observed 45
Aluminum Panel; Compromise along the Seam/Roofing Tape 45
Aluminum Panel Screws Need Maintenance 46
Excess Debris Buildup/Screw Oxidation Observed 46
Fractured Plank Board Decking Observed in the Attic System at the Time of the Inspection 46
Modified Bitumen Roll Roofing 46
Rolled Roofing 46
Modified Bitumen Roll Roof has "Bubbles" Observed 46
Modified Bitumen Roll Roof has "Ponding" Observed 47
Visible Compromise to the Drip Edge Flashing at the Soffit/Fascia Viewed from the Exterior Eaves .. 47
Rusted/Corroded Galvanized Drip Edge Flashing Observed 47
UV Exposure Appears to have Caused Significant Wear to the Skylight Dome,
    Causing Cracking/Damage 47
Screws/Nails Penetrating the Roof Deck at Vent Hoods are Not Sealed 47
Screws/Nails at the Eaves Observed Penetrating the Roof Cover/Flashing 47
Curling Asphalt Shingles Observed 47
Compromises/Lifting along the Seams 48
PVC/TPO Roofing Membrane 48
Post 2000 Installed Membrane: Crescent Fractures Observed to the Roof Surface 48
Post 2000 Installed Membrane: Star Fractures Observed to the Roof Surface 48
Compromises/Lifting along the Seams 48
Tree Limbs Observed Touching the Roof Surface 48
PRE 2001 Roof Covers Installation; Star or Crescent Damages 48
End Caps to Ridge Vent Missing 49
Wood Fascia Paint is Peeling/Chipping is and Appears Unsealed at Sections with Surface Fungi 49
Seals at Vents/Stacks and Roof Transitions are Insufficient/Antiquated 49
Compromise Suspected at the Apron/Counter Flashing/Exterior Wall Abutment. Visible Water Stains 49
Metal Roof Panel is Rusted/Corroded. Galvanized Fasteners Observed Rusting/Corroded 49
Loose Railing Observed 50

LANDSCAPE 51

Yard Shows Signs of Loss of Life Possibly Due to Pests, Disease and/or Poor Maintenance 51
Weeds Growing Through Xeriscape 51
Yard Shows Signs of Loss of Life at Front Possibly Due to Poor Maintenance from Inoperable Sprinkler(s) 51
Excessive Overgrowth and Leaf Debris Buildup 51
Swales Observed Intermittently in the Yard 51
Tree/Brush Overgrowth Encumbering Walkways 52
St. Augustine Grass, Associated Issues and Things to Preempt 52
Bahia Lawns, Associated Issues and Things to Preempt 52
Bermuda, Associated Issues and Things to Preempt 52
Carpet Grass, Associated Issues and Things to Preempt 53
Kentucky Bluegrass, Associated Issues and Things to Preempt 53

Perennial Ryegrass, Associated Issues and Things to Preempt 53

GRADING 55

The Structure is on a Hill and Lacks Proper Run Off at/around the Walls Facing the Uphill Location 55
Tree Roots Encumbers the Building 55
Widespread Sogginess near Landscaping around the Building 55
Tree Roots Encumber Building/Yard Furrows 56
Tree(s) Heaving Grading around Building - No Heaving of Foundation Yet 56
Vinyl Siding Abuts Grading; Moisture is inhibited from Expelling at the Siding Base 56
Grading Slope appears Progressive; Caused by Erosion or was Formed Improper during Construction 56
Rot/Mossy Surfaces Observed, Indicative of Ponding 56
Erosion around the Perimeter of the Building from Lack of Gutters/Partial Gutters 56
Erosion around the Perimeter of the Building under the Eaves Due to Lack of Guttering 57
Swales Observed at the Corners of the Building; where Downspouts Terminate 57
Swales Observed at the Corners of the Building 57

EXTERIOR 58

No Deficiencies; Commercial Buildings 58
No Deficiencies; Standard Buildings 58
Vegetation Growth through Cracks/Joints and Excess Algae found at the Time of Inspection 58
No Expansion Joint Sealant Observed at the Expansion Joints 58
Concrete Stairways; Moisture Cracking from Weathering Observed 59
Algae Growth on Stairway 59
Iron Stains Observed on Stairway(s) 59
Loose Hand Rail Mounts/Fasteners Observed 59
No Graspable Hand Rail at the Stairway 59
Wood Rot Observed at the Exterior Wood Stairs 59
Excessive Wood Warping Observed 60
Wood Stairs; Suspected Termite Damage. No Live Termites Observed 60
Stair Treads are coated with a Slippery Gloss Coating 60
Potential Termite Damage Observed. Live Formosan Subterranean Termites Observed 60
Potential Termite Damage Observed. Live Drywood Termites Suspected/Observed 61
Stairway Path/Width is Insufficient 61
Stair Treads, Rise/Runs are Uneven 61
Loose/Damaged Stair Treads Observed 61
Balustrade; Various Loose Balusters Observed 61
Bannister/Rail Dilapidated 61
Bannister/Rail Insufficient to Safety Standards 62
Railing is Greater than 36 inches in Height 62
Railing is Less than 36 inches in Height 62
Ballasts are Spread Too Far Apart, Exceeding 3 ½ inches Width 62
Wood Stringer Attachment(s); Missing/Damaged Support(s) 62
Bannister/Rail Not Observed at Stairway(s) 62
Newell Post(s) Loose 62
Tree Roots from the Neighboring Tree appear to be Causing Significant Heaving to the Stairs 62
No Railing Observed at the Time of the Inspection 63

WINDOWS/DOORS; TRIM 64

Flashing at the Window Suspected Improper. Water Intrusion found at the Windows Interior/Trim 64
Improperly Installed Integral Finned Window. Drywall Screws Used/Application Improper 64
Improperly Installed Window. Drywall Screws Used 65
Broken Glass Pane(s) Observed. Suspect Sheer Stresses 65
Iron Stains Observed on Window/Door Trim 65
Sliding Door Lock Latch Damaged 65
Sliding Doors Inoperable due to Excess Dirt, Debris and Resin Causing the Track to be Obstructed 65
Defective/Loose Single Hung Balance Spring Observed at the Window 65
Various Defective/Loose Single Hung Balance Springs Observed at the Window 65
Laminated Cabinet Doors Delaminating Starting at the Edges/Seams 65
Missing Glass Pane(s) Observed 65
Windows Sealed Shut 66
Various Crank Windows will Not Open Due to Inoperable/Missing Mechanical Components 66
Hollow Core Door used on the Egress to the Buildings Garage 66

Windows Seals and Weather Stripping Compromised/Antiquated 66
Various Screens were Observed Cut/Ripped at Window(s) 66
Windows/Doors Need Basic Lubricants/Servicing 66
Sliding Doors Need Basic Lubricants/Servicing 66
Single Hung Windows Were Not Operable at the Time of the Inspection 66
Wood Rot Observed at the Base of the Egress Door Frame 66
Wood Rot Observed at and Around the Window(s) Frame 67
Window Screen Missing 67
Wood Warping Observed at the Windows/Trim 67
Wood Warping Observed at the Doors/Trim 67
Suspected Formosan Subterranean Termites/Tunnels (Coptotermes formosanus) Observed 68
Drywood Termites/Damage Suspected 68
Older Subterranean/Drywood Damage Suspected 68
Hollow Core Door Used on the Exterior Egress to the Building 68
Wood Window Screwed/Sealed Shut 68
Broken Glass Pane(s) Observed 69
Double Dead Bolt Observed at the Door(s) 69
Window Lock Latch Handle Broke 69
Various Window Lock Latch(es) were Observed Broke at Multiple Windows 69
Sticking Doors and Windows Observed. Possible Differential Settlement 69
Interior; Forced Entry Damage Observed at the Door/Frame 69
Interior Door(s) Missing 69
Window Servicing Tilt Latch(es) were Observed Broke at Several Windows 69
Drywall Screws Observed Fastening Most Windows 69
Decorative Exterior Window Sashes Broken, Displaced or Missing 69
Base Board Door Stops Damaged/Missing 69
Window(s) Double Pane Seals Compromised 69
Window/Door Trim Observed has Paint Chipping/Peeling and Various Caulk Seals Compromised 70
Exterior Window Head Cap Flashing Not Observed 70
Doors Seals and Weather Stripping Compromised/Antiquated 70
Screens Weathered/Antiquated at Window(s) 70
Door Knob/Hardware was Loose at the Time of the Inspection 71

HOSE BIBS 72

Back Flow Preventers-Equipped-No Deficiencies 72
No Back Flow Preventers Observed at the Time of the Inspection 72
PR or Pressure Relief Valve at Spigot Leaks at Threading 72
Low Water Pressure Observed 72
Spigot/Pipe Loose at the Wall 72
PR or Pressure Relief Valve at Spigot Leaks at the Relief Hole 72
Spigot Shut off Handle for the Gate Valve is Missing/Damaged 73
Hose Spigot; Leak at Stem 73
Lime Scale or Calcium Carbonate fouling on Spigot Valve Joint 73
Spigot Seized/Inoperable at the Time of the Inspection 73
Spigot Inoperable at the Time of the Inspection 73
Low Pressure Observed. Suspect Galvanized Pipe Oxidation Is Constricting 73

SPRINKLERS 74

With Pump 74
Sprinkler Pump was Observed Not Mounted/Secured 74
Sprinkler System has a Manual Operation Style. Could Not Inspect 74
Without Pump 74
Sprinkler Head Partial Damage Observed at the Sprinkler Head Apparatus 75
Iron Stains Observed Due To "Hard" Well Water Sprinkler System 75
System Appears Antiquated and Inoperable at the Time of the Inspection 75
Pipe Fitting Rupture Suspected. Erosion of Soil and Water Flow Observed 75
Sprinkler Head Broken off, Small Geyser Observed at the Sprinkler Apparatus 75
Sprinkler Head Broken off, Water Bubbling from the Surface Observed at the Sprinkler Apparatus 75
Browning of Lawn; Suspect Improper Precipitation/Application Rates 75
Exposed Wires Observed, Spliced but not Sealed from the Elements 76
Recommend Installing a Rain Shut Off Device on the Irrigation System 76

Inoperable Zone(s) Observed in the Sprinkler System ... 76
Sprinkler Annunciator Control Rated Interior; Control Mounted at Exterior ... 76
Exposed PVC Pipes at Grade ... 76
Pipe Fitting/Elbow Rupture Suspected. Erosion of Soil and Water Flow Observed ... 76
Maintenance and Upkeep Considerations for your Systems ... 76
Sprinkler Controller Fuses Stated to Blow Too Often ... 77
The Timer's Display was Observed Blank when the Unit was Plugged In ... 77
The Irrigation System Does Not Water the Yard ... 77
Zone Not Working; Suspect Damaged Zone Connection ... 77

GUTTERS ... 78

Galvanized Gutters Heavily Oxidized/Rusting ... 78
Gutters Observed are Full of Debris ... 78
Compromises to Gutters/Seams. Algae/Degradation Observed to the Exterior Wall/Cladding ... 78
Loose Fasteners Observed Intermittently ... 78
Loose Fasteners Observed to the Gutter System Causing Sag/Compromises ... 79
Good Grading but No Diverters for Downspouts ... 79
Downspouts Mounting Brackets are Loose/Missing ... 79
Compromises at Various Gutters/Seams Locations ... 79
Downspouts Terminate at Foundation Wall ... 79
Downspouts/Diverters Divert Water over Walkways/Driveways; Slip Hazard ... 79
Loose Diverter(s) at the Attachment to the Downspout(s) ... 79
Erosion around the Perimeter of the Dwelling from Lack of Gutters/Partial Gutters ... 79
Erosion around the Perimeter of the Dwelling under the Eaves Due to Lack of Guttering ... 79
Erosion around the Perimeter of the Dwelling from Partial Guttering, where Gutters Are Not Present ... 79
New Structure; No Gutters Observed at the Time of the Inspection ... 80
Downspouts Missing ... 80
Sheathing Separation Observed at the Wall. Wall is bowing. No Vapor Barrier Observed ... 80

POOLS/FILLING AND COATINGS ... 81

Pool Marcite/Plaster Coating was Observed Etching at the Time of the Inspection ... 81
Pool Wall Inlet(s) Apparatus Observed Damaged/Missing ... 81
Concrete Pool Deck; Moisture and Basic Settlement Cracks Observed ... 81
No Expansion Joint Sealant Observed at the Expansion Joints on Pool Deck ... 81

EXTERIOR WALLS ... 83

Aluminum Siding ... 83
Inadequate Fastening; Loose Metal Siding at Exterior Wall ... 83
Aluminum Siding Abuts Grading; Moisture is inhibited from Expelling at the Siding Base ... 84
Siding Compromises Observed. Pipes, Conduit and Other Cut Outs through the Siding Need Sealants ... 84
Stone ... 84
Galvanized Steel Siding ... 84
Hardboard ... 84
No Expansion Joint Sealant Observed at the Expansion Joints ... 84
Previous Porch Addition; Floor Band Joist Protrudes Past the Exterior Wall ... 85
Buckling and Cracking in Hardboard Siding ... 85
Wood Siding Abuts Grading; Moisture is inhibited from Expelling at the Siding Base ... 85
Expansion and Contraction of Wood ... 85
Chalking Observed to the Exterior Vinyl Siding ... 85
Wood Siding General Comments/Maintenance ... 86
Vinyl Siding ... 86
Concrete Block Wall Cracking Suspected to be Associated with Thermal/Moisture Movement ... 86
Tree Roots Heaving/Subsidence Suspected ... 87
Vinyl Siding Chips/Damage Observed at the Base of the Wall ... 87
Vinyl Siding Abuts Grading; Moisture is inhibited from Expelling at the Siding Base ... 87
Wood Shingles and Shakes ... 87
Plywood Siding ... 87
OSB Siding ... 87
Uneven Settlement Observed at the Building Protrusion/Transition ... 87
Uneven Settlement Observed at the Building Transition/Abutment ... 88
Wood Shingle/Shake Splits Observed ... 88
Wood Shingle/Shake Warping Observed ... 88

Wood Siding Needs Various Nails Replaced 88
Pressure Treated Wood; Wood Rot Observed 88
Suspected Formosan Subterranean Termite Damage Observed. (Coptotermes Formosanus) 89
Cement Fiber Siding (Hardi-Siding) 89
Stucco and EIFS 89
Suspected Dry Wood Termite Damage Observed 89
Suspected Subterranean/Dry Wood Damage Observed 89
Missing Caulk/Sealants Fiber Cement Siding at Vertical Trim Joints and Nailing Locations Throughout 90
Inadequate Nailing of Fiber Cement Siding; Loose Siding at Exterior Wall 90
No Weep Screeds Observed at the Base of the Framed Walls Stucco Cladding 90
No Weep Screeds Observed at the Base of the Framed Walls Cladding 90
No Weep Screeds Observed at the Band Joist/2nd Floor Framed Wall to Masonry 1st Wall 90
Manufactured Stone 90
Asphalt Shingle Siding 90
Suspected Asbestos Cement-Based Siding 91
Suspected Asbestos Cement-Based Siding is Chipping, Grinding and Needs Repair 91
Siding and Trim Seams/Nails; Recommended to be Resealed where Needed 91
Efflorescence Observed on the Suspected Asbestos Cement-Based Siding 92
Suspected Asbestos Cement-Based Siding; Fasteners are Corroded, Loose or Broken 92
Clay Siding Damage Observed 92
Galvanized Stucco Casing Bead Shows Rust Oxidation/Expansion 92
Clay and Slate Siding General Comments 92
Slate Siding Damage Observed 93
Masonry Block Recladding 93
General Cracks Observed in the Masonry Wall(s) 93
Spalling Observed 93
Salt Spalling Observed to the Masonry Wall 93
Common/General Stucco Cracks Observed Due to Lack of Maintenance 94
Mortar Deterioration Observed 94
Paint Peeling Throughout the Exterior Wall Surface Intermittently 94
Paint Chalking Observed to the Exterior Paint Sealant 94
Expansion Cracks Observed at the Window Sill 94
Hairline Cracks Observed at the Window Sills 94
Progressive Expansion Cracks Observed at the Window Sill 95
Paint/Primer Seal Insufficient at the Base of the Exterior Wall 95
Significant Settlement/Spalling Cracks 95
Significant Heaving Observed to the Exterior Wall 95
Iron Stains Observed On Sidewalks 95
Brick Wall Cracking Suspected to be Associated with Thermal/Moisture Movement 95
Stucco Cladding Observed on Frame Structure Abutting Grading; Inhibited from Expelling Moisture 96
Brick Veneer 96
Hardi-Siding Lap Board Fasteners Missing at Various Joints/Areas 96
Suspect Stucco is Delaminating. No Foundation Weep Screed 96
Sheathing Separation Observed at the Wall. Wall is bowing. No Vapor Barrier Observed 96

FOUNDATION 97
No Foundation Deficiencies Observed 97
Post in Ground 2566TM 97
Stilts/Pilings 97
Concrete Slab Footing 97
Staddle Stones 98
Stem Wall Slab 98
Stem Wall Crawlspace 98
Uneven Settlement Observed at Different Slab/Level Abutments 98
Suspect Water Intrusion from Roof Compromise(s) and Runoff at the Roof/Eaves 98
No Expansion Joint Sealant Observed at the Expansion Joints 99
Masonry Brick Piers 99
Stone Foundation 99
Masonry Piers 99
Pier(s) Observed Off Center 99

MASONRY FOUNDATION/WALLS 100
Basement Concrete and Concrete Block Sealers for Basement Waterproofing.................................. 100
Rear Porch Suspected Converted to Living Area; Foundation Protrudes Past Siding 100
Dampness in Basement; Suspect Rising Damp from the Flower Base 100
Tree Roots Heaving/Subsidence Suspected 101
Suspect Water Intrusion from Rain Runoff at the Roof/Eaves; Deposits on Walls Upper Mortar Joints 101
Suspect Water Intrusion at the Mid to Lower Foundation Wall; Efflorescence at the
    Walls Mortar Joints Observed 101
Pressure Treated Wood; General Wood Rot Comments to Damaged Wood Observed 101
Formosan Subterranean Termite Damage Suspected. (Coptotermes Formosanus) 102
Suspected Dry Wood Termite Damage Observed.. 102
Suspected Subterranean/Dry wood Damage Observed 102
General Wood Rot Comments to Damage Wood Observed 102
Wood Rot Suspected at the Crawlspace/Basement of the Subfloors Outer Wood Sill, Band Joist
    and/or Band Joist Abutment 103
Salt Spalling Observed.. 103
Efflorescence Observed 103
Greenish Colored Efflorescence Suspected at the Basement/Foundation Wall 103
General Concrete Moisture Cracks... 103
General Cracks in the Concrete Floor... 104
Mortar and Step Crack Patterns in the Dwellings Exterior, Crawl Space or Foundational Walls Observed 104
No Significant Settlement Cracks to the Wall; Foundation Cracks Observed Through the Interior Tile.
    No Exterior Wall Settlement Observed... 104
Tree(s) Heaving Grading around Building; No Heaving of the Foundation Observed 104
Foundation Drainage Panels Recommended around the Building for Proper Drainage 104
Pier Settlement Observed.. 105
Masonry Wall Cracks Observed; Suspect Pier Settlement 105
Horizontal Foundation Wall Cracks Located at Mid-Wall Height.. 105
Horizontal Foundation Cracks Located Low on a Foundation Wall 105
Pier Settlement Observed; Vertical Cracking or Bulging to the Piers Observed............................... 105
Frost-Heaving of the Footing or Piers 105
Tree Roots Encumbering the Foundation 105

ADDITIONAL CRAWL/SUBFLOOR COMMENTS 106
No Railing Observed at the Time of the Inspection.. 106
No Metal Termite Flashing Observed 106
Floor/Joists Sagging Observed 106
Brick Piers are Eroding and should be Replaced 106
Piers Appear Insufficient for the Dead and Live Load Requirements 106
Girder Observed Shows a Visible Sag... 107
Joist(s) Observed appear to have Slid Off the Ledger/Sill 107
Improper Shimmying at the Pier(s) Observed 107
Floor/Joists Sagging Observed. Abutting Joists did not appear to be Supported at the Abutment/Joint............ 107

ROOFING 108
Basic Architectural Shingle Comments 108
Basic Composition Shingle Comments 108
Spray Polyurethane Foam Roofing System with Elastomeric Basic Comments............................... 108
Tar and Gravel Roof Cover is Antiquated and Should Be Replaced 109
Various Concrete Tiles Observed with Hairline Chips/Cracks 109
Suspected Tree Limb Damaged/Missing Shingle Tab Observed at the Eave 109
Metal Panel Roof Compromises along the Seams 109
Metal Panel Roof Upkeep Comments... 109
Damaged/Missing Shingle Tab(s) Observed at the Eave(s) 109
Common Black Algae/Lichen Observed on the Concrete Tile 109
Cracked Tile Observed 109
Leaf Debris at Valleys and Various Locations on the Roof.. 109
Trees Touching/Encumbering Roof Eave 109
Ridge Vent Nailing Sealant Missing/Insufficient.. 110
Cracking/Damage and Chipping was evident at the Skylight Dome/Fasteners Area 110
Tree Limbs Observed Touching the Roof Surface 110

Popped Nail(s) Observed at the Roof Cover...110
Wood Fascia Paint is Peeling/Chipping and Appears Unsealed at Sections with Suspected Surface Fungi.....110
Loose Screws Observed at the Roof Cover...110
End Caps to Ridge Vent Missing 110
UV Exposure Appears to have Caused Significant Wear to the Skylight Dome, Causing Cracking/Damage....110
Second Layer/Overlay on the Roof. Drip Edge and Valley Seams Appear Loose 110
Second Layer/Ply on Three Tab Roof Basic Comments...111
Architectural Shingle Second Layer/Ply over Three Tab Roof Basic Comments 111
Rusted/Corroded Galvanized Drip Edge Flashing Observed 111
Side Gable Wall Cladding/Sheathing shows Moisture Compromises at Seams/Gable Vent 111
Room Addition; Roof Cover Suspected Not Installed to Code with Compromises 111
Curling Asphalt Shingles Observed 112
Vent Stacks/Service Mast Sealant at Roof Abutment Needs Redressing; Compromise Observed 112
Raised Flashing at Valley..112
Modified Bitumen Roll Roof has "Ponding" Observed..112
Fractured Plank Board Decking Observed in the Attic System at the Time of the Inspection 112
South Code; Shingle at the Drip Edge Overlaps the Drip Edge throughout the Eaves 112
Concrete Tile Valley, Ridge Tiles Observed with Mortar/Joint Cracks..112
Visible Compromise to the Ridge Vent Flashing Viewed from Exterior/Attic Interior 112
Ridge Vent End Caps Missing 113
Vent Stack Caps Observed have Rodent Damage...113
Porch Metal Roof over Unpermitted Enclosures 113
Aluminum Panel Seam at Fascia Compromised and Screws Oxidizing 113
Aluminum Panel Foil Seam and Screw Maintenance Tips 113
Seals at Vents/Stacks and Roof Transitions are Insufficient/Antiquated 113
Debris Buildup Observed/Screw Fastener Oxidation Observed 113
Termite Damage Suspected. Live Drywood Termites Suspected Within the Wood Soffit/Fascia 114
Flashing at Asphalt Roof/Wall Transition Appears to be Improperly Installed 114
Asphalt Shingle; Black Algae/Lichen on the Roof Substrate 114
Black Algae-Flat Roofs M.B. Roll with Main Roof Cover Being Shingle 114
Black Algae Main Roof Shingle...114
Service Mast Rubber Boot is Dry Rotted/Degraded around the Circumferential Area.
    Repair/Replace As Needed 115
Roof End of Life. Various Missing Damaged Shingles, Excess Granule Loss and Drip Edge Damage............115
Excess Granule Loss Observed Intermittently throughout the Roof Surface..115
Roof End of Life. Various Missing and Damaged Shingles. Excess Granule and Surface Loss 115
Various Missing and Damaged Shingles Observed at the Time of the Inspection 115
Various Cracked/Missing/Damaged Tiles Observed at the Time of the Inspection 115
Architectural Shingle Prior Roof Leak Damage Observed on a Second Ply Roof Cover 115
Compromise Suspected at the Apron/Counter Flashing/Exterior Wall Abutment. Visible Water Stains..........116
Metal Roof Panel is Rusted/Corroded. Galvanized Fasteners Observed Rusting/Corroded..........................116

FASCIA/EAVES/TRIM 117

No Deficiencies Observed...117
Wood Fascia is Bare and Appears Unsealed with Surface Fungi 117
Loose Aluminum Fascia Cover Observed. Loose/Missing Fasteners Observed 117
Displaced Vinyl/Aluminum Soffit at the J-Channel 117
Visible Compromise to the Drip Edge Flashing to the Soffit/Eave Viewed from Exterior/Attic........................117
Visible Compromise to the Drip Edge Flashing to the Soffit/Eave Viewed from Interior/Attic 117
Aluminum Fascia Cover Oxidizing Due to Interaction with PT Wood 118
Insufficient Eave Venting/Perforated Soffit...118
Ducting Antiquated; Insulation Loose Throughout 118
Antiquated/Damaged Eave Venting Screen/Perforated Soffit 118
Attic Mold Suspected; Fungi Observed at Eave Vents 118
Improperly Installed Vinyl Soffit...118
Improperly Installed Interlocking Aluminum Soffit 119
Heavily Rusted/Corroded Galvanized Drip Edge Flashing Observed 119
Displaced/Loose Wood Soffit..119
Rodent Damage to the Roof Eaves Soffit Vents Observed 119
Rodent Damage to the Roof Eaves Soffit 119

Aluminum Panel Seam at Fascia compromised and Screw Maintenance Needed 119
Missing/Damaged Crown Shingle(s) Observed 119
End Cap Crown Shingle(s) Nail Fasteners Need Sealant 119
Missing/Damaged Shingle(s) Observed 119
Missing/Loose Soffit at Roof Wedge 120
Soffit Section Observed Damaged at the Roof Eave 120

ATTIC 121

Access Hatch Improper/Damaged Cover 121
No Attic Access, Could Not Inspect 121
No Attic Access; Notable Sag Observed at the Main Ridge Beam to the Rafters 121
Insufficient Insulation in Attic. Thermal Bridging Observed 121
Fractured Plank Board Decking Observed in the Attic System at the Time of the Inspection 121
Suspected Live Drywood Termites Observed 121
Drywood Termite Damage Suspected at Ceiling Joists 122
Access Hatch Improper/Missing Fasteners 122
Access Hatch Improper Size/Location or Missing 122
Access Hatch has Improper Framing 122
Thermal Bridging Observed Intermittent throughout the Attic 122
Attic Insufficiently Ventilated, Excess Heat Buildup Evident at Time of Inspection 122
Displaced Radiant Heat Barriers Observed in the Attic 123
Displaced Section of Insulation Observed in the Attic System 123
Attic Insulation Mold Suspected; Beginning Accumulative Evidence found in Various Locations 123
Leak Observed at Valley Flashing 123
Popcorn Textured Ceiling Texture/Tape Peeling 123
Attic Insufficiently Insulation/Ventilated at Time of Inspection 123
Blown-In, Loose-Fill 124
Blankets 124
Cellulose 124
Foam Insulation 124

ROOF FLASHING 125

Ridge Vent End Caps Missing 125
Ridge Vent Missing/Damaged 125
Screws Oxidizing on Ridge Vent Cap 125
Ridge Vent(s) Fasteners Observed Loose with Insufficient Sealants 125
Weather Hood Observed Heavily Corroded with Rust Oxidation 125
Service Mast Flashing Not Installed 125
Kick out Flashing Not Observed 125

PLUMBING 127

Copper Plumbing 127
Pipe Type CPVC 127
HDPE 127
Galvanized Pipe 128
Cross-Linked Polyethylene (PEX/XLPE) 128
Stainless Steel 128
Ductile Iron 128
Polypropylene 129
Polyvinyl Chloride (PVC) 129
Polybutylene 129

MAIN SERVICE PIPE 130

Pressure and Basic Comments 130
High/Elevated Pressure Observed when Tested 130
Handle and Stem Turn But Do Not Engage the Closed Position. Gate Valve Needs Replacing 130
Low Pressure when Faucet is Actuated; Suspect Aerator is Obstructed 130
Erratic/Spitting of Water at the Faucet, Suspect Aerator Obstructed 130
Main PVC Valve Shut-Off Handle was Observed Damaged 131
Missing/Damaged Gate Valve Handle at the Main Shut-Off 131
No Main Shut Off Valve Observed 131
Waste Pipe Observed Buried At/Near the Potable Water Pipe Less than 10 Feet 131
Unknown Plumbing Connection Leading from/to the Main Potable Water System Pipe 131

Leak at Main Shut off Valve Stem 131
Water Service Pipe Observed Buried Too Shallow then allowed by Most Locale Code Requirements 131
Water Service Pipe Observed Installed Above Grade at the Exterior 131
Suspected Asbestos Insulation Lining Pipes 132
Leak at Gate Valve/Joint 132
Galvanized Pipe Rusting at Threaded Joints 132
Lime Scale or Calcium Carbonate Fouling Observed 132
Lime Scale or Calcium Carbonate Fouling on Valves/Joints 132
PR or Pressure Relief Valve Leaks. Pressure Serviceable 132
High PSI. PR or Pressure Relief Valve Recommended 133
Low Pressure Observed. Suspect Galvanized Pipe Oxidation is Constricting 133

DISTRIBUTION PIPE 134

Pressure and Basic Comments 134
Distribution Service Pipe Observed Installed Above Grade at the Exterior 134
Water Service Pipe Observed Buried Too Shallow then Allowed by Most Locale Code Requirements 134
Dishwasher Not/Improperly Mounted at Top Front 134
Improper Installation of Tub/Shower Valve 134
Shut-Off Gate Valve under the Sink was Observed Leaking at the Stem 134
Missing/Damaged Gate Valve Handle at the Sink Shut-Off Valve 135
Loose Piping Observed 135
Jacuzzi Tub Access Panel is Grouted Shut 135
Jacuzzi Tub Access Panel was Not Observed 135
Suspected Asbestos Insulation Lining Pipes 135
Bathroom Sink Drain Plunger(s) Missing 136
PR or Pressure Relief Valve Leaks 136
Recommend Installing a Temperature Relief Valve 136
Recommend Installing a Thermostatic Mixing Valve 136
Leak at Gate Valve/Joint 136
Leak at Shower Handle Valve/Joint 136
Leak at Faucet Handle Valve/Joint 136
Leak at Faucet Joints/Abutments 136
Leak at the Shower Head(s) 136
Washer Hot Shut-Off Gate Valve Leaks 137
Toilet Shut-Off Gate Valve Leaks when Actuated 137
Upward Knocking at Shut-Off Valve 137
Knocking at Toilet Valve Observed 137
Lime Scale or Calcium Carbonate Fouling Observed 137
Lime Scale or Calcium Carbonate Fouling on Shower Walls 137
Lime Scale or Calcium Carbonate Fouling on Valves/Joints 137
Interior Gate Valves Seized and will Not Engage/Disengage when Actuated 138
Loose CPVC Pipe Raceways Observed at the Crawl Space 138
Galvanized Pipe Rusting at Threaded Joints 138
Low pressure Observed. Suspect Galvanized Pipe Oxidation Is Constricting 138
Tub/Shower Valve do not Totally Engage/Disengage. Suspect Lime Scale Etc. 138

WASTE SYSTEM 139

Cast Iron Drainage System is Original, has Excessive Exterior Corrosion and
    is recommended to be replaced 139
Toilet Gasket at the Tank/Bowl Abutment was Observed Leaking when Flushed 139
Drainage System Pipe: PVC 139
Drainage System Pipe: PVC with System Comments 139
Drainage System Pipe: ABS 140
Drainage System Pipe: ABS with System Comments 140
Cast Iron Pipe 140
Copper Plumbing 140
Polypropylene 141
Pipe Type CPVC 141
HDPE 141
Washer Gate Valve Leaks 141
Galvanized Pipe 141

Dielectric fitting not Present at Pipe Transition 142
Cross-Linked Polyethylene (PEX/XLPE) 142
Ductile Iron 142
Leak at Sink Basin 142
Stainless Steel 142
Polybutylene 143
Waste Line Observed Passes across Egress at Step 143
Basin of Sink has Excess Corrosion. Leak/Corrosion at Sink Basin Observed 143
Washer Drain Not Equipped with P-Trap, Standpipe or Vent 143
Garbage Disposal was Seized Up at the Time of the Inspection 143
Bathroom Sink Drain Trip Lever Sticks 143
Bathroom Sink Drain Trip Inoperable 143
Toilet Drainage Bubbles Observed 143
Sink Drains Slowly 144
Drain Vent Stack Suspected at the Exterior Wall under the Eaves 144
Double Trap Observed at the Sink Basin 144
Very Slow Draining at the Bathroom Tub Drain. Suspect Sediment/Hair Clog 144
No Cleanout Observed at the Time of the Inspection 144
Corroded P-Trap Leak Observed at the Sink Drain 144
P-Trap Observed at the Sink Drain is Leaking at a Fitting/Threaded Joint 144
No P-Trap Observed at the Washer Drain 144
No P-Trap Observed at the Washtub Drain 145
Basin of Sink has Excess Corrosion at Locknut to the Drain, located beneath the Strainer Housing 145
Bathroom Sink Drain Trip Inoperable. Bath Drain Stop is Missing 145
Bath Tub Drain Stopper is Loose from Its Mounted Lever and No Longer Suits Its Purpose 145
Toilet Handle/Chain/Flap Inoperable at the Time of the Inspection 145
Toilet Valve Body Damaged 145
No P-Trap Observed at the Sink Drain 145
Septic System could not be inspected. Drains were Tested where Accessible 145

GAS/FUEL SYSTEM LINES 146

Prior Leak at Gas Ignition Area. Water Heater was off and could not be Tested for Heating Adequacy 146
No Gas Drip Leg Observed at the Water Heater Gas Pipe Inlet 146
Suspected Abandoned Buried Fuel Tank Observed 146
Pipe Threaded Joints have no Joint Compound Observed 146
Gas Fuel Leak Suspected at the Pipe Threaded Joint(s) Observed 147
No Dielectric Fittings Observed at Pipe Material Transition 147
No Oil Gauge for the Fuel Tank Observed 147
No Fuel-Oil Relief Valve Observed on the Heating Appliances Discharge Line 147
Natural Gas Fuel Pipe was Observed Loose/Insufficiently Fastened 147
Natural Gas Fuel Pipe Observed in Disrepair 148

WATER HEATER 149

Surface Rust Observed at the Water Heater Tank Pipe Inlets Galvanized Nipples 149
Main Shut Off; Leak Observed at the Gate Valve/Joint 149
Prior Leak at Gas Ignition Area. Water Heater was off and could not be Tested for Heating Adequacy 149
No Gas Drip Leg Observed at the Water Heater Gas Pipe Inlet 149
No Temperature Relief Valve Drain Pipe 149
Element Service Panel Cap is Loose 150
Element Service Panel Cap is missing 150
Gas Water Heater Vent Straps/Fasteners were Observed Loose 150
Draft Hood Loose/Displaced at the Water Heater Abutment 150
No Temperature Relief Valve Drain Pipe or Pan 150
No Main Shut Off Valve to Hot Water Heater 150
Recommend Installing a Temperature Pressure Relief Valve 150
TPR or Temperature Pressure Relief Valve Leaks 150
PVC Flue Observed in Use for the Gas Heater Exhaust 151
No Barometric Damper Observed at the Gas Water Heater Flue Pipe 151
Flue Collar was Observed Not Attached Properly to the Exhaust Flue for the Gas Fired Water Heater 151
Water Heater was Observed Enclosed/Inaccessible at the Time of the Inspection 151
No Main Shut Off Valve Installed at Water Heater 151

Worn TPR Valve Observed. Water Leaking from the Valve Stem 151
TPR-Overflow Pipe Terminates at Floor 152
No TPR-Overflow Pipe Present 152
Water Heater is Antiquated; has Reached or Exceeded its known Life Expectancy 152
No Exhaust Flue observed connected to the Water Heater 152
No Exhaust Flue observed connected to the Boiler 152
TPR Valve has Reducer Installed-Overflow Pipe Insufficient 152
Lime Scale or Calcium Carbonate Fouling on Pipe Inlet Joints 152
Leak Observed and Lime Scale/Calcium Carbonate Fouling on Pipe Inlet/Outlet Joints 153
Glass Lined Water Heater in Operable Condition 153
Water Heaters Gate Valve Shut Off was observed Seized/Hard to Actuate when Testing 153

HVAC 154
Gas Furnace Inspection, Service and Maintenance 154
Floor Vent in Bedroom is obstructed by the Bed 154
Particulate Build Up on Evaporator Coil/Fins Observed at the Time of the Inspection 155
Particulate Build Up on Various Components within the Handler Unit Observed 155
Particulate Build Up on Blower Blades Observed at the Time of the Inspection 155
Duct Pinched/Obstructed by Truss/Joist Wood Member in Attic 155
Return is Located Adjacent to an Egress Door 155
No P-Trap Observed at Condensate Drain Line 155
No Drain Lines Installed at the Wall/Window HVAC Units Drain Hole 155
No Condensate Drain Line Observed from the Catch Pan under the Handler Unit to the Exterior 156
Structural Framing/Support of the Handler Unit is Improper 156
Central A/C Coolant Lines - Metal Box Conduit Cover Needs Cover to Defer Rodent Intrusion 156
HVAC Coolant Lines Metal Box Conduit Cover is Loose at the Wall 156
Central HVAC Exterior Unit Observed Appears Undersized 156
Central HVAC Interior Unit Observed Appears Undersized 156
Central HVAC Exterior Unit Observed Appears Oversized 156
Door to Handler Unit Closet Space Needs to be Air Sealed 156
Exposed Thermostat Wires Observed Spliced but not Sealed from the Elements at the Exterior 156
Exterior Condensing Unit Coil Fins Observed Damaged Intermittently 156
Handler Unit; Particulates and Suspected Microbes on Wires Observed 157
No Exhaust Flue Observed connected to the Heating Furnace 157
Service Hatch to the Handler in the Attic Appears Insufficient 157
No Service Hatch to the Handler in the Attic Observed 157
No Ducting Sleeve Observed at the Coolant Line Running Through the Concrete Floor 157
Condensate Drain Line Observed Terminating at and on the Exterior Wall 158

HVAC DUCTING 159
Replacement of HVAC equipment post 2009, no Mastic Observed on Collars/Joints
    within the Ducting System 159
Interior Handler Return/Distribution Seal at the Duct/Wall Abutment was not Properly Sealed 159
Loose Seal Observed at a Ducting Collar 159
No Filter Observed at the Hinged Air Filter Grill 160
No Service Hatch to the Attic Observed. Could Not Inspect Ducting 160
Handler Return/Distribution Ducting Enclosures Not Properly Sealed at the Air Handler 160
Distribution Ducting Not Properly Mastic Sealed at the Abutting Joints/Collars 160
No Service Hatch to the Attic System to Inspect Ducting 160
Return is Located Adjacent to an Egress Door 161
Handler in Closet; Louvered Door. Filter Door Fasteners Missing at the Handler Filter Hatch 161
Filter Door Fasteners Missing at the Handler Filter Hatch 161
Rodent Damage Observed at the Ducting in the Attic 161
Recommend Installing a Pleated Air Filtration System to the HVAC System 161
Recommend Installing a New Pleated Air Filter in the System 161

EXHAUST SYSTEMS 162
Exhaust Vent Terminates in the Attic 162
Gas Water Heater Vent Straps/Fasteners were Observed Loose 162
Draft Hood Loose/Displaced at the Water Heater Abutment 162
No Barometric Damper Observed at the Gas Water Heater Flue Pipe 162
Flue Collar Observed not Attached Properly to the Exhaust Flue for the Gas Fired Water Heater 162

PVC Flue Observed In Use for the Gas Heater Exhaust 162
Dryer Vent, Vents under the Building in the Crawl Space 163
No Exhaust Flue Observed Connected to the Heating Furnace 163
No Barometric Damper Observed at the Gas Water Heater Flue Pipe... 163
Clothes Dryer Exhaust Expels into the Interior/Garage 163
Dryer Vent Observed Expels into the Attic Space... 163
Chimney Flue Appeared Displaced at the Time of the Inspection 164
Masonry Chimney Airspace Clearance/Fire Protection. No Liner Observed 164
Chimney and Fireplace Appear to have Extensive Ware.. 164
Kitchen Exhaust Vent Terminates in the Attic 164
No Heat Exhaust Vent Observed in the Bathroom.. 164

MAIN SERVICE 165

Basic Breaker Service Panel Comments Accessible 165
Basic Fuse Service Panel Comments Accessible... 165
Main Breaker Suspected to be Undersized for the Load Requirement... 165
Extension Cords Used Throughout the Building 165
Stab-Lok Service/Distribution Panel is a Defective Panel Type and should be Replaced ASAP 165
Occupied with GFCI Outlets.. 166
Occupied; Basic System Remarks Passing Inspection without GFCI Receptacles....................................... 166
Unoccupied Basic Passing Inspection with GFCI Receptacles 166
Unoccupied Basic Passing Inspection without GFCI Receptacles 166
Loose Breakers/Breakers Not Seated Properly 166
Solid Strand Aluminum Wiring Observed.. 166
Various Brand Breakers Observed in the Service Panel 167
Panel is Loose at the Wall... 167
Double Taps in Service Panel... 167
Exposed Spliced Wire Junction Observed with Excess Sheathing Stripped 167
Exposed Wires Observed in the Service Panel 167
Overcrowding at Service Panel Abutting Screw Fasteners Area for the Panel Cover 167
Panel is not Fastened Evenly at the Wall.. 167
Conduit/Armored Cable Leading to the Panel is not Properly Braced 167
Service Mast Leading to the Panel is not Properly Braced 168
Panel Punch Outs Are Missing 168
Service Lateral is Loose Leading to the Panel and is not Properly Braced 168
Stranded Wire at Grounding Bus Observed with Multiple Crimps/Cuts.. 168
Circuits Entering the Panel are not Properly Secured. Fasteners are Missing 168
Stranded Wire at the Wire/Breaker Abutment Observed with Multiple Crimps/Cuts...................................... 168
Stranded Wire at the Main Breaker/Wire Abutment Observed with Multiple Crimps/Cuts............................. 168
Spliced Stranded Wire Observed within the Panel with Multiple Crimps/Cuts 169
Panel is of a Known Defective Type and is recommended to be Replace ASAP 169

DISTRIBUTION SERVICE 170

Solid Strand Aluminum Wiring Observed.. 170
Various Brand Breakers Observed in the Distribution Panel 170
Circuits Entering the Panel are not Properly Secured. Fasteners are missing 170
Loose Breakers/Breakers Not Seated Properly 170
Double Taps in Distribution Panel... 171
Exposed Spliced Wires Junction Observed with Excess Sheathing Stripped 171
Stranded Wire at Grounding Bus Observed with Multiple Crimps/Cuts.. 171
Stranded Wire at the Breaker/Wire Abutment Observed with Multiple Crimps/Cuts...................................... 171
Spliced Stranded Wire Observed Within the Panel with Multiple Crimps/Cuts 171
Conduit/Armored Cable Leading to the Panel is not Properly Braced 171
Double Taps in Distribution Panel... 171
Exposed Wires Observed in the Distribution Panel 172
Overcrowding at the Distribution Panel Abutting Screw Fasteners Area for the Dead Front Cover 172
Panel is Loose at the Wall... 172
Panel Is Not Fastened Evenly at the Wall... 172
Panel Punch Outs Are Missing 172
Circuits Entering the Panel are not Properly Secured. Fasteners are missing 172

BRANCH CIRCUITS DEFICIENCIES.. 173

No Anti-Tip Bracket Observed at the Range/Oven 173
Range/Oven Receptacle was Observed Unmounted and Lying on the Floor 173
Loose Gang Box Observed at the Master Bathroom Sink Counter Back Splash 173
No GFCI Receptacles Observed 173
No GFCI Receptacles Observed in the Bathrooms 173
Grounding Observed. Two Prong Polarized Outlets throughout the Building 174
Loose Receptacle(s) Contact(s) 174
Ducted Kitchen Exhaust was Inoperable at the Time of the Inspection 174
Insufficient Outlets at the Kitchen Peninsular Counter/Cabinet 174
Insufficient Outlets Observed in the Kitchen 174
Can Lighting Appears Antiquated? Thermal Leaks/Bridging Suspected 174
Reverse Neutral/Reverse Polarity Observed when the Outlets Tested 174
Jacuzzi Tub Access Panel is Grouted Shut 175
Jacuzzi Tub Access Panel Was Not Observed 175
Exterior Grade UF Branch Circuit Wire Observed Exposed at Grade 175

INTERIOR FLOORING 177
Drywood Termite Frass/Damage Suspected at the Floors and Sills 177
Floor Tile Suspected to have been Applied Over Tile 177
Various Staining Observed Throughout the Carpeting 177
Loose Floor Boards Observed 177
Subfloor Particle Board Decking Suspected to be Fractured/ Punctured 177
Subfloor Particle Board Subfloor Decking Suspected to be Loose 178
Laminate Flooring Observed Buckling 178
Cracked/Loose Tiles Observed on Wood Subfloor 178
Cracked/Loose Tiles Observed on Slab Floor 178
Tile Grouting Joints appear to be filled with a Mortar or Thin Set, Not Grout 178
Subfloor Particle Board Decking Suspected to be Fractured/Punctured 178

WALLS 179
Chinese Drywall Suspected 179
Wall Tile Suspected to have been Applied Over Tile 179
WL Elevated Moisture, Water Damage and Suspected Microbial Growth Observed 180
Kitchen Cabinets have Observed Drywall Screws Installed Improperly 180
Bathroom Shower Wall has Wide Grout Joint(s) Abutting the Wall with Cracks/Compromises 180

CEILINGS 181
Chinese Drywall Suspected 181
Thermal Leaks/Bridging Suspected at the Older Can Lights 181
Garage Ceiling Fastening Observed Loose 182
Water Stains and Moisture Elevated and Suspected Molds on the Gypsum Board 182
Older Existing Construction-Ingress to the Home from the Garage
 Leads Directly Into a Room 182
Water Stains on the Ceilings Gypsum Board, Moisture Levels Nominal 182
Popcorn Ceiling Texture was Observed Peeling 183
Popcorn Ceiling Peeling. Water Stains Observed. Suspect Roof Leak 183
Popcorn Ceiling Peeling. Water Stains Observed. Suspect Plumbing Leak 183
Popcorn Ceiling Peeling. Suspect Improper Treatment for Drywall Dust Prior 183

SMOKE/FIRE DETECTORS & SUPPRESSION SYSTEMS 184
Smoke Detectors Appear Antiquated and should be Replaced per NFPA Recommendations 184
Various Missing Smoke Detectors Observed in the Multi Unit Building 184
No Deficiencies Observed at the Time of the Inspection 184
No Fire Extinguishers Observed 185
No Fire Extinguishers Observed at the Common Areas to the Multi Unit Building 185
No Smoke Detectors Observed in the Multi Unit Building 185
No Smoke Detectors Observed within the Building 185
No Fire Extinguishers Observed In/On the Building at the Time of the Inspection 185
No Carbon Monoxide Detectors Observed 186
Smoke Detectors were Antiquated and Inoperable within the Building 186
Insufficient Smoke Detectors Observed within the Building 186

GARAGE 187
Concrete Slab; Cubicle/Moisture Cracking from Weathering Observed 187

Garage Door Buck, Wood Jams Lag Bolted to the Wall Improperly, Missing Fasteners at the Top.................187
Automatic Door Torsion Spring is Broke, Visible on the Torsion Tube 187
Sensor Guards Not Present on the Garage Door 187
New Construction; Improper Ceiling Fastening Methodology Observed 187
Moisture and Basic Settlement Cracks Suspected on the Ceiling at Tape Joints 187
Garage Door/Panel Observed with Suspected Vehicle Damage..188
New Construction; Improper/Loose Ceiling Fasters/Tape Joints Observed 188
Ceiling Fastening Observed Loose 188
Center Crack in Poured Concrete. No Control Joints Observed..188
Common Cracks Observed in Garage Poured Concrete Slab..188
Base Wall Seal Compromised; Foundation Protrudes Past Siding 188

FIREPLACES...189
Backdraft..189
Heavy Creosote Observed in the Flue...189
Heavy Creosote Resin Observed in the Firebox, Flue and Smoke Chamber..................................189
Refractory Panel has Observed Serviceable Hairline Cracks...189
Refractory Panel has Observed Cracks...190
Chimney Pointing Observed to be Eroding...190
Refractory Brick in the Firebox Appears Loose, Points Damage Observed 190
Efflorescence Observed in the Firebox...190
Chimney Flue Appeared Displaced at the Time of the Inspection 190
Masonry Chimney Airspace Clearance/Fire Protection. No Liner Observed 190
Chimney and Fireplace Appear to have Extensive Ware..190
Chimney Cap appears Loose..191
Chimney Suspected to Terminate too Close to the Roof/Slope...191
Masonry Chimney Liner Was Not Observed at the Time of the Inspection 191
Masonry Chimney Liner was Observed Heavily Corroded at the Time of the Inspection..............191
Dryer Vent Not Observed at the Exterior/Roof of the Building 191

Fences; Types

PVC Fence
PVC/VINYL FENCING: Vinyl was invented in the mid-20th century, but vinyl fencing came into being closer to the 1980's. Now vinyl fences come with warranties for many years and after they outlive their utility, they can be recycled putting to rest all fears of impending and future ecological danger. They are the ideal choice for those who do not have much time or interest in caring for their fence periodically. Vinyl is nearly five times as strong as wood and thus it takes much more to bring down a vinyl fence than a wooden one. The flexibility of vinyl makes it a good choice in places that witness extreme weather conditions such as strong winds and rain. Wood fences are more likely to break and collapse in such weather. Vinyl fences are also preferred in seaside locations which see a significant amount of salt water exposure. They are also suitable for fencing in animals like horses as the animals can neither chew through it nor hurt themselves if they attempt to run through it. The maintenance required in vinyl fences is next to nothing. Just some general cleaning with soap and water is sufficient to keep your vinyl fence clean and sparkling. Since it does not change color or lose its color, there is no need to repaint it often. You do not have to apply any primer on it or protect it from rust. There is also no danger of rotting or termite attacks when you have vinyl fencing.

Wood Privacy Fence
Note: All-wood privacy fencing has long been the standard of the typical home and many businesses. Fence designs can vary from a basic board fence to one that is beautifully detailed with finials and elaborate carpentry. At first, the wide availability of redwood and cedar made these a logical choice due to their affordability and resistance to decomposition. Today the rising cost of redwood and overall increase of lumber prices have made property owners consider other manufactured products to replace the traditional wood fence. A shadowbox or board on board fence is the age old solution that looks equally good on both sides, both for you and your neighbor. This open design also allows greater air circulation which increases the life of the fence and keeps your yard more comfortable. Cedar is the most common fence wood due to its resistance to decomposition. Depending on the location, installers may use red cedar, white cedar or inland cedar and out west redwood is available. Treated pine is also very common. When replacing rotted wood posts, it's important to note what the best replacement post is. With wood, even if done right they rot and they wobble creating lean in the fence. With steel posts that won't happen.

Tips for Making your Wooden Fence Last Longer
Use a wood species that has proven itself outdoors (cedar, redwood, cypress or pressure treated pine). Select the best wood grade you can afford, the clearer the wood the better. Use steel posts rather than wooden ones; they will last longer and provide stronger support for your fence. Have the fence built so that the wood does not touch the ground; this will reduce the risk of moisture problems such as rotting, warping and splitting.

Stock Fencing
This type of fencing is high tensile or mild steel mesh for strength and durability for keeping in livestock. With cattle for example, corral fences need to be tougher and stable than pasture fences. Pasture fencing for cattle require simple barbed-wire or high-tensile fences, whereas for pigs, goats and sheep, pasture fencing requires page wire up to a 3 to 5 feet tall, respectively. Pasture fencing for horses can also be barbed wire or high-tensile.

Various Burrows Observed at Various Fencing Sections at Grade
Recommend reinstalling where applicable, high tensile mesh under grade to deter further burrows.

Loose Post Observed
Recommend a licensed contractor repair as needed.

No Post Concrete Footers Observed; Posts Enter Grade
Recommend Supporting at Minimum, All Progressively Loose Fence Posts As Needed, To Prevent Progressive Leaning and Warping. Generally, two pieces of 1/2" rebar are placed on opposite corners of the post and can be held in place during installation by special rebar clips. It is essential that this be done on every post of 7' and 8' high fence if vinyl fence, to add structural integrity to the vinyl fence. On shorter heights, only end, gate and corner posts should be set this way for vinyl fence. Gate posts would require filling the post to the bottom of the top rail hole so the hardware will adhere better to the post. After bracing a wood post at level position, concrete can be poured into the perimeter of the post hole and water can then be applied or concrete can be premixed. A post should be allowed to set in accordance with the concrete dry time. Recommend a state or county licensed contractor, perform all repairs as recommended or better per local codes.

PVC Post Caps Broken/Missing at Posts
PVC post caps are used to prevent intrusion of the elements into the hollow interior of the posts and prevent rodent nesting within the posts. Caps prevent the water moisture from trapping and filling in the posts breaking down concrete footings and wood inserts where applicable and rodents from nesting. Small rodents such as mice or even fruit rats can nest, often making further damage to provide additional holes/corridors through railing etc. Additionally fasteners adjoining fencing components to the posts at the top sections have sharp edges. Caps can provide protection from unknowing children and elderly reaching their hands in the hollow section and harming them. Recommend replacing as soon as possible.

Neighboring Tree Heaving Fence Section/Post
Heaving from trees is commonly associated with the tree trunk encumbering and/or the tree roots system uprooting the grading at/near the fence and posts. The roots ultimately encroach on the fence/posts and cause the fence to lean. Recommend a licensed arborist repair all as needed to mitigate the heaving issue.

Foliage Encumbers Fencing Sections
One cannot fully inspect the fencing due to excessive foliage encumbering the fence. It is likely areas encumbered by organic material such as this that will undergo a more expedient oxidation process. Recommend removing all foliage as needed.

Gate Obstructed by Walkway
Gate is obstructed at the walkway and does not fully open/shut. Recommend repairing the gate issue at the base of the gate to allow the proper and full open/close of the gate.

Gate Obstructed by Grading/Vegetation
Gate is obstructed at the grading and does not fully open/shut. Recommend repairing the grading/vegetation issue at the base of the gate to allow the proper and full open/close of the gate.

Gate Latches Do Not Engage; Door is not Aligned/Sags uneven from Latching Properly when Closing
Gate Latches do not engage when the gate is shut. This is because it is not aligned properly and is likely due to the post(s) sagging over time from warping and the weight of the gate, causing the uneven alignment and the inability of latching the gate(s) properly when closing. Recommend repairing the issue at the gate to allow the proper and full open/close of the gate.

Gate Hardware Missing
When Gate hardware are missing, recommend replacing the hardware and repairing as needed.

Gate Hardware Appeared Loose
Gate hardware should be properly fastened to prevent failure during operation in an emergency. Recommend a licensed contractor assess the area further and position and refasten as needed.

Gate Hardware Appeared Loose; Wood Appeared Rotted at the Fasteners Locations
Gate hardware should be properly fastened to prevent failure during operation in an emergency. The suspected rotted areas at the fasteners greatly reduces the tensile strength of the wood resulting in compromised or loose fasteners and potential damage in addition to the present deficiencies. Recommend a licensed contractor assess the area further, replace all wood members heavily damaged, and/or position and refasten all hardware as needed. Recommend a licensed contractor treat all suspected rot as needed.

Wood Members Suspected to be Rotting
Wood rot is caused by undue exposure of untreated wood to moisture. Consequently, prevention constitutes both avoiding such exposure and employing a prevention and treatment program where rot already exists. Wood with 20 percent moisture content and green lumber remain at risk. Two types of rot trouble owners. The first is white and yellow with a stringy and spongy look. The other is brown and crumbly in appearance, and a tendency to break into cubes has earned it the nickname "brown cubical rot." These visible manifestations of wood rot are called "fruiting bodies." About 3 inches in diameter, these crusts or brackets are evidence that the particular decay fungi are present within the wood. Serpula lacrimans, Poria incrassata and Gleophyllum trabeum each have singular fruiting-body appearances. Fruiting bodies produce spores, which spread the decay fungus throughout the wood. To prevent wood rot, use treated wood or the heartwood of a decay-resistant species. Pacific yew, juniper, redwood epoxy, wood hardener and know-how, rotted areas of wood on decks, fences, doorways, and windows can be healthy again! There are many websites that provide adequate direction as to how to treat the wood rot.

Iron Stains Observed on Fencing
The reddish brown rusty stains are a common problem readily seen on siding, sidewalks, walkways, patios, stepping stones, window and door frames in areas where irrigation water has a high iron content. The sprinkler system and/or hoses that are used and water the grounds are also spraying iron particles that create these rust stains wherever they land. Iron is a chemical element that is abundant in soils and aquifers in many parts of the country. And it is the element that, when exposed to air and moisture, oxidizes or rusts. Where the tap water is "hard" or mineral-rich and we irrigate with well water, sprinkler water is probably causing rust stains. The irrigation systems will often "over spray" which means water ends up on the fence, patio, deck, porch, building, windows, doors, concrete walkways, stepping stones or paths, lawn furniture and also on parked vehicles if exposed to overspray. Once iron particles from the water in your sprinkler come in contact with the air, they will begin to oxidize; rust. The stains that result have likely developed over time and can be very stubborn to remove. Recommend installing a rust inhibitive filtration treatment system to the sprinkler system to prevent this and treat as needed.

Excessive Wood Warping Observed
Wood has many outstanding properties, but it is a natural, porous material with individual characteristics, and it can warp. When wood gets wet, it swells. When wood dries out after being sawn from the tree, after being pressure-treated and after rain showers, it shrinks. Uneven drying creates stresses in wood, which results in warping (e.g., bowing, cupping or twisting) or cracking. The degree of warping depends on the species of wood, its grain pattern, uniformity of drying and construction techniques, among other factors. There is not much a user can do to truly un-warp a warped piece of wood. It is possible to position bowed fence boards so that its weight flattens it, using screws to fasten securely an otherwise warped piece. Recommend re-supporting or replacing the displaced section with deck/exterior wood screws per each post and fencing horizontal bracing rails where applicable, as needed.

Wood Warping
Wood has many outstanding properties, but it is a natural, porous material with individual characteristics, and it can warp. When wood gets wet, it swells. When wood dries out after being sawn from the tree, after being pressure-treated and after rain showers, it shrinks. Uneven drying creates stresses in wood, which results in warping (e.g., bowing, cupping or twisting) or cracking. The degree of warping depends on the species of wood, its grain pattern, uniformity of drying and construction techniques, among other factors. There is not much a user can do to truly un-warp a warped piece of wood. It is possible to position bowed fence boards so that its weight flattens it, using screws to fasten securely an otherwise warped piece. Recommend re-supporting or replacing the displaced section with deck/exterior wood screws per each post and fencing horizontal bracing rails as needed.

Top Railing to Chain Link Fence is Damaged
Recommend a licensed contractor repair all as needed.

Various Boards are Broken, Several Posts are Leaning/Warped and Fence Shows Excessive Algae Accumulation
Various sections of fence are starting to warp in the mid sections due to rot (weakening wood/sagging) and uneven drying to some. As the posts warped and/or were not set correctly, this allowed gravity to set as well as the natural contortion to the pressure treated wood as it dries. Additionally, some fence sections were moving away from their posts as the nails were loosening and the sections sag as the wood contorts. Wood has many outstanding properties, but it is a natural, porous material with individual characteristics, and it can warp. When wood gets wet, it swells. When wood dries out after being sawn from the tree, after being pressure-treated and after rain showers, it shrinks. Uneven drying creates stresses in wood, which results in warping (e.g., bowing, cupping or twisting) or cracking. The degree of warping depends on the species of wood, its grain pattern, uniformity of drying and construction techniques, among other factors. There is not much a user can do to truly un-warp a warped piece of wood. It is possible to position bowed deck lumber so that its weight flattens it, or to use screws to fasten securely an otherwise warped piece. Recommend re-supporting the displaced/loosening sections with the prescribed deck screws per each post. Replace all excessively rotted or warped/broken boards. Reset all posts that are in need. Pressure wash and reseal the wood with a translucent wood sealer or prime and paint/stain or replace as needed.

Oxidation Visible on Fittings and Hinges to the Gate/Fence Sections
Recommend recoating any weathered/oxidized part with a rust inhibitor after sanding. Oxidation is defined as the interaction between oxygen molecules and all the different substances they may contact, from metal to living tissue. Technically, however, with the discovery of electrons, oxidation came to be more precisely defined as the loss of at least one electron when two or more substances interact. Those substances may or may not include oxygen. (Incidentally, the opposite of oxidation is reduction — the addition of at least one electron when substances come into contact with each other.) Sometimes oxidation is not such a bad thing, as in the formation of super-durable anodized aluminum. Other times, oxidation can be destructive, such as the rusting of an automobile or the spoiling of fresh fruit. We often used the words oxidation and rust interchangeably, but not all materials which interact with oxygen molecules actually disintegrate into rust. In the case of iron, the oxygen creates a slow burning process, which results in the brittle brown substance we call rust. When oxidation occurs in copper, on the other hand, the result is a greenish coating called copper oxide. The metal itself is not weakened by oxidation, but the surface develops a patina after years of exposure to air and water. When it involves oxygen, the process of oxidation depends on the amount of oxygen present in the air and the nature of the material it touches. This is why stainless steel doesn't rust and ordinary steel does. The stainless steel has a thin coating of another metal which does not contain free radicals. Regular steel may be painted for protection against oxidation, but oxygen can still exploit any opening, no matter how small. This is why you may find a painted metal bicycle still damaged by rust. Treat all oxidation as recommended or better per local code.

Oxidation Visible on Fittings and Aluminum Fence Sections
Recommend recoating any weathered/oxidized part with an aluminum oxidation inhibitor after sanding. Corrosion attack on aluminum surfaces is usually quite obvious, since the products of corrosion are white and generally more voluminous than the original base metal. Even in its early stage, aluminum corrosion is evident as general etching, pitting, or roughness of the aluminum surfaces. General surface attack of aluminum penetrates relatively slowly, but is speeded up in the presence of dissolved salts. Considerable attack can usually take place before serious loss of structural strength develops. When the aluminum has a powder coating on it, a retouch of a flat base metal sealant/ oxide inhibiting paint will aid in sealing the affected areas from further degradation.

Fencing: Potential Termite Damage Observed. No live Termites Observed
This appears to be older remnants/canals and/or suspected subterranean tubes on the fencing intermittently. There were no new signs of damage or present intrusion of these termites. It is unknown if the structure was treated for subterranean or dry wood termites in the recent past. There were old termite burrows found on the wood but there were no suspected signs of live dry wood or subterranean termites. This could have been from an exterior swarm intruding or from an interior swarm attempting to exit. After considering the length of time between treatments, if it is known, it is warranted and recommended to have a licensed pest professional treat the structure and/or provide a routine treatment and inspection plan. Note: Evidence in the fencing may not be an indication of the building being infested or affected with termites. Additionally, there are many termite control companies that will provide free inspections. If needed, termite control can be done with liquid termite control, termite bait systems, or both. Liquid Termite Control products are fast acting, can be applied closer to the

infestation, and require less maintenance. For subterranean, when needed, termite Bait Systems are less intrusive, no drilling or trenching is needed, no expensive equipment is required, and bait systems can help you identify a problem before the termites reach the building. You can do your own termite control and prevention. Advantages to dry wood alternative treatments are: The structure does not have to be unoccupied during treatment, just the immediate work area. There is a residual effect to the termiticide. If re-infestation occurs and the insects come in contact with the treated area, the transfer effect will start again and the colony will be eliminated. Most important, this method uses material much lower in mammalian toxicity. Removing any suspected termite affected fencing is recommended, in hopes to quarantine the area from further spreading. Repair as needed.

Potential Termite Damage Observed. Suspected Live Formosan Subterranean Termites Observed

Suspect Termite damage was evident at and within the wood fencing. The Formosan subterranean termite (Coptotermes formosanus) is an invasive species of termite. It has been transported worldwide from its native range in southern China to Formosa (Taiwan, where it gets its name) and Japan. In the 20th century it became established in South Africa, Hawaii and in the continental United States. The Formosan subterranean termite is often nicknamed the super-termite because of its destructive habits. This is because of the large size of its colonies, and the termites' ability to consume wood at a rapid rate. A single colony may contain several million (compared with several hundred thousand termites for other subterranean termite species) that forage up to 300 feet (100 m) in soil. A mature Formosan colony can consume as much as 13 ounces of wood a day (ca. 400 g) and severely damage a structure in as little as three months. Because of its population size and foraging range, the presence of colonies poses serious threats to nearby structures. Once established; Formosan subterranean termite has never been eradicated from an area. By the 1950's, it was reported in South Africa and Sri Lanka. During the 1960's it was found in Texas, Louisiana, and South Carolina. In 1980, a well-established colony was thriving in a condominium in Hallandale Beach, Florida. Recommend further inspection and treatment if possible, or full removal of any infected area as needed.

Potential Termite Damage Observed. Suspected Live Drywood Termites Observed

Suspected Termite damage was evident at and within the wood fencing. Drywood termites swarm in the evening and at night during the warmer months of the year. It is very hard to find where they are coming from because they live so deeply in the lumber. Drywood termite colonies are small colonies only about 3,000 termites. When the colony reaches about 3,000 termites then they will swarm to start a colony elsewhere. They need very little moisture and are often found in the attic wood framing, wall studs, door casings and window frames. Drywood termites obtain moisture from the water produced by the digestion of cellulose, no matter how old the wood is. Spot treatments, such as orange oil applications, use insecticides applied to control known Drywood termite colonies, such as those found in a door casing, windowsill or piece of furniture. Advantages to Drywood alternative treatments are: The wood fencing needn't be cordoned off and the structure does not have to be unoccupied during treatment, just the immediate work area. There is a residual effect to the termiticide. If re-infestation occurs and the insects come in contact with the treated area, the transfer effect will start again and the colony will be eliminated. Most important, this method uses material much lower in mammalian toxicity.

Retaining Walls

Reinforced Retaining Wall
Traditional retaining walls are built with steel reinforcing bars embedded in concrete, grouted between two widths of solid brick, or grouted in the hollow cores of concrete block. A concrete footing anchors the wall and resists overturning and sliding forces. This type of wall is called a reinforced *cantilever retaining wall* because the stem of the wall is essentially cantilevered from the footing in much the same way that a beam might be cantilevered from a column. Cantilever retaining walls are rigid structures of solid construction. Allowances must be made for expansion and contraction of the materials and for drainage of soil moisture, which may build up behind the wall. The strength of these walls derives from the combination of steel for tensile strength and concrete or masonry for compressive strength and corrosion protection.

Masonry and Concrete: Residential Construction
Retaining walls are typically used to stabilize an earth embankment and protect it from erosion or create terraces in a sloping yard. They can also be used to build a tree well and build raised planting beds. Retaining walls may be built of brick, concrete block, concrete, or stone. Some designs incorporate reinforcing steel or rebar and others rely solely on gravity to resist soil pressures. Newer systems of special concrete masonry retaining wall blocks have greatly simplified the design and installation of retaining walls, and there are a number of proprietary products available.

Mechanically Stabilized Earth Retaining Walls
Mechanically stabilized earth retaining walls built today use a lot of the same knowledge that was used in the Great Wall of China built as much as 1,600 years ago. While the earth between the parallel walls that make up the Great Wall was stabilized with water reeds, laid horizontally between layers of soil, current Mechanically Stabilized Earth retaining walls are built by placing layers of metal straps or strong synthetic meshing or grid material in a zone of earth behind the face stones. This is done to stabilize the soil in the retaining wall as the reeds have done for 1,600 years in the Great Wall of China. Stabilizing the earth behind the face stones makes this stabilized earth zone become the principal part of the retaining wall. The face stones are a minor structural component of the stability of a Mechanically Stabilized Earth retaining wall.

Gravity Retaining Walls
Gravity retaining walls depend on the face stones to "retain" the fill soil behind the stones. The greater the setback slope [batter] of the gravity retaining wall, to a limit, the greater the ability of the stones to retain the soil placed behind the stones. Retaining walls are frequently 5 to 8 degrees off straight up. It is obvious that gravity retaining walls that are built with 0 degrees of batter, straight up, will fail with little horizontal force from the soil pressures behind the stones at the face. It is important to attend care with practices that will minimize the horizontal force that the soil behind the stones may apply to the face stones. Typically, when the batter of a wall or series of tired wall exceeds 30 degrees off straight up the structure referred to as Reinforced Soil Slope [RSS] and is designed with different formulas than the formulas used to design retaining walls.

Basic Comments Overview/Degradation Process: Retaining Walls

The main culprit in the destruction of all retaining walls is water. Referred to as hydrostatic pressure, water that is in the retained soil zone behind the retaining wall and/or the select soil zone can produce forces that will exceed or destroy the wall's design. The principal reason is because, unlike unsaturated and compacted soil that imposes a small horizontal force on the face stones of a retaining wall, water that invades the retained soil zone or the select soil zone will put a horizontal force on the face stones that is equal to the water's vertical force or weight. Also, too much water in the select soil zone will reduce the frictional characteristic of the select soil and then the select soil cannot provide the designed strength of the engineer's design. Soil saturated by water will lose the internal forces that hold it in place, therefore the soil's horizontal force on the face stones increases. Control of water in any of the soils and rock behind the face stones is perhaps the single most critical factor of both gravity and mechanically stabilized earth retaining walls. Design and construction of a swale at the surface behind the face stones of either type of retaining wall is critical if the surface soil does not slope away from the face stone toward the rear of the wall area. The swale must be designed to capture rain or other surface water and carry it away from the retaining wall. A drain tile system can be used for the same purpose.

Preemptions and Maintenance Comments for Sea Walls

A FEW CONSIDERATIONS TO MAINTAIN A SEA OR LAKE RETAINING WALL IS AS FOLLOWS: If you boat, maintain "Idle Speed" in the bays, waterways and canals. This protects berms securing the lower end or toe of the slabs or panels. Encourage your friends and neighbors with boats to do the same. Encourage your neighbors to properly maintain their seawalls. A sagging seawall adjacent to yours may cause you some damage. Avoid the placement of large trees adjacent to seawalls, and avoid the use of heavy equipment traveling along seawall perimeter so as to reduce pressure on the seawall. Adjust sprinkler heads in the vicinity of seawalls to minimize water application behind the wall. Try to redirect drainage from yard and roof so that it does not flow directly into French Drains or pond behind the seawall structure. Avoid continual use of davits installed adjacent to a seawall for hoisting heavy boats as this will also create additional pressure behind seawalls.

Treated Wood and Retaining Walls

Pressure treated wood comes in many dimensions and because it is chemically infused with Chromium Copper Arsenate (CCA) or Alkaline Copper (ACQ) while under pressure, it resists damage from water and boring insects. Although it reduces the likelihood of damage, pressure treated lumber will eventually succumb to water, rotting and insects, although much slower than it would have if left untreated. Pressure treated wood should only be used for low retaining walls and limited to areas that have good drainage. Since wood does not bear an equal amount of pressure, per square inch as does concrete or other masonry, opt for a stronger material if your wall will be higher than 2-feet. Until 2003, the preservative most commonly used in residential pressure-treated lumber was chromate copper arsenate (CCA), an extremely toxic chemical. Remember "Arsenic and Old Lace"? How about that old box of rat poison you have lurking in the garage? CCA is so toxic that the Environmental Protection Agency, over 20 years ago, imposed strict guidelines regarding the manufacturing practices of companies using CCA. However, one must distinguish between the toxicity of the chemical and the toxicity of the wood product in everyday use. Extensive studies were done since the mid 1980's concerning the potential dangers of pressure-treated wood. And rightfully so! Large volumes of CCA were being used, and the treated wood products were beginning to be widely distributed, justifying the need for some hard research. The research was mixed, but the typical hysteria ensued as attorneys and plaintiffs lined up to claim damages from exposure to CCA. In the end, the industry agreed to voluntarily eliminate use of CCA for residential use. Your local building store or lumberyard is now selling lumber treated with (hopefully) less toxic alternatives... amine copper quat (ACQ) and copper azone (CA).though you may find other chemical combinations in specific areas. CCA is still being used in certain marine and industrial applications since it is still the best preservative available at the present time. Whether these new chemicals will turn out to be less hazardous in the long term is anyone's guess.

Vinyl Composite Sea Wall

A vinyl seawall is an excellent option due to its longevity and inability to corrode and deteriorate. Vinyl sheet pilings are a high performance, eco-friendly, and cost effective product compared to wood, concrete and steel. Water jetting is often used to drive vinyl pilings into granular soil or with specialized equipment to drive sheeting into some rock bed applications. Vinyl sheeting currently typically offers two color options, gray and tan, as well as three seawall cap options, such as wood, aluminum or concrete.

Heavy Surface Oxidation to Exposed Thread Bar, Bolt and Plates that Fasten the Deadman/Tie Backs
Recommend treating the rust and applying rust inhibitive marine grade paint as directed per the manufacturer and local code ordinance requirements.

Foliage Overgrowth Encumbers the Retaining Wall. Cannot Fully Inspect
Foliage/vegetation overgrowth was observed encumbering the retaining wall. One cannot fully inspect the retaining wall. Recommend a licensed landscaping contractor remove all foliage and further inspection be completed.

Expansion Cracks Observed. Suspect Steel Oxidation Expansion from Rebar
Recommend consulting a licensed seawall contractor to assess further and mediate eventual concrete expansion breaks at the crack location.

No Expansion Joint Sealant Observed at the Expansion Joints
Expansion joints are those big joints in concrete that typically have either a piece of wood or have an asphalt fiberboard. When pouring the concrete driveway or sidewalk they place these expansion joints to allow the concrete to expand and contract and are also places they have stopped pouring the concrete for the day. Typically there is a piece of rebar going through the expansion strip to prevent the two concrete slabs from moving away from each other. Liquid sealants are the most commonly used sealant product for filling joints in building components and structural joints. Yet their performance, particularly in dynamic joints, can suffer from a variety of shortcomings that often begin with awkward installation factors such as badly prepared substrates and movement during the curing phase. Finally, tensile stresses at bond lines, as well as within the cured liquid sealant elastomer, often result in premature failure. The problem with these expansion strips is that they allow water to migrate down through the joint causing the rebar to rust. Eventually the rebar will break and allow the two concrete slabs to move independently. Another problem with these joints is that they can collect dirt and provide an area for weeds to grow. There is a solution to these problems; you can have a joint sealant placed over the expansion joint. This will help prevent water migrating down, causing the rebar to rust and will also prevent weeds from growing in the joint. Unless otherwise recommended by a licensed professional for this area, the material used is typically a polyurethane caulk that bonds to both side of the concrete slab creating a complete water seal. Other products such as plastic or foam that are placed in-between the joint do not create that watertight seal like the polyurethane caulking.

Repairing/Replacing Wood Retaining Wall
Retaining walls of wood are probably the least expensive and easiest to build. Because the wood contacts the soil directly, when replacing any component, you'll need a rot-resistant type such as redwood, cypress or pressure-treated wood rated for ground contact (the longest lasting of the three). Most walls have posts made from 4-by-4s, 4-by-6s or landscape timber. They are set in a deep, concrete-lined hole to provide support. A perforated pipe behind the wall provides drainage. Any properly designed and built retaining wall involves some quantity of digging. For a timber retaining wall, there is extra digging for the Deadman. If you were to replace that wall with timber, you'd have to do a lot of digging. But materials would be cheap. If you were to replace with stacking wall units, you'd still have to dig a sound base, and dig out enough room behind it for the gravel, fabric, drain and stone. Stacking wall units may be easier to apply for more novice installers. It cannot be fully determined as to what the underlying problems are and is beyond the scope of this inspection. It is highly recommended to have a county/state registered/licensed structural engineer to assess the area further prior to any financial decisions.

Retaining Wall is Overturning (eccentricity) and/or the Bearing Capacity is Insufficient
Hydrostatic pressure, water that is in the retained soil zone behind the retaining wall and/or the select soil zone can produce forces that will exceed or destroy the wall's design in some cases. The principal reason is because, unlike unsaturated and compacted soil that imposes a small horizontal force on the face stones of a retaining wall, water that invades the retained soil zone or the select soil zone will put a horizontal force on the face stones that is equal to the water's vertical force or weight. Also, too much water in the select soil zone will reduce the frictional characteristic of the select soil and then the select soil cannot provide the designed strength of the engineer's design. Soil saturated by water will lose the internal forces that hold it in place, therefore the soil's horizontal force on the face stones increases. This may be the cause amongst other variables, such as poor engineering design during the initial stages of its inception. It cannot be fully determined as to what the underlying problems are and is beyond the scope of this inspection. It is highly recommended to have a county/state registered structural engineer to assess the area further prior to any financial decisions.

Retaining Wall is Sliding
Hydrostatic pressure, water that is in the retained soil zone behind the retaining wall and/or the select soil zone can produce forces that will exceed or destroy the wall's design in some cases. The principal reason is because, unlike unsaturated and compacted soil that imposes a small horizontal force on the face stones of a retaining wall, water that invades the retained soil zone or the select soil zone will put a horizontal force on the face stones that is equal to the water's vertical force or weight. Also, too much water in the select soil zone will reduce the frictional characteristic of the select soil and then the select soil cannot provide the designed strength of the engineer's design. Soil saturated by water will lose the internal forces that hold it in place, therefore the soil's horizontal force on the face stones increases. This may be the cause amongst other variables, such as poor engineering design during the initial stages of its inception. It cannot be fully determined as to what the underlying problems are and is beyond the scope of this inspection. It is highly recommended to have a county/state registered structural engineer to assess the area further prior to any financial decisions.

Small Retaining Wall is overturning (eccentricity) and/or the Bearing Exceeds its Structural Capacity
The wall was not properly constructed for the application. The retaining wall is leaning forward and has separation between the individual stones. It appears that the wall stones may or may not have been set with batter. In this case, that water may have flowed into the area directly behind the wall and saturating the soil behind the wall. This wall, in addition to potential hydrostatic pressure, may have been surcharged due to excess earth loading near and directly behind the wall. This application may have required a design engineer that would have designed the wall with geo-grid to hold the surcharge of the area behind it and a drainage system to assure that water did not collect in the soil behind the wall. A gravity retaining wall [no geo-grid] may not have been adequate for this application. It cannot be fully determined as to what the underlying problems are and is beyond the scope of this inspection. It is highly recommended to have a county/state registered structural engineer to assess the area further prior to any financial decisions.

Small Retaining Wall at the Parking Area is overturning (eccentricity) and/or the Bearing Exceeds its Structural Capacity
The wall does not appear properly constructed for the application. The retaining wall is leaning forward and joint compromises were observed. This wall appeared to be surcharged due to the parking area near and directly behind the wall. It is likely that this application may have required a design engineer that would have designed the wall with geo-grid to hold the surcharge of the parking lot and a drainage system to assure that water did not collect in the soil behind the wall. A gravity retaining wall [no geo-grid] may not have been adequate for this application. It cannot be fully determined as to what the underlying problems are and is beyond the scope of this inspection. It is highly recommended to have a county/state registered structural engineer to assess the area further prior to any financial decisions.

Suspect Improper Swale at the Retaining Wall Back Face Top
The swale is such that it will flow surface water away from the wall rather than allowing the water to soak into the soil behind the retaining wall and saturating the compacted soil and rock behind the retaining wall. A drain tile system can be designed if a swale cannot be built to carry surface water away. The drain tile may collect surface water behind the wall and carry the water away through tubes that are installed under the footing of the wall. Please remember, it cannot be fully determined as to what the underlying problems are and is beyond the scope of this inspection. It is highly recommended to have a county/state registered structural engineer to assess the area further prior to any financial decisions.

Excessive Wood Rotting Observed
Wood rot is caused by undue exposure of untreated wood to moisture. Consequently, prevention constitutes both avoiding such exposure and employing a prevention and treatment program where rot already exists. Wood with 20 percent moisture content and green lumber remain at risk. Two types of rot trouble building owners. The first is white and yellow with a stringy and spongy look. The other is brown and crumbly in appearance, and a tendency to break into cubes has earned it the nickname "brown cubical rot." These visible manifestations of wood rot are called "fruiting bodies." About 3 inches in diameter, these crusts or brackets are evidence that the particular decay fungi are present within the wood. Serpula lacrimans, Poria incrassata and Gleophyllum trabeum each have singular fruiting-body appearances. Fruiting bodies produce spores, which spread the decay fungus throughout the wood. To prevent wood rot, use treated wood or the heartwood of a decay-resistant species. There are many websites that provide adequate direction as to how to treat the wood rot. Please remember, it cannot be fully determined as to what the underlying problems are and is beyond the

scope of this inspection. It is highly recommended to have a county/state registered structural engineer to assess the area further prior to any financial decisions.

Tree Roots from Neighboring Tree(s) are Causing Significant Heaving to the Retaining Wall

Tree roots from a neighboring tree(s) are causing significant heaving to the retaining walls mid-section and heaving will continue until the tree roots are removed. Serious cracking and compromises can occur from heaving stresses and moisture degradation from long-term exposure. Please remember, it cannot be fully determined as to what the underlying problems are and is beyond the scope of this inspection. It is highly recommended to have a county/state registered structural engineer to assess the area further prior to any financial decisions.

Potential Termite Damage Observed. Suspected Live Formosan Subterranean Termites Observed

Termite damage was suspected at and within the wood fencing. The Formosan subterranean termite (Coptotermes formosanus) is an invasive species of termite. It has been transported worldwide from its native range in southern China to Formosa (Taiwan, where it gets its name) and Japan. In the 20th century it became established in South Africa, Hawaii and in the continental United States. The Formosan subterranean termite is often nicknamed the super-termite because of its destructive habits. This is because of the large size of its colonies, and the termites' ability to consume wood at a rapid rate. A single colony may contain several million (compared with several hundred thousand termites for other subterranean termite species) that forage up to 300 feet (100 m) in soil. A mature Formosan colony can consume as much as 13 ounces of wood a day (ca. 400 g) and severely damage a structure or retaining wall in as little as three months. Because of its population size and foraging range, the presence of colonies poses serious threats to nearby structures. Once established; Formosan subterranean termite has never been eradicated from an area. By the 1950's, it was reported in South Africa and Sri Lanka. During the 1960's it was found in Texas, Louisiana, and South Carolina. In 1980, a well-established colony was thriving in a condominium in Hallandale Beach, Florida. Recommend further inspection and treatment if possible, or full removal of any infected area as needed. Please remember, it cannot be fully determined as to what the underlying problems are and is beyond the scope of this inspection. It is highly recommended to have a county/state registered structural engineer to assess the area further prior to any financial decisions.

Concrete Retaining Wall Horizontal Cracking Observed

Cracks which are horizontal are most likely caused by an applied load. Vertical cracks which are significantly wider at the top or bottom could indicate heaving or settlement. With these cracks it is very likely that the crack itself is not the problem, but rather the result of an external problem such as poor drainage, overloading, etc. Direct concern should be made under various conditions. Temperature and shrinkage cracks in walls or slabs are likely to occur in nearly all structures. When the width of a crack exceeds 1/4" in width; when they show 1/4" in lateral dis-placement; when water leaks through the cracks; or you find long horizontal cracks, it is probably time to seek professional assistance. The contractor that built the wall or your local CFA member should be able to help you. Please remember, it cannot be fully determined as to what the underlying problems are and is beyond the scope of this inspection. It is highly recommended to have a county/state registered structural engineer to assess the area further prior to any financial decisions.

Retaining Wall Vertical/Diagonal Cracks Observed

Tremendous forces can build up inside the wall due to any of these causes. When the forces exceed the strength of the material, cracks will develop. Each of these causes normally leaves a "signature" in the type of crack it creates. The vast majority of cracks are of little concern by themselves. Shrinkage and Temperature cracks are most often vertical to diagonal. Cracks of this type are called reentrant cracks. These are very common and, unless they leak or show significant lateral displacement, are typically of no structural concern.

Gravity Retaining Wall is in Disrepair, Sliding/Displaced Sections Throughout

Gravity retaining walls depend on the face stones to "retain" the fill soil behind the stones. The greater the setback slope [batter] of the gravity retaining wall, to a limit, the greater the ability of the stones to retain the soil placed behind the stones. Retaining walls are frequently 5 to 8 degrees off straight up. It is obvious that gravity retaining walls that are built with 0 degrees of batter, straight up, will fail with little horizontal force from the soil pressures behind the stones at the face. It is important to attend care with practices that will minimize the horizontal force that the soil behind the stones may apply to the face stones. Typically, when the batter of a wall or series of tired wall exceeds 30 degrees off straight up the structure referred to as Reinforced Soil Slope [RSS] and is designed with different formulas than the formulas used to design retaining walls.

Sliding/Displaced Sections Throughout
Please remember, it cannot be fully determined as to what the underlying problems are and is beyond the scope of this inspection. It is highly recommended to have a county/state registered structural engineer to assess the area further prior to any financial decisions.

Sidewalks

Pavers: General Comments

Concrete pavers give you the versatility to form sidewalks and walkways with gentle curved configurations and can be made to accommodate any width you desire. They also allow you to replicate the traditional aesthetics of a natural stone or brick walkway, but come in a wider array of colors and shapes. Concrete pavers also help define planting beds, making them ideal for garden paths and entryways. Many pavers are available with textured finishes to improve traction and slip resistance. One of the drawbacks of pavers is the cost, which tends to be higher than decorative poured-in-place concrete. Unlike poured-in-place concrete, concrete pavers can be walked on immediately after installation. Paver sidewalks require minimal maintenance if they are protected with a good sealer and the joints are filled with a polymer sand, which contains a special polymeric additive that binds and hardens the sand and helps to prevent erosion. The only regular maintenance required is sweeping and occasional rinsing to remove dirt and leaves. Concrete pavers may settle in spots over time if they aren't installed properly over a stable sub-base but they can easily be reset with no noticeable patchwork. Simply remove the affected pavers, re-grade and re-compact the sub-base, and reinstall the pavers as needed/when needed.

Exposed Aggregate

The sidewalk was comprised of poured concrete with an exposed aggregate surface. An exposed aggregate surface is durable and skid resistant making it ideal for: Pool Decks, Driveways, Patios, Porches and Sidewalks. The decorative process of exposing aggregate has been around since the early 1900's, well before pattern stamping, stenciling, and decorative overlays became trendy. But this method is far from being ready for retirement. An exposed aggregate finish offers numerous advantages and many of today's contractors are finding creative ways to take exposed aggregate to a new level. Exposed aggregate is a popular finish. This design choice can complement a variety of exterior treatments of the building. It typically is applied to a concrete deck, sidewalk or driveway. Exposed aggregate is an excellent sidewalk material. It is versatile, preferred for durability, appearance, low maintenance and when installed correctly, can indicates quality construction from the first glance. A concrete sidewalk is an essential part of an exposed aggregate texture. This texture type imparts an inviting image. Concrete's wide variety of texture, color, or patterns has brought this sidewalk material to the status of a landscape design element of today's building owner's demands.

Concrete

Concrete is an excellent sidewalk material. It is versatile, preferred for durability, appearance, low maintenance, and indicates quality construction from the first glance. Concrete has become an essential part of a landscaping plan that imparts an inviting image. Concrete's wide varieties of textures, color and patterns have brought this material to the status of a landscape design element for today's building owner's demands. Concrete is functional and it lends itself to a wide variety of options for design, which can make a dramatic difference in landscaping plans, as well as boost property values. In addition to the traditional look, concrete can have the decorative appearance, and color of brick, tile, slate, or stone. It is important to learn more about the product to maintain it and treat it when necessary.

Concrete Pavers
Some details about pavers In general: A paver sidewalk is a series of brick pavers laid dry upon an aggregate (gravel) and leveling base, contained by a locking border system. When installed properly, it is a permanent alternative to poured concrete which is prone to cracking and asphalt which is subject to weathering and requires substantial maintenance and or repaving every few years. Paver sidewalks that are installed properly are beautiful and add substantial value to the structure and the exterior aesthetics. However, most paver sidewalks are not installed properly by many DIY guys or "carpenters" with little to no technical understanding as to why or where they went wrong. While most of the install and material process cannot be seen at the time of the inspection, paver sidewalks require a specific amount of excavation, typically 8-10" below grade. A general rule of thumb is one 15 yard roll off container of excavated material for every five hundred square feet of sidewalk. A 1,000 square foot sidewalk should fill two 15 yard containers when excavated properly. The area should be backfilled with gravel that is "clean" which allows for proper drainage under the pavers. The existence of water under the pavers and the hydrostatic conditions caused by the lack of drainage is at the heart of problems with defective paver sidewalks. Very few paver sidewalks installed by unlicensed contractors are installed to these specifications.

Brick
Although good-quality bricks may outlast civilizations, the mortar that bonds them can crack and crumble after a number of years. Water penetration is the greatest degrader of mortar, and different mortar joints allow for varying degrees of water resistance. Mortar joints in brickwork also take up a large amount of the sidewalks layout/surface area and have a significant influence on the sidewalks overall appearance. Some joint profiles accentuate their individual designs, while others merge the bricks and mortar to form a flush, homogeneous surface.

Treated Wood
Pressure treated wood comes in many dimensions and because it is chemically infused with Chromium Copper Arsenate (CCA) or Alkaline Copper (ACQ), while under pressure, it resists damage from water and boring insects. Although it reduces the likelihood of damage, pressure treated lumber will eventually succumb to water, rotting and insects, although much slower than it would have if left untreated. Pressure treated wood should only be used for sidewalks limited to areas that have good drainage. Since wood does not bear an equal amount of pressure, per square inch as does concrete or other masonry, opt for a stronger material if your walk will be higher than 2-feet until 2003, the preservative most commonly used in residential pressure-treated lumber was chromate copper arsenate (CCA), an extremely toxic chemical. Remember "Arsenic and Old Lace" or that old box of rat poison you may have lurking in the garage? CCA is so toxic that the Environmental Protection Agency, over 20 years ago, imposed strict guidelines regarding the manufacturing practices of companies using CCA. However, one must distinguish between the toxicity of the chemical and the toxicity of the wood product in everyday use. Extensive studies were done since the mid 1980's concerning the potential dangers of pressure-treated wood. And rightfully so! Large volumes of CCA were being used, and the treated wood products were beginning to be widely distributed, justifying the need for hard research. The research was mixed, but the typical hysteria ensued as attorneys and plaintiffs lined up to claim damages from exposure to CCA. In the end, the industry agreed to voluntarily eliminate use of CCA for residential use. Your local building store or lumberyard is now selling lumber treated with (hopefully) less toxic alternatives... amine copper quat (ACQ) and copper azone (CA)... though you may find other chemical combinations in specific areas. CCA is still being used in certain marine and industrial applications since it is still the best preservative available at the present time.

Fiberglass/Composite Decking
Fiberglass/Composite decking is an attractive, **low-maintenance** architectural decking that offers alternatives to traditional decking materials. The panels **do not rot**, rust or mildew, which make them typically ideal for high moisture environments, including ocean inlets exposed to saltwater. The deck panels are easily installed with conventional or hidden fasteners that can create a smooth, attractive surface.

Trip Hazard. Uneven Pavers Observed
Pavers observed were uneven, often by natural settlement and placement. This may happen more where rain run off or ponding may occur.

Vegetation Growth through Brick/Paver Joints and Excess Algae found at the Time of Inspection
Recommend removing all weeds/vegetation at the cracks/joints and pressure wash the sidewalk as needed. Alternatively, some landscape managers have used liquid zinc or other natural algaecide to remove the algae because of its effectiveness, fast and very easy application process.

Concrete Walkways; Moisture Cracking from Weathering Observed
The cracks appear to be from weathering of the concrete. Cubicle and Web Cracks will form and progress many times in a web fashion if they and the concrete surrounding them are not treated. Caulking/sealing the cracks may also aid in reducing erosion underneath the walkway. Where cracks are larger, expansion joint sealant is recommended. Recommend the use of concrete walkway sealants NOT mortar/concrete unless directed by the state licensed contractor.

Small Stone Gravity Retaining Wall at the Sidewalk is Overturning and/or Bearing Exceeds Structural Capacity
The wall may not be properly constructed for the application. The retaining wall is leaning forward and has separation between the individual stones. It appears that the wall stones may or may not have been set with batter. In this case, water may have flowed into the area directly behind the wall, saturating the soil behind the wall. This wall appeared to be surcharged due to the sidewalk area near and directly behind the wall. This application may have required a design engineer that would have designed the wall with geo-grid to hold the surcharge of the sidewalk and a drainage system to assure that water did not collect in the soil behind the wall. A gravity retaining wall [no geo-grid] may not have been adequate for this application. Please note, it cannot be fully determined as to what the underlying problems are and is beyond the scope of this inspection. It is highly recommended to have a county/state registered structural engineer to assess the area further prior to any financial decisions.

Center Crack in Sectioned/Jointed Poured Concrete
Common hairline cracks observed. This is common of areas of wet soils likely to be earth-loading or earth loading exacerbated by water or frost. It appears to be from the shift of the outer soil region as the crack formed in the center. Inciting perhaps progressive soil movement, which is fairly common in the construction industry, as natural settlement is replaced by artificial compounding of the excavated areas. It is also most often after pouring that the natural settlement occurs.

Slight Algae Growth on Walkway
Slight algae growth on walkway is very common. However, you will want to treat or pressure wash mainly the darker areas as this growth tends to cause a slip hazard if allowed to grow. You may pressure clean it or add regular bleach in a sprayer with water, give it a little brushing and let it sit for a few minutes then you can hose it down and let it dry. Depending on neighboring vegetation, exterior grade bleach diluted per manufacturer's Instructions may be good. You may also look for liquid zinc for it's very easy to apply, natural properties.

Excessive Suspected Algae Growth on Walkway
This is very common. However, you will want to treat or pressure wash mainly the darker areas as this growth tends to cause a slip hazard if allowed to grow. You may pressure clean it or add regular bleach in a sprayer with water, give it a little brushing and let it sit for a few minutes then you can hose it down and let it dry. Depending on neighboring vegetation, exterior grade bleach diluted per manufacturer's Instructions may be good. You may also look for liquid zinc for it's very easy to apply, natural properties.

No Expansion Joint Sealant Observed at the Expansion Joints
Expansion joints are those big joints in concrete that typically have either a piece of wood or have an asphalt fiberboard. When pouring the concrete driveway or sidewalk they place these expansion joints to allow the concrete to expand and contract and are often places they have stopped pouring the concrete for the day. Typically, there is a piece of rebar going through the expansion strip to prevent the two concrete slabs from moving away from each other. Liquid sealants are the most commonly used sealant product for filling joints in building components and structural joints. However, their performance, particularly in dynamic joints, can suffer from a variety of shortcomings that often begin with awkward installation factors such as badly prepared substrates and movement during the curing phase. Finally, tensile stresses at bond lines, as well as within the cured liquid sealant elastomer, often result in premature failure. The problem with these expansion strips is that they allow water to migrate down through the joint causing the rebar to rust. Eventually the rebar will break and allow the two concrete slabs to move independently. Another problem with these joints is that they can collect dirt and provide an area for weeds to grow. There is a solution to these problems; you can have a joint sealant

placed over the expansion joint. This will help prevent water migrating down causing the rebar to rust and will also prevent weeds from growing in the joint. The material used is a polyurethane caulk that bonds to both side of the concrete slab creating a complete water seal. Other products such as plastic or foam are also placed in-between these joints, but they do not create that watertight seal like the polyurethane caulking.

Tree Roots from Neighboring Tree and Significant Heaving to the Sidewalk(s) Midsection

This is a liability hazard as it is considered a trip hazard. Fortunately, the walk can be shaved and filled, temporarily eliminating the problem. Heaving will likely continue to raise the walk, requiring further maintenance, until the tree roots are removed.

Tree Roots from Neighboring Tree and Significant Settlement to the Sidewalk(s) Midsections

There was significant settlement and cracks to the concrete sidewalk slabs. This appears to be caused from an alleged tree removed with left roots under the walkway. The roots will decay once the tree is removed or cut down. The decay allows hollowed cavities and loose soil to form under the walkway and eventual settlement of the walkway may occur as suspected at the time of the inspection. To assure no additional settlement will occur and confidence, recommend obtaining subsidence coverage from your insurance carrier. Recommend monitoring all areas of concern should any new occurrences arise. Recommend a licensed structural engineer, assess further all areas with apparent settlement to assure no additional settlement will occur and no structural compromises are present beyond the scope of this basic building inspection.

Paver Joint Sand Appears Insufficiently Applied Between the Pavers/Joints

Various pavers have exposed joints, gapped 1/16th to 1/8th of an inch. The joints of pavers do not require to be filled for the walkway to have integrity as it is a dry laid system. A small amount of the leveling base is swept in to prevent pavers from "rocking" back and forth in place. Adhesive sand is a tricky product and has a minimal application in paver installation under specific circumstances. In most cases it is not needed, can cake up in the corners of the joints and ruin the aesthetics of a beveled paver. Recommend a licensed specialist review this area further and remediate the deficiency as needed.

Iron Stains Observed on Sidewalks

The reddish brown rusty stains are a common problem readily seen on siding, sidewalks, walkways, patios, stepping stones, window and door frames in areas where irrigation water has a high iron content. The sprinkler system and/or hoses that are used to water the grounds may also be spraying iron particles that create these rust stains wherever they land. Iron is a chemical element that is abundant in soils and aquifers in many parts of the country. And it is the element that, when exposed to air and moisture, oxidizes or rusts. Where the tap water is "hard" or mineral-rich and we irrigate with well water, sprinkler water is probably causing rust stains. The irrigation systems will often "over spray" which means water ends up on the fence, patio, deck, porch, building, windows, doors, concrete walkways, stepping stones or paths, lawn furniture and also on parked vehicles if exposed to overspray. Once iron particles from the water in your sprinkler come in contact with the air, they will begin to oxidize or rust. The stains that result have likely developed over time and can be very stubborn to remove. Recommend installing a rust inhibitive filtration treatment system to the sprinkler system to prevent this.

Foliage Obstructs the Path of the Walkway

Recommend cutting back all trees/shrubs to prevent a trip hazard and provide adequate path(s) for walking purposes and access to egresses.

Trip Hazard; Concrete Sidewalk was observed Dilapidated with Cubicle Cracking and Spalling

The side walk was observed with extensive cracking/block cracking and spalling. The sidewalk poses a trip hazard and is recommended to be removed/replaced by a licensed contractor as is needed.

Driveways

Concrete
Concrete is an excellent driveway material. It is versatile, preferred for durability, appearance, low maintenance and indicates quality construction from the first glance. A concrete driveway has become an essential part of a landscaping plan that imparts an inviting image. Concrete's wide varieties of texture, color and patterns have brought this driveway material to the status of a landscape design element of today's building owner's demands. Concrete is functional and it lends itself to a wide variety options for design. This can make a dramatic difference in landscaping plans, as well as boost property values. In addition to the traditional look, concrete can have the decorative appearance (Decorative Flatwork) and color of brick, tile, slate or stone. It is important to learn more about the product to maintain it and treat it when necessary.

Concrete Pavers
Some comments about pavers in general: A paver driveway is a series of brick pavers laid dry upon an aggregate (gravel) and leveling base, contained by a locking border system. When installed properly, it is a permanent alternative to concrete which is prone to cracking and asphalt which is subject to weathering and requires substantial maintenance and or the repaving of such every few years. Paver driveways that are installed properly, are beautiful and add substantial value to the building and exterior aesthetics. However, most paver driveways are not installed properly by many DIY guys or "carpenters" with little to no technical understanding as to why or where they went wrong. While most of the install and material process cannot be seen at the time of the inspection, paver driveways require a specific amount of excavation, typically 8-10" below grade. A general rule of thumb is one 15 yard container of excavated material for every five hundred square feet of driveway. A 1,000 square foot driveway should fill two 15 yard containers when excavated properly. The area should have been backfilled with gravel that is "clean" which allows for proper drainage under the pavers. The existence of water under the pavers and the hydrostatic conditions caused by the lack of drainage is at the heart of problems with defective paver driveways. Very few paver driveways installed by unlicensed contractors are installed to these specifications.

Exposed Aggregate
Exposed aggregate is another popular finish. This design choice can complement a variety of exterior treatments of the house. It typically is applied to a concrete deck/driveway. Concrete is an excellent driveway material. It is versatile, preferred for durability, appearance, low maintenance and may indicate quality construction from the first glance. An exposed aggregate driveway has become an essential part of a landscaping plan that imparts an inviting image. Exposed Aggregate's wide variety of color and patterns has brought this driveway material to the status of a landscape design element to some of today's building owner's demands.

Brick
Although good-quality bricks may outlast civilizations, the mortar that bonds them can crack and crumble after a number of years. Water penetration is the greatest degrader of mortar, and different mortar joints allow for varying degrees of water resistance. Mortar joints in brickwork also take up a large amount of the driveways layout/surface area and have a significant influence on the driveways overall appearance. Some joint profiles accentuate their individual designs, while others merge the bricks and mortar to form a flush, homogeneous surface.

Treated Wood
Pressure treated wood comes in many dimensions and because it is chemically infused with Chromium Copper Arsenate (CCA) or Alkaline Copper (ACQ) while under pressure, it resists damage from water and boring insects. Although it reduces the likelihood of damage, pressure treated lumber will eventually succumb to water, rotting and insects, although much slower than it would have if left untreated. Pressure treated wood typically should only be used for patios, porches, balconies and occasionally, sidewalks. All areas should be limited to locations that have good drainage. Since wood does not bear an equal amount of pressure, per square inch as does concrete or other masonry, opt for a stronger material to endure the live load of vehicles daily. Note: Until 2003, the preservative most commonly used in residential pressure-treated lumber was chromate copper arsenate (CCA), an extremely toxic chemical. Remember "Arsenic and Old Lace" or that old box of rat poison you may have lurking in the garage? CCA is so toxic that the Environmental Protection Agency, over 20 years ago, imposed strict guidelines regarding the manufacturing practices of companies using CCA. However, one must distinguish between the toxicity of the chemical and the toxicity of the wood product in everyday use. Extensive studies were done since the mid 1980's concerning the potential dangers of pressure-treated wood. Large volumes of CCA were being used, and the treated wood products were beginning to be widely distributed, justifying the need for some hard research. In the end, the industry agreed to voluntarily eliminate use of CCA for residential use. Your local building store or lumberyard should now selling lumber treated with (hopefully) less toxic alternatives; amine copper quat (ACQ) and copper azone (CA) though you may find other chemical combinations in specific areas. CCA is still being used in certain marine and industrial applications since it is still the best preservative available at the present time.

Asphalt
Note: A properly installed asphalt driveway will perform much like concrete, but at a much lower cost and typically at a reduced life expectancy. Another trade-off is that you will need to seal coat the asphalt every few years. Asphalt is a petroleum product and that makes it flexible, which makes it less susceptible to cracking. But asphalt can also get very hot in the summer. Asphalt driveways typically last 12 to 35 years, depending on the quality of the installation, climate, usage, and how well they have been maintained. Like most everything else, the better care you take of the asphalt, the longer it will remain in service.

Fiberglass/Composite Decking
Fiberglass/Composite decking is an attractive, **low-maintenance** architectural decking that offers alternatives to traditional decking materials. The panels **do not rot**, rust or mildew, which make them typically ideal for high moisture environments, including ocean inlets exposed to saltwater. The deck panels are easily installed with conventional or hidden fasteners that can create a smooth, attractive surface.

Iron Stains Observed on Driveways
The reddish brown rusty stains are a common problem readily seen on siding, sidewalks, walkways, patios, stepping stones, window and door frames in areas where irrigation water has a high iron content. The sprinkler system and/or hoses that are used to water the grounds may also be spraying iron particles that create these rust stains wherever they land. Iron is a chemical element that is abundant in soils and aquifers in many parts of the country. And it is the element that, when exposed to air and moisture, oxidizes or rusts. Where the tap water is "hard" or mineral-rich and we irrigate with well water, sprinkler water is probably causing rust stains. The irrigation systems will often "over spray" which means water ends up on the fence, patio, deck, porch, building, windows, doors, concrete walkways, stepping stones or paths, lawn furniture and also on parked vehicles if exposed to overspray. Once iron particles from the water in your sprinkler come in contact with the air, they will begin to oxidize or rust. The stains that result have likely developed over time and can be very stubborn to remove. Recommend installing a rust inhibitive filtration treatment system to the sprinkler system to prevent this.

No Expansion Joint Sealant Observed at the Expansion Joints
Expansion joints are those big joints in concrete that typically have either a piece of wood or have an asphalt fiberboard. When pouring the concrete driveway or sidewalk they place these expansion joints to allow the concrete to expand and contract and are also places they have stopped pouring the concrete for the day.

Typically there is a piece of rebar going through the expansion strip to prevent the two concrete slabs from moving away from each other. Liquid sealants are the most commonly used sealant product for filling joints in building components and structural joints. Yet their performance, particularly in dynamic joints, can suffer from a variety of shortcomings that often begin with awkward installation factors such as badly prepared substrates and movement during the curing phase. Finally, tensile stresses at bond lines as well as within the cured liquid sealant elastomer, often result in premature failure. The problem with these expansion strips is that they allow water to migrate down through the joint causing the rebar to rust. Eventually the rebar will break and allow the two concrete slabs to move independently. Another problem with these joints is that they can collect dirt and provide an area for weeds to grow. There is a solution to these problems; you can have a joint sealant placed over the expansion joint. This will help prevent water migrating down causing the rebar to rust and will also prevent weeds from growing in the joint. The material used is a polyurethane caulk that bonds to both side of the concrete slab creating a complete water seal. Other products include plastic or foam are placed in-between the joint but these typically do not create that watertight seal like the polyurethane caulking.

Gravel is Displaced Throughout

Dirt and gravel driveways have less overall form than concrete, asphalt or brick driveways and walkways. Dips, bumps and potholes are unfortunately, just as great a nuisance. Because they are simple in there form and structure, it's very easy to fill a pothole in dirt or gravel driveways/walkways and requires very little effort to smooth out. Potholes won't fix themselves and if they get big enough, they can cause damage to your car or other vehicles and pose a trip hazard. It is best to attack the problem as soon as it is evident, not just for your vehicle or liability from trips and falls, but for the appearance of your driveway as well.

Center Crack in Sectioned/Jointed Poured Concrete

Common hairline cracks observed. This is common of areas of wet soils likely to be earth-loading or earth loading exacerbated by water or frost. It appears to be from the shift of the outer soil region as the crack formed in the center, inciting perhaps progressive soil movement fairly common in the construction industry. As natural settlement is replaced by artificial compounding of the excavated areas, it is more often after pouring, that the natural settlement occurs. This may have been exacerbated by vehicle loading as well as when the sectioned joints are longer than 10' feet in length before an expansion joint on the opposing horizontal/vertical lengths. Cracks will form where shrinkage occurs and settlement will usually exploit them. Filling cracks with an expansion joint sealant can reduce soil shift at the location.

Pavers Appeared Installed Improperly Over Sand

Many paver driveways are improperly installed on sand as a leveling base which is the wrong application. It quickly becomes obvious as piles of sand mount up in the street or corners of the driveway depress or displace after a single or multiple storms. Recommend having the area assessed further by a licensed driveway paver installation professional as needed.

Adhesive Sand Appears Liberally Applied Between the Pavers/Joints

Some contractors, and owners alike, ruin their finished product with the use of adhesive sand assuming the joints should appear "filled" like a mortar joint. The joints of pavers do not require to be filled for the driveway to have integrity as it is a dry laid system. A small amount of the leveling base is swept in to prevent pavers from "rocking" back in forth in place. Adhesive sand is a tricky product and has a minimal application in paver installation under specific circumstances. In most cases it is not needed and can cake up in the corners of the joints ruining the aesthetics of a beveled paver. Recommend a licensed specialist review this area further and remediate the deficiency as needed.

Tree(s) Heaving Grading at the Driveway

Tree roots from the neighboring tree are causing notable heaving to the driveway. This can be a liability hazard as the raised pad and crack(s) may be considered a trip hazard as well as it defacing the aesthetics of the driveway and curb appeal. Fortunately, the driveway can be shaved and filled, temporarily eliminating the problem but heaving will continue until the tree roots are removed and damages will progress. Recommend a licensed specialist review this area further and remediate the deficiency as needed.

Excessive Oil Spots Observed

Excessive oil spots are a safety hazard as it is considered a trip hazard. Recommend treating the area(s) as soon as possible to reduce potential liability.

Vehicle Loading Cracks Observed on the Driveway
This cracking is due to vehicles weighing and moving on the concrete coupled with daily heat and moisture exposure to increase degradation of the concrete. Recommend having a license contractor repair the driveway cracks with expansion joint sealants etc. Progressive cracks can also be attributed to heavier vehicles and/or loads than normal being parked or driven on the driveway.

Progressive Vehicle Loading Cracks on Driveway
This cracking is likely due to vehicles weighing and moving on the concrete coupled with daily heat and moisture exposure to increase degradation of the concrete. Recommend having a license contractor repair the driveway primarily at all progressive cracking and open cracks/joints. Progressive cracks can also be attributed to heavier vehicles than normal being parked or driven on the driveway.

Parking Markings Faded/Missing
Recommend designated marking material applications be applied per DOT requirements to provide clear parking designations and handicap parking designation(s) as needed.

Vegetation Growth through Cracks/Joints and Excess Algae Found at the Time of Inspection
When vegetation growth through cracks/joints and excess algae are found at the time of inspection, recommend removing weeds at the cracks/joints and pressure wash the driveway as needed. For the algae, you will want to treat or pressure wash mainly the darker areas as this growth tends to cause a slip hazard if allowed to grow. Recommend pressure washing/ treating the area as needed.

Algae Growth on Driveway
This is very common. However, you will want to treat and/or pressure wash mainly the darker areas as this growth tends to cause a slip hazard if allowed to grow. You may pressure clean it or add regular bleach in a sprayer with water, give it a little brushing and let it sit for a few minutes then you can hose it down and let it dry. Exterior grade bleach diluted per manufacturer's Instructions may suffice. You may also look for liquid zinc for it's very easy to apply, natural properties.

Subsidence Suspected; Significant Settlement and Cracks Observed
There was a significant settlement crack(s) in the concrete slab. Concrete chipping at these cracks may indicate caving in at these locations, erosion around the areas can be causing more degradation and exacerbation and/or are being induced by water eroding the soils around it. Exposed cracks in an exterior slabs or walls may allow moisture to intrude. If constructed to code, this driveway should have metal mesh reinforcement in it. Recommend for surety, confidence and personal safety, to have a structural engineer, review all areas of concern further before making any financial decisions. At minimum, recommend filling the cracks with expansion joint sealant or better as directed per the manufacturer.

Concrete Driveways; Moisture Cracking from Weathering Observed
The cracks appear to be from weathering of the concrete. Cubicle and Web Cracks will form and progress many times in a web fashion if they and the concrete surrounding them are not treated. Caulking/sealing the cracks may also aid in reducing erosion underneath the slab. Where cracks are larger, expansion joint sealant is recommended. For cubicle cracking resulting in wide gaps of 1/8th inch or more, major repairs or complete replacement may be required. Recommend the use of concrete sealants NOT mortar/concrete unless recommended by a state licensed contractor. Recommend a licensed contractor assess the driveway further and repair all as needed.

Asphalt Comments

Asphalt Fatigue (Alligator) Cracking Observed
Excessive loading suspected. This can be caused by weak surface, base, or subgrade typically conducive to the age of the asphalt. Weak subgrade may be to poor drainage and displacement, often induced by water infiltration by other cracking. A thin surface or base can also be a culprit or apart of the problem as the asphalt off gasses, washes away and ultimately breaks down due to use or any combination of the aforementioned. The asphalt industries may recommend the surface to have a full depth patch repair.

Block Cracking Observed on the Asphalt
Block cracking on asphalt is estimated to be from an old and dried out mix. The mix may have also been placed too dry initially. Fine aggregate mix with low penetration asphalt and absorptive aggregates may also cause this.

Any surface treatment or thin overlay treatment can generally fill and treat these locations as prescribed by the asphalt industry or as recommended by a licensed asphalt parking and driveway installing technician.

Edge Cracks to Asphalt Observed
This is estimated to be an excessive lack of lateral support, settlement of underlying material, shrinkage of drying out soil, weak base or subgrade layer, poor drainage and/or present vegetation along the edge of the asphalt. Per the asphalt industry, it is recommended to improve drainage. It is recommended to remove vegetation close to the edge/if any and maintain it, fill cracks with asphalt emulsion slurry or emulsified asphalt crack seal/fill.

Settlement/Grade Depression(s) Observed in the Asphalt
The asphalt industry assesses this as settlement or failure in the lower pavement layers and can also be contributed from improper construction techniques at the time the asphalt was poured. The asphalt industry states recommendations to cold mill and overlay, apply a thin surface patch or an infrared patch.

Patios

Decks/Patios Surface Types

Exposed Aggregate
The Deck was comprised of poured concrete with an exposed aggregate surface. An exposed aggregate surface is durable and skid resistant making it ideal for: Pool Decks, Driveways, Patios, Porches and Sidewalks. The decorative process of exposing aggregate has been around since the early 1900's, well before pattern stamping, stenciling, and decorative overlays became trendy. But this method is far from being ready for retirement. An exposed aggregate finish offers numerous advantages and many of today's contractors are finding creative ways to take exposed aggregate to a new level.

Concrete
Concrete is an excellent patio material. It is versatile, preferred for durability, appearance, low maintenance, and indicates quality construction from the first glance. A concrete patio has become an essential part of a landscaping plan that imparts an inviting image. Concrete's wide variety of texture, color, or patterns has brought this patio material to the status of a landscape design element of today's building owner's demands. Concrete is functional and it lends itself to a wide variety options for design, which can make a dramatic difference in landscaping plans, as well as boost property values. In addition to the traditional look, concrete can have the appearance, and color of brick, tile, slate, or stone. It is important to learn more about the product to maintain it and treat it when necessary.

Fiberglass/Composite Decking
Fiberglass/Composite decking is an attractive, **low-maintenance** architectural decking that offers alternatives to traditional decking materials. The panels **do not rot**, rust or mildew, which make them typically ideal for high moisture environments, including ocean inlets exposed to saltwater. The deck panels are easily installed with conventional or hidden fasteners that can create a smooth, attractive surface.

Concrete Pavers
Some details about pavers in general: A paver patio is a series of brick pavers laid dry upon an aggregate (gravel) and leveling base, contained by a locking border system. When installed properly, it is a permanent alternative to concrete which is prone to cracking and asphalt which is subject to weathering and requires substantial maintenance and or the repaving of such every few years. Paver patios that are installed properly, are beautiful and add substantial value to the structure and exterior aesthetics. However, since many patios are installed by DIY guys or "carpenters" with little to no technical understanding as to why or where they went wrong, most paver patios are not installed properly. While most of the install and material process cannot be seen at the time of the inspection, paver patios require a specific amount of excavation, typically 8-10" below grade. A general rule of thumb is one 15 yard roll container of excavated material for every five hundred square feet of patio. A 1,000 square foot patio should fill two 15 yard containers when properly excavated. The area should be backfilled with gravel that is clean of soils etc., which allows for proper drainage under the pavers.

The existence of water under the pavers and the hydrostatic conditions caused by the lack of drainage is at the heart of problems with defective paver patios.

Door Closer Inoperable on Screened/Storm Door to the Patio Enclosure
When door closer is inoperable on the screened/storm door, recommend installing a new one or repair the existing one as needed to prevent young children/pets etcetera, from entering/exiting when there may be hazards present as well as to prevent insects entering like mosquitoes or wasps.

Door Closer Missing on Screened/Storm Door to Patio
When the door closer is missing on screened/storm door of the screen enclosure to the patio, recommend installing to prevent young children/pets from entering/exiting when there may be hazards present or insects entering like mosquitoes or wasps.

Treated Wood
Pressure treated wood comes in many dimensions and because it is chemically infused with Chromium Copper Arsenate (CCA) or Alkaline Copper (ACQ) while under pressure, it resists damage from water and boring insects. Although it reduces the likelihood of damage, pressure treated lumber will eventually succumb to water, rotting and insects but much slower than it would have if left untreated. Pressure treated wood should only be used for patios limited to areas that have good drainage. Until 2003, the preservative most commonly used in residential pressure-treated lumber was chromate copper arsenate (CCA), an extremely toxic chemical. Remember "Arsenic and Old Lace" or that old box of rat poison you may have lurking in the garage? CCA is so toxic that the Environmental Protection Agency, over 20 years ago, imposed strict guidelines regarding the manufacturing practices of companies using CCA. However, one must distinguish between the toxicity of the chemical and the toxicity of the wood product in everyday use. Extensive studies were done since the mid 1980's concerning the potential dangers of pressure-treated wood. And rightfully so! Large volumes of CCA were being used, and the treated wood products were beginning to be widely distributed, justifying the need for some hard research. In the end, the industry agreed to voluntarily eliminate use of CCA for residential use. Your local building store or lumberyard is now selling lumber treated with (hopefully) less toxic alternatives... amine copper quat (ACQ) and copper azone (CA)... though you may find other chemical combinations in specific areas. CCA is still being used in certain marine and industrial applications since it is still the best preservative available at the present time. Whether these new chemicals will turn out to be less hazardous in the long term is anyone's guess.

Leaf Debris Observed Covering the Patio
Leaf debris can draw rodents, insects and other pests toward the building. Recommend cleaning off all debris and any algae accrued because of the debris mulching etc.

Tree Roots Heaving/Subsidence Suspected
Encumbering tree roots provide enough concern that there might be heaving involved that can cause far greater damage given enough time and warrants further review by an engineer. Alternatively, cracks may be the result of sudden settlement and as well can be caused by the roots. The roots can starve the neighboring grading of moisture, causing soil shifts etc. Recommend a licensed/insured tree and ROOT removal specialist assess this area further and remove as is needed all roots/trees as needed. Recommend a licensed structural engineer assess the structural stress cracks and thermal conditions etc. as needed and estimate repairs prior to any financial considerations.

Concrete Pool Deck; Moisture and Basic Settlement Cracks Observed
Concrete will crack as a normal outcome of the curing process. Cracking can be worsened if uneven bearing conditions exist under the slab, such as un-compacted fill areas. Excessive water used for the workability of cement tends to produce excessive cracking, which can allow moisture to more readily penetrate the concrete slab, weakening the concrete, and leading to differential drying issues and cracking. Excessive cracking can allow additional moisture, to penetrate more easily through the slab. The use of welded wire-fabric reinforcement provides a means of controlling the severity of cracking. Concrete control joints may also be used to control random cracking by creating planned lines of weakness in the slab. Shrinkage or curing cracks generally occur in any continuous length of concrete longer than about 12 feet. These cracks are easily maintained and virtually eliminated with proper maintenance including proper mitigation of storm water away from the slab. Additionally, recoating or re-texturing the deck, may provide a more uniform elimination of the cracks appearance/if any.

Trip Hazard. Uneven Pavers Observed
Pavers observed were uneven, often by natural settlement and placement. This may happen more where rain run off or ponding may occur. Since many patios are installed by DIY guys or "carpenters" with little to no technical understanding as to why or where they went wrong, most paver patios are not installed properly. It is recommended to have a licensed paving contractor review this area further and repair all as needed.

Pool Wall Inlet(s) Apparatus Observed Damaged/Missing
Damaged or missing inlets can change the distribution process of the pool water. Additionally, the inlet location may aid in water leaks etcetera, at the compromised location. Recommend a state licensed pool service and repair company repair as needed.

Pool Marcite/Plaster Coating was Observed Etching at the Time of the Inspection
The Plaster is also called white coat or Marcite. Pool plaster is a process of finishing the gunite or shotcrete pool structures. Used underwater, it provides the watertight seal that the porous gunite or shotcrete beneath it cannot. Pool Plaster/Marcite finishes provide an average estimate of twenty years of service under ideal conditions. Our world however, is rarely ideal and many variables can cause the progression of degradation to include how it was initially applied. The pool plaster surface is meant to degrade slowly, eventually requiring a fresh coat of Marcite. If your pool plaster has surface irregularities, which may take on a beige hue, you may have what's commonly called etching. This etching can be caused by low pH or alkalinity; an acidic condition. It may begin within the plaster, from the original mix on application, or etching may start from the gunite side of the plaster and work itself from the outside in. In instances were a yellow stain is present and appears in a small cluster at one location or a single spot, chlorine tablets may be the culprit. Left to sit directly on pool plaster, they can also create a yellowish stain and can be difficult to remove. Common costs for re-plastering can vary greatly by the size of the pool.

Iron Stains Observed on Patio
The reddish brown rusty stains are a common problem readily seen on siding, sidewalks, walkways, patios, stepping stones, window and door frames in areas where irrigation water has a high iron content. The sprinkler system and/or hoses that are used to water the grounds may also be spraying iron particles that create these rust stains wherever they land. Iron is a chemical element that is abundant in soils and aquifers in many parts of the country. And it is the element that, when exposed to air and moisture, oxidizes or rusts. Where the tap water is "hard", or mineral-rich and we irrigate with well water, sprinkler water is probably causing rust stains. The irrigation systems will often "over spray" which means water ends up on the fence, patio, deck, porch, building, windows, doors, concrete walkways, stepping stones or paths, lawn furniture and also on parked vehicles if exposed to overspray. Once iron particles from the water in your sprinkler come in contact with the air, they will begin to oxidize or rust. The stains that result have likely developed over time and can be very stubborn to remove. Recommend installing a rust inhibitive filtration treatment system to the sprinkler system to prevent this.

No Expansion Joint Sealant Observed at the Expansion Joints
Expansion joints are those big joints in concrete that typically have either a piece of wood or have an asphalt fiberboard imbedded in them. When pouring the concrete driveway or sidewalk they place these expansion joints to allow the concrete to expand and contract and are also places they have stopped pouring the concrete for the day. Typically there is a piece of rebar going through the expansion strip to prevent the two concrete slabs from moving away from each other. Liquid sealants are the most commonly used sealant product for filling joints in building components and structural joints. Yet their performance, particularly in dynamic joints, can suffer from a variety of shortcomings that often begin with awkward installation factors such as badly prepared substrates and movement during cure. Finally, tensile stresses at bond lines, as well as within the cured liquid sealant elastomer, often result in premature failure. The problem with these expansion strips is that they allow water to migrate down through the joint causing the rebar to rust. Eventually the rebar will break and allow the two concrete slabs to move independently. Another problem with these joints is that they can collect dirt and provide an area for weeds to grow. There is a solution to these problems; you can have a joint sealant placed over the expansion joint. This will help prevent water migrating down causing the rebar to rust and will also prevent weeds from growing in the joint. The material used is a polyurethane expansion joint sealant that bonds to both side of the concrete slab creating a complete water seal. Other products such as plastic or foam that are placed in-between the joint do not typically create that watertight seal like the polyurethane sealant.

Algae Growth on the Patio Observed
Algae growth on the patio is very common. However, you will want to treat or pressure wash mainly the darker areas as this growth tends to cause a slip hazard if allowed to grow. You may pressure clean it or scrub the areas using exterior grade bleach diluted per manufacturer's Instructions. You may also look for a liquid zinc or

other natural algaecide that will not harm neighboring plants etcetera. See Online for additional information from the manufacturers and correct, thorough manners to apply any products noted or better.

Tree(s) Heaving Grading at the Patio
Tree roots from the neighboring tree are causing notable heaving to the patio. This is can be a liability hazard as it may be considered a trip hazard by your insurance company and it is also defacing the aesthetics of the patio. Heaving will likely continue until the tree roots are removed and damages will likely progress. Recommend a licensed specialist review this area further and remediate the deficiency as needed. Installing a root barrier system involves trenching between the tree and target to be protected. Trenching around existing trees needs to be done with extreme caution both to prevent excessive root loss and tree dieback and also to protect the structural integrity and wind firmness of the tree. This is usually best done by a professional arborist or landscape service company that is licensed to contract this service.

Pavers Appeared Installed Improperly Over Sand
Many paver patios are improperly installed on sand as a leveling base which is the wrong application. It quickly becomes obvious as piles of sand mount up in the street or corners of the patio depress or displace after a single or multiple storms. Recommend having the area assessed further by a licensed patio paver installation professional as needed.

Adhesive Sand Appears Liberally Applied Between the Pavers/Joints
Some contractors and owners alike, ruin their finished product with the use of adhesive sand assuming the joints should appear "filled" like a mortar joint. The joints of pavers do not require to be filled for the patio to have integrity as it is a dry laid system. A small amount of the leveling base is swept in to prevent pavers from "rocking" back and forth in place. Adhesive sand is a tricky product and has a minimal application in paver installation under specific circumstances. In most cases it is not needed and can cake up in the corners of the joints and ruin the aesthetics of a beveled paver. Recommend a licensed specialist review this area further and remediate the deficiency as needed.

Vegetation Growth through Cracks/Joints and Slight Algae found at the Time of Inspection
Recommend removing weeds at the cracks/joints and pressure wash the patio as needed. Alternatively, some landscape managers have used liquid zinc or other natural algaecide to remove the algae because of its effective, fast and very easy application process.

Erosion Observed at the Patio from Lack of Gutters/Downspouts at the Location
Lack of gutters, downspouts and diverters for rain run off can cause erosion depressions which in trade pond water after storms and then further exacerbate the erosion. When rain falls, the water runs along the surface of the topsoil, and it will collect in the depression or furrow. The water will slowly seep into the soil and collect in underground pockets that will supply the roots of plants through weeks and even months without rain. Displacement of soil at the foundation will also occur more progressively, causing cracks in the foundation. This unfortunately, is not what you want around the perimeter. Ponding will progressively grow, more so with each rain, and be a feeding spot for roots, like a beacon calling them to the buildings foundation from any trees, if any. Recommend Gutters, downspout and diverters be installed throughout this location to prevent further grade erosion and remediating the ponding with the corrective aggregate as needed.

Concrete Moisture Cracks Observed
There are two guarantees with concrete. One, it will get hard and two, it will crack. Cracking is a frequent cause of complaints in the concrete industry. The Concrete Foundations Association has produced a new flyer to help contractors educate their customers and building owners to know about the causes of cracks and when they should be a concern. Cracking can be the result of one or a combination of factors such as drying shrinkage, thermal contraction, restraint (external or internal) to shortening, subgrade settlement and applied loads. Cracking cannot be prevented but it can be significantly reduced or controlled when the causes are taken into account and preventative steps are taken. Cubicle cracks were found intermittently throughout. Recommend having a licensed concrete treatment contractor assess further and treat/seal as needed.

Brick Mortar Deterioration Observed
Although good-quality bricks may outlast civilizations, the mortar that bonds them can crack and crumble after a number of years. Water penetration is the greatest degrader of mortar, and different mortar joints allow for varying degrees of water resistance. Mortar joints in brickwork also take up a large amount of the patios layout/surface area and have a significant influence on the patios overall appearance. Some joint profiles

accentuate their individual designs, while others merge the bricks and mortar to form a flush, homogeneous surface.

Deterioration of Brick Observed
The spalling, dusting or flaking of brick masonry units may be due to either mechanical or chemical damage. Mechanical damage is caused by moisture entering the brick and freezing, resulting in spalling of the brick's outer layers. Spalling may continue, or it may stop on its own after the outer layers that trapped the interior moisture have broken off. Chemical damage is due to the leaching of chemicals from the ground into the brick, resulting in internal deterioration. External signs of such deterioration are a dusting or flaking of the brick. Very little can be done to correct existing mechanical and chemical damage except for actually replacing the brick. Mechanical deterioration can be slowed or stopped by directing water away from the masonry surface and by pointing mortar joints to slow water entry into the Decking.

Uneven Settlement Observed at the Patio/Building Abutment
Uneven or differential settlement refers to when the slab or other surface settles faster or at a different rate than that of the building, resulting in a separation of the two, noticeable at the abutment point. Serious settlement problems are relatively uncommon. Many signs of masonry distress are incorrectly diagnosed as settlement-related when, in fact, they are due to moisture and thermal movements. It is recommended to have the crack/joint at the building, be sealed with joint sealant at the abutting joint. Recommend non-shrinking, serviceable sealants to prevent moisture and insect intrusion.

Salt Spalling Observed
Salt spalling is a specific type of weathering that can occur in brick, natural stone, tiles and concrete. Dissolved salt is carried through the material in water and then crystallizes inside the material near the surface as the water evaporates. As the salt crystals expand, this builds up shear stresses that break away and create spalling at the surface. Some believe that porous building materials can be protected against salt spalling by treatment with water-repellent sealants that penetrate deeply enough to keep water with dissolved salts well away from the surface. Expert advice should be sought to ensure that any coating applied is compatible with the substrate in terms of its breathability, which is the ability to allow the release of vapors from inside while preventing water intrusion, or other serious problems can be created.

Basic Cracks in the Concrete Floor
Concrete will crack as a normal outcome of the curing process. Cracking can be worsened if uneven bearing conditions exist under the slab, such as un-compacted fill areas. Excessive water used for the workability of cement tends to produce excessive cracking, which can allow moisture to more readily penetrate the concrete slab, weakening the concrete, leading to differential drying issues and cracking. Excessive cracking can allow additional moisture as well as radon gas to penetrate more easily through the slab. The use of welded wire-fabric reinforcement provides a means of controlling the severity of cracking. The use of fiber-reinforced concrete may also provide adequate crack control. Concrete control joints may also be used to control random cracking by creating planned lines of weakness in the slab. Shrinkage or curing cracks generally occur in any continuous length of concrete longer than about 12 feet.

Settlement Crack Observed
Common Hairline Cracks Observed. This is common of areas of wet soils likely to be earth-loading or earth loading exacerbated by water or frost. It appears to be from the shift of the outer soil region as the crack formed in the center, inciting perhaps progressive soil movement, fairly common in the construction industry as natural settlement is replaced by artificial compounding of the excavated areas. It is more often after pouring that the natural settlement occurs. Patio concrete slabs are generally not poured with proper footings like buildings. If the soil below was not proper or properly compacted, this natural settlement effect is more progressive.

Erosion Observed at the Patio from Gutter Downspouts Terminating at the Location
These downspouts caused erosion depressions which in trade pond water after storms and then further exacerbate the erosion. When rain falls, the water runs along the surface of the topsoil, and it will collect in the depression or furrow. The water will slowly seep into the soil and collect in underground pockets that will supply the roots of plants through weeks and even months without rain. Displacement of soil at the foundation will also occur more progressively, causing cracks in the foundation. This unfortunately, is not what you want around the perimeter. Ponding will progressively grow, more so with each rain, and be a feeding spot for roots, like a beacon calling them to the buildings foundation from any trees, if any. Recommend Gutter downspout diverters be installed on downspout location to prevent further grade erosion and remediating the ponding with the corrective aggregate as needed.

Trip Hazard. Uneven Pavers Observed
Pavers observed were uneven, often by natural settlement and placement. This may happen more where rain run off or ponding may occur and may be considered a trip hazard liability by your insurance company. Recommend repairing as is needed.

Loose/Leaning Rail Observed
Rails must properly fastened per the ICC guidelines and/or your local code ordinances. Insurance companies may take issue when rails are leaning and/or are not have properly fastened. Rail systems and handrails must be surfaced to prevent injuries typically, to meet the insurance and OSHA standards. Loose railing can allow the structural integrity to give way and allow a person to fall or become impaled if parts fall with and in relation to the individual, engaging them upon impact with the surface or landing that terminates the fall. Recommend a licensed contractor repair all as needed.

Exposed Rebar Observed at the Patio Concrete Slab
Rebar expansion can occur through the rust/oxidation process, this expansion can in trade cause cracks to appear in the concrete when the expansion pushes ever so slightly on the concrete. Since concrete is susceptible to cracks from the rebar expansion, cracks will occur typically. If, when they do, it is important to seal those cracks to prevent further cracking.

Concrete Patios; Cubicle/Moisture Cracking from Weathering Observed
The cracks appear to be from weathering of the concrete. Additionally, bad concrete batch or too much water in the initial pouring, was applied. Cubicle and Web Cracks will form and progress many times in a web fashion if they and the concrete surrounding them are not treated. Caulking/sealing the cracks may also aid in reducing erosion underneath the slab. Where cracks are larger, expansion joint sealant is recommended. For cubicle cracking resulting in wide gaps of 1/8th inch or more, major repairs or complete replacement may be required. Recommend the use of concrete sealants NOT mortar/concrete unless recommended by a state licensed contractor. Recommend a licensed contractor assess the concrete further and repair all as needed.

Wood Deck Plank Boards are Warping/Loose and Can Pose a Trip Hazard
Wood plank board decking fasteners eventually corrode and cause boards to become loose. If the boards are laid crown up, warping can be progressive. These raised boards can pose a trip hazard. Wood has many outstanding properties, but it is a natural, porous material with individual characteristics, and it can warp. When wood gets wet, it swells. When wood dries out after being sawn from the tree, after being pressure-treated and after rain showers, it shrinks. Uneven drying creates stresses in wood, which results in warping (e.g., bowing, cupping or twisting) or cracking. The degree of warping depends on the species of wood, its grain pattern, uniformity of drying and construction techniques, among other factors. There is not much a user can do to truly un-warp a warped piece of wood. It is possible to position bowed boards so that its weight flattens it, using screws that are load adequate to fasten securely an otherwise warped piece. Recommend re-supporting or replacing the displaced section with deck/exterior wood screws per each section effected and any horizontal bracing and straps on stringers, balustrade, treads and rails where applicable, as needed, as directed by a state licensed contractor/structural engineer.

No Railing Observed at the Time of the Inspection
2012 IRC (International Residential Code) Section R311.7.8 HANDRAILS - In addition, most insurance companies require handrails and railing for decking and where stairs have 3 or more risers to include the decking/landing. R311.7.8 (Handrails) Handrails having a minimum and maximum heights of 34 inches and 38 inches respectively, measured vertically from the sloped plain adjoining the tread nosing or finished surface of ramp slope. Shall be provided on at least one side of stairways with a total rise of 30" or more. Spiral stairways shall have the required handrail located on the outside radius. All required handrails shall be continuous the full length of the stairs. Ends shall be returned or shall terminate in newel posts or safety terminals. Handrails adjacent to a wall shall have a space of not less than 1½ inch between the wall and the handrail. For this reason and for general safety standards, it is highly recommended to remediate ASAP by a licensed contractor per IRC guidelines and/or state and local codes.

Loose Railing Observed
OSHA Regulations: Railing must be properly fastened per the ICC guidelines and/or your local code ordinances. Insurance companies may take issue when railing for balconies railings are not have properly fastened. Stair rail systems and handrails must be surfaced to prevent injuries typically, to meet the insurance and OSHA standards. Loose railing can allow the structural integrity to give way and allow a person to fall or become impaled if parts fall with and in relation to the individual, engaging them upon impact with the surface or landing that terminates the fall. Recommend a licensed contractor repair all as needed.

Patio Covers

Thermoplastic Polyolefin (TPO) Membrane
PVC roofing is one of the best single-ply membranes and has a long history of excellent performance. CRC has observed 20-years old PVC roofs and they are still performing well and still in service. Compared to many roofing products, PVC is contractor friendly both in quality and ease of application. Properly formulated and manufactured PVC and other roofing materials give years of good service.

Modified Bitumen Roll Roofing
The Asphalt Roofing Manufacturers' Association (ARMA) describes Modified Bitumen Roofing as follows: "Modified bitumen membranes MBS combine the features of a built-up roof with the added tensile strength from its polymer modification. Using a reinforced sheet that is prefabricated in the plant, modified bitumen systems require a less labor-intensive application and can be applied cross-platform in both commercial and certain residential applications. A modified bitumen roofing system is composed primarily of polymer-modified bitumen membrane reinforced with one or more plies of fabric such as polyester, fiberglass or a combination of both. Factory surfacing, if applied, includes mineral granules, slag, aluminum or copper. The bitumen determines the membrane's physical characteristics and provides primary waterproofing protection, while the reinforcement adds strength, puncture resistance and overall system integrity. Factory-assembled, modified bitumen membranes undergo strict quality control standards to ensure uniform thickness and consistent physical properties throughout the membrane. The finished roofing system is usually a two to four-ply system consisting of a modified bitumen membrane and a base sheet, with additional plies for added strength if needed. The substrate often determines which ply system is best specified. The finished roofing membrane may consist of one or more modified bitumen sheets, or it may be comprised of a combination of built-up roofing (BUR) felts and one or more modified bitumen sheets.

Bitumen Rolled Roofing
This consists of a heavy, asphalt-saturated organic or fiberglass felt with a granular surface. Rolls are typically 36 inches wide and weigh 90 pounds. Single-coverage roll roofing typically has a 2-inch lap with exposed nails and is used mainly on utility structures. Double-coverage roll roofing is installed with a full 19-inch lap joint, leaving a 17-inch exposure, with a 2-inch head-lap.

Spray Polyurethane Foam Roofing with Elastomeric
Seams are one of the major sources of leaks in roof systems and SPF roofs are totally seamless. Polyurethane foam is applied as a liquid, creating a single monolithic membrane that covers the entire roof – no seams and no joints when installed correctly. Also, the foam is easy to replace when stacks or other roof penetrations need to be moved or added. Additionally, foam roofing typically weighs around 50 lbs. per square, versus 800 lbs. for a built-up roof and 1,000 lbs. for ballasted single-ply roofs. This reduces the structural dead load on your roof.

Galvanized Metal Panel Roof Upkeep Comments
Be careful not to let metals of different types touch each other. Chemical reactions between different materials can invite corrosion. Keep paint touched up to keep rust at bay. Repair holes and open seams as soon as possible. Cover very small holes with roofing cement. Solder a patch of the same metal over larger holes. Only use screws made of the same metal as the roof. Also, always use screws with washers and install them in raised areas, not low areas where water can pool and leak.

Aluminum Panel Screws Need Maintenance
The roof cover is an aluminum panel with a silicone sealed screws aligning the roof to wall abutment and are observed at the roof top. These screws have an applied silicone sealant. Though the screws appear to not be leaking or defective, it appears the sealant is loosening and is recommended to be treated and the screws to be redressed with silicone. Monitor annually. Typically, retreatment is required every 10-15 years or better dependent on product type. It would be prudent to apply a silicone based or better patch/caulk to all screw heads and seams. Apply in accordance with local code and to manufacturer's instructions.

Aluminum Raised Seam Metal Roof
Standing seam is a succession of vertical sheet metal roofing panels connected side-by-side by a vertical locking mechanism called the seam. The seams can be seen from the ridge of a roof all the way down to the eaves. The locked seam is raised by an inch or two above the panels in order to maintain water-tightness of the system. The raised seam also provides for a unique and distinctive appearance. As with most metal roofs featuring concealed fasteners, standing seam roofs are virtually maintenance-free, fire-retardant and resistant to strong winds, and are just as quiet as asphalt shingles, clay tikes, or wooden shingles/shakes when it rains when insulated correctly. Standing seam roofs are very energy efficient, environmentally safe and long lasting. They are a popular choice in "green" construction projects. Since many standing seam metal roofs can easily last longer than 50 years, with virtually no to very low maintenance compared to asphalt shingles that have an average lifespan of 20 to 25 years. Thus, standing seam beats traditional asphalt roofing competition by a factor of three in terms of its expected service life.

UV Exposure Appears to have Caused Significant Wear to the Skylight Dome, causing Cracking/Damage
The skylight dome appears to be at end of life. The plastic is "yellowed" or foggy, indicative of U.V exposure long term. In addition, the perimeter fastening nails are heavily oxidized/rusted with various nails loose. There were also cracks forming at the perimeter cap/lip where the nails are fastened that degrades the uplift resistance and makes it far more susceptible to uplift damage. The internal dome/ plexi glass appears to also have heat stress cracks. Sun and UV exposure will cause significant wear to most originally installed external skylight domes and then rain, hail or snow can often cause cracking or damage in some other way. U.V. radiation degrades the elasticity of the dome(s) and makes them susceptible to crack and fray from far less impact than they were once designed for. Since the progressive degradation conducive to a weathered skylight was present, and given the high probability for water resistance failure in the near future, it is highly recommended to have the skylight glass/dome changed to prevent any water loss and to provide maximum efficiency for lighting purposes.

Rusted Galvanized Drip Edge Flashing Observed
The oxidation rust has penetrated past the zinc coating and has compromised the flashing. A properly applied rust treatment and metal roofing waterproofing sealant may remediate further present and future degradation. Recommend a licensed contractor assess the area further and repair as needed.

Basic Shingle Maintenance Comments (Architectural)
Roof was comprised of an architectural asphalt shingle (3 dimensional). This shingle typically has a 30 year manufacturer's warranty or higher. All valleys, vent stacks and weather hoods appeared to be in serviceable condition. Overall condition to the roof cover was good. The shingle should be resistant to black algae starting to form on the roof surface for ten years from the install date. This algae degrades the life of the roof by years. If observed, it is very easy to apply algae remover. This should be applied to the roof shingle surface as directed by the manufacturer. Your roof cover (architectural/3-Dimensional shingle) is the newer type and likely has a 30 year life warranty or better by the manufacturer. The "black" part of the fungi draws more heat which acts as an additive in the cocktail toward degrading your roof. A good algae removing application is a liquid Ion of Zinc, made for roofing materials. You can search online for the "liquid zinc" products for more information. It is recommended to apply when algae appears to be just setting or when first observed. To obtain full life of the shingle, treat as recommended or better. It is not recommended to use bleaching agents with a higher alkalinity

due to their corrosive behavior and that they can void many roof cover types' warranties. Check your roof material type and warranty details before using/applying any products.

Popped Nail(s) Observed at the Roof Cover
Popped nails are nails that have worked upward, generally, from thermal expansion. While this can happen because the nail or girth is insufficient for the roofing material or the decking type it is. Also, if there is multiple ply roofing materials. It also happens from general tweaks in the wood from the thermal expansion process. Recommend a licensed contractor repair all as needed.

Missing/Damaged Crown Shingle(s) Observed
Recommend a licensed roofer replace the shingle(s) as needed to prevent water intrusion and further degradation.

Basic Shingle Maintenance Comments (3 Tab)
Roof was comprised of a composition asphalt shingle. All valleys, vent stacks and weather hoods appeared to be in serviceable condition. Overall condition to the roof cover was good. This shingle typically has a 25 year manufacturer's warranty or higher. Dark Lichen, Fungi and Algae degrade the life of the roof by years. If observed to be progressive, there is an easy to apply natural algae remover. This should be applied to the roof shingle surface. Your roof cover (composition asphalt shingle) has a standard warrantied life for the shingle by the manufacturer. This life expectancy can be reduced by years if algae is left to grow and eat away at the shingle may negate some warranties depending on severity and conditions/lack of maintenance. Additionally, the "black" part of the algae draws more heat which acts as an additive in the cocktail toward degrading your roof. A good algae removing application is a liquid Ion of Zinc, made for roofing materials. You can search "liquid zinc" online for more information. Use when algae appears to be just setting. To obtain full life of the shingle, treat as recommended or better. It is not recommended to use bleaching agents with a higher alkalinity due to their corrosive behavior and that they can void many roof cover types' warranties. Check your roof material type and warranty details before using/applying any products.

Basic Tile Algae/Fungi Maintenance Comments.
Roof was comprised of a concrete tile. This algae harbors moisture at the roof surface and draws more heat to the roof and may degrade the life of the roof by years. There is an excellent and very easy to apply algae remover. This should be applied to the roof surface. If your roof cover is the newer grade coated tile and has a minimum 30 year life typical warranty by the manufacturer or better for the tile, this life expectancy can be reduced if algae is left to grow and degrade the integrity of the tiles. Additionally, the "black" part of the algae draws more heat which acts as an additive in the cocktail toward degrading your roof. A good algae removing application is a liquid Ion of Zinc, made for roofing materials. You can search online for "liquid zinc" for more information. Use when algae becomes apparent. To obtain full life of the shingle, treat as recommended by the manufacturer or better. It is not recommended to use bleaching agents with a higher alkalinity due to their corrosive behavior and that they can void many roof cover types warranties including coated concrete tile. Check your roof material type and warranty details before using/applying any products.

End Cap Crown Shingle(s) Nail Fasteners Need Sealant
Recommend a licensed roofer treat the fasteners with a rust inhibiting treatment if needed and seal all as needed unless or as recommended by the roofer, to prevent water intrusion and further degradation to fasteners, underlayment etc.

Missing/Damaged Shingle(s) Observed
Recommend a licensed roofer replace the shingle(s) as needed to prevent water intrusion and further degradation to nails, underlayment etc.

Compromise along the Seam/Flashing, where the Patio Roof meets the Fascia
The flashing/counterflashing seals can be a constant preemptive maintenance requirement for this roof cover/transition, requiring coating/sealing or better every 3-7 years depending on the product used. It is recommended for a licensed contractor to apply an elastomeric patch/caulk or DYCO #20/20 Seam Sealer or better to seal around screw heads where needed. Follow label instructions. Apply to manufacturer's instructions.

Posts/Columns Span is Too Far Spaced and can be Structurally Compromised
Normal porches with columns where the posts in a post and beam like construction are compromised. The weight that is being supported and what the beam structure is like, determines if you can span wider than 8-10'. Your posts/columns were exceeding this. Each column should be on a foundation properly mounted and secured to both the mount and the beam. On some older buildings, this is only a pier and the location of the

piers will dictate the location of the columns. The beams might be designed to hold a great deal of weight but may be spliced at certain locations. These splices are typically covered by aesthetic wood covering. The splices will then determine the column locations. The actual size and type of the beam required to span a certain length on a porch is determined not only by engineering but by your local building codes and the type of beam. Your local building codes, an engineer and the local building inspector can assist you further.

Aluminum Panel Seam and Screws Need Maintenance
The roof cover is an aluminum panel with a foil tape seal at the seams. The seals are a constant preemptive maintenance requirement for this roof cover, requiring coating/taping or better every 3-7 years depending on the product used. It would be prudent to apply a silicone based caulk seal or better patch/caulk to all screw heads and seams prior to any tape or other product application. Apply to manufacturer's instructions.

Excess Debris Buildup/Screw Oxidation Observed
Recommend removing debris to prevent backflow and mulching issues. Roof Sheathing Screws Oxidizing, this is typical as they are directly exposed to the elements; however, the corrosion is accelerated when leaf debris is present as it holds moisture. If untreated, water can/will enter the patio at screws and roof transition points conducive to the mulching/back flow issues addressed above. Recommend removing all debris, cleaning the surface of the fascia and roof transition area where the porch roof meets the dwellings fascia board and properly resealing the length of the transition area if applicable. Treat screw heads for any existing rust. Recommend sealing from further oxidation with a Rustoleum/rust inhibiting paint or better after removing excess rust and silicone after as needed by a licensed contractor.

Modified Bitumen Roll Roof has "Bubbles" Observed
Bubbles (air pockets) occur where the roofing no longer adheres well to the surface below it; if you push on the bubble, you may hear a squishy sound where water has leaked under the membrane. Alternatively, it may have been trapped moisture under the area during installation, perhaps if it rained and the cover was applied before it could be fully dried. Sometimes, sealed bubbles are better left alone, but most of the time, it is best to have it cut out and patch or replace the section. Recommend a licensed roofing contractor review further and repair as needed.

End Caps to Ridge Vent Missing
Recommend installing end caps to prevent rodent intrusion into the attic and/or building envelope.

Compromise to the Aluminum Ridge Vent Flashing Viewed from Exterior/Interior
Wood damage/water marks were observed below the ridge vent within the attic. This is indicative of fastener/seam compromises to the aluminum ridge vent. The deficiency can progress into further water damage to the wood, insulation and further damage into the building if left untreated. Recommend resealing all screws/fasteners and seams with an industrialized silicone caulk sealant or better and/or as recommended by a duly licensed professional contractor.

Ridge Vent(s) Fasteners Observed Loose with Insufficient Sealants
Sealants on the ridge vent fasteners appeared compromised/antiquated. Additionally, various fasteners were observed loose. During a high wind storm, the vent could uplift and damage if not adequately fastened, allowing water to enter the home. Recommend a licensed roofing contractor assess the area further and repair as is needed.

Kick out Flashing Not Observed
Kick out flashing, also known as diverter flashing, is a type of flashing that diverts rainwater away from the cladding abutment and into a gutter or away from the cladding. When installed correctly, it provides excellent protection against the penetration of moisture/water into the building envelope. The needs for kick out flashing at wall/roof eave transitions are an imperative. With increased amounts of insulation and building wraps that are used in modern construction, it is making buildings less breathable and more likely to sustain water damage. Kick out flashing prevents rainwater from being absorbed into the wall and is more essential than ever. Recommend a licensed contractor assess the area further and properly install kick out flashing in order to divert rainwater away from the cladding.

Lanai Fastener/Mounting Screws Oxidation Observed
Various screw fasteners observed oxidizing/rusting on the screened lanai. This is typical as they are directly exposed to the elements. If untreated, water can/will enter the patio at screws and roof transition points. Heavy corrosion is more prominent on low lying screws/fasteners. Recommend replacing any heavily corroded screws/fasteners and treat all serviceable screw/fastener heads with a rust inhibitive sealant after treating rust.

You may treat screw heads with a Rustoleum/rust inhibiting paint or better after removing excess rust and silicone seal after as needed or as directed.

Modified Bitumen Roll Roof has "Ponding" Observed

Ponding (standing water) occurs where there are low spots in the roofing. If more than 10 – 15% of the roof remains water-covered 24 hours after a rain, you should build up the low spots to prevent water from working through the seams of the roof caused by excess water pressures. On large areas, 10x15', tapering boards and reroofing may be recommended to prevent a cave in or an excessive leak in the event of a torrential rain onset.

Fractured Plank Board Decking Observed in the Attic System at the Time of the Inspection

Fractured boards can allow a worker accessing the roof or inspector to unknowingly damage the roof. If the boards are fractured enough that they can no longer withstand a live load of an individual or the individual is heavier than average, they can step on the board and send their foot right through the roof system. This can be a costly repair. It is always a good idea to reinforce fractured boards or replace them at the time of the roof replacement. When the roof is newer however, it is unlikely to be replaced anytime soon and thus, the repair can only be done from the inside of the attic, scabbing reinforcing wood members under the board. This repair is also risky (nails can penetrate the roof decking/cover if not applied correctly) so it is always recommended to leave it to the professionals. If there are protruding nails or if the wood support is nailed improperly, nails can pop through the shingle or be driven through accidently when reinforcing the area.

Visible Compromise to the Drip Edge Flashing to the Soffit/Eave Viewed from Exterior

Visible inspection to the underbelly of the eaves not accessible, however, exterior observation shows particulates and oxidation at the soffit/venting holes conducive to wood rot and is typically known to start at the drip edge. Water trails under the roof cover, at the drip edge via fluidic capillary action, rotting the wood, causing a depression at the eaves and progressing the rot process. Recommend a licensed contractor repair all as needed.

Compromises/Lifting along the Seams

The roof cover seams seals can be at a constant preemptive maintenance requirement for this roof cover. Lifting seams or present water intrusion at the eaves is an evident potential implication that the seals may be deficient, possibly throughout the eaves, requiring resealing and/or coating or better every 3-7 years depending on the product(s) used. When the product is a PVC, TPO, M.B Roll, Composition roll roofing etc., It would be prudent to apply an elastomeric patch/caulk or DYCO #20/20 Seam Sealer or better/as directed by a licensed contractor. Also, seal around screw heads where needed. Follow label instructions. Apply per manufacturer's instructions by a licensed contractor.

Potential Termite Damage Observed. Suspected Formosan Termites Observed

Termite damage was suspected at and within the wood fencing. The Formosan subterranean termite (Coptotermes formosanus) is an invasive species of termite. It has been transported worldwide from its native range in southern China to Formosa (Taiwan, where it gets its name) and Japan. In the 20th century it became established in South Africa, Hawaii and in the continental United States. The Formosan subterranean termite is often nicknamed the super-termite because of its destructive habits. This is because of the large size of its colonies, and the termites' ability to consume wood at a rapid rate. A single colony may contain several million (compared with several hundred thousand termites for other subterranean termite species) that forage up to 300 feet (100 m) in soil. A mature Formosan colony can consume as much as 13 ounces of wood a day (ca. 400 g) and severely damage a structure or retaining wall in as little as three months. Because of its population size and foraging range, the presence of colonies poses serious threats to nearby structures. Once established, Formosan subterranean termite has never been eradicated from an area. By the 1950's, it was reported in South Africa and Sri Lanka. During the 1960's it was found in Texas, Louisiana, and South Carolina. In 1980, a well-established colony was thriving in a condominium in Hallandale Beach, Florida. Recommend a licensed pest control technician inspection further and treatment if possible, or full removal of any infected area as needed. Please remember, it cannot be fully determined as to what the underlying problems are and is beyond the scope of this inspection. It is highly recommended to have a county/state registered structural engineer and/or a licensed pest control specialist to assess the area further.

Post 2000 Installed Membrane; Crescent Fractures Observed to the Roof Surface

Crescent Fractures observed on roofing membranes installed after 2000 are typically not considered defects with the material, but rather, foot traffic damage pressing down on the insulation plate lip under the membrane causing a small/large puncture that can progress or installation practice damage during the install process. It is highly recommended, however, to have these compromises reviewed by the manufacturer to ensure no material defects are the culprit. Additionally, it is recommended to have these areas of compromise inspected throughout by a licensed PVC/TPO membrane roofing specialist and repaired as needed.

Post 2000 Installed Membrane; Star Fractures Observed to the Roof Surface
"Star" fractures observed to the roof surface observed on roofing membranes installed after 2000 are typically not considered defects with the material, but either foot traffic damage, installation practice damage during the install process or more commonly from hail impact or other impact damage to the roofing material. It is highly recommended, however, to have these compromises reviewed by the manufacturer to ensure no material defects are the culprit. Additionally, it is recommended to have these areas of compromise inspected throughout by a licensed PVC/TPO membrane roofing specialist and repaired as needed.

Compromises/Lifting along the Seams – PRE 2001 Roof Covers
The roof cover seams seals can be at a constant preemptive maintenance requirement for this roof cover if/when lifting seams are observed or present water intrusion is evident, implying the seals may be deficient throughout, requiring resealing and/or coating or better every 3-7 years depending on the product(s) used. When the product is a M.B Roll or Composition roll roofing, an elastomeric patch/caulk or DYCO #20/20 Seam Sealer or better may work if as per the roofer's recommendations. Additionally, for aluminum roof vents screws, seal around screw heads where needed. Follow label instructions. Apply to manufacturer's instructions.

PRE 2001 Roof Covers Installation; Star or Crescent Damages
These fractures start developing within a 4 to 8 year period after the PVC roof system is installed. The PVC roof often begins with a small number of fractures of this type. The membrane fractures may leak during heavy rainfall or during slow snow melts and in ponded areas. The fractures continue to increase in number from a few fractures to hundreds of fractures in a few short years as the membrane prematurely ages. The manufacturers of the basic PVC formulation during this time period, regarding the problem age/stress fracturing, is the result of ineffective and poor production controls during the manufacturing process which introduced wide variations in membrane plasticizer content and key performance compounds and seemed to occur at random times. Poor post QA product testing was a contributing factor as company (ies) did not test all membrane production runs. During this study on other roofs, we found roofs with all membrane rolls affected with a small number of fractures and stiff membrane. While other roofs had a mixture of both good and bad PVC with some rolls with no fractures and other rolls covered with fractures. The PVC membrane may show signs of shrinkage with the membrane taut between fastener attachment points on mechanically fastened systems. Perimeter sheets may have shrunk and pulled away from wall flashings and can be above the roof substrate surface under tension. The PVC membrane may become less flexible as it ages and will feel stiff and brittle in cold temperatures. The membrane scrim becomes more pronounced as the membrane becomes thinner due to faster plasticizer losses. On Many roofs, the owner may have started patching the fractures thinking the fractures were caused by mechanical damage. Not until the roofs became covered with hundreds of patches over a period of several years did the owner realize they had a material performance problem. The membrane manufacturer responded to these material problems and provided either a product replacement/installation, or coating the roofs with an elastomeric roof coating at no cost to the owners, once the building owners or roofing contractors discovered the fractures and reported them. The membrane materials that fractured were manufactured over a time span covering 5 or 6 years ending mid-2000. Once the production control problems and testing were discovered and identified. The roof system manufacturer changed their manufacturing process and quality control. To the best of our knowledge, we know of no similar problems with the manufacture's current roofing products. If your PVC roof was installed prior to mid-2000 and begins to develop the type of problems stated, please contact a certified roofing consultant that can test and identify the roofing membrane to determine what is causing the fractures and help you secure a valid warranty claim provided the PVC membrane is defective if your roofing warranty supplied guidelines are met. A fracture(s) on any manufacturer's roofing products does not mean the resulting fractures are caused by defective materials. Foot traffic, hail damage, windblown objects and equipment servicing can be the fracture source. These damages cannot be fully ascertained as being defected or not defective at the time of the inspection and is considered beyond the scope of the inspection. PVC roofing is one of the best single-ply membranes and has a long history of excellent performance. CRC's have observed 20-year old PVC roofs and they are still performing well and still in service. Compared to many roofing products, PVC is contractor friendly both in quality and ease of application. The key is identifying the problem and making a warranty claim prior to the warranty expiration.

Wood Fascia Paint is Peeling/Chipping is and Appears Unsealed at Sections with Surface Fungi

Wood fascia is exposed. It may have had a treatment to the wood prior; however, the wood presently shows signs of suspected algae and fungi fruiting bodies indicative of the onset of wood rot. Recommend treating the algae/fungi and sealing the wood as needed.

Various Areas of the Lanai were Observed Cut/Ripped or Worn

Screen was observed ripped/cut or worn at various areas of the screened lanai at the time of the inspection. Recommend repairing/replacing this screen section as is needed.

Tree Limbs Observed Touching the Roof Surface

Tree limbs can and will damage any surface they are allowed to contact. Tree limbs can grow into the roof cover, fascia and soffit, eventually compromising its water resistance, making it susceptible to water intrusion. They also more notoriously perhaps, brush the material surface, diminishing the life of the roof cover in the affected area by damaging the protective coating of the roofing material i.e. granules, zinc plating on galvanized steel, glazing on tiles etc. Recommend a licensed arborist assess further and trim all branch from the roof a recommended 5 feet or more to compensate for wind gusts and the trees malleable swaying motion in a storm. Recommend a licensed roofer assess the roof after the tree limbs are removed to assess damages, if any and repair as needed.

Composition Asphalt Roof Cover Observed On a Slight Slope/Flat Roof

Roof geometry that is considered flat is not permitted to have shingle applied as a viable roof cover under the ICC and most state/local codes. Flat roofs are roof shapes with a pitch less than 2 inches for every 12 inches. Recommend a licensed roofing character assess further and repair as needed.

Seals at Vents/Stacks and Roof Transitions are Insufficient/Antiquated

Recommend a licensed roofing contractor assess the roof protrusion abutments and repair/reseal at all transitions as is needed.

Compromise Suspected at the Apron/Counter Flashing/Exterior Wall Abutment. Visible Water Stains

Roof compromise suspected at the apron/counter flashing. Water stains/damage was observed at the ceiling/roof and wall abutment from within the porch. Recommend licensed roofer assess further and repair as needed.

Metal Roof Panel is Rusted/Corroded. Galvanized Fasteners Observed Rusting/Corroded

The oxidation rust has penetrated past the zinc chromate coating and has compromised the flashing. Recommend replacing any heavily corroded sections, sanding and treating all else with a rust inhibitor and sealing all as is needed. Recommend replacing all screws with new stainless steel with rubber gasket washers or better. With proper care, metal roofs may not need replacing; the biggest question is cost for repair verse replacement. Recommend a licensed roofing contractor assess the roof further and repair as needed.

Decks/Porches

Exposed Aggregate
The siding was comprised of an exposed aggregate surface. An exposed aggregate surface is durable and skid resistant making it ideal for: Pool Decks, Driveways, Patios, and Porches and Sidewalks and sometimes, exterior siding. The decorative process of exposing aggregate has been around since the early 1900's, well before pattern stamping, stenciling, and decorative overlays became trendy. But this method is far from being ready for retirement. An exposed aggregate finish offers numerous advantages and many of today's contractors are finding creative ways to take exposed aggregate to a new level as seen on this exterior wall.

Aluminum Siding
Aluminum is among the common siding materials for porch and balcony enclosures. Aluminum siding can be made to appear like wood, including vertical shingle and shake styles. Aluminum expands and contracts with temperature changes, so installation by a licensed and skilled installer is important. Aluminum does not add to the structural strength of a structure. It is installed over sheathing. Aluminum siding can dent easily. To protect against this, many manufacturers offer a thin backer board of insulation that fits behind each panel. This insulation can reduce overall chatter or noise and can slightly increase the insulation value of the siding. If scratched, the exposed aluminum will not rust. Scratches may be touched up with a certain paint or material. Aluminum siding can conduct electricity, and grounding may be an installation requirement. Grounding the metal siding is a safety measure. Check with the local authority having jurisdiction as to whether grounding the metal siding is a requirement. Also, repainting aluminum is similar to repainting vehicles. It requires preparation, appropriate paint selections and proper application.

Stone
Stone has been used for centuries as an exterior siding material. Stone is durable and it comes in many sizes, colors and patterns. Manufactured stone is a combination of cement, colored oxides and light aggregates. It can sometimes be difficult to distinguish manufactured stone from real natural stone.

Galvanized Steel Siding
Steel siding is less common than aluminum siding. Popular styles of steel siding look like smooth or textured bevel-wood siding. Many styles and colors are available. The installation of steel siding requires special skill and the right tools. Steel siding is more resistant to dents, but if the finish becomes scratched or chipped, it will need to be repaired to prevent rust from developing. Galvanized steel siding can be repainted. Galvanized steel siding can conduct electricity, and grounding may be an installation requirement. Check with the local authority having jurisdiction as to whether grounding the metal siding is a requirement. Repainting aluminum is similar to repainting vehicles. It requires preparation, appropriate paint selections for the right application.

Hardboard
Hardboard is a common type of fiberboard that is made from wood fibers designed with specific density. It is compressed into a wood fiberboard. Synthetic adhesives provide the bonding between the fibers. Hardboard

has a uniform composite and look. There are no grains, knots or natural deficiencies. Hardboard siding is more dense than wood lap siding or other natural wood siding types. Hardboard does not split or warp like natural, conventional wood boards. It does not expand and contract as much as natural wood does and it holds paint well. Hardboards are sometimes pre-finished. It can be embossed and textured to give the appearance of natural wood, plywood or stucco. It may be installed over sheathing or directly to wall framing in the past. Lapped hardboard does not strengthen the house structure it can be affected by moisture. It can rot and it also swells more than natural wood when it is wet.

Masonry Block Recladding

Concrete bricks and blocks are created by the chemical reaction between Portland cement, sand, aggregate and water. Concrete may be plain or decorative, large or small, pre-cast or poured-in-place. Concrete may be made to look like stone or shaped like bricks. Advantages of Masonry siding is that it provides good fire protection as it can increase the thermal mass of a building, which can increase comfort in the heat of summer especially on a porch, and the cold of the winter. Masonry can be effectively used for passive solar applications. Masonry walls are also more resistant to missiles or foreign projectiles (such as debris from strong winds and impact from hail) than walls made of wood or other softer substrates/ materials. Some disadvantages include frost damage that can deteriorate masonry exterior walls. This type of damage is common with certain types of brick too. Masonry is a heavy building material and requires structural support from a strong foundation to avoid settling and cracking. Some common problems with masonry exteriors include cracking, spalling, clearance, mortar deterioration weep holes, moisture, efflorescence and bowing.

Brick Veneer

When it comes to brick veneer walls, you should understand some of the best practices that may be applied to prevent moisture problems. The following are some of the best practices that you may see in a brick veneer: The appropriate brick type and mortar for the weather conditions should be present. This is not readily ascertainable during a typical building inspection. Some installers create an air space of 1 2 inches wide. It should be wide enough to accommodate rigid insulation board. A flexible and strong through-wall flashing membrane could be installed. The membrane should be one that will not disintegrate over time (5 ounces per square foot of copper is time-proven). It should run to the exterior face of the mortar joint. All that you will usually see is the outer edge of the flashing popping through the mortar joint surface. The through-wall flashing should be lapped. The overlaps may be a minimum of 6 inches, and fully sealed. Upright legs 12 inches high may be installed on the supporting wall. End dams should be provided at all corners and discontinuities. Also, the end dams should be sealed.

Asphalt Shingle Siding

Asphalt shingles are sometimes used for siding material. The shingles used are the same used for a roof-covering system. When the roof-covering asphalt shingles are installed as siding, they need to be installed differently. The self-sealing tabs of asphalt shingles will not function because the shingles are installed vertically. The overlying shingle will not adhere to the shingle below. Roofing cement is commonly used to secure the layers of shingles to each other. Loose shingle tabs are susceptible to being blown or torn off by the wind. Asphalt shingles installed as siding generally need six nails per shingle. This is because gravity pulls more on shingles installed vertically, and more fasteners are needed when the shingles are installed on a wall. Asphalt shingles deteriorate over time and as the asphalt shingle gets older, the granules are lost. The protective layering that wears away exposes the asphalt material to heat and further degradation to fungus and lichen. The volatiles in the asphalt evaporate away, and the shingle becomes brittle and shrinks, and quickly deteriorates. It is important to preserve the shingle as best as possible. Some products like liquid zinc can mitigate fungus and lichen growth, while not being corrosive to the granule protective layers adhesion, like bleaches.

Manufactured Stone

Manufactured stone, cultured stone, and man-made stone veneers are popular alternatives to natural stone. Natural stone has become very expensive in many areas. Manufactured stone veneers are typically made from concrete. Natural stones are re-created using molds, aggregate, and colorfast pigments. To the untrained eye, there may be no obvious, visual difference between veneers of natural stone and manufactured stone.

Cement Fiber (Hardi) Siding

FIBER CEMENT SIDING. A manufactured, fiber-reinforcing product made with an inorganic hydraulic or calcium silicate binder formed by chemical reaction and reinforced with organic or inorganic non-asbestos fibers, or both. Additives which enhance manufacturing or product performance are permitted. Fiber cement siding products have either smooth or textured faces and are intended for exterior wall and related applications.

Stucco

Stucco is used as an exterior covering or coating on residential buildings and porches. Stucco is common in many parts of the U.S. Stucco is a durable cladding type. Traditional stucco is made of lime, sand and water. Modern stucco is made of Portland cement, sand and water. Lime can also be added to decrease its permeability rate and increase the workability of modern stucco. Sometimes, proprietary additives such as synthetic acrylics and glass fibers, are added to improve the stucco's strength and flexibility.

Asbestos Cement-Based Siding

Siding is estimated to be the original, asbestos-cement shake siding. This can be hazardous if mishandled. No determination of asbestos content could be rendered as no lab tests are conducted for a standard building inspection. Asbestos and cement were first combined in the United States in the early 1900's to form an innovative, new building material. Asbestos cement is a composite material that consists of cement reinforced with asbestos fibers. Asbestos-cement siding shingles can be made to imitate the appearance of wood siding shingles in shape and appearance. Asbestos fibers are a health hazard when inhaled. Asbestosis is a form of lung cancer that is caused by inhaling asbestos fibers. Because of the health risk, strict environmental regulations on working with asbestos were established in the U.S. Health risks were shown to be greatest during mining and production processes, but minimal during the installation and use of asbestos-cement products. According to the U.S. EPA, a material containing asbestos is deemed potentially hazardous only in its friable state, which is when the material can be crumbled, pulverized, or reduced to a powder by hand pressure. Asbestos cement is not considered friable and, therefore, not hazardous because the cement binds the asbestos fibers and prevents their release into the air under normal-use conditions. However, asbestos-cement products are classified as friable when deterioration disturbs the asbestos. Asbestos-cement products are classified as friable when mechanical means are used for chipping, grinding, sawing or sanding, thereby allowing particles to become airborne. If the asbestos-cement siding material is not disturbed, no hazard exists and no precautions are required. It is highly recommended that periodic inspections be conducted.

Clay and Slate Siding General Comments

Clay and slate shingles are one of the most historic building materials. Traditionally, clay tiles were formed by hand and, later, by machine-extrusion of natural clay, then textured or glazed with color, and fired in high-temperature kilns. The inherently fragile nature of clay shingles dictates that special care and precautions be taken to preserve and repair them. Clay roofing materials are commonly curved, whereas clay siding material is typically flat. Clay and slate are resistant to water, sunlight and wind. They are not combustible. They are heavy and not prone to uplift by wind. Clay and slate shingles, when correctly installed, require little or no maintenance. The fastening system used to secure the shingles to the wall often fails and needs to be replaced, as opposed to the shingles themselves. When the fastening system has deteriorated, or the wall support structure has failed, clay and slate shingles can be removed relatively easily, then necessary repairs can be made, and the shingles can be re-installed with new corrosion resistant fasteners. Broken and damaged shingles should be replaced promptly to prevent further damage to adjacent shingles tiles and the supporting wall structure. Clay and slate shingles have the longest life expectancies among siding materials – generally, 100 to 400 years. But regular maintenance is still recommended to prolong their life. If water damage has occurred behind the clay or slate siding materials, the evidence of damage may not be readily visible at the time of the inspection. A regular maintenance inspection of the clay or slate siding can help determine the condition, potential causes of failure, and the source of any leaks, and will help in developing a program for the preservation and repair of the shingles. Clay and slate siding can be damaged by various things and ways, including branches, stones, balls, and heavy/large hail. Patching a clay or slate shingle with materials such as roofing tar, caulks, asphalt shingle, pieces of metal, or non-matching clay tiles etc. is inappropriate. Such treatments are aesthetically incompatible. They also have the potential to cause physical damage. Water can collect behind the unmatched material and progress the deterioration of the wooden components of the wall and the fastening systems of the structural lumber. During expansion and contraction of a freeze-thaw cycle, ice buildup at patches can cause surrounding tiles to break. Patching is not recommended. The replacement of clay or slate siding pieces that are in poor condition is always best.

Slab on Grade, Exposed Aggregate Finish

The foundation/floor was comprised of poured concrete with an exposed aggregate surface. An exposed aggregate surface is durable and skid resistant making it ideal for: Pool Decks, Driveways, Patios, Porches and Sidewalks. The decorative process of exposing aggregate has been around since the early 1900's, well before pattern stamping, stenciling, and decorative overlays became trendy. But this method is far from being ready for retirement. An exposed aggregate finish offers numerous advantages and many of today's contractors are finding creative ways to take exposed aggregate to a new level.

Fiberglass/Composite Decking
Fiberglass/Composite decking is an attractive, low-maintenance architectural decking that offers alternatives to traditional decking materials. The panels do not rot, rust or mildew, which make them typically ideal for high moisture environments, including ocean inlets exposed to saltwater. The deck panels are easily installed with conventional or hidden fasteners that can create a smooth, attractive surface.

Concrete
Concrete is an excellent material for open or enclosed patios, porches and balconies. It is versatile, preferred for durability, appearance, low maintenance, and indicates quality construction from the first glance. A concrete patio has become an essential part of a landscaping plan that imparts an inviting image. Concrete's wide variety of texture, color, or patterns has brought this patio material to the status of a landscape design element of today's building owner's demands. Concrete is functional and it lends itself to a wide variety options for design, which can make a dramatic difference in landscaping plans, as well as boost property values. In addition to the traditional look, concrete can have the appearance, and color of brick, tile, slate, or stone. It is important to learn more about the product to maintain it and treat it when necessary.

Concrete Pavers
Some details about pavers in general: A paver patio is a series of brick pavers laid dry upon an aggregate (gravel) and leveling base, contained by a locking border system. When installed properly, it is a permanent alternative to concrete which is prone to cracking and asphalt which is subject to weathering and requires substantial maintenance and or the repaving of such every few years. Paver patios that are installed properly, are beautiful and add substantial value to the structure and exterior aesthetics. However, since many patios are installed by DIY guys or "carpenters" with little to no technical understanding as to why or where they went wrong, most paver patios are not installed properly. While most of the install and material process cannot be seen at the time of the inspection, paver patios require a specific amount of excavation, typically 8-10" below grade. A general rule of thumb is one 15 yard roll container of excavated material for every five hundred square feet of patio. A 1,000 square foot patio should fill two 15 yard containers when properly excavated. The area should be backfilled with gravel that is clean of soils etc., which allows for proper drainage under the pavers. The existence of water under the pavers and the hydrostatic conditions caused by the lack of drainage is at the heart of problems with defective paver patios.

Treated Wood
Pressure treated wood comes in many dimensions and because it is chemically infused with Chromium Copper Arsenate (CCA) or Alkaline Copper (ACQ) while under pressure, it resists damage from water and boring insects. Although it reduces the likelihood of damage, pressure treated lumber will eventually succumb to water, rotting and insects but much slower than it would have if left untreated. Pressure treated wood should only be used for patios limited to areas that have good drainage. Until 2003, the preservative most commonly used in residential pressure-treated lumber was chromate copper arsenate (CCA), an extremely toxic chemical. Remember "Arsenic and Old Lace" or that old box of rat poison you may have lurking in the garage? CCA is so toxic that the Environmental Protection Agency, over 20 years ago, imposed strict guidelines regarding the manufacturing practices of companies using CCA. However, one must distinguish between the toxicity of the chemical and the toxicity of the wood product in everyday use. Extensive studies were done since the mid 1980's concerning the potential dangers of pressure-treated wood. And rightfully so! Large volumes of CCA were being used, and the treated wood products were beginning to be widely distributed, justifying the need for some hard research. In the end, the industry agreed to voluntarily eliminate use of CCA for residential use. Your local building store or lumberyard is now selling lumber treated with (hopefully) less toxic alternatives... amine copper quat (ACQ) and copper azone (CA)... though you may find other chemical combinations in specific areas. CCA is still being used in certain marine and industrial applications since it is still the best preservative available at the present time. Whether these new chemicals will turn out to be less hazardous in the long term is anyone's guess.

Paint/Primer Seal Insufficient at the Base of the Wall
Without a proper water seal at the base of the wall, the cladding is susceptible to moisture intrusion, algae and degradation from the elements. Recommend a licensed painter treat the substrate(s), prime and seal all as needed.

Significant Settlement/Spalling Cracks
There was significant settlement crack(s) observed. Notable exterior cracks observed, exceeding and at 1/8th inch in a settlement and stress fashion. Though standard cracks are common amongst new construction and old alike, for some differing reasons, these exhibited stress like conditions and they should not go unmaintained and

should as well, be reviewed by a licensed structural engineer. Exposed cracks in an exterior wall can allow moisture to intrude. Recommend for surety and confidence, to obtain a state licensed structural engineer to inspect and diagnose the deficiencies where needed. Do the maintenance to the exterior crack as prescribed and monitor all areas of concern should any new occurrences arise.

Stucco Cladding on Frame Structure Abuts Grading; Inhibited from Expelling Moisture
Moisture between the stucco cladding and the buildings house wrap can accumulate. This moisture must be allowed to expel from the wall or it can accumulate behind the siding. Moisture that gets in behind the wall at windows, doors and trim or where humidity is prevalent in the area can otherwise aid in progressing web cracks and other damage to the siding and wood framing where applicable. The siding needs a suggested 6 inches above the grading to allow the wall to relieve the moisture and is high enough to theoretically, defer foliage from getting behind the siding. If not present, Weep Screeds should be installed per state codes. Recommend excavating at this wall area and/or applying an aggregate of rocks so that water does not stay at the abutting sight. Redressing the siding on the wall to allow a proper wall bond seal and raising the siding may also be an option.

Loose Posts Suspected at the Wood Dock
When loose post is suspected at the wood dock: Because you will achieve a different load bearing in different bottom materials, there is no rule of thumb for how deep the piling should be installed, but a minimum of four feet would be reasonable or what the local/state code calls for. It is most important if the piling seems "tight", or secure. It is possible the post could have been loosened but appeared secured or eroding processes at the base may have displaced soil. Other variables may be present. Recommend a licensed dock installer assess the area(s) further and repair all as needed.

Vinyl Siding Abuts Grading; Moisture is inhibited from Expelling Moisture at the Siding Base
Siding should be installed tight enough to prevent problems related to water intrusion, but it should be loose enough to allow it to adequately dry after a rainstorm. Additionally, moisture must be allowed to expel from the wall that accumulates behind the vinyl siding. Moisture that gets in behind the wall at windows, doors and trim or where humidity is prevalent in the area, moisture and water can accumulate behind the siding. The siding needs a suggested 6 inches above the grading to allow the wall to relieve the moisture and is high enough to theoretically, defer foliage from getting behind the siding. Recommend excavating at this wall area and/or applying an aggregate of rocks so that water does not stay at the abutting sight. Redressing the siding on the wall to allow a proper wall bond seal and raising the siding may also be an option and is recommended.

Iron Stains Observed on Porches
The reddish brown rusty stains are a common problem frequently observed on siding, sidewalks, walkways, patios, stepping stones, window and door frames in areas where irrigation water has a high iron content. The sprinkler system and/or hoses that are used to water the grounds, may also be spraying iron particles that create these rust stains wherever they land. Iron is a chemical element that is abundant in soils and aquifers in many parts of the country. It is the element that, when exposed to air and moisture, oxidizes or rusts. Where the tap water is "hard" or mineral-rich and we irrigate with well water, sprinkler water is probably causing rust stains. The irrigation systems will often "over spray" which means water ends up on the fence, patio, deck, porch, building, windows, doors, concrete walkways, stepping stones or paths, lawn furniture and also on parked vehicles if exposed to overspray. Once iron particles from the water in your sprinkler come in contact with the air, they will begin to oxidize or rust. The stains that result have likely developed over time and can be very stubborn to remove. Recommend installing a rust inhibitive filtration treatment system to the sprinkler system to prevent this.

Iron Stains Observed on Decking
The reddish brown rusty stains are a common problem frequently observed on siding, sidewalks, walkways, patios, stepping stones, window and door frames in areas where irrigation water has a high iron content. The sprinkler system and/or hoses that are used to water the grounds may also be spraying iron particles that create these rust stains wherever they land. Iron is a chemical element that is abundant in soils and aquifers in many parts of the country. It is the element that, when exposed to air and moisture, oxidizes or rusts. Where the tap water is "hard" or mineral-rich and we irrigate with well water, sprinkler water is probably causing rust stains. The irrigation systems will often "over spray" which means water ends up on the fence, patio, deck, porch, building, windows, doors, concrete walkways, stepping stones or paths, lawn furniture and also on parked vehicles if exposed to overspray. Once iron particles from the water in your sprinkler come in contact with the air, they will begin to oxidize or rust. The stains that result have likely developed over time and can be very

stubborn to remove. Recommend installing a rust inhibitive filtration treatment system to the sprinkler system to prevent this.

Suspected Excessive Wood Rotting Observed
According to the most current studies and scientific findings, generally, wood rot is caused by undue exposure of untreated wood to moisture. Consequently, prevention constitutes both avoiding such exposure and employing a prevention and treatment program where rot already exists. Wood with 20 percent moisture content and green lumber remain at risk. Two types of rot trouble building owners. The first is white and yellow with a stringy and spongy look. The other is brown and crumbly in appearance, and a tendency to break into cubes has earned it the nickname "brown cubical rot." These visible manifestations of wood rot are called "fruiting bodies." About 3 inches in diameter, these crusts or brackets are evidence that the particular decay fungi are present within the wood. Serpula lacrimans, Poria incrassata and Gleophyllum trabeum each have singular fruiting-body appearances. Fruiting bodies produce spores, which spread the decay fungus throughout the wood. The wood members may have had a treatment to the wood when the decking was constructed; however, these pressure treatments dissipate typically over a 3-5 year period and can be less in areas where direct contact to moist soil and/or dense vegetation exists. The wood shows signs of suspected algae and fungi fruiting bodies indicative of the onset of wood rot. Recommend a licensed contractor who can treat the algae/fungi and sealing the wood as needed. Routinely resealing and maintaining the wood will mitigate the suspected algae and fungi future growth. To prevent wood rot, use treated wood or the heartwood of a decay-resistant species. There are many websites that provide adequate direction as to how to treat the wood rot. Please remember, it cannot be fully determined as to what the underlying problems are and is beyond the scope of this inspection. It is highly recommended to have a county/state registered structural engineer to assess the area further prior to any financial decisions.

Pool Marcite/Plaster Coating was Observed Etching at the Time of the Inspection
The Plaster is also called white coat or Marcite. Pool plaster is a process of finishing the gunite or shotcrete pool structures. Used underwater, it provides the watertight seal that the porous gunite or shotcrete beneath it cannot. Pool Plaster/Marcite finishes provide an average estimate of twenty years of service under ideal conditions. Our world however, is rarely ideal and many variables can cause the progression of degradation to include how it was initially applied. The pool plaster surface is meant to degrade slowly, eventually requiring a fresh coat of Marcite. If your pool plaster has surface irregularities, which may take on a beige hue, you may have what's commonly called etching. This etching can be caused by low pH or alkalinity; an acidic condition. It may begin within the plaster, from the original mix on application, or etching may start from the gunite side of the plaster and work itself from the outside in. In instances were a yellow stain is present and appears in a small cluster at one location or a single spot, chlorine tablets may be the culprit. Left to sit directly on pool plaster, they can also create a yellowish stain and can be difficult to remove. Common costs for re-plastering can vary greatly by the size of the pool.

Ceramic Tile Flooring Exposed to the Elements and could Pose a Trip Hazard
Porch ceramic tile flooring is exposed to the elements and could pose a trip hazard. This tile is slippery when wet and should be either coated with a non-slip material or replaced with a nonslip tile or other water resistant surface as needed.

Trip Hazard. Uneven Pavers Observed
Pavers observed were uneven, often by natural settlement and placement. This may happen more where rain run off or ponding may occur. Recommend having a state licensed contractor repair all as needed.

Algae Growth on the Porch Observed
This is very common, however, you will want to treat or pressure wash as this growth tends to cause a slip hazard if allowed to grow. See Online for additional information and correct, thorough manners to apply any products. Recommend a licensed contractor treat the areas as is needed.

Erosion Observed at the Porch from Gutter Downspouts Terminating at the Location
These downspouts caused erosion depressions which in trade pond water after storms and then further exacerbate the erosion. When rain falls, the water runs along the surface of the topsoil, and it will collect in the depression or furrow. The water will slowly seep into the soil and collect in underground pockets that will supply the roots of plants through weeks and even months without rain. Displacement of soil at the foundation will also occur more progressively, causing cracks in the foundation. This is not what you want around the buildings perimeter. Ponding will progressively grow, more so with each rain, and be a feeding spot for roots, like a beacon calling them to the buildings foundation from any trees, if any. Recommend Gutter downspout diverters

be installed on all applicable downspout location to prevent further grade erosion and remediating the ponding with the corrective aggregate as needed.

Tree Roots Heaving/Subsidence Suspected
Encumbering tree roots provide enough concern that there might be heaving involved that can cause far greater damage given enough time and warrants further review by an engineer. Alternatively, cracks may be the result of sudden settlement and as well can be caused by the roots. The roots can starve the neighboring grading of moisture, causing soil shifts etc. Recommend a licensed/insured tree and ROOT removal specialist assess this area further and remove as is needed all roots/trees as needed. Recommend a licensed structural engineer assess the structural stress cracks and thermal conditions etc. as needed and estimate repairs prior to any financial considerations.

Posts/Columns Span is too far spaced and can be Structurally Compromised
Normally, porches columns are the posts in a post and beam like construction. The weight that is being supported and what the beam structure is like, determines if you can span wider than 8-10'. Your posts/columns were exceeding this. Each column should be on a foundation properly mounted and secured to both the mount and the beam. On some older buildings, this is only a pier and the location of the piers will dictate the location of the columns. The beams might be designed to hold a great deal of weight but may be spliced at certain locations. These splices are typically covered by an aesthetic wood covering. The splices will then determine the column locations. Post designation depends on what your load is, what size your header/beam is and where/if there is a butt joint. The actual size and type of the beam required to span a certain length on a porch is determined not only by engineering but by your local building codes and the type of beam. Your local building codes, an engineer and the local building inspector can assist you further.

Tree(s) Heaving Grading at the Porch
Tree roots from the neighboring tree appear to be causing notable heaving to the porch. This is a liability hazard as it is considered a trip hazard and it is also defacing the aesthetics of the porch. Heaving will continue until the tree roots are removed and damages will progress. Recommend a licensed specialist review this area further and remediate the deficiency as needed.

Adhesive Sand Appears Liberally Applied Between the Pavers/Joints
Some contractors and owners alike, ruin their finished product with the use of adhesive sand assuming the joints should appear "filled" like a mortar joint. The joints of pavers do not require to be filled for the patio to have integrity as it is a dry laid system. A small amount of the leveling base is swept in to prevent pavers from "rocking" back in forth in place. Adhesive sand is a tricky product and has a minimal application in paver installation under specific circumstances. In most cases it is not needed and can cake up in the corners of the joints and ruin the aesthetics of a beveled paver. Recommend a licensed specialist review this area further and remediate the deficiency as needed.

Door Closer Missing on Screened/Storm Door to Porch
Recommend installing a door closer to prevent young children/pets from entering/exiting when there may be hazards present or insects entering like mosquitoes or wasps.

Moisture and Basic Settlement Cracks Observed on the Concrete Pool Deck
Concrete will crack as a normal outcome of the curing process. Cracking can be worsened if uneven bearing conditions exist under the slab, such as un-compacted fill areas. Excessive water used for the workability of cement tends to produce excessive cracking, which can allow moisture to more readily penetrate the concrete slab, weakening the concrete and leading to differential drying issues and cracking. Excessive cracking can allow additional moisture to penetrate more easily through the slab. The use of welded wire-fabric reinforcement provides a means of controlling the severity of cracking. Concrete control joints may also be used to control random cracking by creating planned lines of weakness in the slab. Shrinkage or curing cracks generally occur in any continuous length of concrete longer than about 12 feet. These cracks are easily maintained and may be virtually eliminated with proper maintenance. Additionally, recoating the pool and/or re-texturing the deck may provide a more uniform elimination of cracks appearances/if any.

Concrete Moisture Cracks Observed
There are two guarantees with concrete. One, it will get hard and two, it will crack. Cracking is a frequent cause of complaints in the concrete industry. The Concrete Foundations Association has produced a new flyer to help contractors educate their customers and building owners to know about the causes of cracks and when they should be a concern. Cracking can be the result of one or a combination of factors such as drying shrinkage,

thermal contraction, restraint (external or internal) to shortening, subgrade settlement, and applied loads. Cracking cannot be prevented but it can be significantly reduced or controlled when the causes are taken into account and preventative steps are taken.

Brick Mortar Deterioration Observed
Although good-quality bricks may outlast civilizations, the mortar that bonds them can crack and crumble after a number of years. Water penetration is the greatest degrader of mortar, and different mortar joints allow for varying degrees of water resistance. Mortar joints in brickwork also take up a large amount of the patios layout/surface area and have a significant influence on the patios overall appearance. Some joint profiles accentuate their individual designs, while others merge the bricks and mortar to form a flush, homogeneous surface.

Deterioration of Brick Observed
The spalling, dusting or flaking of brick masonry units may be due to either mechanical or chemical damage. Mechanical damage is caused by moisture entering the brick and freezing, resulting in spalling of the brick's outer layers. Spalling may continue, or it may stop on its own after the outer layers that trapped the interior moisture have broken off. Chemical damage is due to the leaching of chemicals from the ground into the brick, resulting in internal deterioration. External signs of such deterioration are a dusting or flaking of the brick. Very little can be done to correct existing mechanical and chemical damage except for actually replacing the brick. Mechanical deterioration can be slowed or stopped by directing water away from the masonry surface and by pointing mortar joints to slow water entry into the Decking.

Deterioration of Brick Foundation Piers Observed
The spalling, dusting or flaking of brick masonry units may be due to either mechanical or chemical damage. Mechanical damage is caused by moisture entering the brick and freezing, resulting in spalling of the brick's outer layers. Spalling may continue, or it may stop on its own after the outer layers that trapped the interior moisture have broken off. Chemical damage is due to the leaching of chemicals from the ground into the brick, resulting in internal deterioration. External signs of such deterioration are a dusting or flaking of the brick. Very little can be done to correct existing mechanical and chemical damage except for actually replacing of the brick. Mechanical deterioration can be slowed or stopped by directing water away from the masonry surface and by pointing mortar joints to slow water entry into the Decking.

Uneven Settlement Observed at the Porch/Building Abutment
Uneven or differential settlement can be a major structural problem in small residential buildings, however, typical uneven settlement for porches abutting the main buildings, typically refers to when the slab or other surface settles faster or at a different rate than that of the building, resulting in a separation of the two and is noticeable at the abutment point. Serious settlement problems are relatively uncommon. Many signs of masonry distress are incorrectly diagnosed as settlement-related when, in fact, they are due to moisture and thermal movements.

Salt Spalling Observed
Salt spalling is a specific type of weathering that can occur in brick, natural stone, tiles and concrete. Dissolved salt is carried through the material in water and then crystallizes inside the material near the surface as the water evaporates. As the salt crystals expand, this builds up shear stresses that break away and create spalling at the surface. Some believe that porous building materials can be protected against salt spalling by treatment with water-repellent sealants that penetrate deeply enough to keep water with dissolved salts well away from the surface. Expert advice should be sought to ensure that any coating applied is compatible with the substrate in terms of its breathability, which is the ability to allow the release of vapors from inside while preventing water intrusion, or other serious problems that can be created.

Basic Cracks in the Concrete Floor
Concrete will crack as a normal outcome of the curing process. Cracking can be worsened if uneven bearing conditions exist under the slab, such as un-compacted fill areas. Excessive water used for the workability of cement tends to produce excessive cracking, which can allow moisture to more readily penetrate the concrete slab, weakening the concrete, and leading to differential drying issues and cracking. Excessive cracking can allow additional moisture, as well as radon gas, to penetrate more easily through the slab. The use of welded wire-fabric reinforcement provides a means of controlling the severity of cracking. The use of fiber-reinforced concrete may also provide adequate crack control. Concrete control joints may also be used to control random cracking by creating planned lines of weakness in the slab. Shrinkage or curing cracks generally occur in any continuous length of concrete longer than about 12 feet.

Tree Roots from Neighboring Tree; Significant Settlement to the Porch/Deck Slab Midsection(s)
There was significant settlement and cracks to the concrete patio/porch slab(s). This appears to be caused potentially from trees roots under growing under/encumbering the slab foundation. The roots will decay once the tree is removed or is cut down. The decay allows hollowed cavities and loose soil to form under the slab and eventual settlement of the patio/porch as was evident at the time of the inspection. Recommend, to assure no additional settlement will occur and confidence, to obtain a state licensed structural engineer to assess the area further. Short term mitigation may be recommended by the engineer, such as maintenance to the exterior crack(s) with expansion joint sealant or better as prescribed by a licensed industry contractor and monitor all areas of concern should any new occurrences arise. Recommend a licensed structural engineer, assess further, all areas with apparent settlement to assure no additional settlement will occur and no structural compromises are present beyond the scope of a basic building inspection and prior to any financial decisions.

Balustrade; Various Loose Balusters Observed
Note: Per OSHA Standards; **Balustrade must be fastened correctly. 1917.112(f)** Condition. Railings shall be maintained free of sharp edges and in good repair.

Loose Hand Rail Mounts/Fasteners Observed
OSHA Regulations: Handrails must be graspable and properly fastened per the ICC guidelines and/or your local code ordinances. Insurance companies may take issue when handrails for stairways with more than 3 risers do not have properly fastened handrails. Stair rail systems and handrails must be surfaced to prevent injuries typically, to meet the insurance and OSHA standards. Loose railing can allow the structural integrity to give way and allow a person to fall or become impaled if parts fall with and in relation to the individual, engaging them upon impact with the surface or landing that terminates the fall. Recommend a licensed contractor repair all as needed.

Bannister/Rail to Stairs Dilapidated
Various loose and damaged sections observed throughout. Fasteners are loose/compromised. OSHA Regulations: Top edges of rail systems used as handrails leading to stairs must not be more than 37 inches (94 cm) high nor less than 36 inches. Rails must be enforced per the ICC guidelines and/or your local code ordinances. Rails must be surfaced to prevent injuries. Recommend a licensed contractor repair all as needed.

Corroded Screws Observed. Various Plank Boards Loose Throughout
Recommend replacing all screws with wood screws that are water resistant stainless steel type or better where needed.

Concrete Porch; Cubicle/Moisture Cracking from Weathering Observed
The cracks appear to be from weathering of the concrete. Additionally, bad concrete batch or too much water in the initial pouring, was applied. Cubicle and Web Cracks will form and progress many times in a web fashion if they and the concrete surrounding them are not treated. Caulking/sealing the cracks may also aid in reducing erosion underneath the slab. Where cracks are larger, expansion joint sealant is recommended. For cubicle cracking resulting in wide gaps of 1/8th inch or more, major repairs or complete replacement may be required. Recommend the use of concrete sealants NOT mortar/concrete unless recommended by a state licensed contractor. Recommend a licensed contractor assess the concrete further and repair all as needed.

Ballasts Are Spread Too Far Apart, Exceeding 3 ½ inches Width
Protective handrails and guardrails should have balusters/spindles at intervals of less than three and a half inches or have sufficient protective material to prevent a three and a half inch sphere from passing through if caring for children two years and over. Recommend a licensed contractor review the area and repair as needed ASAP.

Chalking Observed to the Exterior Vinyl Siding
"Chalking" refers to the white, powdery film on the surface of paint and in this case, the polyvinyl composite siding. As the vinyl weathers and the binder slowly degrades by ultraviolet radiation and moisture, chalking can occur. Over time, the binder's hold on the pigment is released. After years of being hit by sunlight, the vinyl surface, simply starts to wear or erode away the surface composite. This exposes the pigments beneath, and since they are no longer bound into the polyvinyl composite, they are easily wiped off. This result is chalking. Older vinyl is likely to be chalky. The chalk is the powder that is deposited on your finger when you rub it over older vinyl siding more prone to sun exposure. Chalk can run down the wall's surface beneath and cause cosmetic streaks or light patches in the wall's appearance. Caulk can be used where the walls about openings

and trim as well as on any hairline, minute cracks. Latex-silicone blends, polyurethane, and polysulfide caulks generally perform satisfactorily. Caulks that are 100% silicone should not be used. Chalk can be removed simply, by a professional licensed contractor pressure washing the surface.

Wood Deck Plank Boards are Warping/Loose and can Pose a Trip Hazard
Wood plank board decking fasteners eventually corrode and cause boards to become loose. If the boards are laid crown up, warping can be progressive. These raised boards can pose a trip hazard. Wood has many outstanding properties, but it is a natural, porous material with individual characteristics, and it can warp. When wood gets wet, it swells. When wood dries out after being sawn from the tree, after being pressure-treated and after rain showers, it shrinks. Uneven drying creates stresses in wood, which results in warping (e.g., bowing, cupping or twisting) or cracking. The degree of warping depends on the species of wood, its grain pattern, uniformity of drying and construction techniques, among other factors. There is not much a user can do to truly un-warp a warped piece of wood. It is possible to position bowed boards so that its weight flattens it, using screws that are load adequate to fasten securely an otherwise warped piece. Recommend re-supporting or replacing the displaced section with deck/exterior wood screws per each section effected and any horizontal bracing and straps on stringers, balustrade, treads and rails where applicable, as needed, as directed by a state licensed contractor/structural engineer.

Hardi-Siding Lap Board Fasteners Missing at Various Joints/Areas
Replacing fasteners where they have become loose, deteriorated or missing is highly recommended to prevent wind damage in the event of a high wind gust or storm. Stainless steel is generally recommended because of its superior corrosion resistance, however, lightweight coated aluminum are favored as well. Fasteners, such as nails, should be long enough to hold the materials securely. All work should be done by properly licensed contractors. Recommend light weight spackle, used for indoor/outdoor applications, to fill the tiny nail holes as directed by the manufacturer.

Suspected Rot Observed at the Base of the Column
Suspected rot is observed at the base of the column and if the column incurs enough wood rot, it may compromise the structural integrity of the support. This can result in the column shifting, fraying, etcetera, that can cause further damage to the porch. In most cases, wood rot can be repaired and the column may be retrofitted with a flashing and/or be raised to prevent moisture interaction at levels that cause wood to rot. Recommend a licensed structural engineer/contractor assess the column further and repair as needed.

Loose Railing Observed
OSHA Regulations: Railing must be properly fastened per the ICC guidelines and/or your local code ordinances. Insurance companies may take issue when railing for balconies railings are not have properly fastened. Stair rail systems and handrails must be surfaced to prevent injuries typically, to meet the insurance and OSHA standards. Loose railing can allow the structural integrity to give way and allow a person to fall or become impaled if parts fall with and in relation to the individual, engaging them upon impact with the surface or landing that terminates the fall. Recommend a licensed contractor repair all as needed.

Porch Roof Covers

Aluminum Panel

Raised Seam Metal Roof
Standing seam is a succession of vertical sheet metal roofing panels connected side-by-side by a vertical locking mechanism called the seam. The seams can be seen from the ridge of a roof all the way down to the eaves. The locked seam is raised by an inch or two above the panels in order to maintain water-tightness of the system. The raised seam also provides for a unique and distinctive appearance. As with most metal roofs featuring concealed fasteners, standing seam roofs are virtually maintenance-free, fire-retardant and resistant to strong winds, and are just as quiet as asphalt shingles, clay tikes, or wooden shingles/shakes when it rains. Standing seam roofs are very energy efficient, environmentally safe and long lasting. They are a popular choice in "green" construction projects. Since many standing seam metal roofs can easily last longer than 50 years, with virtually no maintenance compared to asphalt shingles that have an average lifespan of 20 to 25 years, standing seam beats traditional asphalt roofing competition by a factor of three in terms of its expected service life.

Popped Nail(s) Observed at the Roof Cover
Popped nails are nails that have worked upward generally from thermal expansion. While this can happen because the nail or girth is insufficient for the roofing material or the decking type, it also happens from general tweaks in the wood from the thermal expansion process. Recommend a licensed contractor repair all as needed.

Missing/Damaged Crown Shingle(s) Observed
Recommend a licensed roofer replace the shingle(s) as needed to prevent water intrusion and further degradation.

End Cap Crown Shingle(s) Nail Fasteners Need Sealant
Recommend a licensed roofer treat the fasteners with a rust inhibiting treatment if needed and seal all as needed unless or as recommended by the roofer, to prevent water intrusion and further degradation to fasteners, underlayment etc.

Missing/Damaged Shingle(s) Observed
Recommend a licensed roofer replace the shingle(s) as needed to prevent water intrusion and further degradation to nails, underlayment etc.

Aluminum Panel; Compromise along the Seam/Roofing Tape
The roof cover is an aluminum panel with a foil tape seal at the seams. The seals are a constant preemptive maintenance requirement for this roof cover, requiring coating/servicing or better every 3-7 years depending on the previous product type and life expectancy. It would be prudent to apply an elastomeric patch/caulk or DYCO

#20/20 Seam Sealer or better to all screws as is needed. Recommend a state licensed roofer assess the seams and treat as needed. Follow label instructions. Apply to manufacturer's instructions.

Aluminum Panel Screws Need Maintenance
The roof cover is an aluminum panel. The screw seals are a constant preemptive maintenance requirement for this roof cover, requiring coating/sealing or better every 3-10 years depending on the product used. It would be prudent to apply a silicone based or better patch/caulk to all screw heads and seams prior to any tape or other product application. Apply to manufacturer's instructions.

Excess Debris Buildup/Screw Oxidation Observed
When excess debris is on the roof, recommend removing debris to prevent backflow and mulching issues. Roof Sheathing Screws Oxidizing. This is typical as they are directly exposed to the elements; however, the corrosion is accelerated when leaf debris is present as it holds moisture. If untreated, water can/will enter patio at screws and roof transition points conducive to the mulching/back flow issues addressed above. Recommend removing all debris, cleaning surface of the fascia and roof transition area where the porch roof meets the buildings fascia board and properly resealing the length of the transition area if applicable. Treat screw heads with a Rustoleum rust inhibiting paint or better after removing excess rust and silicone after as needed.

Fractured Plank Board Decking Observed in the Attic System at the Time of the Inspection
Fractured boards can allow a worker accessing the roof or inspector to unknowingly damage the roof. If the boards are fractured enough that they can no longer withstand a live load of an individual or the individual is heavier than average, they can step on the board and send it right through the roof system. This can be a costly repair. It is always a good idea to reinforce fractured boards or replace them at the time of the roof replacement. When the roof is newer however, it is unlikely to be replaced anytime soon and thus, the repair can only be done from the inside of the attic, scabbing reinforcing wood members under the board. This repair is also risky so it is always recommended to leave it to the professionals. If there are protruding nails or if the wood support is nailed improperly, nails can pop through the shingle or be driven through accidently when reinforcing the area.

Rolled Roofs

Modified Bitumen Roll Roofing
The Asphalt Roofing Manufacturers' Association (ARMA) describes Modified Bitumen Roofing as follows: Modified bitumen membranes MBS combine the features of a built-up roof with the added tensile strength from its polymer modification. Using a reinforced sheet that is prefabricated in the plant, modified bitumen systems require a less labor-intensive application and can be applied cross-platform in both commercial and certain residential applications. A modified bitumen roofing system is composed primarily of polymer-modified bitumen reinforced with one or more plies of fabric such as polyester, fiberglass or a combination of both. Factory surfacing, if applied, includes mineral granules, slag, aluminum or copper. The bitumen determines the membrane's physical characteristics and provides primary waterproofing protection, while the reinforcement adds strength, puncture resistance and overall system integrity. Factory-assembled, modified bitumen membranes undergo strict quality control standards to ensure uniform thickness and consistent physical properties throughout the membrane. The finished roofing system is usually a two to four-ply system consisting of a modified bitumen membrane and a base sheet, with additional plies for added strength if needed. The substrate often determines which ply system is best specified. The finished roofing membrane may consist of one or more modified bitumen sheets, or it may be comprised of a combination of built-up roofing (BUR) felts and one or more modified bitumen sheets. The type of substrate and the performance objectives influence the specification of the modified bitumen membrane system.

Rolled Roofing
This consists of a heavy, asphalt-saturated organic or fiberglass felt with a granular surface. Rolls are 36 inches wide and weigh 90 pounds. Single-coverage roll roofing typically has a 2-inch lap with exposed nails and is used mainly on utility structures. Double-coverage roll roofing is installed with a full 19-inch lap joint, leaving a 17-inch exposure, with a 2-inch head-lap.

Modified Bitumen Roll Roof has "Bubbles" Observed
Bubbles (air pockets) occur where the roofing no longer adheres well to the surface below it; if you push on the bubble, you may hear a squishy sound where water has leaked under the membrane. Alternatively, it may have been trapped moisture under the area during installation, perhaps if it rained and the cover was applied before it

could be fully dried. Sometimes, sealed bubbles are better left alone, but most of the time, it is best to have it cut out and replaced by a state licensed roofer.

Modified Bitumen Roll Roof has "Ponding" Observed
Ponding (standing water) occurs where there are low spots in the roofing. If more than 10 – 15% of the roof remains water-covered 24 hours after a rain, you should build up the low spots to prevent water from working through the seams of the roof caused by excess water pressures. On large areas, 10x15', tapering boards and reroofing may be recommended to prevent a cave in or excessive leak in the event of a torrential rain.

Visible Compromise to the Drip Edge Flashing at the Soffit/Fascia Viewed from the Exterior Eaves
Visible inspection to the underbelly of the eaves not accessible, however, exterior observation shows suspected particulates and oxidation at the soffit conducive to wood rot and is typically known to start at the drip edge. Water trails under the roof cover, at the drip edge via fluidic capillary action, rotting the wood, causing a depression and progressing the rot process. Recommend a licensed contractor repair all as needed.

Rusted/Corroded Galvanized Drip Edge Flashing Observed
This flashing is dilapidated and at end-of-life. The oxidation rust has penetrated past the zinc chromate coating and has compromised the flashing. Recommend replacing any heavily corroded sections as is needed. Recommend a licensed roofing contractor repair as needed.

UV Exposure Appears to have Caused Significant Wear to the Skylight Dome, Causing Cracking/Damage
The skylight dome appears to be at end of life. The plastic is "yellowed" or foggy, indicative of U.V exposure long term. In addition, the perimeter fastening nails are heavily oxidized/rusted with various nails loose. There were also cracks forming at the perimeter cap/lip where the nails are fastened that degrades the uplift resistance and makes it far more susceptible to uplift damage. The internal dome/ plexi glass appears to also have heat stress cracks. Sun and UV exposure will cause significant wear to most originally installed external skylight domes and then rain, hail or snow can often cause cracking or damage in some other way. U.V. radiation degrades the elasticity of the dome(s) and makes them susceptible to cracks and fraying and far less impact resistance than they were once designed for. Since the progressive degradation conducive to a weathered skylight was present, and given the high probability for water resistance failure in the near future, it is highly recommended to have the skylight glass/dome changed to prevent any water loss and to provide maximum efficiency for lighting and energy purposes.

Screws/Nails Penetrating the Roof Deck at Vent Hoods are Not Sealed
These material penetrations of the roofing substrate can allow progressive amounts of moisture and water/damage to the roof cover and eventually, leaks into the structure. To prevent this, it is wise to limit any penetrations into the roof cover and decking as these become the paths of least resistance and eventually, can lead to leaks premature of the roofs end of life expectancy. It is highly recommended to have all superficial nails/ones not used to adhere other pertinent items such as Christmas light nailing often observed as the lead cause of eave compromises, avoided and to seal all other screws/nails penetrating the roof surface and flashing with a high temperature resistant silicone sealant or as directed by a state licensed contractor.

Screws/Nails at the Eaves Observed Penetrating the Roof Cover/Flashing
These material penetrations of the roofing substrate can allow progressive amounts of moisture and water/damage to the roof cover and eventually, leaks into the structure. To prevent this, it is wise to limit any penetrations into the roof cover and decking as these become the paths of least resistance and eventually, can lead to leaks premature of the roofs end of life expectancy as designed by the manufacturer(s). It is highly recommended to have all superficial nails/ones not used to adhere other pertinent items, removed or sealed professionally. Light nailing is often observed as the lead cause of eave compromises. Recommend all superficial nails/screws, be removed and to seal all other screws/nails penetrating the roof surface and flashing with a high temperature resistant silicone sealant by a state licensed roofing contractor.

Curling Asphalt Shingles Observed
Shingle curling is a sign of wear on asphalt shingle roofs. Most-common asphalt roof shingles have different asphalt shingle curling patterns, types and causes. Shingle corner curling is quite common and may provide several or more year's life provided granule integrity is good and no compromises to the roof seal are present.

Compromises/Lifting along the Seams

The roof cover seams seals can be at a constant preemptive maintenance requirement for this roof cover if/when lifting seams are observed or present water intrusion is evident, implying the seals may be deficient throughout, requiring resealing and/or coating or better every 3-7 years depending on the product(s) used. When the product is a PVC, TPO, M.B Roll, Composition roll roofing etc., It would be prudent to apply an elastomeric patch/caulk or DYCO #20/20 Seam Sealer or better and/or as per the roofers recommendations. Additionally, for aluminum roof vents screws, seal around screw heads where needed. Follow labeled instructions. Apply to manufacturer's instructions by a state licensed roofer.

TPO/Vinyl Roofing

PVC/TPO Roofing Membrane

PVC/TPO roofing is one of the best single-ply membranes and has a long history of excellent performance. CRC has observed 20-years old PVC roofs and they are still performing well and still in service. Compared to many roofing products, PVC is contractor friendly both in quality and ease of application. Properly formulated and manufactured PVC and other roofing materials give years of good service.

Defects

Post 2000 Installed Membrane: Crescent Fractures Observed to the Roof Surface

Crescent Fractures observed on roofing membranes installed after 2000 are typically not considered defects with the material, but either foot traffic damage, pressing down on the insulation plate lip under the membrane causing a small/large puncture that can progress or installation practice damage during the install process. It is highly recommended, however, to have these compromises reviewed by the manufacturer to ensure no material defects are the culprit. Additionally, it is recommended to have these areas of compromise inspected throughout by a licensed PVC/TPO membrane roofing specialist and repaired as needed.

Post 2000 Installed Membrane: Star Fractures Observed to the Roof Surface

"Star" fractures observed to the roof surface roofing membranes installed after 2000 are typically not considered defects with the material, but either foot traffic damage, installation practice damage during the install process or more commonly from hail impact or other impact damage to the roofing material. It is highly recommended, however, to have these compromises reviewed by the manufacturer to ensure no material defects are the culprit. Additionally, it is recommended to have these areas of compromise inspected throughout by a licensed PVC/TPO membrane roofing specialist and repaired as needed.

Compromises/Lifting along the Seams

The roof cover seams seals can be at a constant preemptive maintenance requirement for this roof cover if/when lifting seams are observed or present water intrusion is evident. This implies the seals may be deficient throughout, requiring resealing, coating or better every 3-7 years depending on the product(s) used. When the product is a PVC, TPO, M.B Roll, Composition roll roofing etc., It would be prudent to apply an elastomeric patch/caulk or DYCO #20/20 Seam Sealer or better and as per the roofers recommendations. Follow label instructions. Apply to manufacturer's instructions.

Tree Limbs Observed Touching the Roof Surface

Tree limbs can and will damage any surface they are allowed to contact. Tree limbs can grow into the roof cover, fascia and soffit, eventually compromising its water resistance, making it susceptible to water intrusion. They also more notoriously perhaps, brush the material surface, diminishing the life of the roof cover in the affected area by damaging the protective coating of the roofing material i.e. granules, zinc plating on galvanized steel, glazing on tiles etc. Recommend a licensed arborist assess further and trim all branch from the roof a recommended 5 feet or more to compensate for wind gusts and the trees malleable swaying motion in a storm. Recommend a licensed roofer assess the roof after the tree limbs are removed to assess damages, if any and repair as needed.

PRE 2001 Roof Covers Installation; Star or Crescent Damages

These fractures start developing within a 4 to 8 years period after the PVC roof system is installed. The PVC roof often begins with a small number of fractures of the type shown in these photos. The membrane fractures may leak during heavy rainfall or during slow snow melts and in ponded areas. The fractures continue to increase in number from a few fractures to hundreds of fractures in a few short years as the membrane prematurely ages. The manufacturer said the basic PVC formulation during this time period performed. However the problem age/stress fracturing, is the result of ineffective and poor production controls during the manufacturing process which introduced wide variations in membrane plasticizer content and key performance compounds and seemed to occur at random times. Poor post QA product testing was a contributing factor as company/ies did not test all membrane production runs. During this study on other roofs, they found roofs with all membrane rolls affected with a small number of fractures and stiff membrane. Many roofs had a mixture of both good and bad PVC with some rolls with no fractures and other rolls covered with fractures. The PVC membrane may show signs of shrinkage with the membrane taut between fastener attachment points on mechanically fastened systems. Perimeter sheets may have shrunk and pulled away from wall flashings and can be above the roof substrate surface under tension. The PVC membrane may become less flexible as it ages and will feel stiff and brittle in cold temperatures. The membrane scrim becomes more pronounced as the membrane becomes thinner due to faster plasticizer losses. On The membrane manufacturer responded to these material problems and provided either a product replacement installation or coated the roofs with an elastomeric roof coating at no cost to the owner, once the building owners or roofing contractors discovered the fractures and reported them. The membranes with defective material typically found, were manufactured over a time span covering 5 or 6 years ending mid 2000's. Once the production control problems and testing were discovered and identified. The roof system manufacturer changed their manufacturing process and quality control. Today we know of no similar problems with the manufacture's current roofing products. If your PVC roof was installed prior to mid-2000's and begins to develop these defect types, please contact Certified roofing consultants that can test and identify the roofing membrane to determine what is causing the fractures and help you secure a valid warranty claim provided the PVC membrane is defective and if your roofing warranty supplied guidelines are met. Fractures on any manufacturer's roofing product does not mean the resulting fractures are caused by defective materials. Foot traffic, hail damage, windblown objects and equipment servicing can be the fracture source. These damages cannot be fully ascertained as being defected or not defective at the time of the inspection and is considered beyond the scope of the inspection. PVC roofing is one of the best single-ply membranes and has a long history of excellent performance. CRC has observed 20-years old PVC roofs and they are still performing well and still in service. Compared to many roofing products, PVC is contractor friendly both in quality and ease of application. The key is identifying the problem and making a warranty claim prior to warranty expiration.

End Caps to Ridge Vent Missing
Recommend installing end caps to prevent rodent intrusion into the attic and structures interior envelope.

Wood Fascia Paint is Peeling/Chipping is and Appears Unsealed at Sections with Surface Fungi
Wood fascia is exposed. It may have had a treatment to the wood prior, however, the wood presently shows signs of suspected algae and fungi fruiting bodies indicative of the onset of wood rot. Recommend treating the algae/fungi and sealing the wood as needed.

Seals at Vents/Stacks and Roof Transitions are Insufficient/Antiquated
Recommend a licensed roofing contractor assess the roof protrusion abutments and repair/reseal at all transitions as is needed.

Compromise Suspected at the Apron/Counter Flashing/Exterior Wall Abutment. Visible Water Stains.
Roof compromise suspected at the apron/counter flashing. Water stains/damage was observed at the ceiling/roof and wall abutment from within the porch. Recommend licensed roofer assess further and repair as needed.

Metal Roof Panel is Rusted/Corroded. Galvanized Fasteners Observed Rusting/Corroded
The oxidation rust has penetrated past the zinc chromate coating and has compromised the flashing. Recommend replacing any heavily corroded sections, sanding and treating all else with a rust inhibitor and sealing all as is needed. Recommend replacing all screws with new stainless steel with rubber gasket washers or better. With proper care, metal roofs may not need replacing, the biggest question is cost for repair verse replacement. Recommend a licensed roofing contractor assess the roof further and repair as needed.

Loose Railing Observed
OSHA Regulations: Railing must be properly fastened per the ICC guidelines and/or your local code ordinances. Insurance companies may take issue when railing for balconies railings are not have properly fastened. Stair rail systems and handrails must be surfaced to prevent injuries typically, to meet the insurance and OSHA standards. Loose railing can allow the structural integrity to give way and allow a person to fall or become impaled if parts fall with and in relation to the individual, engaging them upon impact with the surface or landing that terminates the fall. Recommend a licensed contractor repair all as needed.

Landscape

Yard Shows Signs of Loss of Life Possibly Due to Pests, Disease and/or Poor Maintenance
This may be from weed overgrowth and/or pest (ant) colonies. You can treat the weeds, but it is safer and more effective to hand remove them. This can however, be quite labor intensive. St. Augustine Grass species needs loose soil to flourish. Should you decide to grow this type of grass or sod, you must first aerate the ground. Recommend a state licensed landscaping contractor review the area further and comprise a plan of treatment and maintenance as needed. For more, you can access the internet for a wide variety of helpful sources.

Weeds Growing Through Xeriscape
Old rock beds tend to be rich with soil and grow weeds quite nicely. Sifting some of that soil out and returning to a 3-5" depth of rocks makes things better. If the gravel was put down without a weed barrier (plastic sheeting) first, then one solution would be to move the gravel aside and put down the weed barrier before restoring the gravel. That would also allow getting rid of any sand/soil that may have drifted into the gravel since it was originally put down. Recommend a state licensed landscaping contractor/architect review the area further and determine method of repair to suit your needs.

Yard Shows Signs of Loss of Life at Front Possibly Due to Poor Maintenance from Inoperable Sprinkler(s)
The poor maintenance appears to be due to the lack of an operable sprinkler head at the location(s), however, the yard and plants were kept. There were sections of browning at the locations. Recommend a state licensed sprinkler technician repair the system as is needed.

Excessive Overgrowth and Leaf Debris Buildup
This can cause a multitude of issues if not already. While the leaf debris mulching effect is good for adding nutrient to the soil, it has very little additional good processes. The evenly excessive piles of mulching leaves are like a food bell to all the unwanted insects such as carpenter ants and roaches as well as snakes and even rodents such as mice and rats. The buildup also allows back flow of water back toward the buildings foundation, rotting wood surfaces and breeding algae and fungi which aid in the degradation of many exterior surfaces. Recommend a landscaper remove all leaf debris and overgrowth as needed.

Swales Observed Intermittently in the Yard
Swales may be caused when a tree and its roots are removed, where the cavity was either not filled or filled poorly. Swales are also intentional and manmade at times for the managed drainage of run off and to mitigate flooding as to mimic retention ponds. Swales may also indicate loose grade or previous sink holes depending on the region. For further comments and proper diagnoses, it is recommended to refer to a state licensed geotechnician as further diagnosis is beyond the scope of this inspection. Surveyor may also be warranted to assess flood plain levels in low lying regions.

Tree/Brush Overgrowth Encumbering Walkways
This can cause a hazard to humans and animals as it inhibits proper land area designated for walking, to traverse safely around the building and may inhibit access to the points of egress and fire escapes. Additionally, overgrown foliage may also excite algae and fungi growth and can pose a trip hazard.

St. Augustine Grass, Associated Issues and Things to Preempt
The following is general opinions on maintenance and upkeep. In no way is it recommended to administer any of the recommendations provided. The following recommendations are for review by a licensed landscaper for maintenance purposes and any additional variations or recommendations by the contractor should be taken into consideration; St. Augustine grass is one of the most popular turf grasses. Its tolerance to shade makes it very attractive for use in heavy landscaped gardens. Cultivars differ in their tolerance to plant pests, cold damage, and shade; you must know those differences in order to select the best cultivar for your particular needs. St. Augustine grass is affected by many insect and disease problems. Learning to recognize their symptoms is important because if the damage is allowed to continue for a long period of time, the problem could be more difficult to control and the damage could become very expensive. Chinch bugs are probably one of the most important insects in St. Augustine grass. The best way to control them is to use resistant varieties such as Floratam or Floralawn. There are known cases of chinch bug damage to these cultivars. Therefore, you should be alert of this insect even if you have a resistant variety. Other insect pests are webworm, army worms, grass loopers, and mole crickets. The most recognized diseases in St. Augustine grass are brown patch and gray leaf spot. Brown patch occurs in warm, humid weather (spring and fall months) and is associated with excessive nitrogen levels. Gray leaf spot occurs during the summer rainy season and it is also associated with high nitrogen levels. The use of fertilizers containing slow release forms of nitrogen can be used to minimize the damage caused by these diseases. Fungicides can also be used to control these diseases. Another disease, known as take-all disease, has been reported frequently in St. Augustine and other grasses. This particular disease is harder to diagnose and very difficult to control. It is usually necessary to replace damaged turf. Mowing is a very important practice and many problems arise because of improper mowing practices. Mow the lawn at 3 inches on regular varieties and 2 inches on semi-dwarf varieties. Do not remove more than 1/3 of the leaf blade in each mowing. Make sure that the blades are sharp during the mowing operation, otherwise the leaf blades will be injured more than necessary and the recovery may be slow and predispose the plant to other problems.

Bahia Lawns, Associated Issues and Things to Preempt
The following is general opinions on maintenance and upkeep. In no way is it recommended to administer any of the recommendations provided. The following recommendations are for review by a licensed landscaper for maintenance purposes and any additional variations or recommendations by the contractor should be taken into consideration; Bahia grass can be grown from seed which is abundant and relatively inexpensive. Once established, these grasses develop an extensive root system which makes them one of the most drought tolerant lawn grasses. Bahia grass produces a very durable sod which is able to withstand moderate traffic. In addition, Bahia grass has fewer pest problems than any other Florida lawn grass, although mole cricket can severely damage it. Bahia grass (Paspalum Notatum) is a warm-season perennial grass that is grown on over one million acres in Mississippi. Bahia grass is ideally adapted to the droughty, sandy soils of the lower Coastal Plain. Bahia is a great grass for year-round low maintenance requirements during normal seasons of rainfall. Its most intensive maintenance practice is its need for weekly (5-7 days) mowing intervals during the growing season. **Best mowing height is 2-3 inches**. Use a frequent mowing schedule to keep the lawn looking their best and fertilize as needed. Bahia grass goes dormant and turns brown/tannish color in winter after frost. May be over seeded with ryegrass for year round green color. The annual growing season is early May late August. **Watering;** Bahia is somewhat drought resistant, but requires watering on a regular basis to get the lawn established especially in the seedling stage and also to promote better germination. Argentine requires more water than Pensacola. Irrigation systems may be required in drought prone areas and during dry seasons in the rainy areas. Bahia grass will go dormant and turn brown during drought situations but survives long period of drought very well. It also responds quickly to rainfall after droughts, greening up fast. **Diseases and Pests;** Bahia has only a few disease problems, none of which are severe and can usually be managed through correct fertilization practices. Pests are minor with the exception of Mole Crickets.

Bermuda, Associated Issues and Things to Preempt
Common Bermuda grass is drought resistant, grows on many soils, and makes a good turf if fertilized and mowed right. Common Bermuda grass produces many unsightly seed heads, but in spite of this fault, it frequently is used on lawns due to the ease and economy of establishment. Common Bermuda may be planted from either seed or sprigs and with intensive management will provide a high quality turf. However, the newer hybrid Bermuda's are generally far superior. In Australia, Bermuda grass is known as Couch grass. Prefers full

sun, drought resistant, can withstand heavy traffic. It can easily be planted from grass seed (although it was once only grown from sod and the new seed varieties are not as fine bladed as the sodded varieties). One of the South's favorites grass types grows in tropical, subtropical and transition zone areas. Found extensively on lawns, golf courses, sporting fields and coast areas. Bermuda grass turns brown with the first drop in temperature. There are more cold tolerant varieties available. In warmer tropical areas, Bermuda retains a beautiful green color year round. This is a very aggressive grass and flower beds or other areas will be quickly overrun if not kept in check. Once established it is very difficult to remove due to its extensive root system.

Carpet Grass, Associated Issues and Things to Preempt

The following is general opinions on maintenance and upkeep. In no way is it recommended to administer any of the recommendations provided. The following recommendations are for review by a licensed landscaper for maintenance purposes and any additional variations or recommendations by the contractor should be taken into consideration; Carpet grass is a perennial, coarse-leaved, creeping grass. It grows better on low, wet soils than do other grasses. It will grow well in either sun or shade but is less shade tolerant than St. Augustine and Centipede grass which it resembles. Carpet grass may be planted by seed or sprigs. Carpet grass is ideal for those slightly shadier areas when moist soil is present for long periods. It will withstand higher traffic than many other grasses with these conditions. It is similar to centipede grass in its cold tolerance. It does not tolerate salt. Good option for soil erosion control combined with low maintenance. Carpet grass can be found from the sandy soils of East Texas to Florida and north to Virginia, Alabama and Arkansas. Carpet grass is found in fields, woods, along roadsides, pastures and lawns. Also known as flat grass, Louisiana grass and as "petit gazon" by the Creoles of Louisiana, carpet grass is native to the Gulf Coast states and other tropical climates. It is a creeping, perennial grass that can be recognized by the blunt rounded tips of its leaves, flat stolon's and a tall seed stalk with 2 branches at the apex. It forms a dense mat and will crowd out most other species. Carpet grass is susceptible to common soil borne diseases such as Brown Patch and Pythium and to most leaf spot diseases, but rarely do these diseases justify fungicide applications on carpet grass. The grass usually recovers with little injury when environmental conditions change. The exception might be brown patch in the fall which can produce unsightly turf for several months. White grub and, in the southeastern states, mole crickets, can cause serious injury to carpet grass turf. Again, where infestations of these insects can cause a problem, insecticides are available to effectively control them.

Kentucky Bluegrass, Associated Issues and Things to Preempt

The following is general opinions on maintenance and upkeep. In no way is it recommended to administer any of the recommendations provided. The following recommendations are for review by a licensed landscaper for maintenance purposes and any additional variations or recommendations by the contractor should be taken into consideration; Kentucky bluegrass is the most common cool season grass and probably the best known. Kentucky bluegrass creates a high quality lawn. It has been around for many years and is now available in many different blend formulations. Kentucky bluegrass has a moderate growth pattern and does spread and will fill in bare spots. The grass will go dormant in hot and dry weather as well as during the cold winter month's common in North America. It does poorly in extremely shady areas. Not recommended for extremely hot climates and will require supplemental irrigation during hot, dry periods. Kentucky bluegrass develops a shallow root system that is not drought tolerant and will go dormant during extreme conditions. If given intermittent watering during prolonged drought conditions, it will come back. Bluegrass seed-blends that include perennial ryegrass, produce a tougher wearing lawn. With the addition of creeping red fescue, the lawn will be more tolerate shadier areas. But what actually happens is that for those situations, the Kentucky bluegrass just doesn't fill in as it would normally in a full sun location and the supplemental blends actually fills in. In the southern United States, Kentucky bluegrass is limited to the transition zone from North Carolina, through much of Tennessee, northern Arkansas to the panhandle of Texas and Oklahoma. In the western states, Kentucky bluegrass is grown only with extensive irrigation.

Perennial Ryegrass, Associated Issues and Things to Preempt

The following is general opinions on maintenance and upkeep. In no way is it recommended to administer any of the recommendations provided. The following recommendations are for review by a licensed landscaper for maintenance purposes and any additional variations or recommendations by the contractor should be taken into consideration; Common perennial ryegrass germinates quickly and can be used as a temporary ground cover while the slower growing bluegrass plants take hold. In warm climates it is used as an over seed to maintain winter green in the lawn after the warm season grasses go dormant, however, it will not survive the summer heat. Of all turf grasses used in the South, ryegrass probably has the highest maintenance requirement. Mowing, watering, fertilization and pest management needs of ryegrass are higher than for any southern turf grass. Ryegrass has a rapid growth rate in the spring and requires twice weekly mowing at the taller heights above 1"; mowing at 2 — 3 day intervals at heights around 1" and daily mowing at heights below 1". In warm climates, perennial ryegrass is used as a temporary "winter green" grass for over seeding established warm season grasses, especially zoysia and bermuda, in early fall. Planted in early fall, it maintains a bright green lawn through winter. By summer the perennial rye has died in the heat and the permanent grass is green again. The ryegrasses are best adapted to moist, cool environments where temperatures are not extreme in the winter or summer. In the United States, the northeastern and northwestern states are well suited to ryegrass. In the transition zone, perennial ryegrass may provide a permanent turf grass. But in the southern states, both species serve as cool season annuals.

Grading

The Structure is on a Hill and Lacks Proper Run Off at/around the Walls Facing the Uphill Location
This bombards the facing section of the building with moisture to the surrounding grading and basement/foundation walls that can degrade and compromise the foundation/basements. Efflorescence is commonly associated with improper run off of this nature. When efflorescence is found at elongated horizontal cracks, it can be associated with serious progressive structural issues, in which case, it is highly recommended to have a structural engineer assess the area ASAP. In addition, recommend installing a drainage system at the foundation to reduce and/or eliminate the aforementioned issues as needed.

Tree Roots Encumbers the Building
This can ultimately cause heaving at the footing of the structure. Additionally, settlement can also occur if the tree starves the soil of moisture allowing for soil displacement. Installing a root barrier system involves trenching between the tree and target to be protected. Trenching around existing trees needs to be done with extreme caution both to prevent excessive root loss and tree dieback and also to protect the structural integrity and wind firmness of the tree. This is usually best done by a professional arborist or landscape service company. Recommend having a licensed arborist assess the area further and terminate the roots/growth toward the building as needed. An arbor culturist, is a professional in the practice of arboriculture, which is the cultivation, management, and study of individual trees.

Widespread Sogginess near Landscaping around the Building
For widespread sogginess near landscaping that is too large or difficult to simply fill in, re-grade or replant, there are other solutions. Runoff can be redirected or captured to minimize water accumulation. Redirecting runoff safely takes it to a suitable area. This can be done using swales, French drains, catch basins or downspout extensions. Capturing and storing runoff helps protect streams and rivers and reuses the water. This can be done using rain barrels, cisterns, dry wells, soil amendment or rain gardens. **Grading problems** on your property will prevent water from quickly flowing away into a storm drain or other suitable outlet. Areas around the foundation should slope away from the foundation walls; swales or other flow diversions between neighboring houses should be properly graded so that runoff does not stagnate on your property. Re-dredging any creeks and continued maintenance of the county side of any creeks/drainage should aid greatly in maintaining the proper drainage on your property.

Tree Roots Encumber Building/Yard Furrows
Grading at the building furrows due to neighboring tree/roots encumbering, this can ultimately cause heaving at the footing of the structure. Additionally, settlement can also occur if the tree starves the soil of moisture allowing for soil displacement. Installing a root barrier system involves trenching between the tree and target to be protected. Trenching around existing trees needs to be done with extreme caution both to prevent excessive root loss and tree dieback and also to protect the structural integrity and wind firmness of the tree. This is usually best done by a professional arborist or landscape service company. Recommend having a licensed arborist assess further and terminate the roots/growth toward the building as needed. An arbor culturist is a professional in the practice of arboriculture, which is the cultivation, management, and study of individual trees.

Tree(s) Heaving Grading around Building - No Heaving of Foundation Yet
Various foliage and their roots, are encumbering the foundational wall. Tree roots from the neighboring trees around the foundational wall may cause significant heaving to the footing of the structure. This can be structurally compromising. Tree root growth and potential future heaving may continue until the tree roots are removed. When removing any roots encumbering the foundation be sure to back fill with an industry prescribed fill. Recommend a state licensed contractor and structural engineer assess all further and repair remediate all as needed.

Vinyl Siding Abuts Grading; Moisture is inhibited from Expelling at the Siding Base
Siding should be installed tight enough to prevent problems related to water intrusion, but it should be loose enough to allow it to adequately dry after a rainstorm. Additionally, moisture must be allowed to expel from the wall that accumulates behind the vinyl siding. Moisture that gets in behind the wall at windows, doors and trim or where humidity is prevalent in the area, moisture and water can accumulate behind the siding. The siding needs a suggested 6 inches above the grading to allow the wall to relieve the moisture and is high enough to theoretically, defer foliage from getting behind the siding. Recommend a state licensed contractor assess all further and excavate at the wall area and/or applying an aggregate of rocks so that water does not stay at the abutting sight. Redressing the siding on the wall to allow a proper wall bond seal and raising the siding may also be an option.

Grading Slope appears Progressive; Caused by Erosion or was Formed Improper during Construction
Recommend installing Wire Mesh Confinement System (Nonstandard) at the steep slope of the grading as needed or as recommended by an engineer. Copy and paste the link below for more on this method. Recommend installing a French drain system around the entire perimeter of the premise/structure particularly where the slope is moderate or steep to defer further grading erosion at the foundations perimeter.

Rot/Mossy Surfaces Observed, Indicative of Ponding
The grading location of the building; soil is soggy/wet. Suspect ponding and drainage issues throughout. Mossy surfaces generally indicate moisture resides for prolonged periods. Additionally, soil content is richer than that of other areas and that of this region. The wood rot and moss covered sections define the level of flooding/ponding the yard endures. Soil swelling can be a major problem to a building's foundational footing. Recommend installing a drainage system at the building to reduce and/or eliminate the aforementioned issues as needed.

Erosion around the Perimeter of the Building from Lack of Gutters/Partial Gutters
Where erosion occurs under the eaves that have no guttering, more often, it is a direct result of having no gutters. **The grading furrows around the building and swales may occur at the corners of the building.** In Permaculture, a swale is a method used to harvest rain water. They are long shallow trenches that run along the contour of the land. This means that swales are perfectly level. Swales do not direct water flow, but they collect water. The furrow around the perimeter of the building acts generally like a swale with intermittent deeper pockets. The soil removed from the swale or furrow at the structure, is piled on the downhill side to make a slightly raised bank or berm further aggravating the process. When rain falls, the water runs along the surface of the topsoil, and it will collect in the depression of the swale or furrow. The water will slowly seep into the soil and collect in underground pockets that will supply the roots of plants through weeks and even months without rain. Displacement of soil at the foundation will also occur more progressively, causing cracks in the foundation and walls/cladding. This unfortunately, is not what you want around the perimeter of the structure. Swales and furrows will progressively grow, more so with each rain, and be a feeding spot for roots, like a beacon calling them to the buildings foundation. As stated, this erosion from rain run off can cause cracks to appear in your exterior walls as well as settlement in the foundation that can progress as long as the problem goes untreated. Recommend Gutters be installed on every eave location of the dwelling to prevent further grade erosion and remediating the furrows/swales with the corrective aggregate as needed by a state licensed contractor.

Erosion around the Perimeter of the Building under the Eaves Due to Lack of Guttering
This is a direct result of having no gutters. **The grading furrows around the building and swales may occur at the corners of the building.** In **Permaculture**, a swale is a method used to harvest rain water. They are long shallow trenches that run along the contour of the land. This means that swales are perfectly level. Swales do not direct water flow, but they collect water. The furrow around the perimeter of the building acts generally like a swale with intermittent deeper pockets. The soil removed from the swale or furrow at the building, is piled on the downhill side to make a slightly raised bank or berm further aggravating the process. When rain falls, the water runs along the surface of the topsoil, and it will collect in the depression of the swale or furrow. The water will slowly seep into the soil and collect in underground pockets that will supply the roots of plants through weeks and even months without rain. Displacement of soil at the foundation will also occur more progressively, causing cracks in the foundation and walls/cladding. This unfortunately, is not what you want around the perimeter of the structure. Swales and furrows will progressively grow, more so with each rain, and be a feeding spot for roots, like a beacon calling them to the buildings foundation. As stated, this erosion from rain run off can cause cracks to appear in your exterior walls as well as settlement in the foundation that can progress as long as the problem goes untreated. Recommend gutters be installed on every eave location of the dwelling to prevent further grade erosion and remediating the furrows/swales with the corrective aggregate as needed.

Swales Observed at the Corners of the Building; where Downspouts Terminate
In **Permaculture**, a swale is a method used to harvest rain water. They are long shallow trenches that run along the contour of the land. This means that swales are perfectly level. Swales do not direct water flow, but they collect water. The soil removed from the swale is piled on the downhill side to make a slightly raised bank or berm. When rain falls, the water runs along the surface of the topsoil, and it will collect in the depression of a swale. The water will slowly seep into the soil and collect in underground pockets that will supply the roots of plants through weeks and even months without rain. This unfortunately, is not what you want around the perimeter of the structure. Swales will progressively grow, more so with each rain and be a feeding spot for roots, like a beacon calling them to the buildings foundation.

Swales Observed at the Corners of the Building
In **Permaculture**, a swale is a method used to harvest rain water. They are long shallow trenches that run along the contour of the land. This means that swales are perfectly level. Swales do not direct water flow, but they collect water. The soil removed from the swale is piled on the downhill side to make a slightly raised bank or berm. When rain falls, the water runs along the surface of the topsoil, and it will collect in the depression of a swale. The water will slowly seep into the soil and collect in underground pockets that will supply the roots of plants through weeks and even months without rain. This unfortunately, is not what you want around the perimeter of the structure. Swales will progressively grow, more so with each rain, and be a feeding spot for roots, like a beacon calling them to the buildings foundation. This appears to be from downspouts terminating at the foundation. The rain runoff will continue to erode the area while the swale will also work as described above. Recommend repairing all swales with the appropriate backfill, installing diverters at the building, diverting run off 4-7 feet from the structure or installing French drains where applicable as needed.

Exterior

Exterior Stairs

No Deficiencies; Commercial Buildings
Note: Typically, fire escapes shall be designed to support a live load of 100 pounds per square foot (4788 Pa) and shall be constructed of steel or other approved noncombustible materials. Fire escapes constructed of wood not less than nominal 2 inches (51 mm) thick are permitted on buildings of Type V construction in some localities and state codes. Walkways and railings located over or supported by combustible roofs in buildings of Types III and IV construction are typically permitted to be of wood not less than nominal 2 inches (51 mm) thick in many localities and states. Stair Dimensions; Typically, in many localities and in accordance with the ICC, Stairs shall be at least 22 inches (559 mm) wide with risers not more than, and treads not less than, 8 inches (203 mm). Landings at the foot of stairs shall not be less than 40 inches (1016 mm) wide by 36 inches (914 mm) long and located not more than 8 inches (203 mm) below the door. The Main entrance; typically, in many localities are in accordance with the ICC Group A. All buildings of Group A with an occupant load of 300 or more shall be provided with a main entrance capable of serving as the main exit with an egress capacity of at least one half of the total occupant load. The remaining exits shall be capable of providing one half of the total required exit capacity.

No Deficiencies; Standard Buildings
Note: Typically, fire escapes shall be designed to support a live load of 100 pounds per square foot (4788 Pa) and shall be constructed of steel or other approved noncombustible materials. Fire escapes constructed of wood not less than nominal 2 inches (51 mm) thick are permitted on buildings of Type V construction in some localities and state codes. Walkways and railings located over or supported by combustible roofs in buildings of Types III and IV construction are typically permitted to be of wood not less than nominal 2 inches (51 mm) thick in many localities and states. Stair Dimensions; Typically, in many localities and in accordance with the ICC, Stairs shall be at least 22 inches (559 mm) wide with risers not more than, and treads not less than 8 inches (203 mm). Landings at the foot of stairs shall not be less than 40 inches (1016 mm) wide by 36 inches (914 mm) long and located not more than 8 inches (203 mm) below the door.

Vegetation Growth through Cracks/Joints and Excess Algae found at the Time of Inspection
Recommend removing weeds at the cracks/joints and to pressure wash as needed. Alternatively, some landscape managers have used liquid zinc or other natural algaecides to remove the algae because of its effectiveness, fast, natural and easy application processes.

No Expansion Joint Sealant Observed at the Expansion Joints
Expansion joints are those big joints in concrete that typically have either a piece of wood or have an asphalt fiberboard. When pouring the concrete driveway or sidewalk, they place these expansion joints to allow the concrete to expand and contract and are also places they have stopped pouring the concrete for the day.

Typically there is a piece of rebar going through the expansion strip to prevent the two concrete slabs from moving away from each other. Liquid sealants are the most commonly used sealant product for filling joints in building components and structural joints. Yet their performance, particularly in dynamic joints, can suffer from a variety of shortcomings that often begin with awkward installation factors such as badly prepared substrates and movement during cure. Finally, tensile stresses at bond lines, as well as within the cured liquid sealant elastomer, often result in premature failure. The problem with these expansion strips is that they allow water to migrate down through the joint causing the rebar to rust. Eventually the rebar will break and allow the two concrete slabs to move independently. Another problem with these joints is that they can collect dirt and provide an area for weeds to grow. There is a solution to these problems; you can have a joint sealant placed over the expansion joint. This will help prevent water migrating down causing the rebar to rust and will also prevent weeds from growing in the joint. The material used is a polyurethane caulk that bonds to both side of the concrete slab creating a complete water seal. Other products such as plastic or foam that are placed in-between the joint do not create that watertight seal like the polyurethane caulking.

Concrete Stairways; Moisture Cracking from Weathering Observed
The cracks appear to be from weathering of the concrete. Cubicle and Web Cracks will form and progress many times in a web fashion if they and the concrete surrounding them are not treated. Caulking/sealing the cracks may also aid in reducing erosion to underneath the surface. Where cracks are larger, expansion joint sealant is recommended. Recommend using concrete sealants, NOT mortar/concrete as they may break off or crumble and not properly adhere to the surface.

Algae Growth on Stairway
This is very common. However, you will want to treat or pressure wash mainly the darker areas as this growth tends to cause a slip hazard if allowed to grow. You may pressure clean it or add regular bleach in a sprayer with water. Exterior grade bleach diluted per manufacturer's Instructions applied by a licensed contractor should work. You may also look for liquid zinc for it's very easy to apply, natural properties.

Iron Stains Observed on Stairway(s)
The reddish brown rusty stains are a common problem readily seen on siding, sidewalks, walkways, patios, stepping stones, window and door frames in areas where irrigation water has a high iron content. The sprinkler system and/or hoses that are used to water the grounds may also be spraying iron particles that create these rust stains wherever they land. Iron is a chemical element that is abundant in soils and aquifers in many parts of the country. And it is the element that, when exposed to air and moisture, oxidizes or rusts. Where the tap water is "hard" or mineral-rich and we irrigate with well water, sprinkler water is probably causing rust stains. The irrigation systems will often "over spray" which means water ends up on the fence, patio, deck, porch, building, windows, doors, concrete walkways, stepping stones or paths, lawn furniture and also on parked vehicles if exposed to overspray. Once iron particles from the water in your sprinkler come in contact with the air, they will begin to oxidize or rust. The stains that result have likely developed over time and can be very stubborn to remove. Recommend installing a rust inhibitive filtration treatment system to the sprinkler system to prevent this.

Loose Hand Rail Mounts/Fasteners Observed
OSHA Regulations: Handrails must be graspable and properly fastened per the ICC guidelines and/or your local code ordinances. Insurance companies may take issue when handrails for stairways with more than 3 risers do not have properly fastened handrails. Stair rail systems and handrails must be surfaced to prevent injuries, typically, to meet the insurance and OSHA standards. Loose railing can allow the structural integrity to give way and allow a person to fall or become impaled if parts fall with and in relation to the individual, engaging them upon impact with the surface or landing that terminates the fall. Recommend a licensed contractor repair all as needed.

No Graspable Hand Rail at the Stairway
OSHA Regulations: Handrails must be graspable per the ICC guidelines and/or your local code ordinances. Insurance companies may take issue when handrails for stairways with more than 3 risers do not have graspable handrails. Stair rail systems and handrails must be surfaced to prevent injuries and frequently, to meet the insurance and OSHA standards. Recommend a licensed contractor repair all as needed.

Wood Rot Observed at the Exterior Wood Stairs
Wood rot is caused by undue exposure of untreated wood to moisture. Consequently, prevention constitutes both avoiding such exposure and employing a prevention and treatment program where rot already exists. Wood with 20 percent moisture content and green lumber remain at risk. Though new fungi strains are frequently introduced to our environment that cause many side effects to many different substrates, two types of

rot currently trouble building owners. The first is white and yellow with a stringy and spongy look. The other is brown and crumbly in appearance, and a tendency to break into cubes has earned it the nickname "brown cubical rot." These visible manifestations of wood rot are called "fruiting bodies". About 3 inches in diameter, these crusts or brackets may indicate that the particular decay fungi are present within the wood. Serpula lacrimans, Poria incrassata and Gleophyllum trabeum each have singular fruiting-body appearances. Fruiting bodies produce spores, which spread the decay fungus throughout the wood. To prevent wood rot, use treated wood or the heartwood of a decay-resistant species like pacific yew, juniper, and redwood. For minor damage, epoxy, wood hardener and know-how may help these minor rotted areas of wood on decks, fences, doorways, windows and non-structural rot damage, to be healthy again! There are many websites that provide adequate direction as to how to treat the wood rot. It is always recommended to have a state licensed contractor assess further and repair as needed.

Excessive Wood Warping Observed

Wood has many outstanding properties, but it is a natural, porous material with individual characteristics, and it can warp. When wood gets wet, it swells. When wood dries out after being sawn from the tree, after being pressure-treated and after rain showers, it shrinks. Uneven drying creates stresses in wood, which results in warping (e.g., bowing, cupping or twisting) or cracking. The degree of warping depends on the species of wood, its grain pattern, uniformity of drying and construction techniques, among other factors. There is not much a user can do to truly un-warp a warped piece of wood. It is possible to position bowed boards so that its weight flattens it, using screws that are load adequate to fasten securely an otherwise warped piece. Recommend re-supporting or replacing the displaced section with deck/exterior wood screws per each section affected and any horizontal bracing and straps on stringers, balustrade, treads and rails where applicable, as needed, as directed by a state licensed contractor/structural engineer.

Wood Stairs; Suspected Termite Damage. No Live Termites Observed

Remnants of canals and/or subterranean tubes on the wood intermittently, there were no live termites observed. It is unknown if the structure was treated for subterranean or dry wood termites in the recent past. There were old termite burrows found on the wood but there were no signs of live dry wood or subterranean termites. After considering the length of time between treatments, if it is known, it is warranted and recommended to have a licensed pest professional treat the building and/or provide a routine treatment and inspection plan. Additionally, there are many termite control companies that will provide free inspections. If needed, termite control can be done with liquid termite control, termite bait systems, or both. Liquid Termite Control products are fast acting, can be applied closer to the infestation, and require less maintenance. For subterranean, when needed, termite Bait Systems are less intrusive, no drilling or trenching is needed, no expensive equipment is required, and bait systems can help you identify a problem before the termites reach the building. You can do your own termite control and prevention. Advantages to dry wood alternative treatments are: The structure does not have to be unoccupied during treatment, just the immediate work area. There is a low residual effect to the termiticide. If re-infestation occurs and the insects come in contact with the treated area, the transfer effect will start again and the colony will be eliminated. Most important, this method uses material much lower in mammalian toxicity. Removing any suspected termite affected wood is recommended, in hopes to quarantine the area from further spreading. Repair as needed or better.

Stair Treads are coated with a Slippery Gloss Coating

Recommend all stairs be coated/textured with a non-slip surface and with discernable markings per each tread. For building/structures that are for commercial/industrial applications, there are specific guidelines as to the color and texture minimums and material types. It is recommended to have a licensed contractor that specializes in this coating type to install it as is needed.

Potential Termite Damage Observed. Live Formosan Subterranean Termites Observed

Termite damage was suspected at and within the wood. The Formosan subterranean termite (Coptotermes formosanus) is an invasive species of termite. It has been transported worldwide from its native range in southern China to Formosa (Taiwan, where it gets its name) and Japan. In the 20th century it became established in South Africa, Hawaii and in the continental United States. The Formosan subterranean termite is often nicknamed the super-termite because of its destructive habits. This is because of the large size of its colonies, and the termites' ability to consume wood at a rapid rate. A single colony may contain several million (compared with several hundred thousand termites for other subterranean termite species) that forage up to 300 feet (100 m) in soil. A mature Formosan colony can consume as much as 13 ounces of wood a day (ca. 400 g) and severely damage a structure in as little as three months. Because of its population size and foraging range, the presence of colonies poses serious threats to nearby structures. Once established, Formosan subterranean termite has never been eradicated from an area. By the 1950's, it was reported in South Africa and Sri Lanka.

During the 1960's it was found in Texas, Louisiana, and South Carolina. In 1980, a well-established colony was thriving in a condominium in Hallandale Beach, Florida. Recommend further inspection and treatment if possible/needed or full removal of any infected area as needed/ recommended by a state licensed pest control contractor ASAP.

Potential Termite Damage Observed. Live Drywood Termites Suspected/Observed

Termite damage was suspected at and within the wood. Drywood termites typically swarm in the evening and at night during the warmer months of the year. It is very hard to find where they are coming from because they live so deeply in the lumber. Drywood termite colonies are small colonies only about 3,000 termites. When the colony reaches about 3,000 termites then they will swarm to start a colony elsewhere. They need very little moisture and are often found in the attic wood framing, wall studs, door casings and window frames. Drywood termites obtain moisture from the water produced by the digestion of cellulose, no matter how old the wood is.' Spot treatments, such as orange oil applications, use insecticides applied to control known drywood termite colonies, such as those found in a door casing, windowsill or piece of furniture. Advantages to drywood alternative treatments are: The wood fencing needn't be cordoned off and the structure does not have to be unoccupied during treatment, just the immediate work area. There is a residual effect to the termiticide. If re-infestation occurs and the insects come in contact with the treated area, the transfer effect will start again and the colony will be eliminated. Most important, this method uses material much lower in mammalian toxicity.

Stairway Path/Width is Insufficient

Stair widths appear less than the required width as required typically by many localities and in accordance with the ICC and OSHA standards. Many localities and in accordance with the ICC and OSHA standards, stairs shall be at least 22 inches (559 mm) wide with risers not more than, and treads not less than, 8 inches (203 mm). Landings at the foot of stairs shall not be less than 40 inches (1016 mm) wide by 36 inches (914 mm) long and located not more than 8 inches (203 mm) below the door. Recommend a licensed contractor repair all as needed. Note: Per OSHA Standards; **1917.112(e)(1)** For stairways less than 44 inches (1.12 m) wide, at least one railing; and **1917.112(e)(2)** For stairways more than 44 inches (1.12 m) but less than 88 inches (2.24 m) wide, a stair rail or handrail on each side, and if 88 or more inches wide, an additional intermediate handrail. **1917.112(f)** Condition. Railings shall be maintained free of sharp edges and in good repair.

Stair Treads, Rise/Runs are Uneven

Stairs shall be at least 22 inches (559 mm) wide with risers not more than, and treads not less than, 8 inches (203 mm). Landings at the foot of stairs shall not be less than 40 inches (1016 mm) wide by 36 inches (914 mm) long and located not more than 8 inches (203 mm) below the door. Recommend a licensed contractor review all and repair as needed per the state, local and OSHA standards.

Loose/Damaged Stair Treads Observed

Per the ICC, stairs shall be at least 22 inches (559 mm) wide with risers not more than, and treads not less than, 8 inches (203 mm). Landings at the foot of stairs shall not be less than 40 inches (1016 mm) wide by 36 inches (914 mm) long and located not more than 8 inches (203 mm) below the door. Treads must be secure, without loose or protruding fasteners so as to not cause accidental injury or fall etc. Many insurance companies will require these to be remediated per your insurance policy/requirements. Recommend a licensed contractor review all and repair as needed per the state, local and OSHA standards.

Balustrade; Various Loose Balusters Observed

Note: Per OSHA and the ICC Standards; **1917.112(e)(1)** For stairways less than 44 inches (1.12 m) wide, at least one railing; and **1917.112(e)(2)** For stairways more than 44 inches (1.12 m) but less than 88 inches (2.24 m) wide, a stair rail or handrail on each side, and if 88 or more inches wide, an additional intermediate handrail. **1917.112(f)** Condition. Railings shall be maintained free of sharp edges and in good repair.

Bannister/Rail Dilapidated

Various loose and damaged sections observed throughout. Fasteners were observed loose/compromised. OSHA Regulations: Stairways with four or more risers or rising more than 30 inches (76 cm) in height, whichever is less, must have railing installed. Top edges of stair rail systems used as handrails must not be more than 37 inches (94 cm) high nor less than 36 inches. Handrails must be graspable per the ICC guidelines and/or your local code ordinances. Stair rail systems and handrails must be surfaced to prevent injuries. Recommend a licensed contractor repair all as needed.

Bannister/Rail Insufficient to Safety Standards
OSHA Regulations: Stairways with four or more risers or rising more than 30 inches (76 cm) in height, whichever is less, must have railing installed. Top edges of stair rail systems used as handrails must not be more than 37 inches (94 cm) high nor less than 36 inches. Handrails must be graspable per the ICC guidelines and/or your local code ordinances. Stair rail systems and handrails must be surfaced to prevent injuries. Recommend a licensed contractor repair all as needed.

Railing is Greater than 36 inches in Height
Top edges of stair rail systems used as handrails must not be more than 37 inches (94 cm) high nor less than 36 inches. Stair rail systems and handrails must be surfaced to prevent injuries. Handrails must be graspable per the ICC guidelines and/or your local code ordinances. Recommend a licensed contractor repair all ASAP.

Railing is Less than 36 inches in Height
Per OSHA and the ICC: Stair railings shall be capable of withstanding a force of at least 200 pounds (890 N) applied in any direction, and shall not be more than 36 inches (0.91 m) nor less than 32 inches (0.81 m) in height from the upper top rail surface to the tread surface in line with the leading edge of the tread. Railings and mid-rails shall be provided at any stairway having four or more risers. Stair rail systems and handrails must be surfaced to prevent injuries. Handrails must be graspable per the ICC guidelines and/or your local code ordinances. Recommend repairing ASAP. Note: Per OSHA Standards; **1917.112(e)(1)** For stairways less than 44 inches (1.12 m) wide, at least one railing; and **1917.112(e)(2)** For stairways more than 44 inches (1.12 m) but less than 88 inches (2.24 m) wide, a stair rail or handrail on each side, and if 88 or more inches wide, an additional intermediate handrail. **1917.112(f)** Condition. Railings shall be maintained free of sharp edges and in good repair.

Ballasts are Spread Too Far Apart, Exceeding 3 ½ inches Width
Protective handrails and guardrails should have balusters/spindles at intervals no more than three and a half inches or have sufficient protective material to prevent a three and a half inch sphere from passing through if caring for children two years and over. Recommend a licensed contractor review the area and repair as needed ASAP.

Wood Stringer Attachment(s); Missing/Damaged Support(s)
Stringers/stairs should be designed so the first step is at the same level of the floor platform which gives the stringers full bearing. If this design cannot be accomplished, proper bearing for the stringers should be provided. When straps/fasteners at the top are only toenailed or screwed with the extent of the attachment, they will fail quickly or a split will develop at the inside corner of the bearing point. Proper support at the top, midsection, base and/or all, will be needed for equal load transfer. It is highly recommended to have a licensed contractor remediate ASAP.

Bannister/Rail Not Observed at Stairway(s)
OSHA Regulations: Stairways with four or more risers or rising more than 30 inches (76 cm) in height, whichever is less, must be installed along with railings. Top edges of stair rail systems used as handrails must not be more than 37 inches (94 cm) high nor less than 36 inches. Handrails must be graspable per the ICC guidelines and/or your local code ordinances. Stair rail systems and handrails must be surfaced to prevent injuries. Recommend a licensed contractor repair all as needed.

Newell Post(s) Loose
These posts act as the main supports for the integral parts such as the railing and balustrade. When the posts are loose or compromised they can structurally compromise the safety equipment, railings etc., on the stairs and can possibly compromise the stairs run/risers structurally. It is highly recommended to have a licensed contractor review and repair ASAP.

Tree Roots from the Neighboring Tree appear to be Causing Significant Heaving to the Stairs
This is a liability hazard as it is considered a trip and slip hazard. Per the ICC; Stairs shall be at least 22 inches (559 mm) wide with risers not more than, and treads not less than, 8 inches (203 mm). Landings at the foot of stairs shall not be less than 40 inches (1016 mm) wide by 36 inches (914 mm) long and located not more than 8 inches (203 mm) below the door. Recommend a licensed contractor review all and repair as needed per the state, local and OSHA standards. Heaving will likely continue to raise the stairway, damaging substrates and structural components, requiring further maintenance, until the tree roots are removed.

No Railing Observed at the Time of the Inspection

2012 IRC (International Residential Code) Section R311.7.8 HANDRAILS - In addition, most insurance companies require handrails and railing for stairs and decking where stairs have 3 or more risers to include the decking/landing. R311.7.8 (Handrails) Handrails having minimum and maximum heights of 34 inches and 38 inches respectively, measured vertically from the sloped plain adjoining the tread nosing or finished surface of ramp slope. They should be provided on at least one side of stairways with a total rise of 30" or more. Spiral stairways shall have the required handrail located on the outside radius. All required handrails shall be continuous the full length of the stairs. Ends shall be returned or shall terminate in newel posts or safety terminals. Handrails adjacent to a wall shall have a space of not less than 1½ inch between the wall and the handrail. For this reason and for general safety standards, it is highly recommended to remediate ASAP by a licensed contractor per IRC guidelines and/or state and local codes.

Windows/Doors; Trim

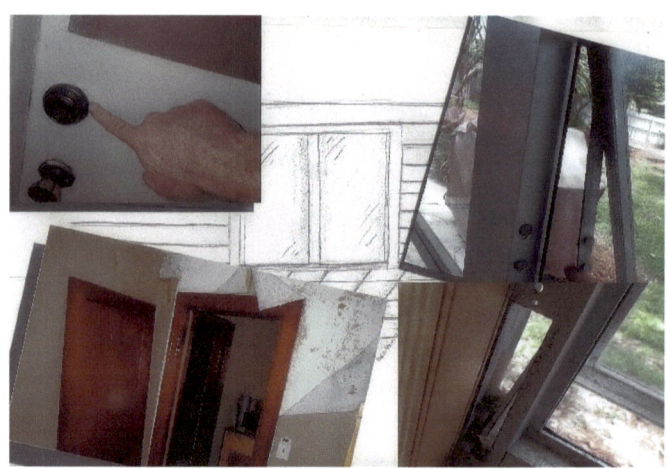

Means of Egress Building Code

2010 FLORIDA BUILDING CODE-EXISTING BUILDING ALTERATIONS-LEVEL 2. Chapter 705.3.1.2.2 Construction; The fire escape shall be designed to support a live load of 100 pounds per square foot (4788 Pa) and shall be constructed of steel or other approved noncombustible materials. Fire escapes constructed of wood not less than nominal 2 inches (51 mm) thick are permitted on buildings of Type V construction. Walkways and railings located over or supported by combustible roofs in buildings of Types III and IV construction are permitted to be of wood not less than nominal 2 inches (51 mm) thick. Chapter 705.3.1.2.3 Dimensions; Stairs shall be at least 22 inches (559 mm) wide with risers not more than, and treads not less than, 8 inches (203 mm). Landings at the foot of stairs shall not be less than 40 inches (1016 mm) wide by 36 inches (914 mm) long and located not more than 8 inches (203 mm) below the door. Chapter 705.3.2 Mezzanines; Travel distance for mezzanines shall comply with Chapter 10 of the *Florida Building Code, Building.* Chapter 705.3.3 Main entrance-Group A; All buildings of Group A with an occupant load of 300 or more shall be provided with a main entrance capable of serving as the main exit with an egress capacity of at least one half of the total occupant load. The remaining exits shall be capable of providing one half of the total required exit capacity.

No Deficiencies Observed at the Doors or Windows

Recommend inspecting exterior windows and doors trim and frames abutments and at all seams annually. When needed, seal all observed cracks/seams that appear breached/compromised as needed. For wood fascia, aluminum covers, vinyl, stucco etc., caulk can be used where siding abuts openings and trim. Latex, latex-silicone blends, polyurethane, and polysulfide caulks generally perform satisfactorily. Caulks that are 100% silicone should not be used. Use per manufacturer's instructions and local code ordinances. For aluminum trim covers, routinely inspect to ensure no nails are loose and the trim cover is intact and not sagging. If a surface rust occurs on any galvanized trim, head flashing or door, sanding and treating the concerning areas is critical to prevent further oxidation using a rust inhibiting sealant treatment. All areas appeared serviceable at the time of the inspection.

Flashing at the Window Suspected Improper. Water Intrusion found at the Windows Interior/Trim

Flashing at the window suspected improper. Water intrusion found at the windows interior/trim. Recommend a licensed window and door technician assess the area further and replace/repair as needed.

Improperly Installed Integral Finned Window. Drywall Screws Used/Application Improper

This Application Type is Improper for the Screw Type. Window(s) were observed installed improperly, using drywall screws instead of the prescribed fastener type. Drywall screws are the favorite for DIY novice carpenters. Unfortunately, they do not have the dead load capacity required to properly retain and maintain a proper flush seal. The window is an integral finned window. These windows are designed for frame buildings with different siding types. Recommend having a licensed window installer assess and replace/repair as needed.

Improperly Installed Window. Drywall Screws Used
Window(s) were observed installed improperly using drywall screws. Drywall screws are the favorite for DIY novice carpenters. Unfortunately, they do not have the dead load capacity required to properly retain and maintain a proper flush seal and are Improper for this application. Windows that are designed for frame buildings use wood screws at all designated predrilled slots within the window frame. Windows installed on a masonry structure, typically with a stucco or brick façade would generally require Tapcon masonry screws. Recommend having a licensed window installer assess and replace/repair all as needed.

Broken Glass Pane(s) Observed. Suspect Sheer Stresses
Broken glass suspected of being broken by settlement stresses evident at this location. Fractured glass can easily break and already broken glass panes with exposed course serrations and sharp edges can break off further and in both cases are extremely hazardous to any child, elderly and animals whom come in contact. It is highly recommended to have a structural engineer review further and a licensed contractor repair as needed.

Iron Stains Observed on Window/Door Trim
The reddish brown rusty stains are a common problem readily seen on siding, sidewalks, walkways, patios, stepping stones, window and door frames and is more prevalent in areas where irrigation water has a high iron content. The sprinkler system and/or hoses that are used to water the grounds may be spraying iron particles that create these rust stains wherever they land. Iron is a chemical element that is abundant in soils and aquifers in many parts of the country. It is also the element that, when exposed to air and moisture, oxidizes or rusts. Where the tap water is "hard" or mineral-rich and we irrigate with well water, sprinkler water is probably causing rust stains. The irrigation systems will often "over spray" which means water ends up on any fence, patio, deck, porch, building, windows, doors, concrete walkways, stepping stones or paths, lawn furniture and also on parked vehicles if exposed to overspray. Once iron particles from the water in your sprinkler come in contact with the air, they will begin to oxidize or rust. The stains that result have likely developed over time and can be very stubborn to remove. Recommend installing a rust inhibitive filtration treatment system to the sprinkler system to prevent this.

Sliding Door Lock Latch Damaged
Recommend a licensed contractor repair/replace the hardware as needed.

Sliding Doors Inoperable due to Excess Dirt, Debris and Resin Causing the Track to be Obstructed
Recommend cleaning and lubricating all parts as needed. Silicone and aluminum sprays or better, used in accordance with the manufacturers specifications, are recommended. Note: Depending on severity, the base/top track system parts may need to be replaced.

Defective/Loose Single Hung Balance Spring Observed at the Window
Defective/Loose Single Hung Balance Spring; the windows use spring balances to help raise and lower the window and keep the window in a raised position. When you have difficulty raising the sash, or it no longer remains open without the help of a prop, one or both of your spring balances could have a broken spring or cord and replacement is needed in order to repair the window(s).

Various Defective/Loose Single Hung Balance Springs Observed at the Window
Defective/Loose Single Hung Balance Springs; your windows use spring balances to help you raise and lower the window sash and keep the sash in a raised position. When you have difficulty raising the sash, or it no longer remains open without the help of a prop, one or both of your spring balances could have a broken spring or cord and replacement is needed in order to repair the window(s).

Laminated Cabinet Doors Delaminating Starting at the Edges/Seams
The Doors are made of a MDF Board (medium density fiberboard) and have a laminated composite applied to the surface. This composite has known issues with delamination and buckling at the seams; at the lips of the doors. This may be able to be remedied nominally before having to replace them if left to progress further.

Missing Glass Pane(s) Observed
This leaves the building vulnerable for break in and can allow rodent intrusion and the elements into the structure. It is highly recommended to have a licensed contractor replace the glass ASAP.

Windows Sealed Shut
Most codes to most localities require means of escape, ventilation etc. Inoperable windows can be a fire hazard to life as they inhibit escape while fire can quickly consume the air in a room. It is highly recommended to have the window repaired to full operability per state and local codes to prevent such hazards, if any.

Various Crank Windows will Not Open Due to Inoperable/Missing Mechanical Components
Most codes to most localities require means of escape, ventilation etc. Inoperable windows can be a fire hazard to life as they inhibit escape etc. It is highly recommended to have the window repaired to full operability per state and local codes to prevent such hazards.

Hollow Core Door used on the Egress to the Buildings Garage
Note: 2010 FLORIDA BUILDING CODE-EXISTING BUILDING ALTERATIONS-LEVEL "2. Chapter 705.3.1.2.2 Construction; The fire escape shall be designed to support a live load of 100 pounds per square foot (4788 Pa) and shall be constructed of steel or other approved noncombustible materials. Fire escapes constructed of wood not less than nominal 2 inches (51 mm) thick are permitted on buildings of Type V construction. Walkways and railings located over or supported by combustible roofs in buildings of Types III and IV construction are permitted to be of wood not less than nominal 2 inches (51 mm) thick. Chapter 705.3.1.2.3 Dimensions; Stairs shall be at least 22 inches (559 mm) wide with risers not more than, and treads not less than, 8 inches (203 mm)." Door should be 2 hour fire rated and UL listed or as directed by you state and local codes. Recommend a licensed contractor replace as needed.

Windows Seals and Weather Stripping Compromised/Antiquated
Recommend lubricating all windows at their hinged or channeled areas and at all moving components. Recommend re-weatherizing with weather stripping and caulk sealants where needed. Latex-silicone blends, polyurethane, Elastomeric and polysulfide caulks generally perform satisfactorily. Caulks that are 100% silicone should not be used as they will not bond to/with any latex paints.

Various Screens were Observed Cut/Ripped at Window(s)
Screen was observed ripped/cut at various windows at the time of the inspection. Recommend repairing/replacing this screen section as soon as possible to defer insect and rodent entry etc. as needed.

Windows/Doors Need Basic Lubricants/Servicing
The windows were observed to be hard to open and shut commonly caused by tensioning/rubbing friction of the plastics, metals 7/or wood of the window frame and balance springs/weights. This can lead to further damage to balance spring mechanisms overtime if not annually lubricated and operated. Recommend a silicone or aluminum to aluminum lubrication spray or as directed by a professional contractor, to all moving components and applied to manufacturer's specifications.

Sliding Doors Need Basic Lubricants/Servicing
Typically, if the door starts to feel tougher to open, it generally means to clean and service the channeling with lubricants, it is commonly caused by tensioning/rubbing friction of the plastics and metals. Recommend a silicone spray (Aluminum to Aluminum Spray for Aluminum Sliders) to all moving components and applied to manufacturer's specifications.

Single Hung Windows Were Not Operable at the Time of the Inspection
Window could not stay open. This could be caused by displaced balanced cartridge(s), springs and other channel components. Recommend repairing/replacing, then lubricating all windows at their hinged or channeled areas and at all moving components. Recommend re-weatherizing with weather stripping and caulk sealants where needed. Latex-silicone blends, polyurethane, elastomeric and polysulfide caulks generally perform satisfactorily. Caulks that are 100% silicone should not be used as they will not bond to/with any latex paints.

Wood Rot Observed at the Base of the Egress Door Frame
Wood rot is caused by undue exposure of untreated wood to moisture. Consequently, prevention constitutes both avoiding such exposure and employing a prevention and treatment program where rot already exists. Wood with 20 percent moisture content and green lumber remain at risk. Two types of rot trouble owners. The first is white and yellow with a stringy and spongy look. The other is brown and crumbly in appearance and has a tendency to break into cubes has earned it the nickname "brown cubical rot". These visible manifestations of wood rot are called "fruiting bodies", about 3 inches in diameter, these crusts or brackets are evidence that the particular decay fungi is present within the wood. Serpula lacrimans, Poria incrassata and Gleophyllum trabeum

each have singular fruiting-body appearances. Fruiting bodies produce spores, which spread the decay fungus throughout the wood. To prevent wood rot at the door base frame or doors themselves, use treated wood or the heartwood of a decay-resistant species. Caulk can be used where the wood siding abuts openings and trim and where cracks are located to fill them. Latex-silicone blends, polyurethane, elastomeric and polysulfide caulks generally perform satisfactorily. Caulks that are 100% silicone should not be used as they will not bond to/with any latex paints. Recommend a licensed contractor repair all as needed.

Wood Rot Observed at and Around the Window(s) Frame
Wood rot is caused by undue exposure of untreated wood to moisture. Cracks in the caulk sealants to the window frames provide access to water intrusion. Consequently, prevention constitutes both avoiding such exposure and employing a prevention and treatment program where rot already exists. Caulk sealants such as elastomeric, polyurethane, siliconized acrylic and other equal or better sealants are made to provide this preventative seal, while still being able to be painted and won't shrink like basic caulks such as standard acrylic. Wood with 20 percent moisture content and green lumber remain at risk. Two types of rot trouble owners. The first is white and yellow with a stringy and spongy look. The other is brown and crumbly in appearance, and a tendency to break into cubes has earned it the nickname "brown cubical rot." These visible manifestations of wood rot are called "fruiting bodies." About 3 inches in diameter, these crusts or brackets are evidence that the particular decay fungi is present within the wood. Serpula lacrimans, Poria incrassata and Gleophyllum trabeum each have singular fruiting-body appearances. Fruiting bodies spread the decay fungus from spore growth throughout the wood. To prevent wood rot at the window(s), window frames, trim and the windows themselves if any part of the windows woods elements, if any, are exposed. Use treated wood or the heartwood of a decay-resistant species. Caulk can be used where the wood siding abuts openings and trim and where cracks are located to fill them. Latex-silicone blends, polyurethane, Elastomeric and polysulfide caulks generally perform satisfactorily. Caulks that are 100% silicone should not be used as they will not bond to/with any latex paints. There are many websites that provide adequate direction as to how to treat the wood rot. Recommend a licensed contractor repair all as needed.

Window Screen Missing
Recommend replacing the window screen(s) to help defer pest intrusion and drywood termite migration into the structure.

Wood Warping Observed at the Windows/Trim
Wood has many outstanding properties, but it is a natural, porous material with individual characteristics, and it can warp. When wood gets wet, it swells. When wood dries out after being sawn from the tree, after being pressure-treated and after rain showers, it shrinks. Uneven drying creates stresses in wood, which results in warping (e.g., bowing, cupping or twisting) or cracking. The degree of warping depends on the species of wood, its grain pattern, uniformity of drying and construction techniques, among other factors. There is not much a user can do to truly un-warp a warped piece of wood. It is possible to position bowed deck lumber, wood paneling, ply wood, conventional lumber etcetera, so that its weight flattens it, or to use screws to fasten securely an otherwise warped piece. It is recommended re-supporting the displaced section with the prescribed deck screws per each post. When caulk seals are broken and water is allowed to enter behind the seal to untreated wood, warping is almost inevitable. Sealing and maintaining these "areas of the weakest link" can prevent further repairs such as the present issues. Recommend a licensed contractor repair as needed.

Wood Warping Observed at the Doors/Trim
Wood has many outstanding properties, but it is a natural, porous material with individual characteristics, and it can warp. When wood gets wet, it swells. When wood dries out after being sawn from the tree, after being pressure-treated and after rain showers, it shrinks. Uneven drying creates stresses in wood, which results in warping (e.g., bowing, cupping or twisting) or cracking. The degree of warping depends on the species of wood, its grain pattern, uniformity of drying and construction techniques, among other factors. There is not much a user can do to truly un-warp a warped piece of wood. It is possible to position bowed deck lumber so that its weight flattens it, or to use screws to fasten securely an otherwise warped piece. Recommend replacing all unrepairable wood sections. Caulk can be used where the wood siding abuts openings and trim and where cracks are located to fill them. Latex-silicone blends, polyurethane, Elastomeric and polysulfide caulks generally perform satisfactorily. Caulks that are 100% silicone should not be used as they will not bond to/with any latex paints. Recommend a licensed contractor repair as needed.

Suspected Formosan Subterranean Termites/Tunnels (Coptotermes formosanus) Observed

The Formosan subterranean termite (Coptotermes formosanus) is an invasive species of termite. It has been transported worldwide from its native range in southern China to Formosa (Taiwan, where it gets its name) and Japan. In the 20th century it became established in South Africa, Hawaii and in the continental United States. The Formosan subterranean termite is often nicknamed the super-termite because of its destructive habits. This is because of the large size of its colonies, and the termites' ability to consume wood at a rapid rate. A single colony may contain several million (compared with several hundred thousand termites for other subterranean termite species) that forage up to 300 feet (100 m) in soil. A mature Formosan colony can consume as much as 13 ounces of wood a day (ca. 400 g) and severely damage a structure in as little as three months. Because of its population size and foraging range, the presence of colonies poses serious threats to nearby structures. Once established, Formosan subterranean termite has never been eradicated from an area. By the 1950's, it was reported in South Africa and Sri Lanka. During the 1960's it was found in Texas, Louisiana, and South Carolina. In 1980, a well-established colony was thriving in a condominium in Hallandale Beach, Florida.

Drywood Termites/Damage Suspected

Termite damage was suspected at and within the wood members. Dry wood termites swarm in the evening and at night during the warmer months of the year. It is very hard to find where they are coming from because they live so deeply in the lumber. Dry wood termite colonies are small colonies only about 3,000 termites. When the colony reaches about 3,000 termites then they will swarm to start a colony elsewhere. They need very little moisture and are often found in the attic wood framing, wall studs, door casings and window frames. Dry wood termites obtain moisture from the water produced by the digestion of cellulose, no matter how old the wood is. Spot treatments, such as orange oil applications, use insecticides applied to control known dry wood termite colonies, such as those found in a door casing, windowsill or piece of furniture. For newer buildings, this is the recommended treatment by honest pest control servicemen and is fairly nominal in price. Advantages to dry wood alternative treatments are: The structure does not have to be unoccupied during treatment, just the immediate work area. There is a residual effect to the termiticide. If re-infestation occurs and the insects come in contact with the treated area, the transfer effect will start again and the colony will be eliminated. Most important, this method uses material chemicals very low in mammalian toxicity.

Older Subterranean/Drywood Damage Suspected

Potential Termite Damage Observed. This appears to be older remnants/canals and/or subterranean tubes on the wood intermittently. There were old termite burrows found on the wood but there were no signs of live dry wood or subterranean termites. This could have been from an exterior swarm intruding or from an interior swarm attempting to exit. After considering the length of time between treatments, if it is known, it is warranted and recommended to have a licensed pest professional treat the building and/or provide a routine treatment and inspection plan. Note: Tenting may not be needed as newer cheaper treatment methods are becoming more readily appeasing to many new and old buyers/owners. Additionally, there are many termite control companies that will provide free inspections. It is unknown if the building was treated for subterranean or drywood termites in the recent past. Termite control can be done with liquid termite control, termite bait systems, or both. Liquid Termite Control products are fast acting, can be applied closer to the infestation, and require less maintenance. For subterraneans, when needed, termite Bait Systems are less intrusive, no drilling or trenching is needed, no expensive equipment is required, and bait systems can help you identify a problem before the termites reach your building. Advantages to drywood alternative treatments are: The structure does not have to be unoccupied during treatment, just the immediate work area. There is a residual effect to the termiticide. If re-infestation occurs and the insects come in contact with the treated area, the transfer effect will start again and the colony will be eliminated. Most important, this method uses material very low in mammalian toxicity.

Hollow Core Door Used on the Exterior Egress to the Building

As per the ICC and most state and local codes, an exterior door generally requires a 2 hour fire rating, must be comprised and tested to prevent minimum wind load and forced entry resistance under the ASTM, ANSI, CFR and other testing and listing laboratories amongst other safety/code requirements. It is highly recommended to have a licensed window and door technician, replace the door to an approved fire rated exterior grade door to code.

Wood Window Screwed/Sealed Shut

Most codes to most localities require means of escape, ventilation etc. Inoperable windows can be a fire hazard to life as they inhibit escape. It is highly recommended to have the window repaired to full operability per state and local codes to prevent such hazards.

Broken Glass Pane(s) Observed
Fractured glass can easily break and already broken glass panes with exposed course serrations and sharp edges can break off further. In both cases, these glass shards are extremely hazardous to any child, the elderly and animals whom come in contact. It is highly recommended to have the broken glass replaced ASAP.

Double Dead Bolt Observed at the Door(s)
This is a direct fire hazard to animal and human life. A double keyed deadbolt inhibits manual operation of the lock without a key. In the event of an emergency, where immediate escape is dire (many people commonly awaken to rooms/houses filled with smoke when it is very difficult to traverse the internal furnishings to find keys) there needs to be a point of escape. All doors and windows should be physically manually able to open without the need of additional keys or tools i.e. a standard unlatching mechanism. Repair as needed ASAP.

Window Lock Latch Handle Broke
This may be considered a fire hazard if the latch is in the lock position. Also, it may leave the building susceptible to break in if the lock is in the open position or displaced. Recommend replacing all damaged lock/latch mechanisms as soon as possible.

Various Window Lock Latch(es) were Observed Broke at Multiple Windows
The locking latches allow the window to be locked in place when the window is fully shut. When this latch is loose or broken off, the window can easily be opened and can be compromised during a break in or from another outside force. Recommend replacing all damaged lock/latch mechanisms as soon as possible.

Sticking Doors and Windows Observed. Possible Differential Settlement
Indications of differential settlement include sticking doors and windows. Settlement most often occurs early in the life of a building, or when there is a dramatic change in underground conditions. Often, such settlement is associated with improper foundation design, particularly inadequate footers and foundation walls. Recommend a licensed structural engineer assess the area further and repair where/if needed.

Interior; Forced Entry Damage Observed at the Door/Frame
Forced entry damage observed at the door/frame. Recommend a licensed contractor repair all damages as is needed per state and local code.

Interior Door(s) Missing
Recommend installing missing door(s) as is needed. Recommend a licensed door technician install all per state and local code requirements or better.

Window Servicing Tilt Latch(es) were Observed Broke at Several Windows
The tilt latches allow the window to be angle positioned for cleaning. The tilt latch also acts as a brace for the top of the window section, aligning it into the channel. When this latch is loose or broken off, the window can be easily pushed in and can be compromised during a storm from wind pressure or other outside force. Recommend a licensed contractor repair the latches as is needed.

Drywall Screws Observed Fastening Most Windows
Drywall screws are for the purpose of hanging drywall, as the name describes. These screws are not made with the proper girth, threading and tensile strength to support windows and to retain structural integrity. The screws will commonly rust soon in their life and can compromise the integrity of the opening/window. Recommend replacing all drywall screws and installing wood screws/Tapcons where required as is needed.

Decorative Exterior Window Sashes Broken, Displaced or Missing
Decorative sashes located at the exterior of the windows observed displaced/broken at the time of the inspection. Recommend a licensed contractor replace all as needed.

Base Board Door Stops Damaged/Missing
Door stops observed damaged/missing at the time of the inspection. Recommend a state licensed contractor install new door stops to prevent drywall damage from door hardware.

Window(s) Double Pane Seals Compromised
Condensation is the accumulation of liquid water on generally cold surfaces. Almost all air contains water molecules, the gas phase of water composed of water droplets. The molecules in warm air are far apart from one another and allow the retention of a generally large amount of water vapor. As air cools, the molecules get closer together and squeeze the tiny vapor droplets closer. The dew point, exists where these water droplets will

be forced so close together and condense into visible liquid in a process called condensation. Double-pane windows have a layer of gas, likely argon or air, trapped between two panes of glass that acts as insulation to reduce heat loss through the window. Other types of gas used in this space have various effects on heat gain or loss through the window. Some windows also have a thin film installed between panes that separate the space between the panes into two spaces, further reducing heat loss and heat. If multiple-pane windows appear misty or foggy, it means that the seal between the window panes has failed. **Solar (Thermal) Pumping or Double-Paned Window Failures happen because the windows** experience a daily cycle of expansion and contraction caused by thermal pumping. Sunlight heats the space between the panes and causes the gas there to heat and expand, pressurizing the space between the panes. At night, the window cools and the area between the panes contracts. This motion acts like bellows of a forge and is called thermal pumping. Over time, the constant pressure fluctuations caused by thermal pumping will stress the seal. Eventually, the seal will develop small fractures that will slowly grow in size, allowing increasing amounts of infiltration and exfiltration of air from the space between the panes. Windows on the sunny side of a building will experience larger temperature swings, resulting in greater amounts of thermal pumping and failure rates. Vinyl window frames have a higher coefficient of expansion resulting in greater long-term stress on the double-pane seal. Windows also experience batch failure, which describes production runs of windows, especially vinyl windows that are defective. If it's allowed to continue, window condensation will inevitably lead to physical window damage. This damage can appear in river bedding, where condensed vapor between the glass panes will form droplets that run down the length of the window. Water that descends in this fashion has the tendency to follow narrow paths and carve grooves into the glass surface. These grooves are formed in a process similar to canyon formation. Silica Haze is another defect. Once the silica gel has been saturated, it will be eroded by passing air and accumulate as white "snowflakes" on the window surface. It is believed that if this damage is present, the window must be replaced. Recommend a state licensed window and door contractor review the compromised seals further and repair/replace as is needed.

Window/Door Trim Observed has Paint Chipping/Peeling and Various Caulk Seals Compromised
One of the most common areas for water intrusion is at windows and doors. Generally, the path of least resistance is at the door and window frame/house trim abutments. Even when properly flashed, windows and doors are meant to be water resistant, not water proof and degradation with lack of maintenance and upkeep can cause caulk seams and paint sealants to become compromised. Recommend a state licensed contractor review further and repair all as needed. Recommend polyurethane, elastomeric or equivalent caulks or as recommended by a licensed contractor.

Exterior Window Head Cap Flashing Not Observed
Many new window and siding installations do not have visible head cap flashing but incorporate a house wrap and flashing tape at the windows surround. The problem with just taping it from the outside is that you're relying on two things: (i) The tape will be installed properly and last a long time, and (ii) no water will get behind the house wrap. Flashing/house wrap cannot typically be observed at a finished window to see the methodology of its installation. Tape can and does last, when you use the correct type and install it properly. But water has a tendency to get into all kinds of places it shouldn't go. If you don't sheath the materials so that they shed water away from the buildings internal materials that are susceptible to moisture damage, you make it more likely that water will get in. Installing the house wrap after the windows means that it's impossible to seal them properly. The omission of head flashing over windows and doors invites leaks behind the siding, rotted windows and door trims, and a need for early exterior window and trim repairs or replacement. Since the head flashing and underlying house wrap/flashing materials could not/were not observed, it is recommended to have a state licensed construction contractor review the areas further.

Doors Seals and Weather Stripping Compromised/Antiquated
Recommend lubricating all doors at their hinged or channeled areas and at all moving components. Recommend re-weatherizing with weather stripping and caulk sealants where needed. Latex-silicone blends, polyurethane, elastomeric and polysulfide caulks generally perform satisfactorily. Caulks that are 100% silicone should not be used as they will not bond to/with any latex paints.

Screens Weathered/Antiquated at Window(s)
Screen was weathered at various windows at the time of the inspection. Recommend repairing/replacing these screens as soon as possible to defer insect and rodent entry etc. as needed.

Door Knob/Hardware was Loose at the Time of the Inspection
Loose hardware can result in permanent damage if neglected, but may be as simple as refastening the screws/fasteners. Additionally, this is considered a fire hazard. In the event of a fire, occupants should have unimpeded escape routes including operable hardware. Recommend a licensed contractor refasten or replace the hardware as needed.

Hose Bibs

Back Flow Preventers-Equipped-No Deficiencies
Back flow preventers are screw on extensions to your hose bibs. When installed they help prevent the back flow of non-potable water into the potable water system. Your spigots are equipped with these back flow prevention devices.

No Back Flow Preventers Observed at the Time of the Inspection
Back flow preventers are screw on extensions to your hose bibs. When installed they help prevent the back flow of non-potable water into the potable water system. You should have a "backflow preventer" screwed onto your outside faucets; at each threaded faucet spout.

PR or Pressure Relief Valve at Spigot Leaks at Threading
PR or Pressure Relief Valve at an exterior spigot is good to have to expel excess pressure that may cause damage to the building's plumbing system when the irrigation pipes are within the main buildings system, however, yours has a constant drip that appears to be coming from the threading. If the building pressure exceeds a certain threshold, typically excess of 80 PSI, hoses and pipe joints may leak or rupture (most systems are rated for 120 psi or greater but can vary, most faults occur from material defects and ware). Recommend repairing the leak and replacing the PR valve if needed. The TPR valve will help relieve pressures that exceed tolerable levels for some pressure joints and faucets in plumbing systems that can lead to hose line ruptures, pipe leaks etc. To mitigate this loss, replace/repair the PR Valve and inspect it routinely.

Low Water Pressure Observed
A reading of 45 to 60/65 psi is ideal. System was tested by hooking up a pressure gauge to an outside water spigot. If a reading is low (less than 40 psi) at the pipes at the well/to the building it is recommended to install a water pressure booster pump. The booster pumps typically cost between $150-$300 at a building supply center or plumbing store, or online. Any setting over 80 psi will wear out the washers on your plumbing fixtures/hoses etc. Typical booster pumps are made to fit 1-in. pipe. Be sure your plumber applies for a plumbing permit so the work will be inspected. Some municipalities require a reduced pressure and backflow preventer to be installed when a water pressure booster is hooked up. Recommend a licensed plumber to evaluate your system and install/repair as needed.

Spigot/Pipe Loose at the Wall
This can allow the pipe and spigot to become damaged and can cause a leak within the fittings/spigot. Recommend securing the pipe/spigot per the National Plumbing Code and the locale/state code as needed.

PR or Pressure Relief Valve at Spigot Leaks at the Relief Hole
PR or Pressure Relief Valve at an exterior spigot is good to have to expel excess pressure that may cause damage to the buildings plumbing system when the irrigation pipes are within the main buildings system, however, yours has a constant drip that appears to be coming from the relief hole, meaning it is likely defective

and needs replacing. If the building pressure exceeds a certain threshold, typically excess of 80 psi, hoses and pipe joints may leak or rupture (most systems components are rated above 110 psi or greater but can vary, most faults occur from material defects and ware). Recommend replacing the PR valve but make sure to install either an equal or better replacement. It will help relieve pressures that exceed tolerable levels for some pressure joints and faucets in plumbing systems that can lead to hose line ruptures, pipe leaks etc. To mitigate this loss, replace/repair the PR valve and inspect it routinely.

Spigot Shut off Handle for the Gate Valve is Missing/Damaged
Gate valves are known to degrade in time predictably and are recommended to be replaced whenever possible. Since repair is needed, it is recommended to replace with a ball joint valve. Minimally, replacing the handle should suffice if the valve is not seized. If able, replace/repair in case of an emergency prior to performing any plumbing work or work in close relation to the spigot/valve.

Hose Spigot; Leak at Stem
When the valve is actuated to close or open, it spits at the stem. This is a gate valve. Gate valves are known to degrade in time, predictably, and are recommended to be replaced whenever possible. Since repair is needed, it is recommended to replace it with a ball valve. Replace in case of an emergency prior to performing any plumbing work or work in close relation to this gate valve/spigot.

Lime Scale or Calcium Carbonate fouling on Spigot Valve Joint
Even in hard water areas, pipes will not scale unless the saturation index of the water is exceeded. If the water is under-saturated or at equilibrium saturation, there will be no scale. Conversely, "soft water" can scale if it becomes over saturated. The saturation index of water is controlled by its acidity (or alkalinity which is the reverse) which we establish by pH measurement. The lower the pH, the more acidic the water and the more it can hold in solution. The higher the pH, the less acid the water, the lower the saturation index, and the less the water can hold dissolved minerals. We raise the pH by heating the water, causing pressure drops (e.g. taps) and adding chemicals. By raising the pH, we are reducing the ability of the water to hold minerals in solution and these minerals are forced to precipitate and cause scale fouling. Recirculating systems (e.g. cooling towers, steam generators, water recovery systems) operate at cycles of concentration with pressure drops and temperature variances causing both super saturation and pH increases simultaneously. Unfortunately, unless installing a mineral filtration system, there is little to resolve the cause of internal scaling, however, the scaling/build up on the spigot valve joint are likely caused by minute orifices at the threading/solder of the joint and is caused by minute amounts of water surfacing, crystallizing/scaling upon breaching the surface. Using Teflon tape or plumbers paste around joint threading will usually remedy the issues to threaded joints and re-sweating soldered joints and repairing as needed should remedy the rest. At times, shark bites are used for copper. PVC and CPVC use special glues to re-fuse the joints. With PVC and CPVC, however, joints/couplings more often cannot be reused and need to be recessed further with additional coupling fittings. Recommend a licensed plumber repair as needed.

Spigot Seized/Inoperable at the Time of the Inspection
The spigot was seized and could not be actuated. Recommend replacing with a ball valve type ASAP.

Spigot Inoperable at the Time of the Inspection
The spigot was actuated and no water dispensed when fully actuated. This spigot may have been adjoined to a now retired portion of the irrigation system. Recommend a licensed plumber assess further. If it is determined to be just in need of replacing, recommend installing a ball valve type, otherwise, if discontinued, recommend closing the shaft completely to differ insect intrusion.

Low Pressure Observed. Suspect Galvanized Pipe Oxidation Is Constricting
Galvanized steel and brass pipes may fail, typically between the 50-75 years range. Galvanized steel can build a lot of corrosion on the interior. The more internal corrosion/rust, the more restricting the flow throughout the building will be. It is mainly for that reason it often gets replaced before it springs a leak. However, if the pipe is not replaced, the galvanized pipe can oxidize and corrode internally, causing leaks from the inside out. The low pressure can be much greater in the hot water service pipe because the hotter the water, the faster it causes the oxidation process as it depletes the zinc galvanized coating on the interior of the pipe. The water treatments can also progress the process. It is highly recommended to have a licensed plumber review the system in full and replace all galvanized pipe.

Sprinklers

General Comments

With Pump
NOTE: Things to consider before you set your sprinklers watering program. The highest water evaporation rates for plant materials and grasses take place during the daytime hours. If you run/operate irrigation systems during the daytime hours, the water you apply does not generally have enough time to soak into the root zone (or fall to the ground from the leaves) for the plant materials to utilize before it evaporates. If you operate most irrigation systems in the first part of the early evening, then the plant material goes to bed wet. Many plant material fungal, disease, freeze, etc. maintenance problems are created by plant materials going to bed wet. Generally, it is a good idea to not irrigate in the early evening hours. The best way to irrigate a project is to work out an operation window in the early dawn hours. This way water is not blown by the wind, it can seep into the ground before the high evaporation rate times, you are not inconvenienced by watering, and the fungi and/or disease maintenance costs are reduced. Also, Sustainable Irrigation begins with knowledge. Sprinkler maintenance, proper sprinkler spacing between heads, correcting water pressure issues, broken heads, leaks, recognizing matching precipitation rates and knowing how to make general repairs are all aspects that lead to a well maintained water conserving sprinkler system. All zones were manually tested. The utility pump was found to be operable with all zones transition as intended. Pressure appeared adequate for proper function. Recommend a licensed sprinkler/plumbing professional review and maintain the unit routinely, repairing all sprinkler heads when needed for proper watering function. System was good/serviceable at the time of the inspection.

Sprinkler Pump was Observed Not Mounted/Secured
Recommend the sprinkler pump be mounted/secured to the floor/slab base to prevent leaks at the joints caused by long term vibration and pressure jolts by. Recommend a licensed sprinkler system contractor to repair as needed.

Sprinkler System has a Manual Operation Style. Could Not Inspect
The system is a manual operating system without solenoids and automatic valve components. These systems are generally concoctions of the building owners and are not tested using the manual apparatus's as it is unknown if the systems components are set to operate without causing unknowing harm or backflow into the main potable water system, the building and/or the premises etc. Because of this, it is recommended that a licensed sprinkler tech review then convert into an automatic system for ease of use, efficiency and safety.

Without Pump
NOTE: Things to consider before you set your sprinklers watering program. The highest water evaporation rates for plant materials and grasses take place during the daytime hours. If you run/operate irrigation systems during the daytime hours, the water you apply does not generally have enough time to soak into the root zone (or fall to the ground from the leaves) for the plant materials to utilize before it evaporates. If you operate most irrigation systems in the first part of the early evening, then the plant material goes to bed wet. Many plant material fungal,

disease, freeze, etc. maintenance problems are created by plant materials going to bed wet. Generally, it is a good idea to not irrigate in the early evening hours. The best way to irrigate a project is to work out an operation window in the early dawn hours. This way water is not blown by the wind, it can seep into the ground before the high evaporation rate times, you are not inconvenienced by watering, and your fungi and/or disease maintenance costs are reduced. Also, Sustainable Irrigation begins with knowledge. Sprinkler maintenance, proper sprinkler spacing between heads, correcting water pressure issues, broken heads, leaks, recognizing matching precipitation rates and knowing how to make general repairs are all aspects that lead to a well maintained water conserving sprinkler system. All zones were manually tested. System was found to be operable in pressure functions with all zones having transitioned as intended. Pressure appeared adequate for proper function. Recommend a licensed sprinkler/plumbing professional review and maintain the unit routinely, repairing all sprinkler heads when needed for proper watering function. System was good/serviceable at the time of the inspection.

Sprinkler Head Partial Damage Observed at the Sprinkler Head Apparatus
This may have been caused by a multiple of reasons e.g. lawn mowers. If installed improperly, it can result in soil getting into the sprinkler head and obstructing the proper flow. It is recommended to have a licensed technician repair this area.

Iron Stains Observed Due To "Hard" Well Water Sprinkler System
The reddish brown rusty stains are a common problem readily seen on siding, sidewalks, walkways, patios, stepping stones, window and door frames in areas where irrigation water has a high iron content. The sprinkler system and/or hoses that are used to water the grounds are also spraying iron particles that create these rust stains wherever they land. Iron is a chemical element that is abundant in soils and aquifers in many parts of the country. And it is the element that, when exposed to air and moisture, oxidizes or rusts. Where the tap water is "hard", or mineral-rich and we irrigate with well water, sprinkler water is probably causing rust stains. The irrigation systems will often "over spray" which means water ends up on the fence, patio, deck, porch, building, windows, doors, concrete walkways, stepping stones or paths, lawn furniture and also on parked vehicles if exposed to overspray. Once iron particles from the water in your sprinkler come in contact with the air, they will begin to oxidize or rust. The stains that result have likely developed over time and can be very stubborn to remove. Recommend installing a rust inhibitive filtration treatment system to the sprinkler system to prevent this.

System Appears Antiquated and Inoperable at the Time of the Inspection
Antiquated and inoperable is due to its age and condition. There was no attempt to actuate the pump to prevent electrical hazards, appliance damage or water damage in the attempt to operate the system. Recommend replacing the entire system to code as is needed.

Pipe Fitting Rupture Suspected. Erosion of Soil and Water Flow Observed
The area appeared eroded. When the zone was actuated, water flow was apparent and consistent at the grading of this location. It is recommended to have a licensed technician repair this area. If installed improperly, it can result in soil getting into the sprinkler head and obstructing the proper flow.

Sprinkler Head Broken off, Small Geyser Observed at the Sprinkler Apparatus
This may have been caused by multiple of reasons e.g. lawn mowers. It is recommended to have a licensed technician repair this area. If installed improperly, it can result in soil getting into the sprinkler head and obstructing the proper flow.

Sprinkler Head Broken off, Water Bubbling from the Surface Observed at the Sprinkler Apparatus
This may have been caused by a multiple of reasons, e.g. lawn mowers. Burst failures usually occur during transient hydraulic conditions that create large pressure variations in the system. Burst failure will, sometimes, occur in a pipe or fitting that was damaged during installation or that is subject to external loads. In these cases the failure may occur at pressures well below the expected burst limit of the product. For elbow joints in Sprinkler systems of residential and light commercial landscape applications, the latter is commonly the issues. It is recommended to have a licensed technician repair this area. If installed improperly, it can result in soil/sand getting into the sprinkler head and obstructing the proper flow.

Browning of Lawn; Suspect Improper Precipitation/Application Rates
Improper precipitation/application rates suspected to be caused by either insufficient watering zone times or improper nozzles/emitters of the rotor, spray, bubbler, drip, micro-irrigation, etc. Example: (1) The nozzles for rotor heads generally have somewhere between 0.10 and 0.25 IPH (inches per hour) precipitation rate. (2) The

nozzles for spray heads generally have somewhere between 1.35 and 2.15 IPH precipitation rate. (3) The nozzles for bubbler heads generally have somewhere between 2.50 and 20.00 IPH precipitation rate. (4) The emitters for drip/micro irrigation generally have somewhere between 0.25 and 1.50 IPH precipitation rate. If you place a lower IPH head (let's say one rotor head at 0.20 IPH) on a zone of higher IPH heads (let's assume all of the spray heads are at 1.60 IPH), then you have created a dry/brown spot in the area watered by the zone. This means that you will have to run this irrigation zone longer to apply enough water in the dry (rotor) spot and oversaturate everything else. Recommend having a licensed technician review and repair the system if/where needed.

Exposed Wires Observed, Spliced but not Sealed from the Elements
Even if the wires are encased at the valves with a box, this is recommended when the area is inflicted with a heavy storm. These boxes installed plumb with grade tend to fill to grade or come in contact with steady moisture elevations. This will cause fluidic capillary action which causes water to enter the wires sheathing and leads back up the wire. Most copper will incur a copper oxide that can inhibit current. Recommend sealing all wire nuts with liquid tape after inspection and cleaning, if any, by a licensed technician.

Recommend Installing a Rain Shut Off Device on the Irrigation System
The proper installation, setting and/or retrofitting of this relatively inexpensive device can prevent an irrigation system from running during a rainstorm and/or after adequate amounts of rain have fallen. These simple devices generally pay for themselves in about one year. Depending on whom you talk to, these rains shutoff devices can save between 3 and 15 percent of the annual operating expenses of an irrigation system. In many parts of the U.S., rain shutoff devices are required by law to be installed on all new irrigation systems with hefty penalties for not installing them because of re-occurring droughts and extreme weather changes.

Inoperable Zone(s) Observed in the Sprinkler System
Inoperable zones can be caused by a multitude of variables. The most common is a bad solenoid caused by oxidation/rust. Further, wiring issues and oxidation can also be the culprit. If wires are submerged or buried, they may be grounded and not providing the proper voltage. Wires can also have breaks or damage at the valve box(es) or further down the line caused by the elements and improper connections, lawn mowers and improper burying, shovels, rodents/squirrels etc. Most of these issues are relatively easy to remedy and typically don't break the bank. If the building has been vacant for a while and/or the sprinkler system has not been used and flushed, there may be additional issues on the horizon such as other solenoids malfunctioning etc. It is highly recommended to have a licensed technician review, test and repair all as needed.

Sprinkler Annunciator Control Rated Interior; Control Mounted at Exterior
This annunciator control is not rated for the elements and does not have an exterior cover to differ water intrusion. Recommend a licensed technician replace the unit as soon as possible.

Exposed PVC Pipes at Grade
Exposed PVC irrigation pipes observed. These pipes, when exposed to the elements, are susceptible to U.V. sun radiation degradation and exposure to accidental damages etc. Recommend burying all pipe per local/state codes/ordinances as needed.

Pipe Fitting/Elbow Rupture Suspected. Erosion of Soil and Water Flow Observed
Burst failure in PVC pipe and fittings is usually rather dramatic. It may begin at a point of stress concentration or weakness and continue by splitting through fittings and pipe. Sometimes, the failures will completely shatter a fitting and the adjacent pipe. Burst failures usually occur during transient hydraulic conditions that create large pressure variations in the system. These include rapid valve closure, pumps starting or stopping, rapid escape of entrapped air, or an air pocket shifting within a pipeline. Burst failure will, sometimes, occur in a pipe or fitting that was damaged during installation or that is subject to external loads. In these cases the failure may occur at pressures well below the expected burst limit of the product. For elbow joints in Sprinkler systems of residential and light commercial landscape applications, the latter is commonly the issues. It is recommended to have a licensed technician repair this area. If installed improperly, it can result in soil/sand getting into the sprinkler head and obstructing the proper flow.

Maintenance and Upkeep Considerations for your Systems
NOTE: Things to consider before you set your sprinklers watering program. The highest water evaporation rates for plant materials and grasses take place during the daytime hours. If you run/operate irrigation systems during the daytime hours, the water you apply does not generally have enough time to soak into the root zone (or fall to the ground from the leaves) for the plant materials to utilize before it evaporates. If you operate most irrigation

systems in the first part of the early evening, then the plant material goes to bed wet. Many plant material fungal, disease, freeze, etc. maintenance problems are created by plant materials going to bed wet. Generally, it is a good idea to not irrigate in the early evening hours. The best way to irrigate a project is to work out an operation window in the early dawn hours. This way water is not blown by the wind, it can seep into the ground before the high evaporation rate times, you are not inconvenienced by watering, and your fungal, disease, etc., maintenance costs are reduced. Also, Sustainable Irrigation begins with knowledge. Sprinkler maintenance, proper sprinkler spacing between heads, correcting water pressure issues, broken heads, leaks, recognizing matching precipitation rates and knowing how to make general repairs are all aspects that lead to a well maintained water conserving sprinkler system.

Sprinkler Controller Fuses Stated to Blow Too Often
Known possible causes for this include; Wires to the valves are damages, valve solenoid(s) or timer is faulty. Recommend a licensed irrigation contractor assess the area further and repair all where needed.

The Timer's Display was Observed Blank when the Unit was Plugged In
Possible Causes Include; the timer and/or the transformer is faulty, a blown fuse in the timer circuit or damaged wiring. Recommend a licensed irrigation contractor assess the area further and repair as needed.

The Irrigation System Does Not Water the Yard
Possible causes can include; Faulty transformer, timer or rain sensor. Replace any faulty components at needed.

Zone Not Working; Suspect Damaged Zone Connection
Recommend a licensed irrigation contractor assess the area further and repair all wiring and/or other deficiencies if needed.

Gutters

General Comments
Gutters and downspouts were observed from the roof during the routine roof inspection and found to be clear of any notable debris or damage. System appeared to be serviceable at the time of the inspection.

Galvanized Gutters Heavily Oxidized/Rusting
Oxidation can be destructive, such as the rusting of an automobile or these gutter types. We often used the words oxidation and rust interchangeably, but not all materials which interact with oxygen molecules actually disintegrate into rust. In the case of iron, the oxygen creates a slow burning process, which results in the brittle brown substance we call rust. In this case, the process of oxidation depends on the amount of oxygen present in the air and the nature of the material it touches. Regular galvanized steel in this case may be painted for protection against oxidation where sections are salvageable, but oxygen can still exploit any opening, no matter how small. This is why you may find a painted metal bicycle still damaged by rust. Recommend a licensed contractor treat all oxidation per local code and replace any compromised sections or replace all gutters with new aluminum or vinyl seamless type as needed.

Gutters Observed are Full of Debris
Gutters filled with leaf debris will mulch and can allow vegetation to grow within them. Additionally, they will allow backflow at the roof line that can ultimately cause leaks. Service as needed. Leaf debris inhibit the proper operation of the guttering system, allow rain run off to backflow toward the roof potentially causing ice damns in colder regions and fluidic capillary action and eaves compromises in general within the warmer regions. Additionally, the leaf debris mulch is providing further nutrients for plant/vegetation to grow. Recommend a licensed contractor service the gutters and routinely as needed for general upkeep.

Compromises to Gutters/Seams. Algae/Degradation Observed to the Exterior Wall/Cladding
Compromises at various locations: Water is trailing down the wall from the roof abutment causing heavy algae and degradation to the stucco cladding and roof surface. If you decide to reuse these gutters, it is recommended to have a licensed contractor seal all seams/screws with gutter sealant or better, inspect guttering at drip edge to ensure proper run off into the guttering is acceptable and repair/seal where needed.

Loose Fasteners Observed Intermittently
Loose fasteners, amongst other reasons, may be because of them being fastened through fascia board only and not into the abutting rafters or trusses. This allows them to work themselves loose over time, sometimes taking years from motion, expansion and retraction. Recommend a licensed contractor re-secure all correctly as is needed.

Loose Fasteners Observed to the Gutter System Causing Sag/Compromises
Loose fasteners, amongst other reasons, may be because of them being fastened through fascia board only and not into the abutting rafters or trusses. This allows them to work themselves loose over time, sometimes years from motion, expansion and retraction. At the time of the inspection, the gutters were observed sagging, indicative of excess weight distribution support compromises and could quickly lead to further damage if not repaired soon. Recommend a licensed contractor re-secure all correctly ASAP.

Good Grading but No Diverters for Downspouts
No ponding or eroded locations observed, however, downspout terminate at or around the foundation. This can increase erosion rather than decrease it and aid in slight settlement allowing stucco cracks etcetera. Recommend installing rain run off diverters at all downspout locations. Optimal diversion of turn off from the building is 4-7 feet.

Downspouts Mounting Brackets are Loose/Missing
This can allow the downspouts to displace and get damaged or leak. Recommend a licensed contractor repair all as needed to local and state codes.

Compromises at Various Gutters/Seams Locations
If you decide to reuse these gutters, seal all seams/screws with gutter sealant or better, inspect guttering at drip edge to ensure proper run off into the guttering is acceptable and repair/seal where needed.

Downspouts Terminate at Foundation Wall
Recommend a licensed contractor install downspout diverters to divert the rain run off at each downspout from the building optimally between 4-7 linear feet to reduce settlement and moisture cracking on foundation walls etcetera. Alternatively, installing French drains and/or partial French drains where the diverters or downspouts would cross the sidewalk, is recommended.

Downspouts/Diverters Divert Water over Walkways/Driveways; Slip Hazard
This can allow algae/fungi to accrue, causing a slip hazard. Recommend a licensed contractor install downspout diverters to divert the rain run off at each downspout from the building and all walkways/driveway optimally between 4-7 linear feet to reduce settlement and moisture cracking on foundation walls etcetera. Alternatively, installing French drains and/or partial French drains where the diverters or downspouts would cross the sidewalk, is recommended.

Loose Diverter(s) at the Attachment to the Downspout(s)
This can allow excess water to leak at the abutting joint, causing erosion to soil at this location. Erosion of perimeter grading around a building is one of the leading reasons for settlement and settlement cracks. Recommend repairing ASAP.

Erosion around the Perimeter of the Dwelling from Lack of Gutters/Partial Gutters
Erosion around the perimeter of the dwelling and under the eaves are due to lack of guttering where applicable. This is a direct result of having no gutters. Erosion from rain run off can cause cracks to appear in your exterior walls as well as settlement in the foundation that can progress as long as the problem goes untreated. Recommend Gutters be installed on every eaves location of the dwelling to prevent further grade erosion. The partial guttering only provides convenience of deferring rain runoff from one or more eave locations typically for people who walk under the eaves and may not reduce overall erosion. Excessive rain bombarding the grade surface around the building can erode and shift the soils, causing latent settlement shifts from newly loosened aggregate. Recommend a licensed contractor install the full gutter system to code.

Erosion around the Perimeter of the Dwelling under the Eaves Due to Lack of Guttering
This is a direct result of having no gutters. Erosion from rain run off can cause cracks to appear in your exterior walls as well as settlement in the foundation that can progress as long as the problem goes untreated. Recommend a licensed contractor install the full gutter system to code on every eave location of the dwelling to prevent further grade erosion.

Erosion around the Perimeter of the Dwelling from Partial Guttering, where Gutters Are Not Present
This is a direct result of having no gutters. Erosion from rain run off can cause cracks to appear in your exterior walls as well as settlement in the foundation that can progress as long as the problem goes untreated.

Recommend a licensed contractor install the full gutter system to code on every eave location without guttering to prevent further grade erosion.

New Structure; No Gutters Observed at the Time of the Inspection
No gutters Observed. Erosion from rain run off can cause cracks to appear in your exterior walls as well as settlement in the foundation that can progress as long as the problem goes untreated. Recommend Gutters be installed on every eave location of the dwelling to prevent grade erosion. No Grade Erosion was found as this is a new building. Recommend a licensed contractor install as needed.

Downspouts Missing
Downspout was not observed at the gutter drop outlet. Water is directed from the roof by the gutter to the drop outlet. Rather than terminating away from the exterior walls and foundation, it directs water at/on the exterior wall and foundation area and is/will progress degradation to the material surfaces. Recommend a licensed gutter installation and repair contractor, assess the area further and repair all as needed per local and state code.

Sheathing Separation Observed at the Wall. Wall is bowing. No Vapor Barrier Observed
The base area of the wall/cladding reveals the plywood sheathing is warping, separating from the wall framing, likely from moisture/humidity and improper installation methodology. The warp or bow may also be indicative of insufficient nailing. No felt paper observed at the base wall, likely indicative of no felt or house wrap used at the bare wood sheathing. Unlike cement shake or other siding overlay, where the vinyl siding is placed over another, a vapor barrier is generally assumed of the first layer of cladding. This cladding, however, was applied over bare wood sheathing. Recommend a licensed structural engineer and contractor assess the area further and repair all as is needed.

Pools/Filling and Coatings

Pool Marcite/Plaster Coating was Observed Etching at the Time of the Inspection
The Plaster is also called white coat or Marcite. Pool plaster is a process of finishing the gunite or shotcrete pool structures. Used underwater, it provides the watertight seal that the porous gunite or shotcrete beneath it cannot. Pool Plaster/Marcite finishes provide an average estimate of twenty years of service under ideal conditions. Our world however, is rarely ideal and many variables can cause the progression of degradation to include how it was initially applied. The pool plaster surface is meant to degrade slowly, eventually requiring a fresh coat of Marcite. If your pool plaster has surface irregularities, which may take on a beige hue, you may have what's commonly called etching. This etching can be caused by low pH or alkalinity; an acidic condition. It may begin within the plaster, from the original mix on application, or etching may start from the gunite side of the plaster and work itself from the outside in. In instances were a yellow stain is present and appears in a small cluster at one location or a single spot, chlorine tablets may be the culprit. Left to sit directly on pool plaster, they can also create a yellowish stain and can be difficult to remove. Common costs for re-plastering can vary greatly by the size of the pool.

Pool Wall Inlet(s) Apparatus Observed Damaged/Missing
Damaged or missing inlets can change the distribution process of the pool water. Additionally, the inlet location may aid in water leaks etcetera, at the compromised location. Recommend a state licensed pool service and repair company repair as needed.

Concrete Pool Deck; Moisture and Basic Settlement Cracks Observed
Concrete will crack as a normal outcome of the curing process. Cracking can be worsened if uneven bearing conditions exist under the slab, such as un-compacted fill areas. Excessive water used for the workability of cement tends to produce excessive cracking, which can allow moisture to more readily penetrate the concrete slab, weakening the concrete, and leading to differential drying issues and cracking. Excessive cracking can allow additional moisture, to penetrate more easily through the slab. The use of welded wire-fabric reinforcement provides a means of controlling the severity of cracking. Concrete control joints may also be used to control random cracking by creating planned lines of weakness in the slab. Shrinkage or curing cracks generally occur in any continuous length of concrete longer than about 12 feet. These cracks are easily maintained and virtually eliminated with proper maintenance including proper mitigation of storm water away from the slab. Additionally, recoating or re-texturing the deck, may provide a more uniform elimination of the cracks appearance/if any.

No Expansion Joint Sealant Observed at the Expansion Joints on Pool Deck
Expansion joints are those big joints in concrete that typically have either a piece of wood or have an asphalt fiberboard imbedded in them. When pouring the concrete driveway or sidewalk they place these expansion joints to allow the concrete to expand and contract and are also places they have stopped pouring the concrete for the day. Typically there is a piece of rebar going through the expansion strip to prevent the two concrete

slabs from moving away from each other. Liquid sealants are the most commonly used sealant product for filling joints in building components and structural joints. Yet their performance, particularly in dynamic joints, can suffer from a variety of shortcomings that often begin with awkward installation factors such as badly prepared substrates and movement during cure. Finally, tensile stresses at bond lines, as well as within the cured liquid sealant elastomer, often result in premature failure. The problem with these expansion strips is that they allow water to migrate down through the joint causing the rebar to rust. Eventually the rebar will break and allow the two concrete slabs to move independently. Another problem with these joints is that they can collect dirt and provide an area for weeds to grow. There is a solution to these problems; you can have a joint sealant placed over the expansion joint. This will help prevent water migrating down causing the rebar to rust and will also prevent weeds from growing in the joint. The material used is a polyurethane expansion joint sealant that bonds to both side of the concrete slab creating a complete water seal. Other products such as plastic or foam that are placed in-between the joint do not typically create that watertight seal like the polyurethane sealant.

Exterior Walls

General Comments
Most cladding types inhibit the observance of the underlying flashing, vapor barrier and/or other components required to ensure proper moisture deflection and resistance. Aside of any aforementioned deficiencies where applicable, the exterior cladding appeared to be in serviceable condition. Recommend sealing where siding abuts openings and trim as well as on any seal breaches/hairline, minute cracks. Latex-silicone blends, polyurethane, and polysulfide caulks generally perform satisfactorily. Caulks that are 100% silicone should not be used. Overall assessment of the exterior wall was serviceable. Many siding problems are caused by improperly applied paint. Paint on siding may blister, peel, crack, fade or chalk. Some paint problems are caused by interior moisture that passes through the wall and lifts the paint. To preempt most issues like this, routinely check for dense vegetation around the building. Vines and ivy that are close to or on the siding should be trimmed or removed. Vegetation holds moisture and water up against the siding, which can be detrimental to the siding's condition over time.

Aluminum Siding
Aluminum is among the common siding materials. Aluminum siding can be made to appear like wood, including vertical shingle and shake styles. Aluminum expands and contracts with temperature changes, so installation by a licensed and skilled installer is important. Aluminum does not add to the structural strength of a structure. It is installed over sheathing. Aluminum siding can dent easily. To protect against this, many manufacturers offer a thin backer board of insulation that fits behind each panel. This insulation can reduce overall chatter or noise and can slightly increase the insulation value of the siding. If scratched, the exposed aluminum will not rust. Scratches may be touched up with a certain paint or material. Aluminum siding can conduct electricity, and grounding may be an installation requirement. Grounding the metal siding is a safety measure. Check with the local authority having jurisdiction as to whether grounding the metal siding is a requirement Repainting aluminum is similar to repainting vehicles. It requires preparation, appropriate paint selections and proper application.

Inadequate Fastening; Loose Metal Siding at Exterior Wall
Left unfastened, the corners of most lightweight metal siding panels can curl or pull away from the building due to wind, the elements and forced entry from rodent intrusion. Loose sections provide large gaps for pests to stage nests or vegetation to grow especially at any low area of the exterior walls. If the product is not properly installed, including end gaps at vertical trim abutments and proper fastening, using the specified fasteners, at the specified intervals and nailed into sound sheathing and house wrap of adequate thickness. Then expansion due to moisture uptake and/or thermal changes resulting in buckling of the material, particularly on sun-exposed walls, won't occur. Recommend a state licensed siding, door and window contractor assess further and repair as needed.

Aluminum Siding Abuts Grading; Moisture is inhibited from Expelling at the Siding Base
Siding should be installed tight enough to prevent problems related to water intrusion, but it should also be loose enough to allow it to adequately dry after a rainstorm. Additionally, moisture must be allowed to expel from the wall that accumulates behind the wood siding. Moisture that gets in behind the wall at windows, doors and trim or where humidity is prevalent in the area, moisture and water can accumulate behind the siding. The siding needs a suggested 6 inches above the grading to allow the wall to relieve the moisture and is high enough to theoretically, defer foliage from getting behind the siding. Recommend excavating at this wall area and applying an aggregate of rocks so that water does not stay at the abutting sight. Replacing all wood damaged siding on the wall and installing weep screed at the base of the wall to code is recommended to allow a proper wall bond seal and raising the siding may also be an option. Recommend a state licensed building contractor repair all as needed.

Siding Compromises Observed. Pipes, Conduit and Other Cut Outs through the Siding Need Sealants
The siding has observed plumbing/electrical entry point exposures that are not sufficiently sealed, if at all. These sections allow moisture to enter behind the siding and can trap within the wall system, causing rot or worse. Recommend a licensed siding contractor assess further and seal/repair as needed. Latex-silicone blends, polyurethane, and polysulfide caulks generally perform satisfactorily. Caulks that are 100% silicone should not be used.

Stone
Stone has been used for centuries as an exterior siding material. Stone is durable and it comes in many sizes, colors and patterns. Manufactured stone is a combination of cement, colored oxides and light aggregates. It can sometimes be difficult to distinguish manufactured stone from real natural stone.

Galvanized Steel Siding
Steel siding is less common than aluminum siding. Popular styles of steel siding look like smooth or textured bevel-wood siding. Many styles and colors are available. The installation of steel siding requires special skill and the right tools. Steel siding is more resistant to dents, but if the finish becomes scratched or chipped, it will need to be repaired to prevent rust from developing. Galvanized steel siding can be repainted. Galvanized steel siding can conduct electricity, and grounding may be an installation requirement. Check with the local authority having jurisdiction as to whether grounding the metal siding is a requirement. Repainting steel is similar to repainting vehicles. It requires preparation, appropriate paint selections and proper application.

Hardboard
Hardboard is a common type of fiberboard that is made from wood fibers designed with a specific density. It is compressed into a wood fiberboard. Synthetic adhesives provide the bonding between the fibers. Hardboard has a uniform composite and look. There is no grains, knots or natural deficiencies. Hardboard siding is more dense than wood lap siding or other natural wood siding types. Hardboard does not split or warp like natural, conventional wood boards. It does not expand and contract as much as natural wood does and it holds paint well. Hardboards are sometimes pre-finished. It can be embossed and textured to give the appearance of natural wood, plywood or stucco. It may be installed over sheathing and has been directly adhered to wall framing in the past. Lapped hardboard does not strengthen the house structure and it can be affected by moisture. It can rot and it also swells more than natural wood when it is wet.

No Expansion Joint Sealant Observed at the Expansion Joints
Expansion joints are those big/long joints in concrete that typically have either a piece of wood or have an asphalt fiberboard wedged in them. When pouring the concrete driveway or sidewalk they place these expansion joints to allow the concrete to expand and contract and are also places they may have stopped pouring the concrete for the day. Typically, there is a piece of rebar going through the expansion strip to prevent the two concrete slabs from moving away from each other. Liquid sealants are the most commonly used sealant product for filling joints in building components and structural joints. Yet their performance, particularly in dynamic joints, can suffer from a variety of shortcomings that often begin with awkward installation factors such as badly prepared substrates and movement during cure. Finally, tensile stresses at bond lines, as well as within the cured liquid sealant elastomer, often result in premature failure. The problem with these expansion strips is that they allow water to migrate down through the joint causing the rebar to rust. Eventually the rebar will break and allow the two concrete slabs to move independently. Another problem with these joints is that they can collect dirt and provide an area for weeds to grow. There is a solution to these problems; you can have

a joint sealant placed over the expansion joint. This will help prevent water migrating down causing the rebar to rust and will also prevent weeds from growing in the joint. The material used is a polyurethane caulk that bonds to both side of the concrete slab creating a complete water seal. Other products such as plastic or foam that are placed in-between the joint do not create that watertight seal like the polyurethane caulking.

Previous Porch Addition; Floor Band Joist Protrudes Past the Exterior Wall

A common occurrence observed when inspecting, is observing a porch that has since been renovated to an enclosed living space. Unfortunately, many conversions are performed out of permit and by DIY building owners or friends that do not have all the prerequisite knowledge in enclosing a porch and the science behind it. Often, the exterior slab or subfloor band joist areas are observed protruding past the exterior siding, whereas the siding/wall is intended to overhang thus deflect water from the floor/foundation and the exterior. Unfortunately, that is the case here. The band joist/wood subfloor protrudes past the exterior siding providing no weep screed, allows water to flow or pond at the wall and will, if not already, allow moisture infiltration. It is highly recommended to have a licensed structural engineer and contractor assess the wall further and repair the defect in full which may require completely reframing the wall. If this is not completed, at minimum, an apron flashing should be installed to deflect the moisture as is needed.

Buckling and Cracking in Hardboard Siding

Buckling and cracking are commonly found with hardboard. When hardboard is used as siding, the wood must be allowed to expand and contract along the length of the board. Buckling and cracking of wood siding materials can be caused by nailing too tightly, or because adjacent boards are butted together too tightly. A space of 1/16-inch to 1/8-inch should exist in between the edges of adjacent sheets of OSB or plywood. The space allows room for expansion and contraction. Hardboard siding should have a space of 3/16-inch in between the pieces. Recommend a licensed contractor assess further and repair as needed.

Wood Siding Abuts Grading; Moisture is inhibited from Expelling at the Siding Base

Siding should be installed tight enough to prevent problems related to water intrusion, but it should also be loose enough to allow it to adequately dry after a rainstorm. Additionally, moisture must be allowed to expel from the wall that accumulates behind the wood siding. Moisture that gets in behind the wall at windows, doors and trim or where humidity is prevalent in the area, moisture and water can accumulate behind the siding. The siding needs a suggested 6 inches above the grading to allow the wall to relieve the moisture and is high enough to theoretically, defer foliage from getting behind the siding. Recommend excavating at this wall area and applying an aggregate of rocks so that water does not stay at the abutting sight. Replacing all wood damaged siding on the wall and installing weep screed at the base of the wall to code is recommended to allow a proper wall bond seal and raising the siding may also be an option. Recommend a state licensed building contractor repair all as needed.

Expansion and Contraction of Wood

One concept to understand about wood siding is that wood moves. If you were to inspect a piece of 2x4 under a microscope, you would see a bunch of tiny parallel tubes. When that 2x4 was part of a tree, those tubes or passageways were used to move nutrients through the tree. Now that it is a 2x4, the tubes tend to expand and contract in relation to the temperature and humidity. Wood tends to expand and contract in one particular direction. The significant expansion and contraction are across the grain – not with the grain. Wood movement parallel with the grain is hardly measurable, whereas expansion and contraction across the grain are significant. The expansion and contraction vary between different wood species. They can vary even from board to board. A general rule of thumb is that a board can move up to 1/16-inch per foot across the grain. Manufactured panels, such as plywood and particleboard, include so much glue that expansion and contraction are virtually nonexistent.

Chalking Observed to the Exterior Vinyl Siding

"Chalking" refers to the white, powdery film on the surface of paint and in this case, the polyvinyl composite siding. As the vinyl weathers and the binder slowly degrades by ultraviolet radiation and moisture, chalking can occur. Over time, the binder's hold on the pigment is released. After years of being hit by sunlight, the vinyl surface, simply starts to wear or erode away the surface composite. This exposes the pigments beneath, and since they are no longer bound into the polyvinyl composite, they are easily wiped off. This result is chalking. Older vinyl is likely to be chalky. The chalk is the powder that is deposited on your finger when you rub it over older vinyl siding more prone to sun exposure. Chalk can run down the wall's surface beneath and cause cosmetic streaks or light patches in the wall's appearance. Caulk can be used where the walls abut openings and trim as well as on any hairline, minute cracks. Latex-silicone blends, polyurethane, and polysulfide caulks generally perform satisfactorily. Caulks that are 100% silicone should not be used. Chalk can be removed simply, by a professional licensed contractor pressure washing the surface.

Wood Siding General Comments/Maintenance
Solid wood or lumber siding may be the most common of siding types and is attractive, durable, readily available and relatively easy to install. Wood siding can be installed diagonally, horizontally, vertically, or in any combination. Wood siding does not strengthen the structure, so corner bracing is needed. However, solid logs on a log structures provide both the siding and structural strength. This cladding type inhibits the observance of the underlying flashing, vapor barrier and other components required to ensure proper moisture deflection and resistance. Many siding problems are caused by improperly applied paint. Paint on siding may blister, peel, crack, fade or chalk. Some paint problems are caused by interior moisture that passes through the wall and lifts the paint. To preempt most issue like this, routinely check for dense vegetation around the building. Vines and ivy that are close to or on the siding should be trimmed or removed. Vegetation holds moisture and water up against the siding, which can be detrimental to the siding's condition over time. Siding should be installed tight enough to prevent problems related to water intrusion, but it should be loose enough to allow it to adequately dry after a rainstorm. Sunlight dries out wood siding, but it does not simply cause evaporation. The sun actually drives the water into the wood. It can drive moisture all the way through the wood siding. This is why it is important for the wood siding to have good drying potential, with air movement on the backside of the wood. Natural wood siding should be installed over building paper regardless of the sheathing materials. Building paper is a water barrier rather than a moisture barrier. It is recommended to prevent water from entering the wall cavity. Foam sheathing is a separate consideration. Caulk can be used where siding abuts openings and trim. Latex, latex-silicone blends, polyurethane, and polysulfide caulks generally perform satisfactorily. Caulks that are 100% silicone should not be used. If repairs are needed, remember correct nails and nailing practices are essential in the proper application of wood siding. In general, siding and box nails are used for face nailing, and casing nails are used for blind nailing. Nails must be corrosion-resistant and, preferably, rust-proof. Stainless steel is the best choice. Aluminum nails may be used. High tensile-strength aluminum is an economical choice. Hot-dipped galvanized nails are the least expensive, but may result in discoloration if precautions are not taken. Hot-dipped nails can rust and stain the wood over time. Other fasteners that are corrosion-resistant may perform satisfactorily. Some fasteners can cause black iron stains, which can be permanent. Nails can be exposed or hidden, depending on the siding type. Overall assessment of the exterior wall was serviceable at the time of the inspection.

Vinyl Siding
This cladding type inhibits the observance of the underlying flashing, vapor barrier and other components required to ensure proper moisture deflection and resistance. Exterior cladding appeared to be in serviceable condition. Recommend using an elastomeric, polyurethane or better caulk sealant around all doors and window treatments where sealant is cracking and degrading. Overall assessment of the exterior wall was serviceable at the time of the inspection. Note: This exterior siding material inhibits the observation of the underlayment such as house wrap, fasteners/methodology and flashing elements. These areas cannot be assessed and are considered beyond the scope of a general building inspection.

Concrete Block Wall Cracking Suspected to be Associated with Thermal/Moisture Movement
Above-ground concrete block walls expand in warm weather, especially on the south or west side elevations, and contract in cool weather regardless of reinforcement. This builds up stresses in the walls that may cause a variety of cracking patterns, depending on the configuration of the structures walls, the number of openings and location of openings. These cracks are normally cyclical and will open and close with the seasons. They will grow wider in cold weather and narrower in hot weather. Cracking can occur at the corners of long walls, walls with abrupt changes in cross-section (such as at a row of windows), walls with abrupt turns or jogs, and in abutments from one to two story areas. These are the weak points or "paths of least resistance" that have the least resistance for stress. Common moisture and thermal movement cracking can include: horizontal or diagonal cracks near the ground at piers in long walls due to horizontal shearing stresses between the upper wall and the wall where it enters the ground. The upper wall can thermally expand, but its movement at ground level is moderated by earth temperatures. These cracks extend across the piers from one opening to the next; along the path of least resistance. This condition is normally found only in walls of extended length. Vertical cracks near the end walls are observed typically due to thermal movement. The contracting wall does not have the strength to pull its end walls with it as it moves inward, causing it or the end walls to crack vertically where they meet vertical cracks in short offsets and setbacks caused by the thermal expansion of the longer walls that are adjacent to them. The shorter walls are "bent" by this thermal movement and crack vertically and vertical cracks near the top and ends of the façade due to the thermal movement of the wall. This may indicate poorly

bonded masonry. Cracks will tend to follow openings upward; and cracks around stone sills and lintels caused by the expansion of the masonry against both ends of a tight-fitting stone piece that cannot be compressed. Cracks associated with thermal and moisture movement are usually only cosmetic problems. Cracks of this nature should be repaired with a flexible sealant, since filling these cyclic cracks with mortar will cause the masonry to crack in another location. Inspectors are not structural engineers. Cracks should be examined by a structural engineer after assessment is made, to ensure there are no unseen or missed issues.

Tree Roots Heaving/Subsidence Suspected
Encumbering tree roots provide enough concern that there might be heaving involved that can cause far greater damage given enough time and warrants further review by an engineer. Alternatively, cracks may be the result of sudden settlement and as well can be caused by the roots. The roots can starve the neighboring grading of moisture, causing soil shifts etc. Recommend a licensed/insured tree and ROOT removal specialist assess this area further and remove as is needed all roots/trees as needed. Recommend a licensed structural engineer assess the structural stress cracks and thermal conditions etc. as needed and estimate repairs prior to any financial considerations.

Vinyl Siding Chips/Damage Observed at the Base of the Wall
There were small chips evident at the bottom section of vinyl siding in various locations. This is commonly caused by unexperienced landscapers in a hurry. It is recommended you hire an experienced, caring landscaper that has an understanding of vinyl siding when weed whacking around the perimeter of the dwelling. Rather than replacing small chipped sections, you can repair them. Recommend a licensed contractor repair or replaced all as needed.

Vinyl Siding Abuts Grading; Moisture is inhibited from Expelling at the Siding Base
Siding should be installed tight enough to prevent problems related to water intrusion, but it should be loose enough to allow it to adequately dry after a rainstorm. Additionally, moisture must be allowed to expel from the wall that accumulates behind the vinyl siding. Moisture that gets in behind the wall at windows, doors and trim or where humidity is prevalent in the area, moisture and water can accumulate behind the siding. The siding needs a suggested 2-6 inches above the grading/surface to allow the wall to relieve the moisture and is high enough to theoretically, defer foliage from getting behind the siding. Recommend excavating at the area and/or applying an aggregate of rocks so that water does not stay at the abutting sight. Redressing the siding on the wall to allow a proper wall bond seal and raising the siding is recommended.

Wood Shingles and Shakes
Shingles and shakes are popular siding materials because they are durable and available in several wood species and types. Shingles/shakes do not add strength to the house structure. They require good nailing to the base, such as plywood or wood sheathing. Western red cedar is one of the most durable wood species for shingles and shakes. Other types are white cedar, redwood or cypress and they all have a natural resistance to wood rot. Pine may be used, but it is usually pressure-treated to resist rot.

Plywood Siding
Plywood is a structural panel. Plywood siding is popular because it is less expensive to install than solid wood siding. It is readily accessible and easily installed. Plywood siding adds to the structural strength of a structure. Most plywood siding requires an exterior wood finish. Rough-surface plywood is ideal for paint and stain. Plywood is made of thin wood veneer sheets or plies that are glued together in layers. The grain of the layers is usually at 90° to the adjacent layers, with the face layer's grain running the length of the panel. The alternating direction of the grain gives the sheet reinforcement and stiffness. Plywood siding is stable more so than solid wood siding with changes in moisture content. Plywood swells only slightly when saturated. Just like other wood, plywood can rot, deteriorate, delaminate and crack at the surface.

OSB Siding
OSB stands for oriented strand board. It is formed of wood wafers mixed that are saturated with a waterproof resin binder. They are then laid flat and oriented. Next, heat is applied and the wafers are compressed into panels. Unlike standard wafer board, the wafers in an OSB panel are oriented so that they align parallel with the length of the panel that give it much more strength. If exposed to the elements, OSB will absorb the moisture quickly, causing it to contort, bow and swell. This in trade causes the wafers and layers to delaminate. The edges of OSB are particularly susceptible to moisture and damage.

Uneven Settlement Observed at the Building Protrusion/Transition
New structures at points of foundation types/transitions and elongated portions to a building are generally points of failure or where common basic settlement may occur. When cracks show diagonal shear stress, spalling or widened cracks in excess of 1/8th inch or when windows/doors are positioned at these locations exhibit operability inhibitions or pane glass cracks/fractures, these cracks are considered a structural risk that are highly recommended to be reviewed further by a structural engineer. The stability of concrete box-buildings will probably depend on the post-cracked strength of the shear walls. Even with unsightly diagonal cracking, a shear wall may still have significant strength. The clamping action of the gravity loads, as well as the vertical rebar will tend to hold the irregular surface of the cracks together, preventing the opposing surface from sliding. In addition, the rebar that cross the crack can also act as dowels.

Uneven Settlement Observed at the Building Transition/Abutment
Uneven or differential settlement can be a major structural problem in small residential buildings, however, typical uneven settlement for patios or additions abutting separately poured slabs or differing foundations/types, refers to when the slab or other surface settles faster or at a different rate than that of the other foundation, resulting in a separation of the two. It generally is most noticeable at the abutment point and will cause more often, a vertical crack at the abutment of the buildings walls/substrates where enclosed walls adjoin, especially on textured cladding such as stucco. Serious settlement problems are relatively uncommon. Many signs of masonry distress are incorrectly diagnosed as settlement-related when, in fact, they are due to moisture and thermal movements. Recommend sealing all cracks as needed. Caulk can be used where stucco abuts openings and trim as well as on these hairlines, minute cracks. Latex-silicone blends, polyurethane, and polysulfide caulks generally perform satisfactorily. Caulks that are 100% silicone should not be used.

NOTE: Inspectors are not structural engineers. It is always recommended to have a structural engineer review any and all cracks further.

Wood Shingle/Shake Splits Observed
Water can easily travel through splits in boards. There is open, exposed wood inside the split that can result in deterioration at that area. Split wood can be caused by rusting nails, shrinkage of the wood, butt ends too tight, physical damage, poor nailing schedule etc. Butt-ends should be spaced about 3/8-inch apart to allow for swelling. Recommend a licensed contractor repair all as needed.

Wood Shingle/Shake Warping Observed
Warping usually appears because one side of the wood is wet or the other side is dry. Warped wood is not weather-tight and can allow water to penetrate the wall. Sometimes, a warped piece of siding can be nailed back into place, however, flattening the warped wood usually results in creating a crack. Screws or nails already present along a crack in a warped piece of wood siding may be an indication of an attempt to flatten it. Recommend a licensed contractor repair all as needed.

Wood Siding Needs Various Nails Replaced
Correct nails and nailing practices are essential in the proper application of wood siding. In general, siding and box nails are used for face nailing and casing nails are used for blind nailing. Nails must be corrosion-resistant and preferably rust-proof. Stainless steel is the best choice. Aluminum nails may be used. High tensile-strength aluminum is an economical choice. Hot-dipped galvanized nails are the least expensive, but may result in discoloration if precautions are not taken. Hot-dipped nails can rust and stain the wood over time. Other fasteners that are corrosion-resistant may perform satisfactorily. Some fasteners can cause black iron stains, which can be permanent. Nails can be exposed or hidden, depending on the siding type.

Pressure Treated Wood; Wood Rot Observed
Any time wood is allowed to get moist and stay moist, wood rot can emerge. To prevent this, many lumber companies treat their wood so that it will resist moisture, often adding chemicals that if the wood does get damp, fungi cannot settle on it. Proper ventilation of wooden structures is also critical, to keep fresh air blowing across the wood so that it stays dry, and wood-to-ground contact is generally to be avoided, as wood which sits on the soil will eventually attract fungi, causing rot. Classically, wood rot causes the wood to become crumbly, spongy, or stringy. Sometimes the outer layers remain intact, and the rot only becomes apparent when catastrophic failure appears. In some cases, the fungi in the wood may put out fruiting bodies, making the problem readily apparent. While it may be tempting to scrape off the fruiting bodies and call it a day, the presence of fungus on wood indicates the need to address the underlying wood rot. Rotten wood generally needs to be removed. People can repair wood rot by taking out and replacing rotten wood, or by removing an area of rot and filling it

with epoxy or another wood filler. Addressing the problem which led to the rot is also important, or the wood will simply start to rot all over again in the future. Recommend repairing any densely rotted wood as needed.

Suspected Formosan Subterranean Termite Damage Observed. (Coptotermes Formosanus)

The Formosan subterranean termite (Coptotermes Formosanus) is an invasive species of termite. It has been transported worldwide from its native range in southern China to Formosa (Taiwan, where it gets its name) and Japan. In the 20th century it became established in South Africa, Hawaii and in the continental United States. The Formosan subterranean termite is often nicknamed the super-termite because of its destructive habits. This is because of the large size of its colonies, and the termites' ability to consume wood at a rapid rate. A single colony may contain several million (compared with several hundred thousand termites for other subterranean termite species) that forage up to 300 feet (100 m) in soil. A mature Formosan colony can consume as much as 13 ounces of wood a day (ca. 400 g) and severely damage a structure in as little as three months. Because of its population size and foraging range, the presence of colonies poses serious threats to nearby structures. Once established, Formosan subterranean termites have never been eradicated from an area, recommend a licensed pest control specialist assess and treat as needed.

Cement Fiber Siding (Hardi-Siding)

Fiber cement siding is a manufactured, fiber-reinforcing product made with an inorganic hydraulic or calcium silicate binder formed by chemical reaction and reinforced with organic or inorganic non-asbestos fibers, or both. Additives which enhance manufacturing or product performance are permitted. Fiber cement siding products have either smooth or textured faces and are intended for exterior wall and related applications.

Stucco and EIFS

Stucco is used as an exterior covering or coating on residential buildings and is common in many parts of the U.S. Stucco is a durable cladding type. Traditional stucco is made of lime, sand and water. Modern stucco is made of Portland cement, sand and water. Lime can also be added to decrease its permeability rate and increase the workability of modern stucco. Sometimes, proprietary additives such as synthetic acrylics and glass fibers, are added to improve the stucco's strength and flexibility.

Suspected Dry Wood Termite Damage Observed

Termite damage was suspected at and within the wood member(s). Dry wood termites swarm in the evening and at night during the warmer months of the year. It is very hard to find where they are coming from because they live so deeply in the lumber. Dry wood termite colonies are small colonies only about 3,000 termites. When the colony reaches about 3,000 termites then they will swarm to start a colony elsewhere. They need very little moisture and are often found in the attic wood framing, wall studs, door casings and window frames. Dry wood termites obtain moisture from the water produced by the digestion of cellulose, no matter how old the wood is. This damage may indicate further damages that are not observable or readily accessible during the standard building inspection. Spot treatments, such as orange oil applications, use insecticides applied to control known dry wood termite colonies, such as those found in a door casing, windowsill or piece of furniture. For newer buildings, this is the recommended treatment by honest pest control servicemen and is fairly nominal in price. Advantages to dry wood alternative treatments are: The structure does not have to be unoccupied during treatment, just the immediate work area. To date, there is no known residual effect to the natural termiticide. If re-infestation occurs and the insects come in contact with the treated area, the transfer effect will start again and the colony will be eliminated. Most important, this method uses material extremely low in mammalian toxicity. Recommend a licensed pest control contractor treat all as needed.

Suspected Subterranean/Dry Wood Damage Observed

There were suspected old termite burrows found on the wood but there were no signs of live dry wood or subterranean termites. Where dry wood termite damage is present, this could have been from an exterior swarm intruding or from an interior swarm attempting to exit. For subterranean, tubes aligning walls and abutting surface joints of the exterior may route the infesting intruders from the exterior to the interior and back to the exterior again. It is warranted and recommended to have a licensed pest professional treat the building and/or provide a routine treatment and inspection plan. There are many termite control companies that will provide free inspections/quotes. Termite control can be done with liquid termite control, termite bait systems, or both. Liquid Termite Control products are fast acting, can be applied closer to the infestation, and require less maintenance. For subterranean, when needed, termite Bait Systems are less intrusive, no drilling or trenching is needed, no expensive equipment is required, and bait systems can help you identify a problem before the termites reach your building. Advantages to dry wood alternative treatments are: The structure does not have to be unoccupied during treatment, just the immediate work area. There is minimal residual effects to the termiticide. If re-infestation occurs and the insects come in contact with the treated area, the transfer effect will start again and the colony can be neutralized. Most important, this method uses material extremely low in mammalian toxicity.

Missing Caulk/Sealants Fiber Cement Siding at Vertical Trim Joints and Nailing Locations Throughout

Failure to follow the manufacturer's installation instructions was observed. The siding appears to not be caulked at its abutment to vertical trim locations i.e. corner, window and door trim. Recommend caulking at the abutment of the horizontal siding boards to *vertical trim boards*. CertainTeed's installation guide has the same recommendations. Generally, the manufacturers do not recommend caulking at the factory-painted fiber cement siding butt joints, presumably because it creates a cosmetic defect; some instructions permit caulking at primed (and smooth) siding, presumably because the caulk "cosmetic defect" will be hidden by the finish paint job. Recommend a licensed contractor assess further and seal/repair as needed.

Inadequate Nailing of Fiber Cement Siding; Loose Siding at Exterior Wall

Left un-nailed, the corners of most siding boards will curl away from the building. Loose sections provide large gaps for pests to stage nests or vegetation to grow especially at any low area of the exterior walls. If the product is not properly installed, including end gaps at vertical trim abutments and proper nailing using the specified fasteners, at the specified intervals, and nailed into sound sheathing of adequate thickness or into wall studs, then expansion due to moisture uptake and/or thermal changes may result in buckling of the material, particularly on sun-exposed walls. Recommend a state licensed siding, door and window contractor assess further and repair as needed.

No Weep Screeds Observed at the Base of the Framed Walls Stucco Cladding

Foundation Weep Screed provides a straight and true screed surface at the base of stucco walls, allowing excess moisture to escape the back of the stucco cladding. It is important to note, the water-resistant paper and metal lath must overlap the nailing flange of the weep screed. Check with your local building codes/department for the proper clearance above grade. Building codes require this bead on framed walls. Roof/Wall Screed uses the same design as the Foundation Weep Screed, except it is manufactured with a shorter (2-3/8") nailing flange. This design is ideal for roof-to-wall transitions found in both stucco and stone applications. It is recommended to have this repaired as soon as possible to prevent moisture in the walls and eventual potential molds.

No Weep Screeds Observed at the Base of the Framed Walls Cladding

Foundation Weep Screed provides a straight and true screed surface at the base of siding/walls, allowing excess moisture to escape the back of the cladding. It is important to note, the water-resistant paper/house wrap and metal lath must overlap the nailing flange of the weep screed. Check with your local building codes/department for the proper clearance above grade. Building codes require this bead on framed walls 10' standard length. It is recommended to have this repaired as soon as possible to prevent moisture in the walls and eventual potential molds.

No Weep Screeds Observed at the Band Joist/2nd Floor Framed Wall to Masonry 1st Wall

Weep Screeds provide a straight and true screed surface at the transition of the wall material. These are needed to provide the upper stories stucco cladding over the frame walls an ability to release moisture, allowing excess moisture to escape the back of the stucco cladding. It is important to note, the water-resistant paper and metal lath must overlap the nailing flange of the weep screed. Check with your local building codes/department for the proper clearances and materials used. Building codes require this bead on framed walls that are 10' standard length. Frame to masonry Wall Transition Screed uses the same methodology as the Foundation Weep Screed. Because there is no discernable screed, water builds at the base and causes potential delamination of the stucco especially if the paint sealant to the wall becomes porous. It is recommended to have this repaired as soon as possible to prevent moisture in the walls and eventual potential molds.

Manufactured Stone

Manufactured stone, cultured stone, and man-made stone veneers are popular alternatives to natural stone. Natural stone has become very expensive in many areas. Manufactured stone veneers are typically made from concrete. Natural stones are re-created using molds, aggregate, and colorfast pigments. To the untrained eye, there may be no obvious, visual difference between veneers of natural stone and manufactured stone.

Asphalt Shingle Siding
Asphalt shingles are sometimes used for siding material. The shingles used are the same used for a roof-covering system. When the roof-covering asphalt shingles are installed as siding, they need to be installed differently. The self-sealing tabs of asphalt shingles will not function because the shingles are installed vertically. The overlying shingle will not adhere to the shingle below. Roofing cement is commonly used to secure the layers of shingles to each other. Loose shingle tabs are susceptible to being blown or torn off by the wind. Asphalt shingles installed as siding generally need six nails per shingle. This is because gravity pulls more on shingles installed vertically, and more fasteners are needed when the shingles are installed on a wall. Asphalt shingles deteriorate over time and as the asphalt shingle gets older, the granules are lost. The protective layering that wears away exposes the asphalt material to heat and further degradation to fungus and lichen. The volatiles in the asphalt evaporate away, and the shingle becomes brittle and shrinks, and quickly deteriorates. It is important to preserve the shingle as best as possible. Some products like liquid zinc can mitigate fungus and lichen growth, while not being corrosive to the granules protective layers and adhesion, like bleaches do. Recommend a licensed roofer apply if needed.

Suspected Asbestos Cement-Based Siding
Siding is estimated to be the original, asbestos-cement shake siding. This can be hazardous if mishandled. No determination of asbestos content could be rendered as no lab tests are conducted for a standard building inspection. Asbestos and cement were first combined in the United States in the early 1900's to form an innovative, new building material. Asbestos cement is a composite material that consists of cement reinforced with asbestos fibers. Asbestos-cement siding shingles can be made to imitate the appearance of wood siding shingles in shape and appearance. Asbestos fibers are a health hazard when inhaled. Asbestosis is a form of lung cancer that is caused by inhaling asbestos fibers. Because of the health risk, strict environmental regulations on working with asbestos were established in the U.S. Health risks were shown to be greatest during mining and production processes, but minimal during the installation and use of asbestos-cement products. According to the U.S. EPA, a material containing asbestos is deemed potentially hazardous only in its friable state, which is when the material can be crumbled, pulverized, or reduced to a powder by hand pressure. Asbestos cement is not considered friable and, therefore, not hazardous because the cement binds the asbestos fibers and prevents their release into the air under normal-use conditions. However, asbestos-cement products are classified as friable when deterioration disturbs the asbestos. Asbestos-cement products are classified as friable when mechanical means are used for chipping, grinding, sawing or sanding, thereby allowing particles to become airborne. If the asbestos-cement siding material is not disturbed, no hazard exists and no precautions are required. It is highly recommended that periodic inspections be conducted.

Suspected Asbestos Cement-Based Siding is Chipping, Grinding and Needs Repair
Siding is estimated to be the original, asbestos-cement shake siding. This can be hazardous if mishandled. No determination of asbestos content could be rendered as no lab tests are conducted for a standard building inspection. Asbestos and cement were first combined in the United States in the early 1900's to form an innovative, new building material. Asbestos cement is a composite material that consists of cement reinforced with asbestos fibers. Asbestos-cement siding shingles can be made to imitate the appearance of wood siding shingles in shape and appearance. Asbestos fibers are a health hazard when inhaled. Asbestosis is a lung disease that occurs from breathing in asbestos fibers. Because of the health risk, strict environmental regulations on working with asbestos were established in the U.S. Health risks were shown to be greatest during mining and production processes, but minimal during the installation and use of asbestos-cement products. According to the U.S. EPA, a material containing asbestos is deemed potentially hazardous only in its friable state, which is when the material can be crumbled, pulverized, or reduced to a powder by hand pressure. When repair to asbestos-cement siding is needed, the least amount of siding should be discarded and the greatest possible amount of original material should be retained. Local code enforcement and permitting offices should be notified and inquired with, prior to any work on this material. Replacing is recommended for asbestos-cement siding material that has been deteriorated by cracking and chipping. For this, repairs are not usually performed on cracked or chipped pieces. The replacement piece should be of a non-asbestos, fiber-cement type. Replacing several pieces of asbestos-cement siding is easy to do because it has been manufactured in standard sizes, shapes, colors and textures. There are siding materials that have been manufactured to replicate asbestos-cement siding pieces. There are non-asbestos reinforced cement, fiberboard with asphalt, fiberglass, metal and vinyl available, too. All work should be done by properly licensed contractors coordinating with local code enforcement, ALWAYS!

Siding and Trim Seams/Nails; Recommended to be Resealed where Needed
Because siding components undergo constant heat and cold expansion and moisture bombardment, caulks and sealants can only hold so long before compromises occur. The caulk types also matter. Acrylic standard caulks

are not recommended for exterior use. It is recommended to apply a polyurethane or elastomeric or better type caulk to fill/seal all nails and siding seams where needed.

Efflorescence Observed on the Suspected Asbestos Cement-Based Siding
When Efflorescence appears, this means it has been exposed to weathering. This form of crystalline growth indicates that water is passing through the material, which can promote deterioration of the asbestos cement. Efflorescence is usually observed at the beginning of the material's life. Biological growth on the exterior of asbestos cement can be a problem in sheltered environments and on northern exposures. Shade trees located close to a building can shield sunlight and result in prolonged dampness of the asbestos-cement building product, promoting biological formations, such as moss and algae. These growths can stimulate surface deterioration and staining. All work should be done by properly licensed contractors coordinating with local code enforcement, ALWAYS!

Suspected Asbestos Cement-Based Siding; Fasteners are Corroded, Loose or Broken
Replacing fasteners for the asbestos-cement product, where they have become deteriorated or have broken due to corrosion, they should be replaced with a more durable metal. Stainless steel is generally recommended because of its superior corrosion resistance, however, lightweight coated aluminum are favored as well. Fasteners, such as nails, should be long enough to hold the materials securely. All work should be done by properly licensed contractors ALWAYS!

Clay Siding Damage Observed
Clay and slate siding can be damaged by various things and ways, including branches, stones, balls and heavy/large hail. Patching a clay or slate shingle with materials such as roofing tar, caulks, asphalt shingle, pieces of metal, or non-matching clay tiles etc. is inappropriate. Such treatments are aesthetically incompatible. They also have the potential to cause physical damage. Water can collect behind the unmatched material and progress the deterioration of the wooden components of the wall and the fastening systems of the structural lumber. During expansion and contraction of a freeze-thaw cycle and ice buildup at patches can cause surrounding tiles to break. Patching is not recommended. The replacement of clay or slate siding pieces that are in poor condition is always best.

Galvanized Stucco Casing Bead Shows Rust Oxidation/Expansion
When the paint has become porous or chalky and/ or when the area around the trim portions that are paint sealed exhibit very minute cracks, it may be possible to have water intrude, causing this oxidation to occur. It is important to have this treated immediately with a rust inhibitor and caulked as needed then paint/water sealed as directed by the product manufacturer or a licensed contractor.

Clay and Slate Siding General Comments
Clay and slate shingles are one of the most historic building materials. Traditionally, clay tiles were formed by hand and later, by machine-extrusion of natural clay, then textured or glazed with color, and fired in high-temperature kilns. The inherently fragile nature of clay shingles dictates that special care and precautions be taken to preserve and repair them. Clay roofing materials are commonly curved, whereas clay siding material is typically flat. Clay and slate are resistant to water, sunlight and wind. They are not combustible. They are heavy and not prone to uplift by wind. Clay and slate shingles, when correctly installed, require little or no maintenance. The fastening system used to secure the shingles to the wall often fails and needs to be replaced, as opposed to the shingles themselves. When the fastening system has deteriorated, or the wall support structure has failed, clay and slate shingles can be removed relatively easily, then necessary repairs can be made, and the shingles can be re-installed with new corrosion resistant fasteners. Broken and damaged shingles should be replaced promptly to prevent further damage to adjacent shingles tiles and the supporting wall structure. Clay and slate shingles have the longest life expectancies among siding materials – generally, 100 to 400 years. But regular maintenance is still recommended to prolong their life. If water damage has occurred behind the clay or slate siding materials, the evidence of damage may not be readily visible at the time of the inspection. A regular maintenance inspection of the clay or slate siding can help determine the condition, potential causes of failure, and the source of any leaks, and will help in developing a program for the preservation and repair of the shingles. Clay and slate siding can be damaged by various things and ways including branches, stones, balls and heavy/large hail. Patching a clay or slate shingle with materials such as roofing tar, caulks, asphalt shingle, pieces of metal, or non-matching clay tiles etc. is inappropriate. Such treatments are aesthetically incompatible. They also have the potential to cause physical damage. Water can collect behind the unmatched material and progress the deterioration of the wooden components of the wall and the fastening systems of the structural lumber. During expansion and contraction of a freeze-thaw cycle, ice

buildup at patches can cause surrounding tiles to break. Patching is not recommended. The replacement of clay or slate siding pieces that in poor condition is always best.

Slate Siding Damage Observed
Clay and slate siding can be damaged by various things and ways, including branches, stones, balls and heavy/large hail. Patching a clay or slate shingle with materials such as roofing tar, caulks, asphalt shingle, pieces of metal, or non-matching clay tiles etc. is inappropriate. Such treatments are aesthetically incompatible. They also have the potential to cause physical damage. Water can collect behind the unmatched material and progress the deterioration of the wooden components of the wall and the fastening systems of the structural lumber. During expansion and contraction of a freeze-thaw cycle and ice buildup at patches can cause surrounding tiles to break. Patching is not recommended. The replacement of clay or slate siding pieces that are in poor condition is always best.

Masonry Block Recladding
Concrete bricks and blocks are created by the chemical reaction between Portland cement, sand, aggregate and water. Concrete may be plain or decorative, large or small, pre-cast or poured-in-place. Concrete may be made to look like stone or shaped like bricks. **Advantages of Masonry siding is that it** provides good fire protection as it can increase the thermal mass of a building, which can increase comfort in the heat of summer and the cold of winter. Masonry can be effectively used for passive solar applications. Masonry walls are also more resistant to missiles or foreign projectiles (such as debris from strong winds and impact from hail) than walls made of wood or other softer substrates/ materials. **Some disadvantages** include frost damage that can deteriorate masonry exterior walls. This type of damage is common with certain types of brick too. Masonry is a heavy building material and requires structural support from a strong foundation to avoid settling and cracking. Some common problems with masonry exteriors include cracking, spalling, clearance, mortar deterioration weep holes, moisture, efflorescence and bowing.

General Cracks Observed in the Masonry Wall(s)
Common causes of cracks in the exterior masonry wall include settlement, premature form removal, low-quality concrete, poor backfill practices, thermal expansion and contraction, frost damage and physical damage like from vehicles. Cracks are commonly caused by the house settling. They can also be caused by the masonry unit's thermal expansion and contraction because of the changes in temperature or by the absorption of moisture. Cracks may allow water to penetrate the building. They may be cosmetic but cracks may also indicate major structural problems. While these cracks appeared common, it is always recommended to have a structural engineer review them further prior to any sale or purchase or when observed in the duration that you own the structure. Caulk can be used where the walls abut openings and trim as well as on any hairline, minute cracks. Latex-silicone blends, polyurethane, and polysulfide caulks generally perform satisfactorily. Caulks that are 100% silicone should not be used.

Spalling Observed
Masonry deterioration may happen by spalling, which is mechanical weathering that can be caused by thawing, freezing, thermal expansion and contraction, and salt deposition. Direct spraying of water onto masonry may cause mechanical damage and spalling. Spalling can be described as crumbling or flaking at the masonry's surface. Freeze-thaw cycles can cause damage by moisture freezing inside cracks in the masonry. Upon freezing, its volume expands, causing large forces that spall and crack off the outer surface. As this cycle repeats, the outer surface undergoes spalling and can result in major damage. The severity of the damage is related to the amount of moisture absorbed, the porosity or permeability of the brick, and the number of freeze-thaw cycles. Spalling can be caused by moisture being wicked up from the ground, entering the masonry wall as a vapor, exposure to direct rainfall, water spilling onto the surface from the gutter system or roof surface, sandblasting, pressure-washing, chemical cleaning of the masonry wall surface and the application of a non-breathable wall sealer. Recommend a licensed contractor review further and repair and prevent further as needed.

Salt Spalling Observed to the Masonry Wall
Salt spalling is a specific type of weathering and can occur in brick, natural stone, tiles and concrete. Dissolved salt is carried through the material in water and then crystallizes inside the material near the surface as the water evaporates. As the salt crystals expand, this builds shear stresses that break away and create spalling at the surface. Porous building materials may be protected against salt spalling by treatment with water-repellent sealants that penetrate deeply enough to keep water with dissolved salts away from the surface. Expert advice should always be sought to ensure that any coating applied is compatible with the substrate and its breathability,

which is the ability to allow the release of vapors from inside while preventing water intrusion, or any serious problems that can be created. Repair as needed.

Common/General Stucco Cracks Observed Due to Lack of Maintenance
Cracking is one of the largest complaints from building owners with stucco cladding. Cracks are unsightly and can lead to major water intrusion issues if they aren't addressed in a timely manner. All stucco cracks are caused when the stucco releases stresses placed on it by moisture, shrinkage, expansion, or other movement. Usually, stucco releases stress through a series of small cracks spread over the wall surface or at predetermined locations where control joints are placed. However, errors in stucco application can cause the stucco to store the stress until it's forced to crack. These cracks can run deep, exposing the building materials beneath the stucco, such as house wrap, to the elements. Because these materials aren't built to withstand prolonged exposure, water will eventually be able to penetrate them and move toward the interior of the building. The amounts of water and cement are usually tightly controlled by the manufacturer's specifications. With sand, there's more opportunity for error. Recommend sealing all cracks as needed. Caulk can be used where stucco abuts openings and trim as well as on these hairline, minute cracks. Latex-silicone blends, polyurethane, and polysulfide caulks generally perform satisfactorily. Caulks that are 100% silicone should not be used.

Mortar Deterioration Observed
Good-quality bricks may outlast civilizations; however, the mortar that bonds them can crack and crumble after a number of years. Water penetration is the greatest degrader of mortar. Different mortar joints allow varying degrees of water resistance. Mortar joints in brickwork can take up a large amount of a wall's surface area and take on a significant influence on the wall's overall appearance. Some joint types accentuate their individual designs, while others merge the bricks and mortar to form a flush, homogeneous surface. Recommend a licensed contractor assess the area further, remedy any unseen and present issues and repoint as needed.

Paint Peeling Throughout the Exterior Wall Surface Intermittently
Paint was observed peeling at the base and intermittently throughout the exterior walls of the structure's perimeter. This is usually caused by improper priming, too much moisture when applying sealant, improper treatment of the surface etc. Paint is a surface finish of a liquid or mastic composition that contains pigments. After applying in a thin layer to a substrate, such as wood siding or masonry block/stucco, it is converted to an opaque, solid film. Recommend a licensed painter repair all as needed.

Paint Chalking Observed to the Exterior Paint Sealant
"Chalking" refers to the white, powdery film on the surface of paint. As the paint weathers and the binder slowly degrades by ultraviolet radiation and moisture, chalking can occur. Over time, the binder's hold on the pigment is released. After years of being hit by sunlight, paint simply starts to wear or erode away. This exposes the pigments beneath, and since they are no longer bound into the paint film, they are easily wiped off. This result is chalking. Old paint is likely to be chalky. The chalk is the powder that is deposited on your finger when you rub it over old, chalky paint. Chalk can run down the wall's surface beneath and cause cosmetic problems with the wall's appearance. Caulk can be used where the walls abut openings and trim as well as on any hairline, minute cracks. Latex-silicone blends, polyurethane, and polysulfide caulks generally perform satisfactorily. Caulks that are 100% silicone should not be used. Chalk can be removed. Once removed, the surface can be primed and re-painted.

Expansion Cracks Observed at the Window Sill
The masonry window sills are comprised of reinforced rebar for structural stability, however, when hairline cracks occur, typically at the base corners or when the paint sealant becomes chalky or both, the concrete allows more and more water intrusion to soak into the concrete sometimes taking days to dry out. This moisture contacts the rebar and causes expansion of the rebar through the oxidation process that in trade, causes small minute cracks at first, but progressively gets bigger the longer it is untreated. Recommend sealing all hairline cracks. Caulk can be used where the walls abut the openings and trim as well as on any hairline, minute cracks. Latex-silicone blends, polyurethane, and polysulfide caulks generally perform satisfactorily. Caulks that are 100% silicone should not be used. Recommend a licensed contractor repair all as needed per manufacturer's specifications.

Hairline Cracks Observed at the Window Sills
The masonry sills are comprised of reinforced rebar for structural stability, however, when hairline cracks occur, typically at the base corners of the sill or when the paint sealant becomes chalky or both, the concrete allows more and more water intrusion to soak into the concrete sometimes taking days to dry out. This moisture

contacts the reinforcing rebar in the sill and causes expansion of the rebar through the oxidation process that in trade, causes small minute cracks at first, but progressively gets bigger the longer it is untreated. Recommend sealing all hairline cracks. Caulk can be used where the walls abut the openings and trim as well as on any hairline, minute cracks. Latex-silicone blends, polyurethane, and polysulfide caulks generally perform satisfactorily. Caulks that are 100% silicone should not be used. Recommend a licensed contractor repair all as needed per manufacturer's specs.

Progressive Expansion Cracks Observed at the Window Sill
The masonry window sills are comprised of reinforced rebar for structural stability, however, when hairline cracks occur, typically at the base corners or when the paint sealant becomes chalky or both, the concrete allows more and more water intrusion to soak into the concrete sometimes taking days to dry out. This moisture contacts the rebar and causes expansion of the rebar through the oxidation process that in trade, causes small minute cracks at first, but progressively gets bigger the longer it is untreated. Sills appear cracked through/missing portions. Latex-silicone blends, polyurethane, and polysulfide caulks generally perform satisfactorily. Caulks that are 100% silicone should not be used. Recommend a licensed contractor repair all as needed per manufacturer's specifications.

Paint/Primer Seal Insufficient at the Base of the Exterior Wall
Recommend a licensed painter treat the substrate/s, prime and seal all as needed.

Significant Settlement/Spalling Cracks
There appeared to be significant settlement crack observed. Notable exterior cracks to the exterior walls mid-section and paths of least resistance, exceeding and at 1/8th inch in settlement and stress fashioned, spalling cracks. Though standard cracks are common amongst new construction and old alike for some differing reasons. Exposed cracks in an exterior wall can also allow moisture to intrude. These cracks appear to be exhibited stress like conditions and they should not go unmaintained and as well, be reviewed by a licensed structural engineer.

Significant Heaving Observed to the Exterior Wall
Cracks observed exceed 1/8th inch and appear adjacent to the tree/roots encumbering the building. Recommend a state licensed structural engineer assess all further before any financial decisions are made.

Iron Stains Observed On Sidewalks
The reddish brown rusty stains are a common problem readily seen on siding, sidewalks, walkways, patios, stepping stones, window and door frames in areas where irrigation water has a high iron content. The sprinkler system and/or hoses that are used to water the grounds may also be spraying iron particles that create these rust stains wherever they land. Iron is a chemical element that is abundant in soils and aquifers in many parts of the country. It is the element that, when exposed to air and moisture, oxidizes or rusts. Where the tap water is "hard" or mineral-rich and we irrigate with well water, sprinkler water is probably causing rust stains. The irrigation systems will often "over spray" which means water ends up on the fence, patio, deck, porch, building, windows, doors, concrete walkways, stepping stones or paths, lawn furniture and also on parked vehicles if exposed to overspray. Once iron particles from the water in your sprinkler come in contact with the air, they will begin to oxidize or rust. The stains that result have likely developed over time and can be very stubborn to remove. Recommend installing a rust inhibitive filtration treatment system to the sprinkler system to prevent this.

Brick Wall Cracking Suspected to be Associated with Thermal/Moisture Movement
Above-ground brick walls expand in warm weather, especially on the south or west side elevations and contract in cool weather. This builds up stresses in the walls that may cause a variety of cracking patterns, depending on the configuration of the structures walls, the number of openings and location of openings. These cracks are normally cyclical and will open and close with the seasons. They will grow wider in cold weather and narrower in hot weather. Cracking can occur at the corners of long walls, walls with abrupt changes in cross-section (such as at a row of windows), walls with abrupt turns or jogs, and in abutments from one to two story areas. These are the weak points or "paths of least resistance" that have the least resistance for stress. Common moisture and thermal movement cracking can include horizontal or diagonal cracks near the ground at piers in long walls due to horizontal shearing stresses between the upper wall and the wall where it enters the ground. The upper wall can thermally expand, but its movement at ground level is moderated by earth temperatures. These cracks extend across the piers from one opening to next; along the path of least resistance. This condition is normally found only in walls of extended length; vertical cracks near the end walls due to thermal movement. The contracting wall does not have the strength to pull its end walls with it as it moves inward, causing it or the end walls to crack vertically where they meet; vertical cracks in short offsets and setbacks caused by the thermal

expansion of the longer walls that are adjacent to them. The shorter walls are "bent" by this thermal movement and crack vertically; vertical cracks near the top and ends of the façade due to the thermal movement of the wall. This may indicate poorly bonded masonry. Cracks will tend to follow openings upward; and cracks around stone sills and lintels caused by the expansion of the masonry against both ends of a tight-fitting stone piece that cannot be compressed. Cracks associated with thermal and moisture movement are usually only cosmetic problems. Cracks of this nature should be repaired with a flexible sealant, since filling these cyclic cracks with mortar will cause the masonry to crack in another location. Inspectors are not structural engineers. Cracks should be examined by a structural engineer after assessment is made, to ensure there are no unseen or missed issues.

Stucco Cladding Observed on Frame Structure Abutting Grading; Inhibited from Expelling Moisture

Moisture between the stucco cladding and the buildings house wrap can accumulate. This moisture from the wall that accumulates behind the siding must be allowed to expel. Moisture that gets in behind the wall at windows, doors and trim or where humidity is prevalent in the area can otherwise aid in progressing web cracks and other damage to the siding and wood framing where applicable. The siding needs a suggested 6 inches above the grading to allow the wall to relieve the moisture and is high enough to theoretically, defer foliage from getting behind the siding. Recommend a licensed contractor repair as is needed.

Brick Veneer

The main function of the building envelope is to keep out moisture. When it comes to brick veneer walls, you should understand some of the best practices that may be applied to prevent moisture problems. The following are some of the best practices that you may see applied to a brick veneer cladding: The appropriate brick type and mortar for the weather conditions should be present. This is not readily ascertainable during a typical building inspection. Some installers create an air space of 1 2 inches wide. It should be wide enough to accommodate rigid insulation board. A flexible and strong through-wall flashing membrane could be installed. The membrane should be one that will not disintegrate over time (5 ounces per square foot of copper is time-proven). It should run to the exterior face of the mortar joint. All that you will usually see is the outer edge of the flashing popping through the mortar joint surface. The through-wall flashing should be lapped. The overlaps may be a minimum of 6 inches, and fully sealed. Upright legs 12 inches high may be installed on the supporting wall. End dams should be provided at all corners and discontinuities. The end dams should be sealed.

Hardi-Siding Lap Board Fasteners Missing at Various Joints/Areas

Replacing fasteners where they have become loose, deteriorated or missing is highly recommended to prevent wind damage in the event of a high wind gust or storm. Stainless steel is generally recommended because of its superior corrosion resistance, however, lightweight coated aluminum are favored as well. Fasteners, such as nails, should be long enough to hold the materials securely. All work should be done by properly licensed contractors. Recommend light weight spackle, used for indoor/outdoor applications, to fill the tiny nail holes as directed by the manufacturer.

Suspect Stucco is Delaminating. No Foundation Weep Screed

No foundation weep screed observed. Because there is no discernible screed, water builds at the base of the cladding and may be the cause of the suspected delamination of the stucco. This is progressed especially if the paint sealant to the wall becomes porous. It is recommended to have a licensed contractor assess the area further and have this repaired as soon as possible to prevent moisture in the walls and eventual potential molds.

Sheathing Separation Observed at the Wall. Wall is bowing. No Vapor Barrier Observed

The base area of the wall/cladding reveals the plywood sheathing is warping, separating from the wall framing, likely from moisture/humidity and improper installation methodology. The warp or bow may also be indicative of insufficient nailing. No felt paper observed at the base wall, likely indicative of no felt or house wrap used at the bare wood sheathing. Unlike cement shake or other siding overlay, where the vinyl siding is placed over another, a vapor barrier is generally assumed of the first layer of cladding. This cladding, however, was applied over bare wood sheathing. Recommend a licensed structural engineer and contractor assess the area further and repair all as is needed.

Foundation

Types

No Foundation Deficiencies Observed
The exterior of the building was inspected for progressive cracking conducive to subsidence as well as an interior observation of the wall and flooring systems. There were no notable signs conducive to subsidence or active settlement which would compromise the overall integrity of the building that were observed at the time of the inspection. Due to the floor finishes, the observation of the foundation is limited to the foundation wall and observance of the floor finish surfaces. This does not always have signs of underlying problems. Overall assessment based on a limited observation was good/serviceable condition at the time of the inspection.

Post in Ground 2566TM
Post in ground (Also called *Poteau en terre*, post in ground construction, earth fast, hole-set posts), is a type of construction in which vertical, roof-bearing timbers, called posts, are placed into excavated post holes. Earth fast construction is common from the Neolithic period to the present and is used world-wide. Post-in-the-ground construction is sometimes called an "impermanent" form such as for houses which are expected to last a decade or two before a better quality structure can be built. Post in ground construction can also include sill on grade, wood-lined cellars, and pit houses. Most pre-historic and medieval wooden dwellings were built post in ground worldwide. The exterior of the building was inspected for progressive cracking conducive to subsidence as well as an interior observation of the wall and flooring systems. There were no observed signs conducive to subsidence or active settlement which would compromise the overall integrity of the building that were observed at the time of the inspection. Due to the floor finishes, the observation of the foundation is limited to the foundation wall and observance of the floor finish surfaces. This does not always have signs of underlying problems. Overall assessment based on a limited observation was good/serviceable condition at the time of the inspection.

Stilts/Pilings
Stilt structures or pile buildings or palafitte are buildings raised on piles over the surface of the soil or a body of water. Stilt buildings are built primarily as a protection against flooding, but also serve to keep out vermin. The shady space under the building can be used for work or storage. Many Buildings equip this space for vehicle storage. The exterior of the building was inspected for progressive cracking conducive to subsidence as well as an interior observation of the wall and flooring systems. There were no visible signs conducive to subsidence or active settlement which would compromise the overall integrity of the building that were observed at the time of the inspection. Due to the floor finishes, the observation of the foundation is limited to the foundation wall and observance of the floor finish surfaces. This does not always have signs of underlying problems.

Concrete Slab Footing
As the name suggests, a slab is a single layer of concrete, several inches thick. The slab is poured thicker at the edges, to form an integral footing; reinforcing rods strengthen the thickened edge. The slab normally rests on a

bed of crushed gravel to improve drainage. Casting a wire mesh in the concrete then limits the chances of cracking. A slab on grade is suitable in areas where the ground or surface soils do not freeze, but it can also be adapted with insulation to prevent it from being affected by the frost heaves. The slab-on-grade or above grade is monolithic (poured all at one time). The exterior of the building was inspected for progressive cracking conducive to subsidence as well as an interior observation of the wall and flooring systems. There were no notable signs conducive to subsidence or active settlement which would compromise the overall integrity of the building that were observed at the time of the inspection. Due to the floor finishes, the observation of the foundation is limited to the foundation wall and observance of the floor finish surfaces. This does not always have signs of underlying problems. Overall assessment based on a limited observation was good/serviceable condition at the time of the inspection.

Staddle Stones
Staddle stones (variations include Staddle stones) were originally used as supporting bases for granaries, hayricks, game larders, etc. The Staddle stones lifted the granaries above the ground thereby protecting the stored grain from vermin and water seepage. Staddle stone foundations can be mainly found in England, Galicia and Asturias (Northern Spain). The exterior of the building was inspected for progressive cracking conducive to subsidence as well as an interior observation of the wall and flooring systems. There were no notable signs conducive to subsidence or active settlement which would compromise the overall integrity of the building that were observed at the time of the inspection. Due to the floor finishes, the observation of the foundation is limited to the foundation wall and observance of the floor finish surfaces. This does not always have signs of underlying problems.

Stem Wall Slab
Where a slab is desired for cost savings or otherwise in a cold climate, stem wall/slab foundations are common. The footings and foundation are constructed like a crawlspace foundation. Fill is placed inside the foundation and is compacted. The slab is then poured. Sand bags are used occasionally instead of the fill. The exterior of the building was inspected for progressive cracking conducive to subsidence as well as an interior observation of the wall and flooring systems. There were no notable signs conducive to subsidence or active settlement which would compromise the overall integrity of the building that were observed at the time of the inspection. Due to the floor finishes, the observation of the foundation is limited to the foundation wall and observance of the floor finish surfaces. This does not always have signs of underlying problems.

Stem Wall Crawlspace
A continuous block or concrete wall is constructed around the perimeter of the building over the footing. The stem wall crawlspace is more popular in moderate climates such as the Pacific Northwest and the mid-Atlantic coast. The footings are placed below the frost line, and a stem wall is placed on top of the footing. The sub-floor structure is placed on top of the foundation. The exterior of the building was inspected for progressive cracking conducive to subsidence as well as an interior observation of the wall and flooring systems. There were no notable signs conducive to subsidence or active settlement which would compromise the overall integrity of the building that were observed at the time of the inspection. Due to the floor finishes, the observation of the foundation is limited to the foundation wall and observance of the floor finish surfaces. This does not always have signs of underlying problems.

Uneven Settlement Observed at Different Slab/Level Abutments
Uneven or differential settlement can be a major structural problem in small residential buildings, however, typical uneven settlement for slabs abutting each other from two separate pours and levels to a building, is typical and why expansion joints are applied to the foundation in new construction. It refers to when the slab or other surface settles faster or at a different rate than that of the other building section, resulting in a separation of the two, noticeable at the abutment point by a hairline crack. 1/8th inch cracks or greater of this type are considered uncommon or serious settlement problems if found abruptly during the life of the home but are expected within the first ten years of a buildings construction.

Suspect Water Intrusion from Roof Compromise(s) and Runoff at the Roof/Eaves
Water appears to have penetrated the roof surface with deposits through the structures walls and upper mortar joints to the foundation wall in the basement/crawlspace. This water that enters the basement/Crawlspace has caused problems ranging from peeling paint, mold/mildew growth and efflorescence to the stem walls/piers where the leaks occur. The interior basement/crawlspaces air quality is lessened unless the walls and floors are sealed. Recommend sealing the concrete, concrete blocks and other structural materials used in the basement/crawlspace walls and floors at the exterior if possible and stop water and gas migration into the

basement/crawlspace. Recommend repairing the roof as recommended in the roofing section(s). Recommend treating any damaged wood where needed.

No Expansion Joint Sealant Observed at the Expansion Joints
Expansion joints are those big joints in concrete that typically have either a piece of wood or have an asphalt fiberboard. When pouring the concrete driveway or sidewalk they place these expansion joints to allow the concrete to expand and contract and are also places they have stopped pouring the concrete for the day. Typically, there is a piece of rebar going through the expansion strip to prevent the two concrete slabs from moving away from each other. Liquid sealants are the most commonly used sealant product for filling joints in building components and structural joints. Yet their performance, particularly in dynamic joints, can suffer from a variety of shortcomings that often begin with awkward installation factors such as badly prepared substrates and movement during cure. Finally, tensile stresses at bond lines, as well as within the cured liquid sealant elastomer, often result in premature failure. The problem with these expansion strips is that they allow water to migrate down through the joint causing the rebar to rust. Eventually the rebar will break and allow the two concrete slabs to move independently. Another problem with these joints is that they can collect dirt and provide an area for weeds to grow. There is a solution to these problems; you can have a joint sealant placed over the expansion joint. This will help prevent water migrating down causing the rebar to rust and will also prevent weeds from growing in the joint. The material used is a polyurethane caulk that bonds to both side of the concrete slab creating a complete water seal. Other products such as plastic or foam that are placed in-between the joint do not create that watertight seal like the polyurethane caulking. Recommend a licensed contractor repair as needed.

Masonry Brick Piers
Brick piers are vertical structures. They typically act as supports for walls that are built into or for construction built on top of them. Historically, these were widely used and common place in some locales. Other types of foundations that are stronger, however, have been developed over time like masonry block, precast piers and monolithic slab footings etc. Since this is the case, construction using brick piers in building foundations is generally not utilized. It is still commonly used in walls and to support structures such as pergolas.

Stone Foundation
Dry stone and stones laid in mortar to build foundations are common in many parts of the world. Dry laid stone foundations may have been pointed with mortar after construction. Sometimes the top, visible course of stone is hewn, quarried stones. The exterior of the building was inspected for progressive cracking conducive to subsidence as well as an interior observation of the wall and flooring systems. There were no notable signs conducive to subsidence or active settlement which would compromise the overall integrity of the building that were observed at the time of the inspection. Due to the floor finishes, the observation of the foundation is limited to the foundation wall and observance of the floor finish surfaces. This does not always have signs of underlying problems.

Masonry Piers
Masonry piers are often used to support internal loads on small residential buildings, or to support projecting building elements, such as bay windows, porches and additions. In some cases, they support the entire structure. Piers often settle differentially and, over a long period of time, particularly when they are exposed to the weather, they tend to deteriorate. The exterior of the building was inspected for progressive cracking conducive to subsidence as well as an interior observation of the wall and flooring systems. There were no notable signs conducive to subsidence or active settlement which would compromise the overall integrity of the building that were observed at the time of the inspection. Due to the floor finishes, the observation of the foundation is limited to the foundation wall and observance of the floor finish surfaces. This does not always have signs of underlying problems.

Pier(s) Observed Off Center
International Code Council (ICC) States "Centers of piers shall bear in the middle 1/3 of the footings, and girders shall bear in the middle 1/3 of the piers, except exterior girders. Footings shall be full thickness over the entire area of the footing." Recommend a licensed structural engineer assess further and repair all as needed.

Masonry Foundation/Walls

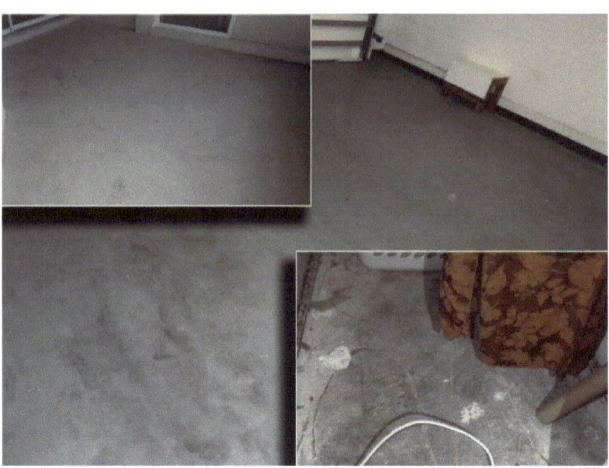

Basement Waterproofing Using Sealers for Concrete Floors and Masonry Foundation Walls

Basement Concrete and Concrete Block Sealers for Basement Waterproofing
Basements are below grade, surrounded by soil. This soil absorbs water during rains and surges where structures are on the coast, and then releases it. By capillary action, water can migrate through a block, brick and even through solid concrete basement walls and floors. This water that enters the basement can cause problems ranging from peeling paint, mold/mildew growth, spalling, and efflorescence. Also, naturally occurring gasses that are released from soils can be transmitted into the basement. The interior basement air quality is lessened unless the walls and floors are sealed. It is possible to seal the concrete, concrete blocks and other structural materials used in basement walls and floors that stop water and gas migration into a basement. It can even be done from the interior of a building. Both old and new structures can be sealed.

Rear Porch Suspected Converted to Living Area; Foundation Protrudes Past Siding
It was not confirmed that there was any permitting for the sidings installation, so it is not confirmed that proper flashing was used at the base of the wall. The foundation at this area may have been constructed for a lightweight aluminum enclosure, with posts that receded in a few inches from the edge of the foundation to allow for better bracing, less water exposure etcetera. Framing of the enclosed area is not generally discernable as the material items are covered and may not have the structural support needed to sustain maximum wind load in the event of a high wind storm. The raised seam aluminum roof is still connected to the wall and flashed at the wall. Structural ties, wiring, flashing and vapor barriers are all covered, if present, behind the walls and cannot be determined. As long as the foundation and masonry protrude beyond the siding you will have moisture wicking up. If the paint and stucco sealant break, water may be able to enter, rotting the underlying wood. Even with a moisture breach, the protruding foundation might allow rain to splash up and keep the bottom of your cladding wet. Getting copper used to form gutters, a contractor may form a custom apron flashing. Cut length wise, into strips, then formed in and fastened/sealed at the wall, going up several inches with the copper flashing filling the gap. Make a 45 +/degree angle toward the base to get out past the foundation extending several inches down the foundation face, like drip edge flashing at the base. Aluminum or copper will probably be best. Recommend a licensed contractor assess further and repair as needed/recommended to local/state codes.

Dampness in Basement; Suspect Rising Damp from the Flower Base
Rising damp is the upward movement of moisture through the pores in masonry, caused by fluidic and capillary action which relies on surface tension of the moisture to draw moisture vertically, upwards into the building foundation and masonry walls, from the ground. Basements/crawl spaces are below grade and surrounded by soil. This soil absorbs water during rains and surges where structures are on the coast and then releases it. By capillary action, water can migrate through a block, brick and even through solid concrete basement/crawl space

walls and floors. This water that enters the basement/ crawl spaces can cause problems ranging from peeling paint, mold/mildew growth, spalling and efflorescence. Also, naturally occurring gasses that are released from soils can be transmitted into the basement. The interior basement/ crawl spaces air quality is lessened and can permeate through floor boards unless the walls and floors are sealed. Recommend to seal the blocks and/or other structural materials used in the basement/ crawl space walls and floors to stop water and gas migration.

Tree Roots Heaving/Subsidence Suspected
Encumbering tree roots provide enough concern that there might be heaving involved that can cause far greater damage given enough time and warrants further review by an engineer. Alternatively, cracks may be the result of sudden settlement and as well can be caused by the roots. The roots can starve the neighboring grading of moisture, causing soil shifts etc. Recommend a licensed/insured tree and root removal specialist assess this area further and remove as is needed, all roots/trees as needed. Recommend a licensed structural engineer assess the structural stress cracks and thermal conditions etc. as needed and estimate repairs prior to any financial considerations.

Suspect Water Intrusion from Rain Runoff at the Roof/Eaves; Deposits on Walls Upper Mortar Joints
Deposits were observed at the walls upper mortar joints to the foundation wall in the basement/crawlspace. If water is leaking into the basement from roof spillage on the ground outside, the best fix starts with the roof gutter and downspout systems. Efflorescence was observed at the upper foundation wall in the basement/crawlspace of the structure indicative of moisture seepage through the wall from moisture at the grade level, typically, caused by improper downspouts and furrowing of the grading around the building. **Efflorescence** or "mineral salts" is a whitish crystalline or powdery deposit on damp masonry walls, especially foundation walls which are located below the grade level. White wall deposits were observed at the mortar joints. This usually-white fluffy material is *efflorescence*, a crystalline mineral salt left behind as moisture comes through the wall and evaporates into the building interior. Efflorescence is an indicator of wet conditions that could contribute to mold problems in the building and should be remediated ASAP. This water that enters the basement can cause problems ranging from peeling paint, mold/mildew growth, spalling and efflorescence. Also, naturally occurring gasses that are released from soils can be transmitted into the basement. The interior basement air quality is lessened unless the walls and floors are sealed. Recommend to seal the concrete, concrete blocks and other structural materials used in the basement walls and floors and stop water and gas migration into a basement/crawlspace. This can even be done from the interior of a building. Both old and new structures can be sealed.

Suspect Water Intrusion at the Mid to Lower Foundation Wall; Efflorescence at the Walls Mortar Joints Observed
If water is leaking into the basement from roof run off on the ground outside, the best fix starts with the roof gutter and downspout system. Efflorescence was observed at the mid to lower foundation wall in the basement of the structure indicative of moisture seepage through the wall from moisture at the soil at the exterior, neighboring the wall, typically caused by improper or degraded water seal to the opposing side of the wall. Additional aggressors to the problem may be improper termination of downspouts, furrowing of the grading around the building caused by no guttering or other reasons. Fixing any of these potential issues may slow its progression, however, a water sealant is preferred to be applied ASAP. **Efflorescence** or "mineral salts" is a whitish or powdery deposit on damp masonry walls, especially foundation walls which are located below the grade level. White wall deposits at the mortar joints is usually a white fluffy material called *efflorescence*, a crystalline mineral salt left behind as moisture comes through the wall and evaporates into the building interior. Efflorescence is an indicator of wet conditions that could contribute to a mold problems somewhere in the building and should be remediated ASAP. This water that enters the basement can cause problems ranging from peeling paint, mold/mildew growth, spalling, and efflorescence. Also, naturally occurring gasses that are released from soils can be transmitted into the basement. The interior basement air quality is lessened unless the walls and floors are sealed. Recommend to seal the concrete, concrete blocks and other structural materials used in the basement walls and floors and stop water and gas migration into a basement. This can even be done from the interior of a building. Both old and new structures can be sealed.

Pressure Treated Wood; General Wood Rot Comments to Damaged Wood Observed
Any time wood is allowed to get moist and stay moist, wood rot can emerge. To prevent this, many lumber companies treat their wood so that it will resist moisture, often adding chemicals which harm fungi so that if the wood does get damp so fungi cannot settle on it. This chemical however, dissipates and no longer is effective after several or more years depending on the product. Proper ventilation of wooden structures is also critical, to keep fresh air blowing across the wood so that it stays dry, and wood-to-ground contact is generally to be

avoided, as wood which sits on the soil, will eventually attract fungi causing rot. Classically, wood rot causes the wood to become crumbly, spongy, or stringy. Sometimes the outer layers remain intact, and the rot only becomes apparent when catastrophic failure appears. In some cases, the fungi in the wood may put out fruiting bodies, making the problem readily apparent. While it may be tempting to scrape off the fruiting bodies and call it a day, the presence of fungus on wood indicates the need to address the underlying wood rot. Rotten wood generally needs to be removed. People can repair wood rot by taking out and replacing rotten wood, or by removing an area of rot and filling it with epoxy or another wood filler. Addressing the problem which led to the rot is also important, or the wood will simply start to rot all over again in the future. Recommend a licensed contractor replacing any densely rotted wood and repairing all as needed.

Formosan Subterranean Termite Damage Suspected. (Coptotermes Formosanus)
The Formosan subterranean termite (Coptotermes Formosanus) is an invasive species of termite. It has been transported worldwide from its native range in southern China to Formosa Taiwan, where it gets its name, and Japan. In the 20th century it became established in South Africa, Hawaii and in the continental United States. The Formosan subterranean termite is often nicknamed the super-termite because of its destructive habits. This is because of the large size of its colonies, and the termites' ability to consume wood at a rapid rate. A single colony may contain several million (compared with several hundred thousand termites for other subterranean termite species) that forage up to 300 feet (100 m) in soil. A mature Formosan colony can consume as much as 13 ounces of wood a day (ca. 400 g) and severely damage a structure in as little as three months. Because of its population size and foraging range, the presence of colonies poses serious threats to nearby structures. Once established, Formosan subterranean termite has never been eradicated from an area. Recommend a licensed termite treatment specialist treat all as needed.

Suspected Dry Wood Termite Damage Observed
Suspected termite damage was evident at and within the wood member(s). Dry wood termites swarm in the evening and at night during the warmer months of the year. It is very hard to find where they are coming from because they live so deeply in the lumber. Dry wood termite colonies are small colonies only about 3,000 termites. When the colony reaches about 3,000 termites then they will swarm to start a colony elsewhere. They need very little moisture and are often found in the attic wood framing, wall studs, door casings and window frames. Dry wood termites obtain moisture from the water produced by the digestion of cellulose, no matter how old the wood is. This damage may indicate further damages that are not observable or readily accessible during the standard building inspection. Spot treatments, such as orange oil applications, use insecticides applied to control known dry wood termite colonies, such as those found in a door casing, windowsill or piece of furniture. For newer structures, this is the recommended treatment by honest pest control servicemen and is fairly nominal in price. Advantages to dry wood alternative treatments are: The structure does not have to be unoccupied during treatment, just the immediate work area. If re-infestation occurs and the insects come in contact with the treated area, the transfer effect will start again and the colony will be eliminated. Most important, this method uses material extremely low in mammalian toxicity.

Suspected Subterranean/Dry wood Damage Observed
There was old suspected termite damage found on the wood but there were no signs of live dry wood or subterranean termites. Where dry wood termite damage is present, this could have been from an exterior swarm intruding or from an interior swarm attempting to exit. As for subterranean, tubes aligning walls and abutting surface joints of the exterior may route the infesting intruders from the exterior to the interior and back to the exterior again. It is warranted and recommended to have a licensed pest professional treat the structure and/or provide a routine treatment and inspection plan. Note: Tenting may not be needed as new cheaper treatment methods are becoming more readily appeasing to many new and old building buyers/owners. Additionally, there are many termite control companies that will provide free inspections/quotes. Termite control can be done with liquid termite control, termite bait systems, or both. Liquid Termite Control products are fast acting, can be applied closer to the infestation, and require less maintenance. For subterranean, when needed, termite Bait Systems are less intrusive, no drilling or trenching is needed, no expensive equipment is required, and bait systems can help you identify a problem before the termites reach your building. Advantages to dry wood alternative treatments are: The structure does not have to be unoccupied during treatment, just the immediate work area, if re-infestation occurs and the insects come in contact with the treated area, the transfer effect will start again and the colony will be eliminated. Most important, this method uses material extremely low in mammalian toxicity.

General Wood Rot Comments to Damage Wood Observed
Any time wood is allowed to get moist and stay moist, wood rot can emerge. Proper ventilation of wooden structures is also critical, to keep fresh air blowing across the wood so that it stays dry, and wood-to-ground

contact is generally to be avoided, as wood which sits on the soil will eventually attract fungi, causing rot. Typically, wood rot causes the wood to become crumbly, spongy, or stringy. Sometimes the outer layers remain intact, and the rot only becomes apparent when catastrophic failure appears. In some cases, the fungi in the wood may put out fruiting bodies, making the problem readily apparent. While it may be tempting to scrape off the fruiting bodies and call it a day, the presence of fungus on wood indicates the need to address the underlying wood rot. Rotten wood generally needs to be removed. People can repair wood rot by taking out and replacing rotten wood, or by removing an area of rot and filling it with epoxy or wood filler. Addressing the problem which led to the rot is also important, or the wood will simply start to rot all over again in the future. Recommend replacing any densely rotted wood and repairing all as needed.

Wood Rot Suspected at the Crawlspace/Basement of the Subfloors Outer Wood Sill, Band Joist and/or Band Joist Abutment

This is typically caused by poor ground clearance at the subfloor and foundation abutment but may also be conducive to rain runoff from the roof terminating at the foundation. Providing adequate clearance to defer run off of rain away from the building is recommended. This should reduce or even eliminate most issues as noted. All damaged wood should be treated and repaired by a licensed contractor as needed.

Salt Spalling Observed

Salt spalling is a specific type of weathering that can occur in brick, natural stone, tiles and concrete. Dissolved salt is carried through the material in water and then crystallizes inside the material near the surface as the water evaporates. As the salt crystals expand, this builds up shear stresses that break away and create spalling at the surface. Some believe that porous building materials can be protected against salt spalling by treatment with water-repellent sealants that penetrate deeply enough to keep water with dissolved salts well away from the surface. Expert advice should be sought to ensure that any coating applied is compatible with the substrate in terms of its breathability, which is the ability to allow the release of vapors from inside while preventing water intrusion, or other serious problems that can be created.

Efflorescence Observed

Efflorescence often occurs on masonry, particularly brick, when water moves through a wall and brings out salts to the surface that are not commonly bound as part of the concrete. As the water evaporates, the salts are left behind. The salts appear as white, fluffy deposits that can usually be simply brushed off by hand. The resulting white deposits are referred to as efflorescence. Efflorescence is sometimes referred to as salt-petering. Since primary efflorescence brings out salts that are not ordinarily part of the cement stone, it is not a structural concern but, rather, an aesthetic concern. Rising damp, however, can be associated with efflorescence in basements, crawl spaces and exterior walls and can be a concern.

Greenish Colored Efflorescence Suspected at the Basement/Foundation Wall

Vanadium salts, common in clay or brick products from some areas such as Southwestern U.S., may produce green efflorescence on white or buff burned clay surfaces. Other efflorescence salts leave white or gray deposits. **Efflorescence** or "mineral salts" is a whitish crystalline or powdery deposit on damp masonry walls, especially foundation walls which are located below the grade level. White wall deposits at the mortar joints; this usually-white fluffy material is *efflorescence*, a crystalline mineral salt left behind as moisture comes through the wall and evaporates into the building interior. Efflorescence is an indicator of wet conditions that could contribute to a mold problems somewhere in the building and should be remediated ASAP. This water that enters the basement can cause problems ranging from peeling paint, mold/mildew growth, spalling, and efflorescence. Also, naturally occurring gasses that are released from soils can be transmitted into the basement. The interior basement air quality is lessened unless the walls and floors are sealed. Recommend to seal the concrete, concrete blocks and other structural materials used in the basement walls and floors to help stop water and gas migration into a basement. This can even be done from the interior of a building. Both old and new structures can be sealed.

General Concrete Moisture Cracks

There are two guarantees with concrete. One, it will get hard and two, it will crack. Cracking is a frequent cause of complaints in the concrete industry. The Concrete Foundations Association has produced a flyer to help contractors educate their customers and building owners to know about the causes of cracks and when they should be a concern. Cracking can be the result of one or a combination of factors such as drying shrinkage, thermal contraction, restraint (external or internal) to shortening, subgrade settlement, and applied loads. Cracking cannot be prevented but it can be significantly reduced or controlled when the causes are taken into account and preventative steps are taken.

General Cracks in the Concrete Floor
Concrete will crack as a normal outcome of the curing process. Cracking can be worsened if uneven bearing conditions exist under the slab, such as un-compacted fill areas. Excessive water used for the workability of cement tends to produce excessive cracking, which can allow moisture to more readily penetrate the concrete slab, weakening the concrete, and leading to differential drying issues and cracking. Excessive cracking can allow additional moisture, as well as radon gas, to penetrate more easily through the slab. The use of welded wire-fabric reinforcement provides a means of controlling the severity of cracking. The use of fiber-reinforced concrete may also provide adequate crack control. Concrete control joints may also be used to control random cracking by creating planned lines of weakness in the slab. Shrinkage or curing cracks generally occur in any continuous length of concrete longer than about 10 feet.

Mortar and Step Crack Patterns in the Dwellings Exterior, Crawl Space or Foundational Walls Observed
These were found on the corner footings and/or at windows/doors. Most solid materials may both expand and contract in response to temperature variations. Masonry blocks may shrink and expand. The diagonal, step cracks appear to be conducive to changes in soil, causing some settlement. Also, they may be directly resulting from moisture retention into the walls after cracking occurred, resulting in further cracks as the paints and water sealants composition that may have aged, that can be compromised and now porous, allowing excessive moisture retention of the concrete that may result in the progressive cracks. These cracks are very minute in nature and follow the path of least resistance, the mortar joints etcetera. Please note: home inspectors are generalist, not structural engineers and cannot determine structural components integrity and/or defects. For any concerns, it is highly recommended to have a state licensed structural engineer assess further to ensure no unseen structural issues may be apparent and licensed contractor treat/water seal all walls and cracks as needed to code.

No Significant Settlement Cracks to the Wall; Foundation Cracks Observed Through the Interior Tile. No Exterior Wall Settlement Observed
Cracks in the tile appears to be from the shift of the outer soil region and/or shrinkage cracks caused when the tile is laid prior to when the concrete fully dries. Both are common at the early stages of the building and typically happen within the first ten years or so as drying and natural settlement occur more prominently at this time and less in the following years. In the construction industry it is common, as natural settlement is replaced by artificial compounding of the excavated areas, more often after pouring, that the natural settlement occurs. Note: these are common presumptions throughout the concrete and construction industry, however, it is highly recommended to attain sink hole coverage for your building as many areas throughout the country are known for anomalies conducive to aquifer over use etc. Note: Home inspectors are generalists, not structural engineers and cannot provide conclusive structural element deficiency determinations. It is always recommended to have a licensed structural engineer review further, any cracks within the structure, to ensure a misdiagnosis is not rendered.

Tree(s) Heaving Grading around Building; No Heaving of the Foundation Observed
Various roots are encumbering the foundational wall. Tree roots from the neighboring trees around the foundational wall may cause significant heaving to the footing of the building. This can be structurally compromising. Structures older than the 1970's/1980's, that is a concrete slab, may have their water proof bond compromised as well, since a water barrier may not have been applied. Tree root growth and potential future heaving may continue until the tree roots are removed. When removing any roots encumbering the foundation be sure to back fill with an industry prescribed fill. Recommend hiring a licensed arborist to evaluate the tree and the roots prior to remediation to assess the trees structural integrity if/ when the roots are recessed/removed for uprooting compromises to the tree itself.

Foundation Drainage Panels Recommended around the Building for Proper Drainage
The foundation is a vulnerable place for water intrusion. Improper drainage around the foundation is a major cause of leaking foundations. When a drainage system is used in residential construction, it is usually a combination of a layer of gravel for drainage with a foundation drain, usually either drain tile or perforated PVC pipe. Months later, as drainage occurs, small soil particles can fill the drainage path, resulting in reduced drainage of ground water. Water pressure then builds up and eventually causes leakage through the foundation wall. The drainage path can be designed using several different methods: a solid drainage board with a porous structure, allowing moisture and water to drain vertically down to the foundation drain. These board-type systems provide protection of the waterproof membrane and thermal insulation; an air space created by a dimpled plastic grid, or "geogrid." Condensation can also be collected in this air space; a traditional gravel

course, with filter fabric to the outside, and a protection board over the foundation waterproofing. Washed pea-gravel and screened crushed stone work well for this drainage course. Panels with an air space help quickly move the water to the drains, reducing hydrostatic pressure against the foundation. Most of these systems also provide protection to the damp-proof or waterproof membrane. Recommend a licensed contractor review further and repair all as needed.

Pier Settlement Observed
Piers should be plumb, without major settlement, in good condition and adequate in accepting bearing loads. When appearance is not a factor (as is often the case), piers can be supplemented by the addition of adjacent supports. Settlement or rotation of the pier footing can cause a lowering or tilting of the pier and subsequent loss of bearing capacity. Wood-frame structures adjust to this condition by flexing and redistributing their loads or by sagging. The pier width-to-height ratio should not exceed 1:10. Those that are deficient should be repaired or replaced.

Masonry Wall Cracks Observed; Suspect Pier Settlement
Masonry walls located over settled piers will crack. Deterioration of the pier could be caused by elements exposure, poor construction, or over-stressing. Piers for many older residential structures are often of poorly constructed masonry that deteriorates over the years. A sign of over-stressing of piers is vertical cracking or bulging. Problems with piers can result in problems with bearing of wooden components. Structural wooden components can lose bearing when piers move or deteriorate. Settlement or rotation of the pier footing can cause a lowering or tilting of the pier and subsequent loss of bearing capacity. Wood-frame structures adjust to this condition by flexing and redistributing their loads, or by sagging. The pier width-to-height ratio should not exceed 1:10. Those that are deficient should be repaired or replaced.

Horizontal Foundation Wall Cracks Located at Mid-Wall Height
Masonry block or stone walls which are cracked and/or bulging inwards at mid-height on the wall are likely to have been damaged by vehicle traffic when a driveway is near the wall or site or history involving movement of heavy equipment near the wall such as an RV parked etc. Earth loading is also common at a hillside or earth loading exacerbated by water or frost common in areas of wet soils. It is highly recommended to have this areas reviewed further by a licensed structural engineer to assess the severity of the present condition and repairs as needed.

Horizontal Foundation Cracks Located Low on a Foundation Wall
The forces exerted by soils against a foundation wall increase geometrically as we move from surface level of the soil against the wall to the areas near the bottom of the wall. In other words, earth pressure is greatest at the bottom of the wall. This fact helps us distinguish between frost or water-related cracking and simple earth loading in some cases since a wall which has become dislocated laterally only at or near its bottom is likely to have been damaged by earth loading.

Pier Settlement Observed; Vertical Cracking or Bulging to the Piers Observed
A sign of over-stressing of piers is vertical cracking or bulging. Problems with piers can result in problems with bearing of wooden components. Structural wooden components can lose bearing when piers move or deteriorate. Settlement or rotation of the pier footing can cause a lowering or tilting of the pier and subsequent loss of bearing capacity. Wood-frame structures adjust to this condition by flexing and redistributing their loads, or by sagging. Masonry walls located over settled piers will crack. Deterioration of the pier(s) could be caused by elements exposure, poor construction, or over-stressing. Piers for many older residential structures are often of poorly constructed masonry that deteriorates over the years. The pier width-to-height ratio should not exceed 1:10. Those that are deficient should be repaired or replaced. Recommend a licensed structural engineer assess further and repair as needed.

Frost-Heaving of the Footing or Piers
Frost-heaving of the footing or pier is a condition caused by the lack of an adequate footing, or one of insufficient depth, can raise or tilt a pier. This could show up as movement similar to that caused by settlement or rotation of the footing. Such a condition is most common under porches and decks. Above-ground piers exposed to the weather are subject to freeze-thaw cycles and subsequent physical damage.

Tree Roots Encumbering the Foundation
Tree roots appear to encumber the foundation. No heaving observed, however, future heaving may occur causing heaving, earth loading cracks, subsidence or breaches in the foundation/wall bond. Recommend mitigating or removing the tree/roots as needed.

Additional Crawl/Subfloor Comments

No Railing Observed at the Time of the Inspection
2012 IRC (International Residential Code) Section R311.7.8 HANDRAILS In addition, most insurance companies require handrails and railing for stairs and decking where stairs have 3 or more risers to include the decking/landing. R311.7.8 (Handrails) Handrails having a minimum and maximum height of 34 inches and 38 inches respectively, measured vertically from the sloped plain adjoining the tread nosing or finished surface of ramp slope. On at least one side of stairways shall be provided with a total rise of 30 inches or more. Spiral stairways shall have the required handrail located on the outside radius. All required handrails shall be continuous the full length of the stairs. Ends shall be returned or shall terminate in newel posts or safety terminals. Handrails adjacent to a wall shall have a space of not less than 1½ inch between the wall and the handrail. For this reason and for general safety standards, it is highly recommended to remediate ASAP by a licensed contractor per IRC guidelines and/or state and local codes.

No Metal Termite Flashing Observed
No Metal Termite Flashing observed from within the crawl space. Recommend retrofitting a deflector flashing to help in deflecting termites from accessing the wood components of the home. There may be additional methods and preventative treatments available that are equally suitable but less cost. Recommend a licensed pest control specialist review the area further and/or a licensed contractor as needed.

Floor/Joists Sagging Observed
Most finished floors will develop squeaks at some time or another. A typical floor consists of joists which stretch from each end of an exterior wall and the subfloor decking ads rigidity. Temperature and humidity changes cause the various floor parts to shrink and swell at different rates. When the subfloor dips or sags, however, it can mean structural issues are present or settlement has and/or is occurring. The structure may have insufficient piers apportioned to distribute the load adequately. This usually causes sagging and tensioning/compressing of the joist(s) at the neighboring piers. A structural engineer, preferably one who works in the foundation and pier installation and repair field, is recommended to evaluate the area further and recommend repairs and cost analysis as needed. Recommend a licensed contractor assess and repair all as needed.

Brick Piers are Eroding and should be Replaced
As with all things in time, the piers and the mortar appear to be eroding away and can give way if the support capability can no longer support the load, causing further weight to be applied to all the other piers that also need replacement/repair. Recommend a licensed contractor and structural engineer assess all areas further and repair/replace as is needed.

Piers Appear Insufficient for the Dead and Live Load Requirements
This may cause the joist(s) to sag and cause additional structural issues. Recommend a structural engineer review all piers further and repair as needed.

Girder Observed Shows a Visible Sag
This typically is indicative of insufficient load distribution and may require new and further support of girders, joists and piers as a structural engineers deems suitable. Recommend a licensed contractor and structural engineer assess the area further and repair/replace as needed.

Joist(s) Observed appear to have Slid Off the Ledger/Sill
This can allow uneven distribution of the structures load, cause sag and progressive additional structural issues and compromises. Recommend a licensed contractor and structural engineer to assess the area further and repair/replace as needed.

Improper Shimmying at the Pier(s) Observed
This can cause the joist(s) to shift, progressing sag and causing additional structural issues. Recommend a licensed contractor and structural engineer to assess the area further and repair/replace as needed.

Floor/Joists Sagging Observed. Abutting Joists did not appear to be Supported at the Abutment/Joint
Abutting joists did not appear to be supported at the abutment/joint. This can cause a structural compromise. It is highly recommended to have a licensed contractor and structural engineer to assess the area further and repair/replace as needed.

Roofing

Basic Architectural Shingle Comments
Roof was comprised of an architectural asphalt shingle (3 dimensional). This shingle typically has a 30 year manufacturer's warranty or higher. All valleys, vent stacks and weather hoods appeared to be in serviceable condition. Overall condition to the roof cover was good. The shingle should be resistant to black algae starting to form on the roof surface for ten years from the install date. This algae degrades the life of the roof by years. If observed, there is an excellent and very easy to apply algae remover. This should be applied to the roof shingle surface. Your roof cover (arch shingle) is the newer grade and has a minimum 30 year life warranty by the manufacturer, for the shingle. This life expectancy can be reduced by 5 years or more if algae is left to grow and eat away at the shingle. Additionally, the "black" part of the algae draws more heat which acts as an additive in the cocktail toward degrading your roof cover. Good algae removing application is a liquid Ion of Zinc, made for roofing materials. You can search "liquid zinc" online for more information. Use as directed. To obtain full life of the shingle, have a licensed contractor treat as directed by the product manufacturer's directions. It is not recommended to use bleaching agents with a higher alkalinity due to their corrosive behavior. Bleaching agents may also void many roof cover type warranties. Check your roof material type and warranty details before using/applying any products.

Basic Composition Shingle Comments
Roof was comprised of a composition asphalt shingle. This shingle typically has a 25 year manufacturer's warranty or higher. All valleys, vent stacks and weather hoods appeared to be in serviceable condition. Overall condition to the roof cover was good. Dark Lichen, Fungi and Algae degrade the life of the roof by years. If observed to be progressive, there is an excellent and very easy to apply algae remover. This should be applied to the roof shingle surface. Your roof cover (composition asphalt shingle) has a standard warrantied life for the shingle by the manufacturer. This life expectancy can be reduced greatly if algae are left to grow and eat away at the shingle. Additionally, the "black" part of the algae draws more heat which acts as an additive in the cocktail toward degrading your roof. Good algae removing application is a liquid Ion of Zinc, made for roofing materials. You can search "liquid zinc" online for more information. Use as directed by the manufacturer. To obtain full life of the shingle, have a licensed contractor treat as recommended or better. It is not recommended to use bleaching agents with a higher alkalinity due to their corrosive behavior and that they can void many roof cover types' warranties. Check your roof material type and warranty details before using/applying any products.

Spray Polyurethane Foam Roofing System with Elastomeric Basic Comments
Seamless: Seams are one of the major sources of leaks in roof systems and SPF roofs are totally seamless. Polyurethane foam is applied as a liquid, creating a single monolithic membrane that covers the entire roof – no seams and no joints. The foam is easy to replace when stacks or other roof penetrations need to be moved or added. Lightweight: Foam roofing typically weighs around 50 lbs. per square, versus 800 lbs. for a built-up roof and 1,000 lbs. for ballasted single-ply roofs. This reduces the structural dead load on your roof.

Tar and Gravel Roof Cover is Antiquated and Should Be Replaced
Tar and gravel roof was observed intermittently with fiberglass meshing observed at various areas where displaced gravel was present. Additionally, drip edge flashing is rusting. Due to the age of the roof and present condition it is recommended to replace the roof as is needed.

Various Concrete Tiles Observed with Hairline Chips/Cracks
Concrete tiles can chip or crack for many reasons like live load (walking the roof), wind chatter on loose tiles, wind born debris, tree limbs falling etc. Recommend a licensed roofing contractor repair all that can be repaired and replacing any cracked tiles where needed.

Suspected Tree Limb Damaged/Missing Shingle Tab Observed at the Eave
Recommend a state licensed roofing contractor replace all damaged shingle tabs per the state and local codes.

Metal Panel Roof Compromises along the Seams
The roof cover seams seals can be at a constant preemptive maintenance requirement for this roof cover if/when lifting seams are observed or present water intrusion is evident, implying the seals may be deficient throughout, requiring resealing and/or coating or better every 3-7 years depending on the product(s) used. When the product is a PVC, TPO roofing etc., an elastomeric patch/caulk or DYCO #20/20 Seam Sealer or better may be recommended. Seal around the screw heads where needed. Recommend a licensed roofer repair all as needed and apply any aforementioned products to the manufacturer's instructions.

Metal Panel Roof Upkeep Comments
Here are basic recommendations to help keep your metal panel roof in good condition. Be careful not to let metals of different types touch each other. Chemical reactions between different materials can invite corrosion. Keep all paints/sealers touched up to keep rust at bay. Be sure to repair holes and open seams as soon as possible, whenever observed. Also, cover very small holes with roofing cement. Don't forget; solder a patch of the same metal only over larger holes. Only use screws made of the same metal as the roof. Finally, always use screws with washers and install them in raised areas, not low areas where water can pool and leak.

Damaged/Missing Shingle Tab(s) Observed at the Eave(s)
Damaged/missing shingle tab observed. High wind gusts/storms can cause vulnerable/loose shingles to flap, when this occurs a sudden gust can press against the shingle with enough force to brake it at the top, since shingles loose there malleability over time and are not designed to bend more than 45 degrees when new. Damages at the drip edge can compromise the drip edge flashing, allowing fluidic capillary action to the exposed wood. Left untreated, this can lead to further damages.

Common Black Algae/Lichen Observed on the Concrete Tile
The "black" part of the algae draws more heat which acts as an additive in the cocktail toward degrading your roof. Good algae removing application is a liquid Ion of Zinc, made for roofing materials. You can search "liquid zinc" online for more information. Use when algae appear visible or as directed by the manufacturer and in accordance with local/state code. To obtain full life of the tile, have a licensed roofing contractor treat as recommended or better. It is not recommended to use bleaching agents with a higher alkalinity due to their corrosive behavior and that they can void many roof cover type's warranties such as most new types of tile that are glazed. Check your roof material type and warranty details before using/applying any products. Roof cleaning companies may or may not follow warranty guidelines and may not be held liable dependent on their license compliance requirements. Because of this, it is always recommended to inquire with the tile cleaning company what products they use and if there is any warranty or advertised best practices policy they employ.

Cracked Tile Observed
Recommend a licensed roofing contractor repair all as needed.

Leaf Debris at Valleys and Various Locations on the Roof
Leaf debris mulch overtime, this creates a nutrient rich sustenance for plant life, algae/fungus's and lichen to thrive, all of which damage the roof surface. Recommend a licensed contractor remove all debris and maintaining a routine servicing program.

Trees Touching/Encumbering Roof Eave
Trees grow and so do their trunks. The tree trunk can continually grow wider into the wood, damaging the eaves. Additionally, when the winds blow, trees sway, this can cause damage if the trunk claps against the structures roof eaves. Recommend removing all trees/limbs within 5 feet of the roof/eaves surfaces.

Ridge Vent Nailing Sealant Missing/Insufficient
Recommend a licensed roofing contractor reseal the ridge vent(s) at all screw/nail fasteners and seams with a silicone sealant to completely protect the nails/screws from oxidation or water penetration. All loose or rusted fasteners should be replaced if/when observed.

Cracking/Damage and Chipping was evident at the Skylight Dome/Fasteners Area
Chipping was evident at the dome/fasteners area. Since the progressive degradation conducive to a weathered skylight was present, and given the high probability for water resistance failure in the near future, it is highly recommended to have the skylight glass/dome changed to prevent any water loss and to provide maximum efficiency for lighting purposes.

Tree Limbs Observed Touching the Roof Surface
Tree limbs can and will damage any surface they are allowed to contact. Tree limbs can grow into the roof cover, fascia and soffit, eventually compromising its water resistance, making it susceptible to water intrusion. They also more notoriously perhaps, brush the material surface, diminishing the life of the roof cover in the affected area by damaging the protective coating of the roofing material i.e. granules, zinc plating on galvanized steel, glazing on tiles etc. Recommend a licensed arborist assess further and trim all branches from the roof a recommended 5 feet or more to compensate for wind gusts and the trees malleable swaying motion in a storm. Recommend a licensed roofer assess the roof after the tree limbs are removed to assess damages, if any and repair as needed.

Popped Nail(s) Observed at the Roof Cover
Popped nails are nails that have worked upward generally from thermal expansion. While this can happen because the nail or girth is insufficient for the roofing material or the decking type, it is applied as well on 2nd layer/ply roofing materials, not allowing proper fastening into the wood and loosening over time through expansion/retraction from the roof material. It also happens from general tweaks in the wood from the thermal expansion process. Recommend a licensed contractor repair all as needed.

Wood Fascia Paint is Peeling/Chipping and Appears Unsealed at Sections with Suspected Surface Fungi
Wood fascia is exposed. It may have had a treatment to the wood prior, however, the wood presently shows signs of suspected algae and fungi fruiting bodies indicative of the onset of wood rot. Recommend treating the algae/fungi and sealing the wood as needed. Routinely resealing and maintaining the wood will mitigate the algae and fungi future growth.

Loose Screws Observed at the Roof Cover
Loose screws are screws that have worked upward generally from thermal expansion. This can happen because the screw or its girth is insufficient or loose at first. Other variables can also be the culprit such as expansion and retraction of the roofing material, the decking type that is applied, if there is multiple ply roofing materials and from general tweaks in the wood from the thermal expansion process. Recommend a licensed contractor repair all as needed.

End Caps to Ridge Vent Missing
Recommend a licensed roofer install end caps to prevent rodent intrusion into the attic/building.

UV Exposure Appears to have Caused Significant Wear to the Skylight Dome, Causing Cracking/Damage
The skylight dome appears to be at the end of its life expectancy. The plastic is "yellowed" or foggy, indicative of U.V exposure long term reducing the malleability and plasticizers. In addition, the perimeter fastening nails are heavily oxidized/rusted with various nails loose. There were also cracks forming at the perimeter cap/lip where the nails are fastened that degrades the uplift resistance and makes it far more likely for uplift damage. Sun and UV exposure will cause significant wear to most originally installed external skylight domes and then rain, hail or snow can often cause cracking or damage in some other way. U.V. Radiation degrades the elasticity of the dome(s) and makes them susceptible to crack and fray from far less impact than they were once designed for. It is highly recommended to have the skylight glass/dome changed to prevent any water loss and to provide maximum efficiency for lighting purposes.

Second Layer/Overlay on the Roof. Drip Edge and Valley Seams Appear Loose
Your shingle is a three tab type that may allow a second layer of like roofing material, depending on the state/county. Weight on trusses is a marginal issue in older buildings. However, newer buildings with plywood

roof decks may present a weight issue depending on truss design and specifications. If the sub roof is 1/2" then a 2nd ply roof is a poor choice because of weight. Condition of existing shingle is a major factor, reduced life of shingle due to heat retention can be an issue but not a consistent factor. Ice and water shield is a concern in northern locations for Ice damming and in the south to resist wind uplift and fluidic capillary action. Second layer roof covers require longer nails (not used sometimes). Second layer roof covers are generally more susceptible to wind damage. Existing sub-roof damage is more difficult to determine. Shingle manufactures tend not to want 2nd layer as additional variables come into play with warranties. Not all roofs are recommended and/or allowed to have the second application and not all roofers can do a good job on 2nd layer install. Architectural shingle for example, due to the uneven surface, is not able to have a second layer of roof cover installed over it. The seams on the second roof cover at the eaves and valleys were observed. Additionally, the valley seaming was observed loose at the valleys. This can allow or progress roof leaks. Recommend a licensed roofer repair as is needed.

Second Layer/Ply on Three Tab Roof Basic Comments
Your shingle is a three tab type that may allow a second layer of like roofing material, depending on the state/county. Weight on trusses is a marginal issue in older buildings. However, newer buildings with plywood roof decks may present a weight issue depending on truss design and specifications. If the sub roof is 1/2" then a 2nd ply roof is a poor choice because of weight. Condition of existing shingle is a major factor; reduced life of shingle due to heat retention can be an issue but not a consistent factor. Ice and water shield is a concern in northern locations for Ice damming and in the south to resist wind uplift and fluidic capillary action. Second layer roof covers require longer nails (not used sometimes). Second layer roof covers are generally more susceptible to wind damage. Existing sub-roof damage is more difficult to determine. Shingle manufactures tend not to want 2nd layer as additional variables come into play with warranties. Not all roofs are recommended and/or allowed to have the second application and not all roofers can do a good job on 2nd layer install. Architectural shingle for example, due to the uneven surface, is not able to have a second layer of roof cover installed over it.

Architectural Shingle Second Layer/Ply over Three Tab Roof Basic Comments
Your shingle is an architectural shingle type. The base ;layer appears to be an older 3 tab shingle type that typically allows a second layer of like roofing material, depending on the state/county. Weight on trusses is a marginal issue in older buildings. However, newer buildings with plywood roof decks may present a weight issue depending on truss design and specifications. If the sub roof is 1/2" then a 2nd ply roof is a poor choice because of weight. Condition of existing shingle is a major factor, reduced life of shingle due to heat retention can be an issue but not a consistent factor. Ice and water shield is a concern in northern locations for Ice damming and in the south to resist wind uplift and fluidic capillary action. Second layer roof covers require longer nails (not used sometimes). Second layer roof covers are generally more susceptible to wind damage. Existing sub-roof damage is more difficult to determine. Shingle manufactures tend not to want 2nd layer as additional variables come into play with warranties. Not all roofs are recommended and/or allowed to have the second application and not all roofers can do a good job on 2nd layer install. Architectural shingle for example, due to the uneven surface, is not able to have a second layer of roof cover installed over it.

Rusted/Corroded Galvanized Drip Edge Flashing Observed
This flashing is dilapidated and at end-of-life. The oxidation rust has penetrated past the zinc chromate coating and has compromised the flashing. This flashing will need to be treated and coated to properly remediate any further present and future degradation where able and replaced where recommended by a licensed roofing contractor.

Side Gable Wall Cladding/Sheathing shows Moisture Compromises at Seams/Gable Vent
This appears due to insufficient paint and caulk sealants and possibly, compromises to the vapor barriers/if any. Recommend a licensed contractor assess the area further and repair all where needed.

Room Addition; Roof Cover Suspected Not Installed to Code with Compromises
It is highly recommended to converse with the permitting office and a licensed third party contractor specializing in local roofing code and possibly an insulation/moisture resistance specialist to assess the area further. Recommend to first contact the permits department to verify if permitting was completed for this addition and the inspections were finalized. If the room was completed with a roof inspection incomplete, improper securing retrofits of the roof structure and framing/decking deficiencies may be present but not visible that can later be costly to remedy.

Curling Asphalt Shingles Observed
Shingle curling is a sign of wear on asphalt shingle roofs. Most-common asphalt roof shingles have different asphalt shingle curling patterns, types and causes. Shingle corner curling is quite common. Curling asphalt shingles are common and can generally provide several or more year's life provided granule integrity is good, no compromises to the roof seals are present, no storm or exterior force or variable causes unforeseen degradation to the roof surface Recommend a licensed roofing contractor review each shingle table for loose adhesives and re-adhere where needed to prevent uplift. Curling shingles are more susceptible to high wind uplift damage.

Vent Stacks/Service Mast Sealant at Roof Abutment Needs Redressing; Compromise Observed
Tar Sealant at the roof abutment is cracking/compromised and needs to be resealed to prevent water intrusion, further degradation to the roof decking and rotting of wood members. Recommend a licensed roofer assess further and repair all where needed.

Raised Flashing at Valley
This can allow water to backflow during a high wind storm and can allow water intrusion and damage to the valley and wood underbelly. Recommend a licensed roofing contractor assess the area further and repair all as needed.

Modified Bitumen Roll Roof has "Ponding" Observed
Ponding (standing water) occurs where there are low spots in the roofing. If more than 10 – 15% of the roof remains water-covered 24 hours after a rain, you should build up the low spots to prevent water from working through the seams of the roof caused by excess water pressures. On large areas, 10x15', tapering boards and reroofing may be recommended to prevent a cave in or excessive leak in the event of a torrential rain.

Fractured Plank Board Decking Observed in the Attic System at the Time of the Inspection
Fractured boards can allow a worker accessing the roof or inspector to unknowingly damage the roof. If the boards are fractured enough that they can no longer withstand a live load of an individual or the individual is heavier than average, they can step on the board and send it right through the roof system. This can be a costly repair. It is always a good idea to reinforce fractured boards or replace them at the time of the roof replacement. When the roof is newer however, it is unlikely to be replaced anytime soon and thus, the repair can only be done from the inside of the attic, scabbing reinforcing wood members under the board. This repair is also risky so it is always recommended to leave it to the professionals. If there are protruding nails or if the wood support is nailed improperly, nails can pop through the shingle or be driven through accidently when reinforcing the area. Recommend a licensed roofing contractor assess the area further and repair all as needed.

South Code; Shingle at the Drip Edge Overlaps the Drip Edge throughout the Eaves
In the southern region of the United States has code restrictions making this practice "out-of-code". This method of installation, though it can prevent fluidic capillary action as it's known in the south or reduce ice damming in the north, it can allow greater uplift potential. Storm wind gusts are increasing all the time throughout the country and it is highly recommended to have all shingle types discontinue precisely at the drip edge. Degradation to the shingle can and will also progress at these overlapping shingles as they age and dry and as well, from ladders and other material interactions like tree limb contact.

Concrete Tile Valley, Ridge Tiles Observed with Mortar/Joint Cracks
Concrete tile roof ridge line tiles and the valley channels have exposed mortar joints. Over time, the home moves and the roof tiles undergo constant ebbs and flows in expansion/retraction from daily heat and nightly cold. These cause wear on the mortar joints resulting in cracks. If given more time without servicing the cracks, the mortar chips off. Further damage such as loose or broken tiles can occur if neglected. Recommend a licensed roofing contractor assess the area further and repair where needed. Be sure all repairs allow a clear, clean and uniform transitioned surface throughout the treated areas to allow proper water flow.

Visible Compromise to the Ridge Vent Flashing Viewed from Exterior/Attic Interior
This is indicative of fastener/seam compromises to the ridge vent. The deficiency can progress into further water damage to the wood, insulation and further damage into the building if left untreated. Recommend resealing all screws/fasteners and seams with an industrialized silicone caulk sealant or better and/or as recommended by a duly licensed professional contractor.

Ridge Vent End Caps Missing
The end cap will just snap in place with a little pressure. They are of a pliable rubber like compound so the fit will hold once the roofing contractor presses it in place. A licensed roofing contractor installs them as needed. You need end caps on the ridge or else wasps, small bugs and animals will find their way in if it is left open as well as potential wind driven rain during high wind storms.

Vent Stack Caps Observed have Rodent Damage
Vent stacks lead caps had progressive rodent damage that is allowing moisture intrusion to evade the shingle cover and streams down the circumferential exterior of the vent pipe(s) damaging substrates and insulation it contacts along the way down. Recommend a licensed roofing contractor repair all stacks with rodent resistant cap sleeves or better.

Porch Metal Roof over Unpermitted Enclosures
It is highly recommended to converse with the permitting office and a licensed third party contractor specializing in local roofing code and insulation/moisture resistance to assess if proper permitting was done and the inspections were finalized. If the room was completed with a roof inspection incomplete, improper securing of retrofits to the roof structure and framing may be present but unseen that can later be too costly to remedy. Typically, shed roofs were not made to prevent moisture vapor and temperature variables from entering the building and if structured aluminum is used for joists, thermal bridging can be occurring especially in the moist rainy season in Florida, drawing moisture condensation to the interior wall frame.

Aluminum Panel Seam at Fascia Compromised and Screws Oxidizing
Compromise along entire seam where the patio roof meats the building's roof fascia. The seals/screws are a constant preemptive maintenance requirement for this roof cover, requiring coating or better every 3-7 years depending on the product used. It would be prudent to apply an elastomeric patch/caulk or DYCO #20/20 Seam Sealer or better. Recommend a licensed roofing contractor apply to manufacturer's instructions and repair as needed.

Aluminum Panel Foil Seam and Screw Maintenance Tips
The roof cover is an aluminum panel with a foil tape seal at the seams. The seals are a constant preemptive maintenance requirement for this roof cover, sometimes requiring redressing the tape or requiring coating or better every 3-7 years depending on the product used. You can roll/spray elastomeric roof mastic on the entire aluminum roof cover to ensure all areas are sealed and recoat every 3-7 years depending on warrantied life of the product. Recommend a licensed roofing contractor assess the area further and repair all as needed.

Seals at Vents/Stacks and Roof Transitions are Insufficient/Antiquated
Recommend a licensed roofing contractor assess the roof protrusion abutments and repair/reseal at all transitions as is needed.

Standing Seam Porch Roofs

Debris Buildup Observed/Screw Fastener Oxidation Observed
Recommend removing all debris to prevent backflow and mulching issues. Roof screw fasteners were observed oxidizing. This is typical as they are directly exposed to the elements, however, the corrosion is accelerated when leaf debris is present as it holds moisture. If untreated, water can/will enter the porch interior at the screws and roof transition points conducive to the mulching/back flow issues addressed above. Recommend a licensed roofing contractor remove all debris, cleaning surface of the fascia and roof transition area where the porch roof meets the dwellings fascia board and properly sealing the length of the transition area. Treat screw heads with a Rust oleum rust inhibiting paint and silicone after as needed or as directed by the licensed roofing contractor.

Termite Damage Suspected. Live Drywood Termites Suspected Within the Wood Soffit/Fascia
Termite damage was suspected at and within the wood soffit/fascia. Drywood termites swarm in the evening and at night during the warmer months of the year. It is very hard to find where they are coming from because they live so deeply in the lumber. Drywood termite colonies are small colonies only about 3,000 termites. When the colony reaches about 3,000 termites then they will swarm to start a colony elsewhere. They need very little moisture and are often found in the attic wood framing, wall studs, door casings and window frames. Drywood termites obtain moisture from the water produced by the digestion of cellulose, no matter how old the wood is. Spot treatments, such as orange oil applications, use insecticides applied to control known drywood termite colonies, such as those found in a door casing, windowsill or piece of furniture. Advantages to drywood alternative treatments are: The building needn't be cordoned off entirely and the structure does not have to be unoccupied during treatment, just the immediate work area. There is a residual effect to the termiticide. If re-infestation occurs and the insects come in contact with the treated area, the transfer effect will start again and the colony will be eliminated. Most important, this method uses material much lower in mammalian toxicity.

Flashing at Asphalt Roof/Wall Transition Appears to be Improperly Installed
Flashing is to be applied under the membrane or asphalt roof cover. Traditionally a counter flashing is applied after to provide adequate moisture deflection at the wall transition. Recommend a licensed roofer assess the area further and repair all as needed.

Asphalt Shingle; Black Algae/Lichen on the Roof Substrate
There was the presence of black algae starting to form on the roof surface. This algae degrades the life of the roof by years. There is an excellent and very easy to apply algae/stain remover. This should be applied to the roof by a licensed roofing contractor. The roof life expectancy can be reduced by years if algae are left to grow and eat away at the shingle. Additionally, the "black" part of the algae draws more heat which acts as an additive in the cocktail toward degrading your roof. The application is a liquid Ion of Zinc. You can search "liquid zinc" online for further guidance and purchase options. To obtain full life of the shingle, treat as recommended or better. It is not recommended to use bleaching agents on any roof cover that is tile, asphalt etc. Some warranties will be negated using bleaching agents that have an excess alkalinity, thus corrosive to the substrate such as tile roofing and can progress granule loss etc. to the shingle. Check with the roof material manufacturer's warranty for further information prior to using any products.

Black Algae-Flat Roofs M.B. Roll with Main Roof Cover Being Shingle
Roof Algae on Rear Flat Roof Cover: There was the presence of black algae starting to form on the flat roof surface. This algae degrades the life of the roof by years. There is an excellent and very easy to apply algae/stain remover. This can be applied to the main roof as well, whenever needed. Your roof cover should have a minimum 10 year life warranty from the date of manufacture, for the flat roofs M.B. Roll from the manufacturer, depending on pitch etc. This life expectancy can be reduced by years or more if algae are left to grow and eat away at the roofing membrane. Additionally, the "black" part of the algae draws more heat which acts as an additive in the cocktail toward degrading your roof. A good algae/lichen removing application is a liquid Ion of Zinc. You can search "liquid zinc" on line for further details and ordering information. The algae are typical of every standard flat roof with M.B. Roll as well as pitched shingle covers. To obtain full life of the roof, treat as recommended or better to the manufacturer's specifications. It is not recommended to use bleaching agents on any roof cover that is tile, asphalt etc. Some warranties will be negated using bleaching agents that have an excess alkalinity, thus corrosive to the substrate such as tile roofing and can progress granule loss etc. to the rolled roofing and shingle.

Black Algae Main Roof Shingle
There was the presence of black algae on the roof surface. This algae degrades the life of the roof by years. There is an excellent and very easy to apply algae/stain remover. This can be applied directly to the roof surface as directed by the manufacturer. The roof life expectancy can be reduced by years or more if algae is left to

grow and eat away at the roofing membrane. Additionally, the "black" part of the algae draws more heat which acts as an additive in the cocktail toward degrading your roof. A good algae/lichen removing application is a liquid Ion of Zinc. You can search "liquid zinc" on line for further details. The algae appear to be just setting and are typical of every standard asphalt shingle. To obtain full life of the roof, treat as recommended or better to the manufacturer's specifications. It is not recommended to use bleaching agents on any roof cover that is tile, asphalt etc. Some warranties will be negated using bleaching agents that have an excess alkalinity, thus corrosive to the substrate such as tile roofing and can progress granule loss etc. to asphalt rolled roofing and shingle.

Service Mast Rubber Boot is Dry Rotted/Degraded around the Circumferential Area. Repair/Replace As Needed

Service Mast rubber boot, a part of the flashing apparatus, has degraded around the circumferential area of the mast and is allowing water to enter the roof system when it rains. This can allow wood rot to the wood decking and trusses around the immediate area and serves as an opening for rodent intrusion.

Roof End of Life. Various Missing Damaged Shingles, Excess Granule Loss and Drip Edge Damage

Various missing/damaged shingles, granule loss exceeds 70+% est. and compromises to the drip edge flashing observed. Recommend a licensed roofing contractor replace the roof cover to code as needed. If installing new, recommend applying a polyglass/peel n stick underlayment. If shingle roof cover, recommend having Woven Valleys or "No-Cut-Valleys Installed as needed.

Excess Granule Loss Observed Intermittently throughout the Roof Surface

Granule loss exceeds 70+% estimated at various locations throughout the roof surface. Recommend a licensed roofer replace the roof cover to code as needed. If installing new, recommend applying a polyglass/peel n stick underlayment. If installing asphalt shingles, recommend having Woven Valleys or "No-Cut-Valleys Installed if/where needed at all valleys.

Roof End of Life. Various Missing and Damaged Shingles. Excess Granule and Surface Loss

Various missing/damaged shingles, granule loss exceeds 70+% est. Recommend a licensed roofing contractor replace the roof cover to code as needed. If installing new, recommend applying a peel n stick underlayment. If installing asphalt shingle, recommend having Woven Valleys or "No-Cut-Valleys Installed as needed.

Various Missing and Damaged Shingles Observed at the Time of the Inspection

The underlying nailing is exposed allowing corrosion to set to the nails and may be intruding in past the nail head onto the roof decking, slowly damaging it and more progressively as it is not remediated/repaired. Recommend replacing/repairing all shingles and monitoring for any future shingle uplift as needed, annually.

Various Cracked/Missing/Damaged Tiles Observed at the Time of the Inspection

The underlying batten nailing and/or primary composition/bituminous rolled roof cover is exposed allowing corrosion to set to any nails if applicable and to potentially compromise the roof at an unobservable location unless noted. Corrosion to unseen flashing and nails may be happening and intruding in past the nail head/flashing onto the roof decking, slowly damaging it and more progressively as it is not remediated/repaired. Recommend replacing/repairing all damaged tiles and monitoring for any future damage as needed by annual inspection and after any storms by a licensed roofing contractor.

Architectural Shingle Prior Roof Leak Damage Observed on a Second Ply Roof Cover

When the attic was inspected, an apparent prior water leaks damage was observed. Prior leaks on a second ply/cover of roofing can be the birth place for future leaks. This is because the old leak presides at a location where as only a second layer of roof cover was applied, as assumed with general 2nd ply installs. The second ply roof degrades faster and the end results usually is; leaks start at the prior covered damaged area/s. Recommend having a licensed roofer review the area further and monitor routinely for the duration of time the roof covers are present, until the roof covers replaced and a single ply, new roof cover and SWR are applied. It is recommended, especially in high wind storm prone areas, to have a "Peel & Stick"/Self Adhering Modified Bitumen Polymer Underlayment installed directly to the roof decking in lieu of standard or synthetic felt/vapor barrier. This is to aid in resisting high wind uplift and water intrusion during a high winds. Insurance companies may provide building owners with an insurance discount in some localities. It is recommended to check with your insurance company to see if this may apply in your area.

Compromise Suspected at the Apron/Counter Flashing/Exterior Wall Abutment. Visible Water Stains

Roof compromise suspected at the apron/counter flashing. Water stains/damage was observed at the ceiling/roof and wall abutment from within the porch. Recommend licensed roofer assess further and repair as needed.

Metal Roof Panel is Rusted/Corroded. Galvanized Fasteners Observed Rusting/Corroded

The oxidation rust has penetrated past the zinc chromate coating and has compromised the flashing. Recommend replacing any heavily corroded sections, sanding and treating all else with a rust inhibitor and sealing all as is needed. Recommend replacing all screws with new stainless steel with rubber gasket washers or better. With proper care, metal roofs may not need replacing, the biggest question is cost for repair verse replacement. Recommend a licensed roofing contractor assess the roof further and repair as needed.

Fascia/Eaves/Trim

No Deficiencies Observed
No deficiencies observed at the eaves or trim/fascia. Recommend inspecting exterior soffit/wall abutments and fascia annually and seal all observed cracks/seams that appear breached/compromised as needed. For wood fascia, a polyurethane, elastomeric caulk or better sealant can be used to waterproof as they are also paintable and will not shrink like acrylic. Recommend a licensed contractor use per manufacturer's instructions and local code ordinances. For aluminum fascia cover, routinely inspect to ensure no nails are loose and fascia cover is intact and not sagging. If a surface rust occurs on the drip edge flashing but the roof is in good repair, sanding and treating the concerning areas is critical to prevent further oxidation using a rust inhibiting sealant treatment.

Wood Fascia is Bare and Appears Unsealed with Surface Fungi
Wood fascia is exposed. It may have had a treatment to the wood fascia when the building was constructed; however, these pressure treatments are dissipated typically over a 3-5 year period. The wood presently shows suspected signs of algae and fungi fruiting bodies indicative of the onset of wood rot. Recommend a licensed contractor, treat the suspected algae/fungi and seal the wood as needed. Routinely resealing and maintaining the wood will mitigate the algae and fungi future growth.

Loose Aluminum Fascia Cover Observed. Loose/Missing Fasteners Observed
This can allow exposure to the elements and eventual water damage if not already. Additionally, rodents and pests may be attracted to damaged fascia/soffit.

Displaced Vinyl/Aluminum Soffit at the J-Channel
Areas of the soffit appear to be displaced from the J-Channel System. Recommend Repairing as needed to prevent rodent intrusion, compromise during a wind storm or further degradation.

Visible Compromise to the Drip Edge Flashing to the Soffit/Eave Viewed from Exterior/Attic
Visible Attic inspection of some eaves not accessible, however, exterior observation shows particulates and oxidation at the soffit venting holes conducive to suspected wood rot and is typically known to start at the drip edge. Water trails under the roof membrane at the drip edge via fluidic capillary action rotting the wood, causing a depression and progressing the rot process. Recommend a licensed contractor assess the area further and repair all as needed.

Visible Compromise to the Drip Edge Flashing to the Soffit/Eave Viewed from Interior/Attic
Visible Attic inspection of some eaves not accessible, however, interior observation shows suspected wood rot at the soffit/fascia conducive to compromises and is typically known to start at the drip edge. Water trails under

the roof cover at the drip edge via fluidic capillary action rotting the wood, causing a depression and progressing the rot process. Recommend a licensed roofing contractor assess the area further and repair all as needed.

Aluminum Fascia Cover Oxidizing Due to Interaction with PT Wood
Aluminum fascia cover is the best way to go but you can't use aluminum if it will be in contact with PT wood because it reacts badly or oxidizes the aluminum. The ACQ that the wood is treated with is the culprit. If you cover the wood with #30 felt or other house wrap type first, so that the aluminum does not contact the wood, then it should separate the two surfaces. PT wood is Pressure Treated wood. It is infused with chemicals under pressure until saturated. The chemical that it is typically/usually infused with is ACQ (alkaline copper quaternary). The alkaline/copper does corrode the aluminum. By "reacts badly", I mean the chemicals in the PT wood have the potential to eat the aluminum, causing it to corrode to the point that the aluminum will "rust" and eventually become eaten with holes. "#30 felt" stands for 30 pound felt, it is a secondary water barrier and will inhibit this interaction. It is the heavy grade of tar paper/felt paper. Strips of felt paper could be used to separate the PT wood from any aluminum you install, so that the two never touch. Recommend a licensed contractor review the fascia in full and repair as needed.

Insufficient Eave Venting/Perforated Soffit
An attic with insufficient ventilation will get warmer than a well-ventilated attic, which may increase the temperature of the roof materials which may decrease the life of the material. In southern humid climates like Florida, humidity will accumulate and can propagate molds and fungi growth on various substrates in the attic like wood members and insulation. This can increase the chances of certain insects wanting to nest within the attic including pests such as rodents. Many inspectors and property owners alike, miss the many variables of consequences that can promulgate due to one bad decision or system component. Proper ventilation will also help to keep the attic space cooler during the winter, which may help to prevent ice dams in northern regions. Proper ventilation may also help to reduce frost in the attic in northern locations, but it won't prevent it. It is highly recommended to have the soffits reviewed by a licensed and experienced attic insulation and ventilation technician to further assess the scope and type of vents needed to properly vent your attic for your climate/region.

Ducting Antiquated; Insulation Loose Throughout
Ducting in the attic was observed to be radial metal ducting with insulation that was observed loose throughout. Ducting is antiquated and inefficient, can allow sweating and moisture to interact with the insulation, leaks in the attic to occur, ware to the handler and condenser, etcetera. Recommend replacing the ducting ASAP.

Antiquated/Damaged Eave Venting Screen/Perforated Soffit
An attic with insufficient ventilation will get warmer than a well-ventilated attic, which may increase the temperature of the roof materials which may decrease the life of the material. In southern humid climates like Florida, humidity will accumulate and can propagate molds and fungi growth on various substrates in the attic like wood members and insulation. This can increase the chances of certain insects wanting to nest within the attic including pests such as rodents. Many inspectors and building owners alike miss the many variables of consequences that can promulgate due to one bad decision or system component. The vent screening/covers at the soffit were antiquated with various compromises. Improper or insufficient vent screens/covers can inhibit natural venting and allow rodents to enter the attic system and thus, the building envelope. Proper ventilation will also help to keep the attic space cooler during the winter, which may help to prevent ice dams in northern regions. It is highly recommended to have the soffits reviewed by a licensed and experienced attic insulation and ventilation technician to further assess the scope and type of vents needed to properly vent your attic for your climate/region.

Attic Mold Suspected; Fungi Observed at Eave Vents
This is commonly caused by improper attic venting or conditioning/venting of the building that may allow hot, humid air to build within the attic and trap. Without proper eave venting, ridge venting becomes less irrelevant. To remediate, it is recommended to ensure all eave vents are unobstructed. For best results, installing a solar, automatic vent fan in addition or in lieu of the present vents is recommended. Recommend treating or removing all effected insulation batts and treating any wood surfaces within the attic by a licensed contractor as needed.

Improperly Installed Vinyl Soffit
Soffit appears to be installed long ways, as long strips aligning the structures walls parallel to the wall and eaves direction, whereas, the soffit needs to be installed aligning from the wall to the eaves. The first step in installing soffit is to install the proper receiving channels. You have several options for receiving channels. You can use accessories such as F-channel or J-channel, or the contractor can make channels using coil stock. The best

approach is for the contractor to select a method that works most effectively with the construction techniques used to create the eave. It is very important to measure from the wall to the fascia board, and then subtract 1/2" to allow for expansion. Insert the panel into the channel on the wall, then into the channel at the fascia board, unlike the present installation. Recommend a licensed contractor repair as needed.

Improperly Installed Interlocking Aluminum Soffit
Soffit appears to be installed long ways, as long strips aligning the structures walls parallel to the wall and eaves direction, whereas, the soffit needs to be installed aligning from the wall to the eaves. The first step in installing soffit is to install the proper receiving channels. You have several options for receiving channels. You can use accessories such as F-channel or J-channel, or the contractor can make channels using coil stock. The best approach is for the contractor to select a method that works most effectively with the construction techniques used to create the eave. It is very important to measure from the wall to the fascia board, then subtract 1/2" to allow for expansion. Insert the panel into the channel on the wall, then into the channel at the fascia board, unlike the present installation. Recommend a licensed contractor repair as needed.

Heavily Rusted/Corroded Galvanized Drip Edge Flashing Observed
This flashing is dilapidated and at end-of-life. The heavy oxidation means the rust has penetrated past the zinc chromate coating and has compromised the flashing to an unrepairable condition. This flashing will need to be replaced to properly remediate any further, present and future degradation.

Displaced/Loose Wood Soffit
Displaced Areas appear to be from loose fastener screws/nails. Recommend Repairing as needed to prevent rodent intrusion or compromise during a wind storm causing further degradation.

Rodent Damage to the Roof Eaves Soffit Vents Observed
This is a common problem in all terrains from the north to the south. Rats or other pests find their way from trees or coolant line opening to roof vents and unprotected soffit locations to enter the attic and into the home. The damage observed on the soffit appeared to be done from a rodent. It is recommended to first contact a licensed pest control specialist or licensed trapper to assess the attic for the particular rodent type and to remove all rodents as needed prior to closing the opening and repairing the damage. After, you will need to repair the openings as needed immediately to prevent any re-infestations or unwanted visits.

Rodent Damage to the Roof Eaves Soffit
This is a common problem in all terrains from the north to the south. Rats or other pests find their way from trees or coolant line openings, roof vents and unprotected soffit locations to enter the attic and into the building. The damage observed on the soffit appeared to be done from a rodent. It is recommended to first contact a licensed pest control specialist or licensed trapper to assess the damage and access to the attic for the particular rodent type and to remove all rodents as needed prior to closing the opening and repairing the damage. After, you will need to close the openings and repair damages to prevent any re-infestations or unwanted visits.

Aluminum Panel Seam at Fascia compromised and Screw Maintenance Needed
The roof cover is an aluminum panel with exposed screws. The seals are a constant preemptive maintenance requirement for this roof cover, requiring coating or better every 3-7 years or longer depending on the product used. It would be prudent to apply caulk or DYCO #20/20 Seam Sealer or better prescribed for these material types. Also, seal around screw heads where needed. Follow label instructions. Apply to manufacturer's instructions.

Missing/Damaged Crown Shingle(s) Observed
Recommend a licensed roofer replace the shingle(s) as needed to prevent water intrusion and further degradation.

End Cap Crown Shingle(s) Nail Fasteners Need Sealant
Recommend a licensed roofer treat the fasteners with a rust inhibiting treatment if needed and seal all as needed or as recommended by a licensed roofing contractor, to prevent water intrusion and further degradation to fasteners, underlayment etc.

Missing/Damaged Shingle(s) Observed
Recommend a licensed roofer replace the shingle(s) as needed to prevent water intrusion and further degradation to nails, underlayment etc.

Missing/Loose Soffit at Roof Wedge
There was a missing/loose section of soffit observed from the roofs wedge, where the roof eave/soffit merges with the roof top of the structure. Exposed eaves can allow rodents to intrude, and as well, other things such as leaf debris when the structure resides under tree cover. Recommend a licensed roofing contractor repair the soffit with wedge flashing or other methodology to differ rodent intrusion as needed.

Soffit Section Observed Damaged at the Roof Eave
Recommend repairing the soffit to prevent the soffit loosening during a storm, causing further damage or allowing rodent intrusion into the building. Recommend a licensed contractor assess the area further and repair as needed.

Attic

Access Hatch Improper/Damaged Cover
This hatch cover was present but damaged prior to the inspection. Recommend installing an aluminum staircase to code or better to provide additional safety when accessing. All work is recommended to be completed per state and local codes by a licensed contractor.

No Attic Access, Could Not Inspect
No attic hatch was observed/present at the time of the inspection. One could not inspect the attic system. Recommend a licensed contractor install a hatch to provide needed access to the attic system, wiring and to routinely inspect the rafter system and insulate the attic system.

No Attic Access; Notable Sag Observed at the Main Ridge Beam to the Rafters
No attic access was observed at the time of the inspection, however, the exterior roof inspection revealed notable sag at the ridge beam. This may be caused by a number of possible conditions. These conditions may include: insufficient or no web bracing, cross bracing or vertical bracing. Additionally, other damages may be present within the attic such as termite damage or water induced damage. Recommend a state licensed structural engineer to review further and repair as needed.

Insufficient Insulation in Attic. Thermal Bridging Observed
Recommend applying additional insulation and/or replacing existing insulation to meet R-30 rating. Wood joists exposed intermittently throughout, meaning thermal bridging is present daily. Installing new insulation over all ceiling/wood members will reduce/eliminate this process, unfortunately common in many buildings.

Fractured Plank Board Decking Observed in the Attic System at the Time of the Inspection
Fractured boards can allow a worker accessing the roof or inspector to unknowingly damage the roof. If the boards are fractured enough that they can no longer withstand a live load of an individual or the individual is heavier than average, they can step on the board and send it right through the roof system. This can be a costly repair. It is always a good idea to reinforce fractured boards or replace them at the time of the roof replacement. When the roof is newer however, it is unlikely to be replaced anytime soon and thus, the repair can only be done from the inside of the attic, scabbing reinforcing wood members under the board. This repair is also risky so it is always recommended to leave it to the professionals. If there are protruding nails or if the wood support is nailed improperly, nails can pop through the shingle or be driven through accidently when reinforcing the area.

Suspected Live Drywood Termites Observed
Live drywood termite damage was suspected at and within the wood members. Drywood termites swarm in the evening and at night during the warmer months of the year. It is very hard to find where they are coming from because they live so deeply in the lumber. Drywood termite colonies are small colonies only about 3,000 termites. When the colony reaches about 3,000 termites then they will swarm to start a colony elsewhere. They

need very little moisture and are often found in the attic wood framing, wall studs, door casings and window frames. Drywood termites obtain moisture from the water produced by the digestion of cellulose, no matter how old the wood is. Spot treatments, such as orange oil applications, use insecticides applied to control known drywood termite colonies, such as those found in a door casing, windowsill or piece of furniture. Advantages to drywood alternative treatments are: The structure does not have to be unoccupied during treatment, just the immediate work area. There is a residual effect to the termiticide. If re-infestation occurs and the insects come in contact with the treated area, the transfer effect will start again and the colony will be eliminated. Most important, this method uses material much lower in mammalian toxicity.

Drywood Termite Damage Suspected at Ceiling Joists
Drywood Termite damage was suspected at and within the wood members. Drywood termites swarm in the evening and at night during the warmer months of the year. It is very hard to find where they are coming from because they live so deeply in the lumber. Drywood termite colonies are small colonies only about 3,000 termites. When the colony reaches about 3,000 termites, they will swarm to start a colony elsewhere. They need very little moisture and are often found in the attic wood framing, wall studs, door casings and window frames. Drywood termites obtain moisture from the water produced by the digestion of cellulose, no matter how old the wood is. Spot treatments, such as orange oil applications, use insecticides applied to control known drywood termite colonies, such as those found in a door casing, windowsill or piece of furniture. Advantages to drywood alternative treatments are: The structure does not have to be unoccupied during treatment, just the immediate work area. There is a residual effect to the termiticide. If re-infestation occurs and the insects come in contact with the treated area, the transfer effect will start again and the colony will be eliminated. Most important, this method uses material much lower in mammalian toxicity.

Access Hatch Improper/Missing Fasteners
Fasteners used to adhere the stairs and attic hatch jam to the ceiling were not correct for this opening type and could become structurally compromised when a person/Live Load is on the ladder. Recommend a licensed contractor assess and at minimum install lag screws/bolts per local codes and the FBC and/or as directed by the licensed contractor in accordance with the aforementioned code.

Access Hatch Improper Size/Location or Missing
There should be an access opening to all attic spaces that exceed 30 square feet and have a vertical height of 30 inches or more. The rough-framed opening should be at least 22 inches by 30 inches. It should be located in a hallway or other readily accessible location. An attic access that is located in a clothes closet is often inaccessible due to permanent shelving installed. There should be headroom that is a minimum of 30 inches above the attic access.

Access Hatch has Improper Framing
The hatch did not have any frame/cross braces at either side of the opening, between the ceiling joists. This is not correct for this opening type and could become structurally compromised when a person/Live Load attempts to enter the attic. Recommend a licensed contractor assess the area further and repair all per local codes and the FBC &/or as directed by the licensed contractor in accordance with the aforementioned code.

Thermal Bridging Observed Intermittent throughout the Attic
Insulation in between studs in a wall does not restrict the heat flow through those studs. This heat flow is called thermal bridging. The overall R-value of that wall may be different from the R-value of the insulation itself. It is recommended that the insulation installed in an attic, covers the tops of the attic floor joists. It is also recommended that insulation sheathing be installed on stud walls. Wood studs can transfer energy through the wall assembly. Metal studs can transfer energy much better than wood studs can. As a result, the metal wall's overall R-value can be as low as half of the insulation's R-value.

Attic Insufficiently Ventilated, Excess Heat Buildup Evident at Time of Inspection
Ventilation of attic areas is intended to prevent the accumulation of moisture vapor in the attic-roof space and to dry low levels of condensation that may form on the underside of a roof deck. Ventilation is also intended to reduce the temperature of the roof deck during hot periods to improve shingle durability. Reducing attic temperature through ventilation and insulation also improves energy efficiency during hot periods. In the case of ice dams, elevated attic and roof temperatures during the winter can cause snow on the roof to melt. Insulation and roof ventilation help to keep the roof's exterior surface cold and minimizes the development of melted water and, consequently, ice dams. Ventilating roofs in hot and humid conditions may add rather than remove moisture from attics and enclosed roof spaces. However, not ventilating a roof may void the manufacturer's warranty and slightly decrease the life expectancy of the asphalt shingles due to the increased temperature of

the roof surface. In colder climates, roof ventilation serves to remove humidity and condensation from the roof-attic space and helps to prevent the chronic formation of ice dams at eaves.

Displaced Radiant Heat Barriers Observed in the Attic
Radiant barriers are installed in buildings, primarily in attics. In recent years, more plywood sheathing has been observed incorporated with it and are now being installed on many buildings and businesses throughout the U.S. primarily to reduce summer heat gain and reduce cooling costs. The barriers consist of a highly reflective material that reflects radiant heat rather than absorbing it. They don't reduce heat conduction however, like thermal insulation materials do. Radiant Heat Barrier(s) were observed loose in the attic at the time of the inspection. Recommend having a licensed contractor re-adhere as needed.

Displaced Section of Insulation Observed in the Attic System
Recommend a licensed contractor install an R-30 equivalent value insulation or better at this location to prevent thermal bridging.

Attic Insulation Mold Suspected; Beginning Accumulative Evidence found in Various Locations
Batts Obstruct Proper Air Flow/Ventilation To The Attic. Additionally, there were only natural venting hoods/opening close to the ridge. This allows hot, humid air to build within the attic and can trap. Without proper eave venting, ridge venting becomes less relevant. To remediate, it is recommended to ensure all eave vents are unobstructed. For best results, installing a solar, automatic vent fan in addition or in lieu of the present vents is recommended. Recommend treating or removing all effected insulation batts within the attic.

Leak Observed at Valley Flashing
Recommend a licensed roofer repair all as needed. If installing asphalt shingles, recommend installing the shingles at the valley with a no-cut valley or "woven" valley technique. This eliminates the seam and thus, virtually eliminates any future leaks at the valleys.

Popcorn Textured Ceiling Texture/Tape Peeling
Removing a textured popcorn ceiling isn't that difficult, if you know how to go about it, but it can be very messy. If the texture was applied before 1978, have it tested for asbestos first. If the texture doesn't contain asbestos, you can proceed with removal. Popcorn applied before 1978 MUST BE TESTED for asbestos and other chemicals common to the product in the 60's/70's. You do **NOT** want those fibers floating around the room to be ingested. If its asbestos based, you should have a professional come in to take care of it. Some municipalities have codes against you doing it yourself, for obvious safety reasons. The reason why the application can peel and crack is that it is susceptible to moisture elevations in the air, in fact, to remove it you only have to use a water sprayer to moisten a 5x5 foot box shape at a time. The compound absorbs a lot of water and a smooth edged scraper will slide through the "oatmeal" easily without leaving the Sheetrock very wet behind it, typically. Over the course of decades, this can wreak havoc on the aesthetic look of a garage ceiling because the garage is not usually conditioned, allowing an abundance of water induced air to pass thru the material all the time and eventually, delaminating the defective style product, causing loose or hanging tape at the joints and peeling of the material. It is highly recommended to have this material first tested, then removed by a licensed professional.

Attic Insufficiently Insulation/Ventilated at Time of Inspection
Ventilation of attic areas is intended to prevent the accumulation of moisture vapor in the attic-roof space and to dry low levels of condensation that may form on the underside of a roof deck. Ventilation is also intended to reduce the temperature of the roof deck during hot periods to improve shingle durability. Reducing attic temperature through ventilation and insulation also improves energy efficiency during hot periods. In the case of ice dams, elevated attic and roof temperatures during the winter can cause snow on the roof to melt. Insulation and roof ventilation help to keep the roof's exterior surface cold and minimizes the development of melted water and, consequently, ice dams. Ventilating roofs in hot and humid conditions may add rather than remove moisture from attics and enclosed roof spaces. However, not ventilating a roof may void the manufacturer's warranty and slightly decrease the life expectancy of the asphalt shingles due to the increased temperature of the roof surface. In colder climates, roof ventilation serves to remove humidity and condensation from the roof-attic space and helps to prevent the chronic formation of ice dams at eaves.

Blown-In, Loose-Fill
The type of insulation used, its R-value, and the thickness needed are all directly related to the nature and location of the spaces in the house that are insulated. Different forms of insulation can be used together. For example, you may find batt or roll insulation over loose-fill insulation. Blown-in, loose-fill insulation may be made of cellulose, fiberglass, rock wool or fiber pellets. The insulation can be blown in using a pump and hose system. This type of insulation can be blown into wall cavities. You may often see it blown onto the attic floor as is the case with your attic.

Blankets
The type of insulation used, its R-value, and the thickness needed are all directly related to the nature and location of the spaces in the house that are insulated. Different forms of insulation can be used together. For example, you may find batt or roll insulation over loose-fill insulation. Blankets come in the form of batts and rolls. They are flexible. They are made from mineral fibers, including fiberglass and rock wool. They are available in different widths and lengths. They are made in standard sizes (widths) for inserting in between studs and floor joists. They are available with or without vapor-retarder faces (paper face). A batt insulation, when installed in the ceiling or a basement with the insulation exposed, may have a flame-resistant face.

Cellulose
The type of insulation used, its R-value, and the thickness needed are all directly related to the nature and location of the spaces in the house that are insulated. Different forms of insulation can be used together. For example, you may find batt or roll insulation over loose-fill insulation. Blown-in, loose-fill insulation may be made of cellulose, fiberglass, rock wool or fiber pellets. The insulation can be blown in using a pump and hose system. This type of insulation can be blown into wall cavities. You may often see it blown onto the attic floor as is the case with your attic.

Foam Insulation
The type of insulation used, its R-value, and the thickness needed are all directly related to the nature and location of the spaces in the house that are insulated. Different forms of insulation can be used together. For example, you may find batt or roll insulation over loose-fill insulation. Foam insulation can be installed by a professional using special equipment that meters, mixes and sprays the foam insulation. Polyicynene is an open-cell foam. Polyisocyanurate and polyurethane are closed-cell foams. In general, open-cell foams allow water to move through the wall more easily than closed-cell foams. Some of the closed-cell foams are, therefore, able to provide a better R-value where the space is limited.

Roof Flashing

Ridge Vent End Caps Missing
The end cap will just snap in place with a little pressure. They are of a pliable rubber like compound so the fit will hold once you press it in. You need end caps on the ridge or else wasps, small bugs and animals will find their way in if it is left open as well as potential wind driven rain during high wind storms.

Ridge Vent Missing/Damaged
It is vital to have a serviceable ridge vent undamaged, to provide proper heat ventilation and water resistance for the roof system. It is highly recommended to have this area repaired as soon as possible.

Screws Oxidizing on Ridge Vent Cap
The seals are a constant preemptive maintenance requirement for this ridge vent type over the life of the roof, requiring silicone caulking every 7 years depending on the product used. It would be prudent to apply a silicone based or better patch/caulk to all screw heads and screws/nails circumferential area. Recommend a licensed roofing contractor apply to manufacturer's instructions.

Ridge Vent(s) Fasteners Observed Loose with Insufficient Sealants
Sealants on the ridge vent fasteners appeared compromised/antiquated. Additionally, various fasteners were observed loose. During a high wind storm, the vent could uplift and damage if not adequately fastened, allowing water to enter the home. Recommend a licensed roofing contractor assess the area further and repair as is needed.

Weather Hood Observed Heavily Corroded with Rust Oxidation
Recommend a licensed roofing contractor assess further, treat if able or replace if needed.

Service Mast Flashing Not Installed
Service mast flashing was not present at the time of the inspection. Without a proper seal and flashing, water can enter the attic and wall system at the circumferential perimeter of the mast pipe. Water can contact the roof sheathing, rotting wood and further widening the gap at the mast. Additionally, water tends to stream down the pipe at the circumferential area, contacting other substrates and insulation in the attic and eventually causing potential fungus and mold growths. It is recommended to have a state licensed roofing contractor review further and repair/replace as needed all deficiencies per state and local codes.

Kick out Flashing Not Observed
Kick out flashing, also known as diverter flashing, is a type of flashing that diverts rainwater away from the cladding abutment and into a gutter or away from the cladding. When installed correctly, it provides excellent protection against the penetration of moisture/water into the building envelope. The needs for kick out flashing at wall/roof eave transitions are an imperative. With increased amounts of insulation and building wraps that are used in modern construction, it is making buildings less breathable and more likely to sustain water damage.

Kick out flashing prevents rainwater from being absorbed into the wall and is more essential than ever. Recommend a licensed contractor assess the area further and properly install kick out flashing in order to divert rainwater away from the cladding.

Plumbing

Copper Plumbing
Since the Safe Drinking Water Act Amendments of 1986 the use of lead-containing solders in potable water systems has effectively been banned nationwide. The major impact of the Act has been on solder containing 50% tin and 50% lead (50-50), until then the most widely used solder for drinking water systems. Lead-base solders have been replaced by tin-antimony and tin-silver solders. The main differences between these solders and 50-50 are that they are stronger and require somewhat higher working temperatures. Many plumbers in the United States have used them in copper plumbing systems for decades. Copper is also antifungal. One major advantage of the tin-antimony and tin-silver solders is that joints made with them are considerably stronger than joints made with 50-50 tin-lead. This superiority is the main reason that tin-antimony and tin-silver solders have long been specified for high-rise installations, for high-temperature service, for commercial refrigeration and air conditioning hook-ups and for soldered copper fire sprinkler systems. Because soldered joints made with tin-antimony and tin-silver are stronger, plumbing systems installed using them can withstand higher pressures and temperatures than systems made with 50-50 tin-lead solder.

Pipe Type CPVC
CPVC (CHLORINATED POLY VINYL CHLORIDE) can withstand corrosive water at temperatures greater than PVC, typically 40°C to 50°C (104°F to 122°F) or higher, contributing to its popularity as a material for water piping systems in residential as well as commercial construction. The principal mechanical difference between CPVC and PVC is that CPVC is significantly more ductile, allowing greater flexure and crush resistance. Additionally, the mechanical strength of CPVC makes it a viable candidate to replace many types of metal pipe in conditions where metal's susceptibility to corrosion limits its use. CPVC is similar to PVC in resistance to fire. It is typically very difficult to ignite and tends to self-extinguish when not in a directly applied flame. Due to its chlorine content, the incineration of CPVC, either in a fire or in an industrial disposal process, can result in the creation of dioxins. Alternatively, however, though petro-chem leeching is known to happen in the potable CPVC water systems, metal oxidative properties/bi products such as rust are dramatically reduced and/or eliminated provided no galvanized junctions are present.

HDPE
High Density Polyethylene (HDPE) is a versatile plastic that has many practical uses, not the least of which is for the fabrication of pipe. English chemists Reginald Gibson and Eric Fawcett created a solid form of polyethylene in 1935. This discovery was first used commercially was an insulating material for radar cables during World War II. In 1953, Karl Ziegler of the Kaiser Wilhelm institute invented high density polyethylene. In 1955 HDPE was first used as a pipe. For his invention of HDPE, Ziegler won the Nobel Prize for Chemistry in 1963. The number one characteristic that sets HDPE apart from other pipe types is that it can be made to be flexible. This quality opens HDPE pipe up to a different world of applications than rigid pipe. Another quality of HDPE is that it can melted and re-solidified a limitless number of times without losing any of its favorable qualities. For this reason, most HDPE pressure pipe is made to be 'butt welded'. This is where the ends of two

sections of pipe are melted and then pushed and held together, forming a single pipe. There is an HDPE product that can be applied to just about any situation. There are a few things that should be noted, though. Because most HDPE is a flexible product, it is not commonly used in sanitary sewer gravity installations. This is because the flexible properties of the pipe can cause dips in the gravity runs. There are several manufacturers that produce a corrugated rigid pipe product that is primarily used for storm drainage. Like PVC, HDPE pipe can be color coated to match installation requirements. Typically for pressure installations, HDPE is black with a color coated stripe. Below you will find a list of common colors and uses: Water Distribution – Blue, Fire Main – Red, Sewer – Green, Gas – Yellow, and Reclaimed Water – Purple.

Galvanized Pipe
When a pipe has been galvanized, it means that the steel or iron has been coated with zinc. Galvanized pipes are silver when they are new, and will dull to gray as they age. This coating is to resist oxidation and any potential rusting of the pipe. However, galvanized pipe will corrode in time. If you have galvanized pipe installed, it will be in working condition for about 40-60 years before joints have been known to rust out or water flow may become severely reduced, allowing more pressure to build in areas. The reason for the limited usage is that the corrosion, which will eventually fill the entire pipe and will restrict the water flow in the pipe. One problem with this type of pipe is that the corrosion can be more rapid whenever a steel galvanized pipe meets any brass or copper. This often happens when the valves are made of brass. One way to combat this effect is to use dielectric unions between copper and steel pipes. However, some of these can close off the flow. The problem occurring is that it can break the grounding if a live wire and a pipe come into contact with each other. Corrosion in galvanized pipes can usually not be cleaned out without causing water leaks.

Cross-Linked Polyethylene (PEX/XLPE)
Cross-linked polyethylene is commonly abbreviated **PEX** or **XLPE**. Almost all PEX used for pipe and tubing is made from high density polyethylene (HDPE). PEX contains cross-linked bonds in the polymer structure, changing the thermoplastic to a thermoset. Cross-linking is accomplished during or after the extrusion of the tubing. Crosslinking improves the elevated-temperature properties of the base polymer. Adequate strength to 120–150 C is maintained by reducing creep, the tendency to flow. Chemical resistance is enhanced by resisting dissolution. Low temperature properties are improved. Impact and tensile strength, scratch resistance, and resistance to brittle fracture are enhanced. PEX tubing is widely used to replace copper in plumbing applications. One estimate is that residential use of PEX for delivering drinking water to faucets has increased by 40% annually, and there is substantial evidence that PEX is or will soon become the dominant technology for carrying water in buildings and businesses in the next decade or so. It is widely accepted among different groups, and has been used by volunteer organizations such as Habitat for Humanity in constructing buildings. In 2006, The Philadelphia Inquirer recommended that plumbing installers switch from copper pipes to PEX. PEX has become a contender for use in residential water plumbing because of its flexibility. It can bend into a wide-radius turn if space permits, or accommodate turns by using elbow joints. In addition, it can handle short-radius turns, sometimes supported with a metal brace; in contrast, PVC, CPVC and copper all require elbow joints. A single length of PEX pipe cannot handle a sharp 90-degree turn, however, so in those situations, it is necessary to connect two PEX pipes with a 90-degree PEX elbow joint. Also, since PEX pipes typically have fewer sharp turns, there is greater water pressure at the sinks and showers and toilets where it is needed.

Stainless Steel
Stainless Steel is an iron based alloy that contains at least 11.5% chromium. Other elements, such as nickel, are also added to modify the properties of the metal. Stainless steel is able to withstand high temperatures. It is also highly resistant to corrosion. Stainless steel pipe and tubing are used for many reasons. They resist corrosion and oxidation. They resist high temperatures. The most common type of stainless used is Type 304. It is used in piping and tubing in chemical plants, refineries, food processing and paper plants.

Ductile Iron
The United States first used CIP in 1817 when Philadelphia utilized it in the installation of a new water system. According to the Ductile Iron Pipe Research Association (DIPRA), today there are more than 600 utilities that have had CIP mains in service for more than 100 years. There are also at least 21 utilities with CIP mains in service for more than 150 years. Ductile Iron Pipe (DIP) emerged on the scene in 1953. DIP is superior to CIP because of an improved manufacturing process. Magnesium is introduced in the smelting process and this changes the form of the graphite particles in the iron. The result is a pipe that is lighter, stronger, more corrosion resistant and more able to machine than CIP. This results in a more cost effective product than CIP too. Because DIP is an iron product, it can have the same corrosion problems prone to all iron products, especially when installed in corrosive environments. DIP is commonly coated in the inside with a cement-mortar lining. This lining enables it to handle the rigors of transporting potable water, sea water, non-septic gravity sewers,

sewer force mains and reclaimed water. DIP is also available with various epoxy liners. This is commonly used for septic sewer and other caustic environments.

Polypropylene

Polypropylene is a type of thermoplastic polymer resin. It is a part of both the average households and is in commercial and industrial applications. The chemical designation is C3H6. One of the benefits of using this type of plastic is that it can be useful in numerous applications including as a structural plastic or as a fiber-type plastic. The history of polypropylene began in 1954 when a German chemist named Karl Rehn and an Italian chemist named Giulio Natta first polymerized it. This led to a large commercial production of the product that began just three years later. Natta synthesized the first syndiotactic polypropylene.

Polyvinyl Chloride (PVC)

Rigid plastic PVC (polyvinyl chloride) and ABS (acrylonitrile butadiene styrene) are the most popular types of plastic plumbing pipe. PVC is usually white or cream colored and ABS is black. Both are typically used only for vents and drains and aren't made to fit directly together. Plastic pipe joints are connected with glue that actually melts the pieces together. The joints for both PVC and ABS are glued the same way, but the types aren't interchangeable and only a special fitting can connect them together. Roughly half of the world's polyvinyl chloride resin manufactured annually is used for producing pipes for various municipal and industrial applications. In the water distribution market it accounts for 66 percent of the market in the US. In sanitary sewer pipe applications, it accounts for 75 percent. Its light weight, high strength, and low reactivity make it particularly well-suited for this purpose. In addition, PVC pipes can be fused together using various solvent cements, or heat-fused (butt-fusion process, similar to joining HDPE pipe), creating permanent joints that are virtually impervious to leakage.

Polybutylene

Polybutylene is a plastic resin that was used for water pipe manufactured in the U.S. from 1978 to 1995. The polybutylene pipe was promoted as the pipe of the future because of its low cost and ease of installation. During the years it was produced, it replaced traditional copper piping for both exterior and interior plumbing use. Industry experts claim the poly piping was installed in approximately six to 10 million new or remodeled buildings and homes or about one in every four during its 17-year reign. Shell Chemical Company was the primary manufacturer of the poly pipe, along with Quest and Vanguard. The fittings were manufactured by Celanese and DuPont. A typical 2,000 square foot residence cost $1,000 to $1,500 less to build with polybutylene than with copper piping so the cost savings was significant. Polybutylene manufacturers initially claimed that their plumbing system would last a lifetime. Not only did it not last a lifetime, it barely lasted a decade and caused extensive property damage when it finally corroded and leaked. On average, poly pipes take between 10-15 years to show signs of severe deterioration. When it fails, it does so without warning. Because of the high damage costs when polybutylene fails, insurance companies have sometimes canceled or refused building policies because of it. The known presence of poly piping can also affect a building's value on the real estate market. It is recommended to preempt the inevitable and prevent a potential, much larger expenditure should a leak occur and have the building re-piped per FPC guidelines.

Main Service Pipe

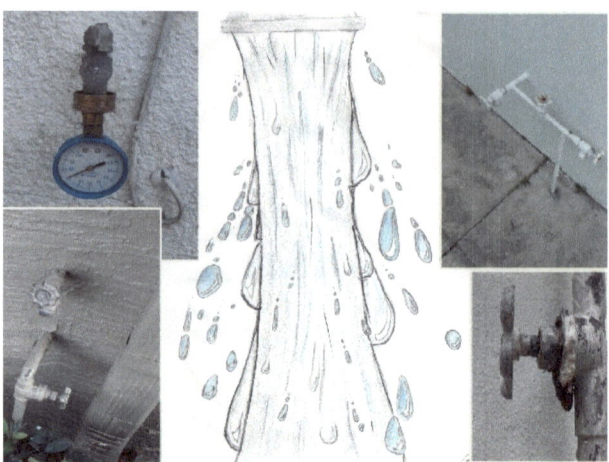

Pressure and Basic Comments
The system was tested for serviceable pressure and signs of leaks. A heat test was performed to test the efficiency of the heating elements in the water heater and the thermostats regulatory function over the heating elements temperature. All tested fixtures and valves were found to be serviceable aside of any deficiencies noted. Overall assessment of the system aside of any aforementioned deficiencies, was good/serviceable condition at the time of the inspection.

High/Elevated Pressure Observed when Tested
High pressures observed may harm weakened fitting, joints and some appliances that are made to attach to the plumbing system. It is recommended to have a pressure relief valve (PRV) installed at the exterior and an expansion tank at the water heater to reduce any potential city back pressure from damaging plumbing system components in the future.

Handle and Stem Turn But Do Not Engage the Closed Position. Gate Valve Needs Replacing
Stem at the main valve appears to be worn and not engaging. This is a gate valve. Gate valves are known to degrade in time predictably and are recommended to be replaced whenever possible. Since repair is needed, it is recommended to replace with a ball valve. Recommend replacing in case of an emergency prior to performing any plumbing work or work in close relation to plumbing.

Low Pressure when Faucet is Actuated; Suspect Aerator is Obstructed
When a faucet has a weak, spitting or intermittent flow, the problem is often with the aerator. Aerators contain a fine wire screen that mixes water with air to provide an even flow. Over time the screen can become clogged by mineral debris deposits lodged above the screen that are too big to pass through or with mineral on the screen(s), reducing the amount of water coming through. To solve the problem of fouling or buildup, a plumber will unscrew the aerator from the end of the faucet and replace it, however, it can be soaked overnight in a cup of white vinegar instead. The acid in the vinegar will dissolve any deposits and make the aerator as good as new.

Erratic/Spitting of Water at the Faucet, Suspect Aerator Obstructed
When a faucet has a weak flow, spitting/jets of water shooting off in an erratic array or intermittent flow, the problem is often with the aerator. Aerators are a mesh of fine wire screen that mixes water with air to provide an even flow. It is found at the tip of the faucet. Over time the screen can become clogged by mineral debris deposits lodged above the screen that are too big to pass through or with minerals on the screen(s), reducing the amount of water coming through. To solve the problem of fouling or buildup, a plumber will unscrew the aerator from the end of the faucet and replace it; however, it can be soaked overnight in a cup of white vinegar instead. The acid in the vinegar will dissolve any deposits and make the aerator as good as new.

Main PVC Valve Shut-Off Handle was Observed Damaged
The main service valves handle was damaged. Recommend replacing the valve to be able to terminate the flow of water in the event there is a leak within the structure in the future.

Missing/Damaged Gate Valve Handle at the Main Shut-Off
Missing/Damaged Handle Gate valves are known to degrade in time predictably and are recommended to be replaced whenever possible. Since repair is needed, it is recommended to replace the gate valve with a ball valve type. Minimally, replacing the handle should suffice if the handle can then be turned. If the valve cannot be actuated, then the valve is seized and needs replacement. Recommend a licensed plumbing contractor to replace the handle in case of an emergency prior to performing any plumbing work or work in close relation to plumbing.

No Main Shut Off Valve Observed
A shut off valve at the main cold feed to the building for new installations is generally required by most local and state codes throughout the US and for insurance companies. The shut off is required for emergency access in case of a very fast gushing leak or a small drip, the building owner can access the immediate area if there is a working shut off for the main line. Recommend a licensed plumbing contractor repair as needed and required by local codes.

Waste Pipe Observed Buried At/Near the Potable Water Pipe Less than 10 Feet
The International Plumbing Code Generally Goes As Follows: "Water service and building drain or building sewer may be installed in separate trenches with a minimum of 10 feet horizontal separation. Material listed in Appendix A. Table-A (Approved Materials for Building Sewer and Approved Materials for Water Service Pipe) shall be used, provided that the material is specific for this type of installation (See Appendix I. Illustration E.). The water service and the building drain or building sewer may be installed in the same trench provided that the water service is placed on a solid shelf a minimum of 18 inches above the building drain or building sewer. The building sewer shall be of material listed in Appendix A. Table-A (Approved Building Drainage/Vent Pipe) for a building drain (See Appendix I. Illustration F for the proper installation of water service, building drain and building sewer.)."

Unknown Plumbing Connection Leading from/to the Main Potable Water System Pipe
The International Plumbing Code Generally Goes As Follows: "There shall be no physical connection between an active potable water supply and an unapproved water supply, or any reclaimed water, wastewater or storm water system, which would allow unsafe water to enter or backflow into the active potable water system by direct pressure, vacuum, gravity or any other means. All potable water services shall be in compliance with all applicable cross connection control regulations. All brass in contact with potable water shall be "Lead Free"." Recommend a licensed plumber repair all as needed.

Leak at Main Shut off Valve Stem
When the valve is actuated to close or open, it spits at the stem. This is a gate valve. Gate valves are known to degrade in time predictably and are recommended to be replaced whenever possible. Since repair is needed, it is recommended to replace the gate valve with a ball valve. Recommend replacing in case of an emergency prior to performing any plumbing work or work in close relation to plumbing.

Water Service Pipe Observed Buried Too Shallow then allowed by Most Locale Code Requirements
The International Plumbing Code Generally Goes As Follows: "The minimum depth for any water service pipe shall be at least 36 inches or the maximum frost penetration of the local area, whichever is of greater depth." Recommend a licensed plumbing contractor to assess further and repair if needed.

Water Service Pipe Observed Installed Above Grade at the Exterior
In States where climates are considered to sustain freezing temperatures and where the locale adhered to strict code as stated by the international plumbing code, the International Plumbing Code generally goes as follows: "No water service pipe shall be installed or permitted outside of a building or in an exterior wall unless the pipe is protected from freezing, in accordance with Section 890.1210(a). For areas that do not adhere strictly to this code and/or do not generally see frost, it is still prudent to have the above grade pipes insulated in such a way that can protect the pipe from both the temperatures as well as the elements.

Suspected Asbestos Insulation Lining Pipes
As per the Florida Department of Environmental Protection: "Often, questions arise concerning compliance with the asbestos regulations. The Asbestos Letters, Determinations and Clarifications web page provides information to assist in answering these compliance questions. The Asbestos Letters, Determinations and Clarifications page contains memoranda issued by the State's Department of Environmental Protection or its agents and the US Environmental Protection Agency on applicability and compliance issues associated with the Asbestos National Emissions Standard for Hazardous Air Pollutant (NESHAP, 40 CFR Part 61, Subpart M)." Recommend contacting a local Asbestos Remediation Company to mitigate the removal of this material ASAP.

Leak at Gate Valve/Joint
Valve/joint appears to be leaking. This is a gate valve. Gate valves are known to degrade in time predictably and are recommended to be replaced whenever possible. Recommend replacing in case of an emergency prior to performing any plumbing work or work in close relation to plumbing.

Galvanized Pipe Rusting at Threaded Joints
Note: The galvanized pipe shows signs of rust at the joints throughout the observed plumbing system. This is a clear sign of potential leaks occurring in the near future. Due to the rapid introduction of mold and other fungi when leaks occur, it is highly recommended that the pipe be replaced with a more durable pipe such as CPVC, PEX and/or copper pipe.

Lime Scale or Calcium Carbonate Fouling Observed
Even in hard water areas, pipes will not scale unless the saturation index of the water is exceeded. If the water is under-saturated or at equilibrium saturation, there will be no scale. Conversely, "soft water" can scale if it becomes over saturated. The saturation index of water is controlled by its acidity (or alkalinity which is the reverse) which we establish by pH measurement. The lower the pH, the more acidic the water is and the more it can hold in solution. The higher the pH, the less acid the water, the lower the saturation index, and the less the water can hold dissolved minerals. We raise the pH by heating the water, causing pressure drops (e.g. taps) and adding chemicals. By raising the pH, we are reducing the ability of the water to hold minerals in solution and these minerals are forced to precipitate and cause scale fouling. Recirculating systems (e.g. cooling towers, steam generators, water recovery systems) operate at cycles of concentration with pressure drops and temperature variances causing both super saturation and pH increases simultaneously.

Lime Scale or Calcium Carbonate Fouling on Valves/Joints
Even in hard water areas, pipes will not scale unless the saturation index of the water is exceeded. If the water is under-saturated or at equilibrium saturation, there will be no scale. Conversely, "soft water" can scale if it becomes over saturated. The saturation index of water is controlled by its acidity (or alkalinity which is the reverse) which we establish by pH measurement. The lower the pH, the more acidic the water is and the more it can hold in a solution. The higher the pH, the less acidic the water, the lower the saturation index, and the less the water can hold dissolved minerals. We raise the pH by heating the water, causing pressure drops (e.g. taps) and adding chemicals. By raising the pH, we are reducing the ability of the water to hold minerals in solution and these minerals are forced to precipitate and cause scale fouling. Recirculating systems (e.g. cooling towers, steam generators, water recovery systems) operate at cycles of concentration with pressure drops and temperature variances causing both super saturation and pH increases simultaneously. Unfortunately, unless installing a mineral filtration system, there is little to resolve the cause of internal scaling, however, the scaling/build up on the valves are likely caused by minute orifices at the threading of the joints and is caused by minute amounts of water surfacing, crystallizing/scaling upon breaching the surface. For threaded plumbing fittings, using Teflon tape or plumbers paste around joint threading will typically remedy the issue. For soldered joints, re-sweating of the joint will be needed.

PR or Pressure Relief Valve Leaks. Pressure Serviceable
PR or Pressure Relief Valve above the main shut off is good to have, however, yours has a constant drip. The buildings pressure appeared optimal. Recommend repairing the leak and replacing the PR valve if needed but make sure to install either an equal or better replacement. It will help relieve pressure that exceed tolerable levels for some pressure joints and faucets within the plumbing systems that can lead to hose line ruptures, pipe leaks etc. To mitigate this loss, have a licensed plumbing contractor replace/repair the PR Valve and inspect it routinely.

High PSI. PR or Pressure Relief Valve Recommended

PR or Pressure Relief Valve above the main shut off is good to have in addition to the TPR valve and expansion tank. The buildings pressure appeared elevated at the time of the inspection. Recommend a licensed plumbing contractor install a PR valve to help relieve pressure that may exceed tolerable levels for some pressure joints and faucets in plumbing systems with lower pressure tolerances or wear, that can lead to hose line ruptures, pipe leaks etc. To mitigate this loss, routinely inspect the systems readily observable plumbing exposures at bathrooms, kitchens, water heaters etc.

Low Pressure Observed. Suspect Galvanized Pipe Oxidation is Constricting

Galvanized steel and brass pipes may fail, typically between the 50-75 years range. Galvanized steel can build a lot of corrosion on the interior. The more internal corrosion/rust, the more restricting the flow throughout the building will be. It is mainly for that reason it often gets replaced before it springs a leak. However, if the pipe is not replaced, the galvanized pipe can oxidize and corrode internally, causing leaks from the inside out. The low pressure can be much greater in the hot water service pipe because the hotter the water, the faster it causes the oxidation process as it depletes the zinc galvanized coating on the interior of the pipe. The water treatments can also progress the process. It is highly recommended to have a licensed plumber review the system in full and replace all galvanized pipe.

Distribution Pipe

Pressure and Basic Comments
The system was tested for serviceable pressure and signs of leaks. A heat test was performed to test the efficiency of the heating elements in the water heater and the thermostats regulatory function over the heating elements temperature. All tested fixtures and valves were found to be serviceable aside of any deficiencies noted. Overall assessment of the system was good/serviceable condition at time of the inspection.

Distribution Service Pipe Observed Installed Above Grade at the Exterior
In States where climates are considered to sustain freezing temperatures and where the locale adhere to strict code as stated by the international plumbing code, the International Plumbing Code generally goes as follows: "No water service pipe shall be installed or permitted outside of a building or in an exterior wall unless the pipe is protected from freezing, in accordance with Section 890.1210(a). For areas that do not adhere strictly to this code and/or do not generally see frost, it is still prudent to have the above grade pipes insulated in such a way that can protect the pipe from both the temperatures as well as the elements.

Water Service Pipe Observed Buried Too Shallow then Allowed by Most Locale Code Requirements
In States where climates are considered to sustain freezing temperatures and where the locale adhere to strict code as stated by the international plumbing code, the International Plumbing Code generally goes as follows: "The minimum depth for any water service pipe shall be at least 36 inches or the maximum frost penetration of the local area, whichever is of greater depth."

Dishwasher Not/Improperly Mounted at Top Front
Recommend a state licensed contractor fasten as needed per state and local codes.

Improper Installation of Tub/Shower Valve
Tub/Shower valve was observed to be installed improperly when tested. Unit does not properly/fully actuate hot and cold as designed. This unfortunately, is a common problem as more often handy men are hired to repair and update plumbing systems and not experienced plumbers. Recommend a licensed plumber repair all as needed.

Shut-Off Gate Valve under the Sink was Observed Leaking at the Stem
Shut off gate valve appears to be leaking at the stem. Additionally, when the valve is actuated to close or open, it can spit/spray at the stem. This is a gate valve. Gate valves are known to degrade in time predictably and are recommended to be replaced whenever possible. Since repair is needed, it is recommended to replace the gate valve with a ball valve. Recommend replacing in case of an emergency prior to performing any plumbing work or work in close relation to plumbing.

Missing/Damaged Gate Valve Handle at the Sink Shut-Off Valve
Missing/Damaged handle observed. Gate valves are known to degrade in time predictably and are recommended to be replaced whenever possible. Since repair is needed, it is recommended to replace the gate valve with a ball valve. Recommend a licensed plumber replace the handle/valve in case of an emergency prior to performing any plumbing work or work in close relation to plumbing.

Loose Piping Observed
Loose piping can jostle suddenly upon termination of water at a faucet caused by pressure. When the pipe is not sufficiently fastened, the sudden pressure jolts will cause "knocking". This knocking will cause potential leaks over time. Additionally, loose pipes can be accidently damaged by live load or other articles coming into contact with them. Recommend re-piping or fastening the loose pipe in accordance with the IPC and/or your local state code requirements.

Jacuzzi Tub Access Panel is Grouted Shut
In accordance with NEC (National Electric Code) all motors and electrical equipment pertaining to the tub need to be "Readily Accessible". Because many potential faults can occur, immediate access to the power and other equipment is needed. The code is as follows: NEC DEFINITIONS; Readily Accessible Capable of being reached quickly for operation, renewal or inspection without requiring those concerned to use a tool, to climb over, remove obstacles or other. Accessible (as applied to wiring methods). Capable of being removed or exposed without damaging the building structure or finish or not permanently closed in by the structure or finish of the building. Accessible (as applied to equipment) admitting close approach; not guarded by locked doors, elevation, or other effective means. NEC 110.3(B) All electrical equipment shall be installed and used in accordance with the listing requirements and manufacturer's instructions. 680.73 Accessibility. Electrical equipment for hydro massage bathtubs must be capable of being removed or exposed without damaging the building structure or finish. Where the hydro massage bathtub is cord-and plug-connected with the supply receptacle accessible only through an access opening, the receptacle must face toward the opening and be within 1 ft. of the opening. Article 430.14(A) states that, "motors shall be located so that adequate ventilation is provided and so that maintenance can be readily accomplished." 314.29 Boxes, Conduit Bodies, and Handhole Enclosures to Be Accessible. Boxes, conduit bodies, and handhole enclosures shall be installed so that the wiring contained in them can be rendered accessible without removing any part of the building NEC 400.8 Uses Not Permitted Flexible cords and cables shall not be used for the following: (5) Where concealed by walls, floors, ceilings or located above suspended or dropped ceilings 430.102 Disconnect Means Location (B) Motor Disconnect. A disconnecting means must be located in sight from the motor location and the driven machinery location. 430.107 Readily Accessible. The disconnecting means shall be readily accessible.

Jacuzzi Tub Access Panel was Not Observed
In accordance with NEC (National Electric Code) all motors and electrical equipment pertaining to the tub need to be "Readily Accessible". Because many potential faults can occur, immediate access to the power and other equipment is needed. The code is as follows: NEC DEFINITIONS; Readily Accessible Capable of being reached quickly for operation, renewal or inspection without requiring those concerned to use a tool, to climb over, remove obstacles or other. Accessible (as applied to wiring methods). Capable of being removed or exposed without damaging the building structure or finish or not permanently closed in by the structure or finish of the building. Accessible (as applied to equipment) admitting close approach; not guarded by locked doors, elevation, or other effective means. NEC 110.3(B) All electrical equipment shall be installed and used in accordance with the listing requirements and manufacturer's instructions. 680.73 Accessibility. Electrical equipment for hydro massage bathtubs must be capable of being removed or exposed without damaging the building structure or finish. Where the hydro massage bathtub is cord-and plug-connected with the supply receptacle accessible only through an access opening, the receptacle must face toward the opening and be within 1 ft. of the opening. Article 430.14(A) states that, "motors shall be located so that adequate ventilation is provided and so that maintenance can be readily accomplished." 314.29 Boxes, Conduit Bodies, and Handhole Enclosures to Be Accessible. Boxes, conduit bodies, and handhole enclosures shall be installed so that the wiring contained in them can be rendered accessible without removing any part of the building NEC 400.8 Uses Not Permitted Flexible cords and cables shall not be used for the following: (5) Where concealed by walls, floors, or ceilings or located above suspended or dropped ceilings 430.102 Disconnect Means Location (B) Motor Disconnect. A disconnecting means must be located in sight from the motor location and the driven machinery location. 430.107 Readily Accessible. The disconnecting means shall be readily accessible.

Suspected Asbestos Insulation Lining Pipes
As per the Florida Department of Environmental Protection: "Often, questions arise concerning compliance with the asbestos regulations. The Asbestos Letters, Determinations and Clarifications web page provides

information to assist in answering these compliance questions. The Asbestos Letters, Determinations and Clarifications page contains memoranda issued by the State's Department of Environmental Protection or its agents and the US Environmental Protection Agency on applicability and compliance issues associated with the Asbestos National Emissions Standard for Hazardous Air Pollutant (NESHAP, 40 CFR Part 61, Subpart M)." Recommend contacting a local Asbestos Remediation Company to Mitigate the Removal of this Material ASAP.

Bathroom Sink Drain Plunger(s) Missing
When engaging the trip lever, the plunger is not present and thus, the drain stopper mechanism is inoperable. It is recommended that the plunger/lever be repaired/replaced.

PR or Pressure Relief Valve Leaks
PR or Pressure Relief Valve above the main shut off is good to have, however, yours has a constant drip that appears to be coming from the threading. The buildings pressure was optimal, exactly 60 pounds per square inches of pressure. Recommend a licensed plumbing contractor repairing the leak and replacing the PR valve if needed. It will help relieve pressure that exceed tolerable levels in some pressure joints and faucets in plumbing systems that can lead to hose line ruptures, pipe leaks etc. To mitigate this loss, replace/repair the PR Valve and inspect it routinely.

Recommend Installing a Temperature Relief Valve
The name is Temperature Pressure Relief Valve (TPR valve). This safety valve releases water (and thus relieves pressure) if either the temperature or pressure in the system/water heater tank gets too high. These valves are very important for places such as on water heaters as they can become bombs if the pressure gets too high and these valves fail to work.

Recommend Installing a Thermostatic Mixing Valve
Series MMV Thermostatic Mixing Valves maintain and limit mixed hot water to a desired, selectable temperature. The MMV series can be set to any temperature between 80°F and 120°F (27°C and 49°C) with flow rates as low as 0.5 gpm and as high as 12 gpm. This mixing valve series is listed under ASSE 1017 for hot water source applications, ASSE 1069 for end use fixture fittings and ASSE 1070 for single or multiple fixture applications. The MMV series uses a double throttling design to control both the hot and cold water supply to the mixed outlet. The superior flow characteristics of this valve provides accurate temperature control (+/-3°F, +/- 1.7°C) with low pressure drop across the rated flow range. As an added feature the MMV series incorporates integral inlet filter washers and check valves in both the hot and cold water inlets to protect against cross flow. The MMV is available with either union thread (-UT), union solder (-US), CPVC, Quick-Connect (-QC) or PEX end connections. Maximum Pressure: 150psi (10.55 bar).

Leak at Gate Valve/Joint
Valve/joint appears to be leaking. This is a gate valve. Gate valves are known to degrade in time predictably and are recommended to be replaced whenever possible. Recommend replacing in case of an emergency prior to performing any plumbing work or work in close relation to plumbing.

Leak at Shower Handle Valve/Joint
Valve/joint appears to be leaking. Water was evident at the handle coming from the stem/valve area. Recommend replacing in case of an emergency prior to performing any plumbing work or work in close relation to the plumbed area.

Leak at Faucet Handle Valve/Joint
The valve/joint appears to be leaking. Water was evident at the handle coming from the stem/valve area. Recommend a licensed plumbing contractor repair/replace in case of an emergency prior to performing any plumbing work or work in close relation to the plumbed area.

Leak at Faucet Joints/Abutments
The faucets internal valve/joint components appear defective and appear to be leaking. Water was evident at the abutments and suspected to be a compromise coming from the stem/valve area. Recommend replacing the faucet in case of an emergency and prior to performing any plumbing work or work in close relation to the plumbed area.

Leak at the Shower Head(s)
Recommend a licensed plumbing contractor reinstall with proper Teflon tape/plumbers paste applied to the threading of the abutting fittings as needed.

Washer Hot Shut-Off Gate Valve Leaks
When the valve is actuated to close or open, it spits at the stem. This is a gate valve. Gate valves are known to degrade in time, predictably, and are recommended to be replaced whenever possible. Since repair is needed, it is recommended to replace the gate valve with a ball valve type.

Toilet Shut-Off Gate Valve Leaks when Actuated
When the valve is actuated to close or open, it spits at the stem. This is a gate valve. Gate valves are known to degrade in time, predictably, and are recommended to be replaced whenever possible. Since repair is needed, it is recommended to replace the gate valve with a ball valve type.

Upward Knocking at Shut-Off Valve
Knocking scales upward and can potentially cause further damage at the valve or further down the pipe. Burst failures usually occur during transient hydraulic conditions that create large pressure variations in the system. Recommend a licensed plumbing contractor assess further and repair/replace the valve ASAP.

Knocking at Toilet Valve Observed
There is an escalating rattle or hard knocking that occurs at the toilets distribution pipe and can be conducive to several things. Possible causes may be the valve at the wall or in the wall are loose, air in the system and will likely require a licensed plumber to tackle. Water hammer, also known as air hammer, is a loud knocking sound that is caused by the pressurization of a water pipe when the water is shut off. Loose or broken valves of all kinds can cause knocking, rattling or other noises in water pipes when water flow is switched on. This is what is suspected to be the case for the distribution pipe for this toilet. Other reasons include water hammer, rust and other problems can lead to broken or loose support straps around water pipes. Once these straps are loose, even normal water pressure will make them rock back and forth. Hammering or knocking noises when a faucet or valve is opened is often caused by high water pressure, with the sound occurring as the pressure inside the pipe builds. Recommend to have a licensed plumber inspect and repair as needed.

Lime Scale or Calcium Carbonate Fouling Observed
Even in hard water areas, pipes will not scale unless the saturation index of the water is exceeded. If the water is under-saturated or at equilibrium saturation, there will be no scale. Conversely, "soft water" can scale if it becomes over saturated. The saturation index of water is controlled by its acidity (or alkalinity which is the reverse) which we establish by pH measurement. The lower the pH, the more acidic the water and the more it can hold in solution. The higher the pH, the less acidic the water, the lower the saturation index and the less the water can hold dissolved minerals. We raise the pH by heating the water, causing pressure drops (e.g. taps) and adding chemicals. By raising the pH, we are reducing the ability of the water to hold minerals in solution and these minerals are forced to precipitate and cause scale fouling. Recirculating systems (e.g. cooling towers, steam generators, water recovery systems) operate at cycles of concentration with pressure drops and temperature variances causing both super saturation and pH increases simultaneously.

Lime Scale or Calcium Carbonate Fouling on Shower Walls
Note: Lime scale or Calcium Carbonate fouling on Shower Walls/Floor Tiles. This can be treated using natural methods. Inquire online. Alternatively, there are readily available chemical products as well. Be sure that any product used does not harm the substrate the fouling is on.

Lime Scale or Calcium Carbonate Fouling on Valves/Joints
Even in hard water areas, pipes will not scale unless the saturation index of the water is exceeded. If the water is under-saturated or at equilibrium saturation, there will be no scale. Conversely, "soft water" can scale if it becomes over saturated. The saturation index of water is controlled by its acidity (or alkalinity which is the reverse) which we establish by pH measurement. The lower the pH, the more acidic the water and the more it can hold in solution. The higher the pH, the less acidic the water, the lower the saturation index, and the less the water can hold dissolved minerals. We raise the pH by heating the water, causing pressure drops (e.g. taps) and adding chemicals. By raising the pH, we are reducing the ability of the water to hold minerals in solution and these minerals are forced to precipitate and cause scale fouling. Recirculating systems (e.g. cooling towers, steam generators, water recovery systems) operate at cycles of concentration with pressure drops and temperature variances causing both super saturation and pH increases simultaneously. Unfortunately, unless installing a mineral filtration system, there is little to resolve the cause of internal scaling, however, the scaling/build up on the valves under the sink are caused by minute orifices at the threading of the joints and is caused by minute amounts of water to surfacing, crystallizing/scaling upon breaching the surface. For threaded plumbing fittings, using Teflon tape or plumbers paste around joint threading will typically remedy the issue.

Interior Gate Valves Seized and will Not Engage/Disengage when Actuated
Gate valves commonly incur problems as they are rarely used. Because of this, the valves tend to develop fouling and inevitable fusing within the packing/shaft components within the valve. This can allow the valve to leak if attempted to be closed. Recommend a licensed plumbing contractor replace all seized valves as needed. Recommend quarter round turn valves to replace the gate valves present.

Loose CPVC Pipe Raceways Observed at the Crawl Space
Pipes running under the building are attached to the bottom of the floor joists. To little pipe fasteners can allow the plastic pipe to sag and may aid in leaks down the road. Additionally, loose pipes undergo more pressure thrusts in the plumbing system do to engaging/disengaging the water. These are called knocks or knocking and can loosen pipes and fittings. Recommend a state licensed contractor fasten/repair all as needed.

Galvanized Pipe Rusting at Threaded Joints
Note: The galvanized pipe showed signs of rust at the joints throughout the observed plumbing system. This is a clear sign of potential leaks occurring in the near future. Due to the rapid introduction of mold and other fungi when leaks occur, it is highly recommended that the pipe be replaced with a more durable pipe such as CPVC, PEX and/or copper pipe.

Low pressure Observed. Suspect Galvanized Pipe Oxidation Is Constricting
Galvanized steel and brass pipes may fail, typically between the 50-75 years range. Galvanized steel can build a lot of corrosion on the interior. The more internal corrosion/rust, the more restricting the flow throughout the building will be. It is mainly for that reason it often gets replaced before it springs a leak. However, if the pipe is not replaced, the galvanized pipe can oxidize and corrode internally, causing leaks from the inside out. The low pressure can be much greater in the hot water service pipe because the hotter the water, the faster it causes the oxidation process as it depletes the zinc galvanized coating on the interior of the pipe. The water treatments can also progress the process. It is highly recommended to have a licensed plumber review the system in full and replace all galvanized pipe.

Tub/Shower Valve do not Totally Engage/Disengage. Suspect Lime Scale Etc.
Shower partially actuates when the tub faucet is actuated and vise verse. Suspect internal calcium and lime scale, inhibiting the functionality of the fixtures/valves. Recommend a licensed plumber assess the area further and repair all as needed per state and local codes.

Waste System

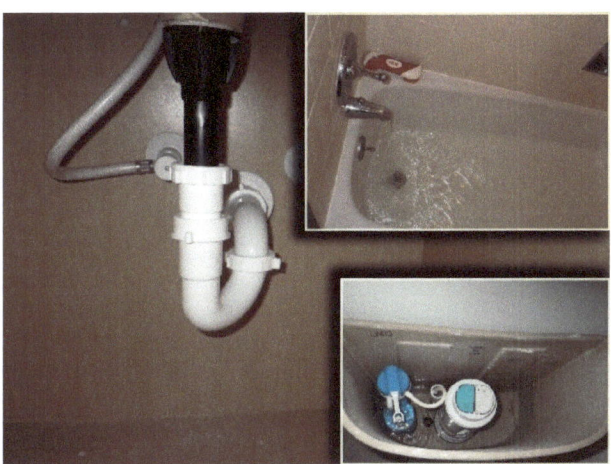

Drainage System Basic Comments
The Drainage System was tested at all waste system drain locations with exception to the one servicing the washer unit as testing the washer connections is beyond the scope of a general building inspection and report. All drains with exception of the aforementioned washer drain and any deficiencies addressed, were found to be working as designed and were in serviceable condition at time of inspection.

Cast Iron Drainage System is Original, has Excessive Exterior Corrosion and is recommended to be replaced
Drainage pipe is the original for the building and has exceeded its known life expectancy. Recommend replacing all antiquated cast iron draining system as is needed.

Toilet Gasket at the Tank/Bowl Abutment was Observed Leaking when Flushed
Leak at the tank/bowl abutment when flushing the toilet typically means the locknut is not tight enough, the rubber washer inside the tank has flashing compromises or the porcelain surface inside the tank is uneven or has a chip, therefore not sealing. This is symptomatic of a leak in the tank-to-bowl seal or around the tank-to-bowl mounting bolts. Tightening the bolts may solve the issue, if not, a new gasket may be needed. Recommend a licensed plumbing contractor assess further and repair as needed.

Drainage System Pipe: PVC
Rigid plastic PVC (polyvinyl chloride) and ABS (acrylonitrile butadiene styrene) are the most popular types of plastic plumbing pipe. PVC is usually white or cream colored and ABS is black. Both are typically used only for vents and drains and aren't made to fit directly together. Plastic pipe joints are connected with glue that actually melts the pieces together. The joints for both PVC and ABS are glued the same way, but the types aren't interchangeable and only a special fitting can connect them together. Roughly half of the world's polyvinyl chloride resin manufactured annually is used for producing pipes for various municipal and industrial applications. In the water distribution market, it accounts for 66% of the market in the US, and in sanitary sewer pipe applications, it accounts for 75%. Its light weight, high strength, and low reactivity make it particularly well-suited to this purpose. In addition, PVC pipes can be fused together using various solvent cements, or heat-fused (butt-fusion process, similar to joining HDPE pipe), creating permanent joints that are virtually impervious to leakage.

Drainage System Pipe: PVC with System Comments
Rigid plastic PVC (polyvinyl chloride) and ABS (acrylonitrile butadiene styrene) are the most popular types of plastic plumbing pipe. PVC is usually white or cream colored and ABS is black. Both are typically used only for vents and drains and aren't made to fit directly together. Plastic pipe joints are connected with glue that actually melts the pieces together. The joints for both PVC and ABS are glued the same way, but the types aren't interchangeable and only a special fitting can connect them together. Roughly half of the world's polyvinyl

chloride resin manufactured annually is used for producing pipes for various municipal and industrial applications. In the water distribution market it accounts for 66% of the market in the US, and in sanitary sewer pipe applications, it accounts for 75%. Its light weight, high strength, and low reactivity make it particularly well-suited to this purpose. In addition, PVC pipes can be fused together using various solvent cements, or heat-fused (butt-fusion process, similar to joining HDPE pipe), creating permanent joints that are virtually impervious to leakage. Drainage System was tested at all waste system drain locations with exception to the one servicing the washer unit as testing the washer unit is beyond the scope of this inspection and report. All drains with exception of the aforementioned washer drain and any deficiencies addressed, were found to be working as designed and were in serviceable condition.

Drainage System Pipe: ABS

Acrylonitrile Butadiene Styrene (ABS) is the polymerization of Acrylonitrile, Butadiene, and Styrene monomers. Chemically, this thermoplastic family of plastics is called "terpolymers", in that they involve the combination of three different monomers to form a single material that draws from the properties of all three. ABS possesses outstanding impact strength and high mechanical strength, which makes it so suitable for tough consumer products. Additionally, ABS has good dimensional stability, excellent resistance (no attack) to Glycerin, inorganic salts, alkalis, many acids, most alcohols and hydrocarbons, limited resistance (moderate attack and suitable for short term use only) to weak acids, poor resistance (not recommended for use with) to strong acids and solvents, ketones, aldehydes, esters, and some chlorinated hydrocarbons properties.

Drainage System Pipe: ABS with System Comments

Acrylonitrile Butadiene Styrene (ABS) is the polymerization of Acrylonitrile, Butadiene, and Styrene monomers. Chemically, this thermoplastic family of plastics is called "terpolymers", in that they involve the combination of three different monomers to form a single material that draws from the properties of all three. ABS possesses outstanding impact strength and high mechanical strength, which makes it so suitable for tough consumer products. Additionally, ABS has good dimensional stability and electrical insulating; excellent resistance (no attack) to glycerin, inorganic salts, alkalis, many acids, most alcohols and hydrocarbons, limited resistance (moderate attack and suitable for short term use only) to weak acids, poor resistance (not recommended for use with) strong acids and solvents, ketones, aldehydes, esters, and some chlorinated hydrocarbons properties. The drainage system was tested at all waste system drain locations with exception to the one servicing the washer unit as testing the washer unit is beyond the scope of this inspection and report. All drains with exception of the aforementioned washer drain and any deficiencies addressed, were found to be working as designed and were in serviceable condition.

Cast Iron Pipe

Cast iron pipe is a pipe which has had historic use as a pressure pipe for transmission of water, gas and sewage, and as a water drainage pipe during the 19th and 20th centuries. It comprises predominantly a gray cast iron tube and was frequently used uncoated, although later coatings and linings reduced corrosion and improve hydraulics. Cast iron pipe was superseded by ductile iron pipe, which is a direct development, with most existing manufacturing plants transitioning to the new material during the 1970's and 1980's. Little cast iron pipe is currently manufactured. The oldest extant water pipes date from the 17th century and were installed to distribute water throughout the gardens of the Chateau de Versailles. This amounts to some 35 km of pipe, typically 1m lengths with flanged joints. The extreme age of these pipes make them of considerable historical value. Following extensive refurbishment in 2008 by Saint-Gobain PAM, 80% remain original. The flanged joints of cast-iron drainpipe were sealed with oakum and molten-lead joints. The first standardization of cast iron water pipes in Britain occurred in 1917 with the publishing of BS 78. This standard specified a dimensionless nominal size, which approximately corresponded with the internal diameter in inches of the pipe, and four pressure classes, Class A, Class B, Class C and Class D, each with a specified wall thickness and outer diameter. It is noted that the outer diameter is identical between classes with the exception of sizes 12 to 27, where Classes A and B share one diameter and Classes C and D have another, larger diameter.

Copper Plumbing

Since the Safe Drinking Water Act Amendments of 1986 the use of lead-containing solders in potable water systems has effectively been banned nationwide. The major impact of the Act has been on solder containing 50% tin and 50% lead (50-50), until then the most widely used solder for drinking water systems. Lead-base solders have been replaced by tin-antimony and tin-silver solders. The main differences between these solders and 50-50 are that they are stronger and require somewhat higher working temperatures. Many plumbers in the United States have used them in copper plumbing systems for decades. Copper is also antifungal. One major advantage of the tin-antimony and tin-silver solders is that joints made with them are considerably stronger than joints made with 50-50 tin-lead. This superiority is the main reason that tin-antimony and tin-silver solders have long been specified for high-rise installations, for high-temperature service, for commercial refrigeration and air conditioning hook-ups and for soldered copper fire sprinkler systems. Because soldered joints made with tin-antimony and tin-silver are stronger, plumbing systems installed using them can withstand higher pressures and temperatures than systems made with 50-50 tin-lead solder.

Polypropylene
Polypropylene is a type of thermoplastic polymer resin. It is a part of both the average household and is in commercial and industrial applications. The chemical designation is C3H6. One of the benefits of using this type of plastic is that it can be useful in numerous applications including as a structural plastic or as a fiber-type plastic. The history of polypropylene began in 1954 when a German chemist named Karl Rehn and an Italian chemist named Giulio Natta first polymerized it. This led to a large commercial production of the product that began just three years later. Natta synthesized the first syndiotactic polypropylene.

Pipe Type CPVC
CPVC (CHLORINATED POLY VINYL CHLORIDE) can withstand corrosive water at temperatures greater than PVC, typically 40°C to 50°C (104°F to 122°F) or higher, contributing to its popularity as a material for water piping systems in residential as well as commercial construction. The principal mechanical difference between CPVC and PVC is that CPVC is significantly more ductile, allowing greater flexure and crush resistance. Additionally, the mechanical strength of CPVC makes it a viable candidate to replace many types of metal pipe in conditions where metal's susceptibility to corrosion limits its use. CPVC is similar to PVC in resistance to fire. It is typically very difficult to ignite and tends to self-extinguish when not in a directly applied flame. Due to its chlorine content, the incineration of CPVC, either in a fire or in an industrial disposal process, can result in the creation of dioxins. Alternatively, however, though petro chem leeching is known to happen in the potable water system, metal oxidative properties/bi products such as rust are dramatically reduced and/or eliminated provided no galvanized junctions are present.

HDPE
High Density Polyethylene (HDPE) is a versatile plastic that has many practical uses, not the least of which is for the fabrication of pipe. English chemists Reginald Gibson and Eric Fawcett created a solid form of polyethylene in 1935. This discovery was first used commercially was an insulating material for radar cables during World War II. In 1953, Karl Ziegler of the Kaiser Wilhelm institute invented high density polyethylene. In 1955 HDPE was first used as a pipe. For his invention of HDPE, Ziegler won the Nobel Prize for Chemistry in 1963. The number one characteristic that sets HDPE apart from other pipe types is that it can be made to be flexible. This quality opens HDPE pipe up to a different world of applications than rigid pipe. Another quality of HDPE is that it can be melted and re-solidified a limitless number of times without losing any of its favorable qualities. For this reason, most HDPE pressure pipe is made to be 'butt welded'. This is where the ends of two sections of pipe are melted and then pushed and held together, forming a single pipe. There is an HDPE product that can be applied to just about any situation. There are a few things that should be noted, though. Because most HDPE is a flexible product, it is not commonly used in sanitary sewer gravity installations. This is because the flexible properties of the pipe can cause dips in the gravity runs. There are several manufacturers that produce a corrugated rigid pipe product that is primarily used for storm drainage. Like PVC, HDPE pipe can be color coated to match installation requirements. Typically for pressure installations, HDPE is black with a color coated stripe. Below you will find a list of common colors and uses: Water Distribution – Blue, Fire Main – Red, Sewer – Green, Gas – Yellow, and Reclaimed Water – Purple.

Washer Gate Valve Leaks
When the valve is fully closed and not actuated to close or open, it appears to leak at the stem. This is a gate valve. Gate valves are known to degrade in time, predictably and are recommended to be replaced whenever possible. Since repair is needed, it is recommended to replace the gate valve with a ball valve type.

Galvanized Pipe
When a pipe has been galvanized, it means that the steel or iron has been coated with zinc. Galvanized pipes are silver when they are new, and will dull to gray as they age. This coating is to resist oxidation and any potential rusting of the pipe. However, galvanized pipe will corrode in time. If you have galvanized pipe installed, it will be in working condition for about 40-60 years averaged, before joints rust out or water flow becomes severely reduced, allowing more pressure to build in areas. The reason for the limited usage is that the corrosion, which will eventually fill the entire pipe and will restrict the water flow in the pipe. One problem with this type of pipe is that the corrosion can be more rapid whenever a steel galvanized pipe meets any brass or copper. This often happens when the valves are made of brass. One way to combat this effect is to use dielectric unions between copper and steel pipes. However, some of these can close off the flow. The problem

occurring is that it can break the grounding if a live wire when the pipe types come into contact with each other. Corrosion in galvanized pipes can usually not be cleaned out without causing water leaks.

Dielectric fitting not Present at Pipe Transition
A dielectric union is a term used to describe two-part fittings of dissimilar metals which are electrically isolated from each other to prevent galvanic corrosion. The term is also used to describe a family of plumbing pipe fittings. Galvanic corrosion occurs when two different metals are placed in contact with each other in an acidic solution, electrolysis occurs which causes an ion flow between the two metals. This flow of electric current causes molecules from one of the metals to be deposited on the other, thereby resulting in what is known as galvanic corrosion. The metal which donates molecules will slowly be eroded away while the one that receives the material will build up a layer of corrosion byproduct. Most domestic water sources are mildly acidic; galvanic corrosion is likely to occur wherever dissimilar metals are used in plumbing fittings. One way of preventing this destructive process is to insulate the two parts of the fitting from each other. One way to combat this effect is to use dielectric unions between copper and steel pipes. Recommend a licensed plumber repair all as needed.

Cross-Linked Polyethylene (PEX/XLPE)
Cross-linked polyethylene is commonly abbreviated **PEX** or **XLPE**. Almost all PEX used for pipe and tubing is made from high density polyethylene (HDPE). PEX contains cross-linked bonds in the polymer structure, changing the thermoplastic to a thermoset. Cross-linking is accomplished during or after the extrusion of the tubing. The required degree of cross-linking, according to ASTM Standard F876, is between 65 and 89%. A higher degree of cross-linking could result in brittleness and stress cracking of the material while a lower degree of cross-linking could result in product with poorer physical properties. Crosslinking improves the elevated-temperature properties of the base polymer. Adequate strength to 120–150 °C is maintained by reducing creep, the tendency to flow. Chemical resistance is enhanced by resisting dissolution. Low temperature properties are improved. Impact and tensile strength, scratch resistance, and resistance to brittle fracture are enhanced. PEX tubing is widely used to replace copper in plumbing applications. One estimate is that residential use of PEX for delivering drinking water to faucets has increased by 40% annually, and there is substantial evidence that PEX is or will soon become the dominant technology for carrying water in buildings and businesses in the next decade or so. It is widely accepted among different groups, and has been used by volunteer organizations such as Habitat for Humanity in constructing buildings. PEX has become a contender for use in residential water plumbing because of its flexibility. It can bend into a wide-radius turn if space permits, or accommodate turns by using elbow joints. In addition, it can handle short-radius turns, sometimes supported with a metal brace; in contrast, PVC, CPVC and copper all require elbow joints. A single length of PEX pipe cannot handle a sharp 90-degree turn, however, so in those situations, it is necessary to connect two PEX pipes with a 90-degree PEX elbow joint. Since PEX pipes typically have fewer sharp turns, there is greater water pressure at the sinks and showers and toilets where it is needed.

Ductile Iron
The United States first used CIP in 1817 when Philadelphia utilized it in the installation of a new water system. According to the Ductile Iron Pipe Research Association (DIPRA), today there are more than 600 utilities that have had CIP mains in service for more than 100 years. There are also at least 21 utilities with CIP mains in service for more than 150 years. Ductile Iron Pipe (DIP) emerged on the scene in 1953. DIP is superior to CIP because of an improved manufacturing process. Magnesium is introduced in the smelting process and this changes the form of the graphite particles in the iron. The result is a pipe that is lighter, stronger, more corrosion resistant and more machinable than CIP. These qualities, thus, make it more cost effective than CIP, too. Because DIP is an iron product, it can have the same corrosion problems prone to all iron products, especially when installed in corrosive environments. DIP is commonly coated in the inside with a cement-mortar lining. This lining enables it to handle the rigors of transporting potable water, sea water, non-septic gravity sewers, sewer force mains and reclaimed water. DIP is also available with various epoxy liners. This is commonly used for septic sewer and other caustic environments.

Leak at Sink Basin
Leak observed at the sink basin/gasket when testing. Recommend repairing as needed.

Stainless Steel
Stainless Steel is an iron based alloy that contains at least 11.5% chromium. Other elements, such as nickel, are also added to modify the properties of the metal. Stainless steel is able to withstand high temperatures. It is also highly resistant to corrosion. Stainless steel pipe and tubing are used for many reasons. They resist corrosion and oxidation. They resist high temperatures. The most common type of stainless used is Type 304. It is used in piping and tubing in chemical plans, refineries, food processing and paper plants. Type 304 has a

maximum carbon content of 0.08%. Another common type is Type 304L. It is similar to Type 304, except that it has a maximum carbon content of 0.03%.

Polybutylene
Polybutylene is a plastic resin that was used for water pipe manufacture in the U.S. from 1978 to 1995. The polybutylene (poly) pipe was promoted as the pipe of the future because of its low cost and ease of installation. During the years it was produced, it replaced traditional copper piping for both exterior and interior plumbing use. Industry experts claim the poly piping was installed in approximately six to 10 million new or remodeled buildings – or about one in every four during its 17-year reign. Shell Chemical Company was the primary manufacturer of the poly pipe, along with Quest and Vanguard. The fittings were manufactured by Celanese and DuPont A typical 2,000 square foot residence cost $1,000 to $1,500 less to build with polybutylene than with copper piping so the cost savings was significant. Polybutylene manufacturers initially claimed that their plumbing system would last a lifetime. In fact, not only did it not last a lifetime, it barely lasted a decade and caused extensive property damage when it finally corroded and leaked. On average, poly pipes take between 10-15 years to show signs of severe deterioration. When it fails, it does so without warning. Because of the high damage costs when polybutylene fails, insurance companies have sometimes canceled or refuse building policies because of it. The known presence of poly piping can also affect a building's value on the real estate market.

Waste Line Observed Passes across Egress at Step
International Plumbing Code; "Location of fixtures and piping: Piping, fixtures or equipment shall not be located in such a manner as to interfere with the normal operation of windows, doors or other means of egress openings. All Stairways and openings to which are a mode of ingress/egress, where foot traffic in known to be, should not be obstructed by any loose or mounted piping or electrical conduit. This can cause a trip hazard to an individual, obstructs the proper run/landing at a door or egress and poses danger of damage to the piping or conduit. Recommend restructuring the stairway/landing at the steps or redirecting the pipe to provide a clear path as prescribed by the ICC and state code.

Basin of Sink has Excess Corrosion. Leak/Corrosion at Sink Basin Observed
Leak observed at the sink basin/gasket when testing. Suspect excess corrosion has compromised the sink at the drain. Recommend replacing as needed.

Washer Drain Not Equipped with P-Trap, Standpipe or Vent
Recommend relocating the drain to extend to the right with a minimum 2 inch diameter drain that does NOT turn with a 90 degree turn in close relation to the service end as it can allow Backflow. Meaning, if the water expels out of the drain hose from the washer using enough pressure (psi) the pipe curve alone can act as an opposing force. With No Ventilation Stack Observed with such a short pipe, the water does not reduce much pressure upon expelling into the narrow chamber. In many jurisdictions, the standpipe height is 36 to 42 inches for proper drainage. The pipe must be 1 1/2 or 2 inches in diameter, depending upon local building and plumbing codes. In most locale code requirements, 2 inches is the standard. See Local Codes for actual dimensions and specs for your region.

Garbage Disposal was Seized Up at the Time of the Inspection
Unit energized but was seized and would not engage its function. This is conductive typical excess oxidation in the unit and typically occurs with ware or lack of use. Recommend replacing the unit.

Bathroom Sink Drain Trip Lever Sticks
When engaging the trip lever, the plunger does not appear to engage. This appears to be an issue with the chain, plunger or trip lever. It is recommended to have a licensed plumbing contractor replace/repair as needed.

Bathroom Sink Drain Trip Inoperable
When engaging the trip lever, the plunger does not appear to engage. This appears to be an issue with the chain, plunger or trip lever. It is recommended to have a licensed plumbing contractor replace/repair as needed.

Toilet Drainage Bubbles Observed
The fact that your toilet bubbles, and you have to have a certain volume of water, for it to drain, are good indicators of this. The volume of water is needed to overcome the vacuum imposed by not having enough ventilation. The bubbles can be from air having been sucked down the drain and then escaping. There may still be a blockage, or other restriction in the flow, too. Recommend a licensed plumbing contractor repair all as needed.

Sink Drains Slowly
Suspect this problem is at the sinks trap. Sink drains very commonly build up sediments from human skin, hair or other particulate such as from paints and building materials or food items etc. more so then other sediments in other drain traps. Because of this, they tend to drain slower and slower as sediments build up and impinge on the natural flow through the trap. Recommend a licensed plumbing contractor assess further. If the trap is determined to be clogged, cleaning out the trap should remediate the issue.

Drain Vent Stack Suspected at the Exterior Wall under the Eaves
The drain vent should terminate above the roof line to prevent vent exhaust of human waste entering the attic system, encouraging rodent nesting and mold/fungi growth potential. Recommend a licensed plumbing contractor assess the pipe further and repair where needed.

Double Trap Observed at the Sink Basin
Double trapping creates an air-lock between the two traps thus impeding flow and not permitting proper air flow in the drainage system that promotes bacterial growth. Hydraulic principles working on the air between the two traps will either prevent drainage entirely, or slow it down initially. Recommend a licensed plumbing contractor repair as is needed.

Very Slow Draining at the Bathroom Tub Drain. Suspect Sediment/Hair Clog
There was excessive hair, soap scum and/or human particulate build up suspected in the drain. Tub and sink drains very commonly build up sediments from human skin, hair etc. more so then other sediments in other drain traps. Because of this, they tend to drain slower and slower as sediments build up and impinge on the natural flow through the trap. Recommend a licensed plumbing contractor cleaning out the trap/repair as needed.

No Cleanout Observed at the Time of the Inspection
This does not always signify there is no cleanout, however, a buried or otherwise non discernable cleanout and its location is essentially mute and does not serve the purpose intended. Recommend having a licensed plumber find or install a cleanout as needed per the international plumbing code or regional/state locale guidelines.

Corroded P-Trap Leak Observed at the Sink Drain
The P-Trap contains a water seal system at the base convex half circle or the 180 degree turn/elbow that allows for water to flow into the overflow pipe, but not to flow backward toward the sink. It is this back flow prevention water seal that sits at the base of the pipe that prevents sewer gas from escaping into the house. Sewer gas can contain many noxious odors which at the least, may smell like rotten eggs and at their worst, can be explosive and poisonous. As a result of the water always contacting the base of the pipe, it is common for these chromed steel traps to oxidize and eventually corrode through and leak as was observed at the time of the inspection. It is highly recommended to have a licensed plumber install a new PVC or non-corrosive P-Trap ASAP.

P-Trap Observed at the Sink Drain is Leaking at a Fitting/Threaded Joint
A P-trap is a plumbing drainage fixture that has several purposes. It traps debris that have drained from the sink and prevents it from forming a clog deeper within the plumbing system, and to stops sewer gases from passing into the building. P-traps can be made from PVC pipe/steel, poly composites etc. The P-Trap contains a water seal system at the base convex half circle or the 180 degree turn/elbow that allows for water to flow into the overflow pipe, but not to flow backward toward the sink. It is this back flow prevention water seal that sits at the base of the pipe that prevents sewer gas from escaping into the house. Sewer gas can contain many noxious odors which at the least, may smell like rotten eggs and at their worst, can be explosive and poisonous. The fittings tend to be loosened or fastened improperly allowing leaks to occur. Additionally, sometimes build ups in the trap and the pipe surrounds can aggravate water back up and pressures to the loose joint at the threading allowing leaks that otherwise would not have been occurring. It is highly recommended to have a licensed plumber repair the P-Trap ASAP.

No P-Trap Observed at the Washer Drain
The P-Trap contains a water seal system at the base convex half circle or the 180 degree turn/elbow that allows for water to flow into the overflow pipe, but not to flow backward toward the sink. It is this back flow prevention water seal that sits at the base of the pipe that prevents sewer gas from escaping into the house. Sewer gas can contain many noxious odors which at the least, may smell like rotten eggs and at their worst, can be explosive and poisonous. The traps installed in the plumbing lines help to form a barrier of water within the P-trap. Without

this vital component, other things such as insects may also backtrack up into the building from sewer locations. It is highly recommended to have a licensed plumber install a P-Trap ASAP.

No P-Trap Observed at the Washtub Drain
A P-trap is a plumbing drainage fixture that has several purposes. It traps debris that have drained from the sink and prevents it from forming a clog deeper within the plumbing system, and to stops sewer gases from passing into the building. P-traps can be made from PVC pipe/steel, poly composites etc. The P-Trap contains a water seal system at the base convex half circle or the 180 degree turn/elbow that allows for water to flow into the overflow pipe, but not to flow backward toward the sink. It is this back flow prevention water seal that sits at the base of the pipe that prevents sewer gas from escaping into the house. Sewer gas can contain many noxious odors which at the least, may smell like rotten eggs and at their worst, can be explosive and poisonous. The fittings tend to be loosened or fastened improperly allowing leaks to occur. Additionally, sometimes build ups in the trap and the pipe surrounds can aggravate water back up and pressures to the loose joint at the threading allowing leaks that otherwise would not have been occurring. It is highly recommended to have a licensed plumber repair the P-Trap ASAP.

Basin of Sink has Excess Corrosion at Locknut to the Drain, located beneath the Strainer Housing
This is typically indicative of present/previous leaks. It is recommended to have a licensed plumbing contractor replace the locknut and/or repair/replace all as needed.

Bathroom Sink Drain Trip Inoperable. Bath Drain Stop is Missing
It is recommended to have a licensed plumbing contractor repair/replace as needed.

Bath Tub Drain Stopper is Loose from Its Mounted Lever and No Longer Suits Its Purpose
Recommended a licensed plumbing contractor assess the components further and replace/repair where needed per the ICC and local and state code requirements.

Toilet Handle/Chain/Flap Inoperable at the Time of the Inspection
Recommend a licensed plumbing contractor replace the internal/external parts as needed.

Toilet Valve Body Damaged
Recommend a licensed plumbing contractor replace/repair the internal/external parts as needed.

No P-Trap Observed at the Sink Drain
A P-trap is a plumbing drainage fixture that has several purposes. It traps debris that has drained from the sink and prevents it from forming a clog deeper within the plumbing system and to stop sewer gases from passing into the building. P-traps can be made from PVC pipe/steel, poly composites etc. The P-Trap contains a water seal system at the base convex half circle or the 180 degree turn/elbow that allows for water to flow into the overflow pipe, but not to flow backward toward the sink. It is this back flow prevention water seal that sits at the base of the pipe that prevents sewer gas from escaping into the house. Sewer gas can contain many noxious odors which at the least, may smell like rotten eggs and at their worst, can be explosive and poisonous. The traps installed in the plumbing lines help to form a barrier of water within the P-trap. Without this vital component, other things such as insects may also backtrack up into the building from sewer locations. It is highly recommended to have a licensed plumber install a P-Trap.

Septic System could not be inspected. Drains were Tested where Accessible
The septic system was not addressed by the client to the inspector prior to arriving on site and could not be inspected. No cap was observed. During the building inspection, water was run through the drains throughout the house during the inspection. Septic tank and percolation drain field could not be located by probing. The building owner and buyer are responsible to ensure the septic cap is located and removed prior to the inspection as well as the city/county need to be informed the inspector will be probing, prior to the inspector's arrival on site. Prior percolation problems or flooding problems were not visible/readily known beyond the aforementioned and do not appear to be related to the septic, if any. The level of sludge within the septic tank can only be determined by removal of the often buried, concrete lid. This procedure is beyond the scope of this inspection, and is generally performed by a septic tank pumping company. You may want to have this done if you have doubts about the level of sludge within the tank. An inquiry to the seller about the date of any prior pumping is often informative.

Gas/Fuel System Lines

Prior Leak at Gas Ignition Area. Water Heater was off and could not be Tested for Heating Adequacy
Inspector was informed a leak at the water heaters gas ignition area was detected prior to the inspection. Water heater was inoperable and could not be tested for heating adequacy. Due to the obvious fire risk, the pilot could not be tested as a result. The unit could not be tested for efficiency in regulating the heating of the water at the time of the inspection. Recommend a licensed plumbing contractor and gas technician assess further and repair/ replace as needed.

No Gas Drip Leg Observed at the Water Heater Gas Pipe Inlet
A sediment trap which is sometimes called a drip leg (although technically different) is a capped off section of gas line which is positioned so that any debris or moisture in the gas line will be caught in the trap where it can be removed easily when serviced. The reason for this is to provide safe operation of an appliance by keeping debris out of the tiny openings of the gas valves. Recommend a state licensed mechanical and gas technician assess the area further and repair as needed.

Suspected Abandoned Buried Fuel Tank Observed
Rusted/heavily corroded tanks, if not filled to code, may collapse from live load and may cause an accidental hazard. Per the IMC, International Mechanical Code; "1301.4 Fuel tanks, piping and valves. The tank, piping and valves for appliances burning oil shall be installed in accordance with the requirements of this chapter. When an oil burner is served by a tank, any part of which is above the level of the burner inlet connection and where the fuel supply line is taken from the top of the tank, an *approved* anti-siphon valve or other siphon-breaking device shall be installed in lieu of the shutoff valve." "1301.5 Tanks abandoned or removed. All exterior above-grade fill piping shall be removed when tanks are abandoned or removed. Tank abandonment and removal shall be in accordance with Section 3404.2.13 of the *International Fire Code.*" Recommend a licensed contractor assess the area further and repair as needed.

Pipe Threaded Joints have no Joint Compound Observed
Threaded joints should have a joint compound or other approved sealant to the threading to inhibit fuel leaks. Per the IMC, International Mechanical Code; "SECTION 1303 JOINTS AND CONNECTIONS 1303.1 Approval. Joints and connections shall be *approved* and of a type *approved* for fuel-oil piping systems. All threaded joints and connections shall be made tight with suitable lubricant or pipe compound. Unions requiring gaskets or packings, right or left couplings, and sweat fittings employing solder having a melting point of less than 1,000°F (538°C) shall not be used in oil lines. Cast-iron fittings shall not be used. Joints and connections shall be tight for the pressure required by test." Recommend a licensed contractor assess the pipes further and repair all where/if needed.

Gas Fuel Leak Suspected at the Pipe Threaded Joint(s) Observed
Threaded joints should have a joint compound or other approved sealant to the threading to inhibit fuel leaks. Per the IMC, International Mechanical Code; "SECTION 1303 JOINTS AND CONNECTIONS 1303.1 Approval. Joints and connections shall be *approved* and of a type *approved* for fuel-oil piping systems. All threaded joints and connections shall be made tight with suitable lubricant or pipe compound. Unions requiring gaskets or packings, right or left couplings, and sweat fittings employing solder having a melting point of less than 1,000°F (538°C) shall not be used in oil lines. Cast-iron fittings shall not be used. Joints and connections shall be tight for the pressure required by test." It is highly recommended to have a licensed mechanical contractor assess the pipes further and repair all where needed ASAP.

No Dielectric Fittings Observed at Pipe Material Transition
A dielectric union is a term used to describe two-part fittings of dissimilar metals which are electrically isolated from each other to prevent galvanic corrosion. The term is also used to describe a family of plumbing pipe fittings. Galvanic corrosion occurs when two different metals are placed in contact with each other in an acidic solution, electrolysis occurs which causes an ion flow between the two metals. This flow of electric current causes molecules from one of the metals to be deposited on the other, thereby resulting in what is known as galvanic corrosion. The metal which donates molecules will slowly be eroded away while the one that receives the material will build up a layer of corrosion byproduct. Most domestic water sources are mildly acidic; galvanic corrosion is likely to occur wherever dissimilar metals are used in plumbing fittings. One way of preventing this destructive process is to insulate the two parts of the fitting from each other. One way to combat this effect is to use dielectric unions between copper and steel pipes. Per the IMC, International Mechanical Code; "SECTION 1303 JOINTS AND CONNECTIONS 1303.1 Approval. Joints and connections shall be *approved* and of a type *approved* for fuel-oil piping systems. All threaded joints and connections shall be made tight with suitable lubricant or pipe compound. Unions requiring gaskets or packings, right or left couplings, and sweat fittings employing solder having a melting point of less than 1,000°F (538°C) shall not be used in oil lines. Cast-iron fittings shall not be used. Joints and connections shall be tight for the pressure required by test." "1303.1.1 Joints between different piping materials. Joints between different piping materials shall be made with *approved* adapter fittings. Joints between different metallic piping materials shall be made with *approved* dielectric fittings or brass converter fittings. Recommend a licensed contractor assess the pipes further and repair all where/if needed.

No Oil Gauge for the Fuel Tank Observed
A gauge is vital to assess fuel levels within the tank. For fuel tanks used in conjunction with a heating furnace, gauges are essential to prevent freezing during a major winter storm. Per the IMC, International Mechanical Code; "SECTION 1306 OIL GAUGING 1306.1 Level indication. All tanks in which a constant oil level is not maintained by an automatic pump shall be equipped with a method of determining the oil level. 1306.4 Gauging devices. Gauging devices such as liquid level indicators or signals shall be designed and installed so that oil vapor will not be discharged into a building from the liquid fuel supply system." Recommend a licensed contractor assess the area further and repair as needed.

No Fuel-Oil Relief Valve Observed on the Heating Appliances Discharge Line
SECTION 1307 FUEL OIL VALVES; "1307.4 Fuel-oil heater relief valve. A relief valve shall be installed on the discharge line of fuel-oil-heating appliances. 1307.5 Relief valve operation. The relief valve shall discharge fuel oil when the pressure exceeds the limitations of the system. The discharge line shall connect to the fuel oil tank." Recommend a licensed contractor assess the area further and repair as needed.

Natural Gas Fuel Pipe was Observed Loose/Insufficiently Fastened
Loose pipes can be damaged and caused to leak, leading to far worse conditions. Per the IMC, International Mechanical Code; "SECTION 305 PIPING SUPPORT 305.1 General. All mechanical system piping shall be supported in accordance with this section. 305.2 Materials. Pipe hangers and supports shall have sufficient strength to withstand all anticipated static and specified dynamic loading conditions associated with the intended use. Pipe hangers and supports that are in direct contact with piping shall be of approved materials that are compatible with the piping and that will not promote galvanic action. 305.3 Structural attachment. Hangers and anchors shall be attached to the building construction in an approved manner. 305.4 Interval of support. Piping shall be supported at distances not exceeding the spacing specified in Table 305.4, or in accordance with MSS SP-69." Recommend a licensed contractor assess the piping throughout the building and fastened to code as needed.

Natural Gas Fuel Pipe Observed in Disrepair
Galvanized pipe were observed in disrepair. Heavy oxidation was observed to the observed piping. To prevent hazardous condition, it is highly recommended to have a licensed contractor assess the area further and repair/replace all as is needed to state & local codes.

Water Heater

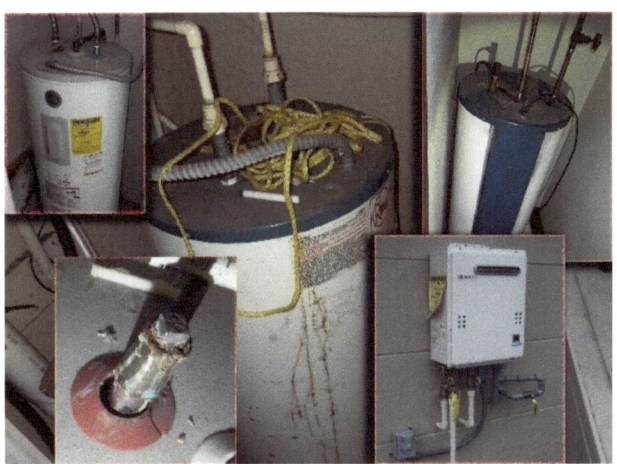

Water Heater General Comments

No deficiencies were found to the water heater itself (internal components conditions cannot be verified beyond an exterior inspection only and the outer casing/housing) or to the distribution or main service inlets/pipes. Pressure was good at the time of the inspection. A heat test was performed at all hot water plumbing exposures where applicable/accessible. Aside of any deficiencies, the unit was serviceable at the time of the inspection.

Surface Rust Observed at the Water Heater Tank Pipe Inlets Galvanized Nipples

This should be monitored for any progression. Rust can be superficial and can be from previous chemical or water exposure. Commonly, water heater storage tanks have been used by building owners as a shelving space, given their common close proximity to washers and wash tub locations. Recommend a licensed contractor monitor and/or treat as needed.

Main Shut Off; Leak Observed at the Gate Valve/Joint

Valve/joint appears to be leaking. This is a gate valve. Gate valves are known to degrade in time predictably and are recommended to be replaced whenever possible. Slow leaks can lead to big bills overall annually. Recommend replacing in case of an emergency and prior to performing any plumbing work or work in close relation to plumbing.

Prior Leak at Gas Ignition Area. Water Heater was off and could not be Tested for Heating Adequacy

Inspector was informed a leak at the water heaters gas ignition area was detected prior to the inspection. Water heater was inoperable and could not be tested for heating adequacy. Due to the obvious fire risk, the pilot could not be tested as a result. The unit could not be tested for efficiency in regulating the heating of the water at the time of the inspection. Recommend a licensed plumbing contractor and gas technician assess further and repair/ replace as needed.

No Gas Drip Leg Observed at the Water Heater Gas Pipe Inlet

A sediment trap which is sometimes called a drip leg (although technically different) is a capped off section of gas line which is positioned so that any debris or moisture in the gas line will be caught in the trap where it can be removed easily when serviced. The reason for this is to provide safe operation of an appliance by keeping debris out of the tiny openings of the gas valves. Recommend a state licensed mechanical and gas technician assess the area further and repair as needed.

No Temperature Relief Valve Drain Pipe

No TPR-Overflow Pipe Present. In case the thermostat fails on the water heater, the water in the tank can heat up to above boiling temperatures (210 degrees) expanding (every inch of water expands into a square foot of steam) this expansion in the tank can cause an explosion. To prevent the possibility of this occurring, a temperature relief valve is installed that can detect temperatures higher than the allowable heat radiance and will relieve the tank of excess pressure by opening. When this happens, boiling water disperses at a 110 pounds per square inch (hot and fast) and needs to be projected within 6" inches of the catch pan under the tank or outside. Installing a permitted pipe type from the temperature relief valve (TPR) to the pan or exterior of the building will divert this hot and fast water from damaging the building or electrical components in the event of a thermostat failure. Recommend a licensed plumbing contractor to complete all work. Minimum drain pipe radius must be the same as the TPR Female fitting and no smaller, typically 3/4 inch. Common piping for this is CPVC for its easy assembly and no solder or torching required, however, any acceptable potable water pipe will work.

Element Service Panel Cap is Loose
There are bare live circuits wires located at the elements and thermostat that can cause shock or death if exposed to a small child or animal. It is recommended a licensed electrician fasten this panel so as to prevent tampering or dislocation of the cover as is needed.

Element Service Panel Cap is missing
There are bare live circuits wires located at the elements and thermostat that can cause shock or death if exposed to a small child or animal. It is recommended to have a new panel cover installed so as to prevent tampering or contact with livened circuits.

Gas Water Heater Vent Straps/Fasteners were Observed Loose
Recommend a state licensed contractor refasten per the NFPA and/or to all state/local code requirements to prevent damage to the vent and potential fire hazards.

Draft Hood Loose/Displaced at the Water Heater Abutment
Recommend a licensed plumbing and mechanical contractor replace/repair the draft hood to assist in stabilizing the vent and to provide proper back draft protection for the water heater unit as is needed.

No Temperature Relief Valve Drain Pipe or Pan
In case the thermostat fails on the water heater, the water in the tank can heat up to above boiling temperatures (210 degrees) expanding (every inch of water expands into a square foot of steam) this expansion in the tank can cause an explosion. To prevent the possibility of this occurring, a temperature relief valve is installed that can detect temperatures higher than the allowable heat radiance and will release this out the TPR drain pipe that is currently only expelling to the floor and not at minimum, to a pan. Installing a permitted pipe type from the temperature relief valve (TPR) to a catch pan under the water heater or exterior of the building will divert this hot and fast water from damaging the building or electrical components in the event of a thermostat failure. Recommend a licensed plumbing contractor assess further and complete all repairs per the IPC and state/local code requirements. Minimum drain pipe radius must be the same as the TPR Female fitting and no smaller, typically 3/4 inches. Any acceptable potable water pipe will work.

No Main Shut Off Valve to Hot Water Heater
Shut off Valve at the cold feed to the water heater is required by most local and state codes throughout the US. The International Plumbing Code States: The cold water branch line from the main water supply line to each hot water storage tank or tank less water heater shall be provided with a valve, located near the equipment and serving only the hot water storage tank or water heater. The valve shall not interfere or cause a disruption of the cold water supply to the remainder of the cold water system. The valve shall be provided with access on the same floor level as the water heater served. Refer to your local code office or website for further details pertaining to code. The shut off is required for emergency access in case of a very fast gushing leak or a small drip, a building owner or plumber can access the immediate area to a working shut off for the hot water line. Recommended a licensed plumbing contractor assess further and repair all as needed and required by local codes and the safety of the structure.

Recommend Installing a Temperature Pressure Relief Valve
The name is Temperature Pressure Relief Valve or TPR valve. This is a safety valve that releases water (and thus relieves pressure) if either the temperature or pressure in the system/ tank gets too high. These valves are very important for places such as water heaters that can become bombs if the pressure gets too high and the heating elements thermostat fails to work as intended or becomes defective. Recommend a licensed plumbing contractor asses the area further and install as needed.

TPR or Temperature Pressure Relief Valve Leaks
TPR Valve has a constant drip. Recommend a licensed plumbing contractor repair/replace the TPR valve as needed.

PVC Flue Observed in Use for the Gas Heater Exhaust
The piping manufacturer recommends that inquiries about the suitability of plastic piping systems for venting combustion gases should be directed to the manufacturer of the water or space heating equipment being installed. As stated in the International Code Council's International Fuel Gas Code 503.4.1.1: **Plastic pipe and fittings used to vent appliances shall be installed in accordance with the appliance manufacturer's installation instructions.** Furthermore, several of the ASTM standards applicable to PVC plastic pipe and fittings that this company manufactures their pipe to include the following note: This standard specification for PVC pipe does not include requirements for pipe and fittings intended to be used to vent combustion gases. Generally, for a new condensing water heater or boiler, the stack temperature will be about 20 degrees higher than the water temperature. The design and efficiency of the unit, along with several other factors, including water quality, will affect the stack temperature. If a water heater is set to store water at 140 F to minimize Legionella bacteria growth, the flue gas temperature will be about 160 F when the heater is new. The PVC Flue is used for venting the water heater exhaust though legal if recommended by the manufacturer. As scale builds up and the heater efficiency falls off, the flue gas temperatures can easily increase to over 350 degrees F. Even if someone had their water heater set at 120 F, with scaling, the flue gas temperatures can rise well above 300 F. Boiler thermostats or burner controls are generally limited to 200 F, commercial water heater thermostats or burner controls to 180 F and residential water heater burner controls to 160 F, and all can overshoot by several degrees. As scale builds up on the heating surfaces, the scale insulates the flue gases from the hot water in the system, causing the flue gas temperatures to increase. For safety, though not required, it is recommended to re-pipe the PVC exhaust flue with a steel type for this vent.

No Barometric Damper Observed at the Gas Water Heater Flue Pipe
Why a Barometric Damper or Draft Regulator Is Needed; During oil burner operation, also on some gas fired equipment, combustion air moves into the burner are and combustion chamber as combustion air. As combustion continues, a mix of air and combustion gases continues onwards, moving out of the combustion chamber, up through the boiler or furnace heat exchanger, through the flue vent connector called the "stack pipe or flue pipe" and on into the chimney where these gases are finally vented outside, usually above the building roof. The force with which this air or combustion gas moves is the "draft" inside of the heating appliance. Too much draft increases heating appliance operating cost by venting heat out through the chimney instead of transferring the heat into the building where it was wanted. Too much draft can also increase chimney temperatures to an unsafe level. Too little draft can result in incomplete combustion, soot-clogging of heating equipment, a dangerous condition. Additionally, more dangerous heating appliance malfunctions can occur such as oil burner puff backs and in some cases dangerous production of carbon monoxide gas that leaks into the building (a potentially fatal problem). Recommend a licensed plumbing and mechanical contractor assess the area further and repair all as needed.

Flue Collar was Observed Not Attached Properly to the Exhaust Flue for the Gas Fired Water Heater
This can allow deadly scentless carbon monoxide to accumulate within the room housing the heater and can further back into the building through breaches in the air seals of the door(s), walls and ceiling where applicable.

Water Heater was Observed Enclosed/Inaccessible at the Time of the Inspection
Per the International Plumbing Code; Water heaters and storage tanks shall be located and connected so as to provide access for observation, maintenance, servicing and replacement. For obvious safety and servicing reasons, it is highly recommended to provide the aforementioned clearance. Recommend a licensed contractor repair as needed ASAP.

No Main Shut Off Valve Installed at Water Heater
Shut off Valve at the cold feed to the water heater is required by Most Local and State Codes throughout the US. Refer to your local code office or website for your State Plumbing Code for further details pertaining to code requirements. The shut off is required for emergency access in case of a very fast gushing leak or a small drip. The building occupant can access the shut off within the immediate area. Repair as needed and required by local codes.

Worn TPR Valve Observed. Water Leaking from the Valve Stem
Water leaking from a temperature/pressure (T/P) relief valve is a sign of a worn or defective temperature/pressure (T/P) relief valve. Recommend a licensed plumbing contractor replace as needed.

TPR-Overflow Pipe Terminates at Floor
In the event that the thermostat fails on the water heater, boiling water disperses at a 110 pounds per square inch (hot and fast) and needs to be projected within 6" inches of the catch pan under the tank or outside. Installing a permitted pipe type from the temperature relief valve (TPR) to the pan or exterior of the building will divert this hot and fast water from damaging the structure or electrical components in the event of a thermostat failure. Minimum drain pipe radius must be the same as the TPR Female fitting and no smaller under most codes, typically 3/4 inch. Recommend a licensed plumbing contractor assess further and repair as needed.

No TPR-Overflow Pipe Present
In case the thermostat fails on the water heater, the water in the tank can heat up to above boiling temperatures (210 degrees) expanding (every inch of water turns into a square foot of steam) this expansion in the tank can cause an explosion. To prevent the possibility of this occurring, a temperature relief valve is installed that can detect temperatures higher than the allowable heat radiance and will relieve the tank of excess pressure by opening. When this happens, boiling water disperses at a 110 pounds per square inch (hot and fast) and needs to be projected within 6" inches of the catch pan under the tank or outside. Installing a permitted pipe type from the temperature relief valve (TPR) to the pan or exterior of the building will divert this hot and fast water from damaging the structure or electrical components in the event of a thermostat failure. Recommend licensed plumber to complete all work. Minimum drain pipe radius typically must be the same as the TPR Female fitting and no smaller, typically 3/4 inch. Any acceptable potable water pipe will work.

Water Heater is Antiquated; has Reached or Exceeded its known Life Expectancy
Water heaters serviceability has exceeded its known life expectancy and is likely to incur a failure of the elements, tank or other component. Recommend a licensed plumbing contractor replace the unit preemptive of a potential leak.

No Exhaust Flue observed connected to the Water Heater
Per the IMC (International Mechanical Code); "502.1 General. An exhaust system shall be provided, maintained and operated as specifically required by this section and for all occupied areas where machines, vats, tanks, furnaces, forges, salamanders and other *appliances, equipment* and processes in such areas produce or throw off dust or particles sufficiently light to float in the air, or which emit heat, odors, fumes, spray, gas or smoke, in such quantities so as to be irritating or injurious to health or safety."

No Exhaust Flue observed connected to the Boiler
Per the IMC (International Mechanical Code); "502.1 General. An exhaust system shall be provided, maintained and operated as specifically required by this section and for all occupied areas where machines, vats, tanks, furnaces, forges, salamanders and other *appliances, equipment* and processes in such areas produce or throw off dust or particles sufficiently light to float in the air, or which emit heat, odors, fumes, spray, gas or smoke, in such quantities so as to be irritating or injurious to health or safety."

TPR Valve has Reducer Installed-Overflow Pipe Insufficient
In case the thermostat fails on the water heater, the water in the tank can heat up to above boiling temperatures (210 degrees) expanding (every inch of water turns into a square foot of steam) this expansion in the tank can cause an explosion. To prevent the possibility of this occurring, a temperature relief valve is installed that can detect temperatures higher than the allowable heat radiance and will relieve the tank of excess pressure by opening. When this happens, boiling water disperses at a 110 pounds per square inch (hot and fast) and needs to be projected within 6" inches of the catch pan under the tank or outside. Installing a permitted pipe type from the temperature relief valve (TPR) to the pan or exterior of the building will divert this hot and fast water from damaging the structure or electrical components in the event of a thermostat failure. The pipe that is currently installed, is reduced from Its original required size. Recommend a licensed plumbing contractor assess the area further and repair as needed. Minimum drain pipe radius must be the same as the TPR Female fitting and no smaller in most codes, typically 3/4 inch. All pipe reducers should be removed where applicable. Any acceptable potable water pipe will work.

Lime Scale or Calcium Carbonate Fouling on Pipe Inlet Joints
Even in hard water areas, pipes will not scale unless the saturation index of the water is exceeded. The saturation index of water is controlled by its acidity (or alkalinity which is the reverse) which we establish by pH measurement. The lower the pH, the more acidic the water and the more it can hold in solution. The higher the pH, the less acidic the water, the lower the saturation index, and the less the water can hold dissolved minerals. We raise the pH by heating the water, causing pressure drops (e.g. taps) and adding chemicals. By raising the pH, we are reducing the ability of the water to hold minerals in solution and these minerals are forced to

precipitate and cause scale fouling. The scaling/build up on the valves are caused by minute orifices at the threading of the joints and is caused by minute amounts of water to surface, crystallizing/scaling upon breaching the surface. For threaded plumbing fittings, using Teflon tape or plumbers paste around joint threading will typically remedy the issue. For soldered joints, re-sweating of the pipe joint will likely be needed.

Leak Observed and Lime Scale/Calcium Carbonate Fouling on Pipe Inlet/Outlet Joints

Present water was observed at the joint. Fouling was observed. Even in hard water areas, pipes will not scale unless the saturation index of the water is exceeded. If the water is under-saturated or at equilibrium saturation, there will be no scale. Conversely, "soft water" can scale if it becomes over saturated. The saturation index of water is controlled by its acidity (or alkalinity which is the reverse) which we establish by pH measurement. The lower the pH, the more acidic the water and the more it can hold in solution. The higher the pH, the less acidic the water, the lower the saturation index, and the less the water can hold dissolved minerals. We raise the pH by heating the water, causing pressure drops (e.g. taps) and adding chemicals. By raising the pH, we are reducing the ability of the water to hold minerals in a solution and these minerals are forced to precipitate and cause scale fouling. Recirculating systems (e.g. cooling towers, steam generators, water recovery systems) operate at cycles of concentration with pressure drops and temperature variances causing both super saturation and pH increases simultaneously. Unfortunately, unless installing a mineral filtration system, there is little to resolve the cause of internal scaling, however, the scaling/build up on the joints, are caused by minute orifices at the threading/ soldered or glued pipe joints depending on material type, allowing small amounts of water to reach the surface, crystallizing/scaling upon breaching the surface. For threaded plumbing fittings, using Teflon tape or plumbers paste around joint threading will typically remedy the issue. For soldered joints, re-sweating of the pipe/fitting will likely be needed. Recommend a licensed plumber assess and repair as is needed.

Glass Lined Water Heater in Operable Condition

Decades ago, water heaters were known to have a minimum life expectancy of 20 years or more. Now, due mostly to plan obsolescence and profit incentives, a standard water heater has an average life of 7-15 years, if you're lucky. For glass lined tanks, tank failure is the only reason to replace a unit unless required by your insurance company due to its age and the stigma given from standard tanks commonly corroding through. Everything else, can be repaired. While there are fiberglass tanks with life time warranties and stainless steel tanks that will last years longer than a standard unit, the most common, longest living tank is by far, the glass lined tank. It suffers no corrosion to the glass. Showers commonly spew heat vapor in the air when showering, these are ingested by breathing. Water and minerals may also absorb in the skin. With standard tanks, that comes with rust etc. but with a glass lined unit, the water is not picking up these oxides and thus, they are not transferred in the air or on your skin. It is recommended to have the unit serviced and maintained. Recommend a licensed plumber assess and treat the tank for other minerals/deposits and check/replace the anode rod as needed.

Water Heaters Gate Valve Shut Off was observed Seized/Hard to Actuate when Testing

Gate valves commonly incur problems as they are rarely used. Because of this, the valves tend to develop fouling and inevitable fusing within the packing/shaft components within the valve. This can allow the valve to leak if attempted to be closed. Recommend a licensed plumbing contractor replace all seized valves as needed. Recommend quarter round turn valves to replace the gate valves present.

HVAC

Central HVAC Full System Basic Comments

The readily observable ducts were inspected and found to be serviceable. The system was tested for proper air distribution for both hot and cold performed at every accessible vent and found to be serviceable. The service panel was removed from the handler. An inspection of the evaporator coils, fins as well as the blower and capacitor where visible was performed. The coils were found to be clean as well as the blower. Both were in good condition at the time of the inspection. Recommend having the unit inspected bi-annually to prevent particulates from clogging the unit, algae/fungi from building up in the condensate pipe and microbes from culturing in the handler unit.

Basic Heat Strip/Heating Comments

The heating was turned on and serviceable. The heat strip was tested at the vent registers at each room for operable heating and found to be operable at the time of the inspection. Recommend having the unit inspected bi-annually to prevent particulates from clogging the unit, algae/fungi from building up in the condensate pipe and microbes from culturing in the handler unit.

Basic Air Conditioning and Condenser Comments

The HVAC cooling portion of the central system was tested at the annunciator/control panel and was serviceable. The air conditioning was tested at the vent registers at each room for operable heating and found to be operable at the time of the inspection. Recommend having a state licensed HVAC contractor inspect and service the unit bi-annually to prevent particulates from clogging the unit, algae/fungi from building up in the condensate pipe and microbes from culturing in the handler unit.

Gas Furnace Inspection, Service and Maintenance

The heating system should be inspected by a qualified service technician every year. It is recommended that the system be inspected before the heating season. The technician can ensure the continued safe operation of the heating system.

Floor Vent in Bedroom is obstructed by the Bed

This will Likely Happen as long as certain size mattresses such as double or greater types are used and the bed is positioned in a way that covers the vent. The coldest air is trapped under the bed, inhibiting flow. Since heat rises, it remains at waist level and higher. When the heat is distributed, it too is trapped and can cause worse problems to substrates etc. It is recommended to reset the vent register to abut the wall best suited for flow in consideration to personal articles such as furniture that may inhibit conditioned air flow or as directed by a licensed HVAC technician.

Particulate Build Up on Evaporator Coil/Fins Observed at the Time of the Inspection
Recommend a licensed HVAC technician to treat the coil and surfaces within the unit as needed. Also recommend having the unit inspected bi-annually to prevent particulates from clogging the unit, algae/fungi from building up in the condensate pipe and microbes from culturing in the handler unit.

Particulate Build Up on Various Components within the Handler Unit Observed
This can promote fungi development and will reduce the overall blower blades curvature countering the contour and ultimately reducing the unit's efficiency. Recommend a licensed HVAC technician service the blower blades and surfaces within the unit as needed. Recommend having the unit inspected bi-annually to prevent particulates from clogging the unit, algae/fungi from building up in the condensate pipe and microbes from culturing in the handler unit.

Particulate Build Up on Blower Blades Observed at the Time of the Inspection
This can promote microbial development and will reduce the overall blower blades curvature countering the contour and ultimately reducing the unit's efficiency. Recommend a licensed HVAC technician service the blower blades and surfaces within the unit as needed. Recommend having the unit inspected bi-annually to prevent particulates from clogging the unit, algae/fungi from building up in the condensate pipe and microbes from culturing in the handler unit.

Duct Pinched/Obstructed by Truss/Joist Wood Member in Attic
Insufficient Strapping Observed at Duct. Duct lye's on the wood bracing of the roof truss/ceiling joist system. This has caused it to pinch/obstruct the proper distribution of air in the duct. Recommend proper strapping be installed at the duct and wherever needed to prevent further obstructions and to ensure operability of the ducting and system.

Return is Located Adjacent to an Egress Door
This area is particularly hot. When the door is not weatherized and especially if the door is hollow core/interior rated, thermal bridging and hot air intrusion is most abundant at these locations. The hot air rises, enters the return and thereby sends unconditioned air to the handler. In the summer, this can cause the unit to run longer to compensate for the returns placement. Recommend a licensed HVAC technician relocate the return where best suited and/or adding additional returns at the room(s) to equal air pressures if needed and afford more compensatory conditioned air into the system, offsetting the amount of air pulled at the door.

No P-Trap Observed at Condensate Drain Line
Problems with primary condensate drain lines stem form plant pollen, fungus spores and other particulate matter entrained in the air stream passing over the wet evaporator coil. They are captured by the condensate draining off the coil and are carried into the drain system. There they produce algae, mildew, and fungus growths which can clog the primary drain system. While the emergency drain lines are normally dry and clear, they are open to the atmosphere. Wasps, called "mud-daubers", are known to nest in these open drain lines, thereby rendering them useless; always at the wrong time. Condensate traps are intended to allow the condensate to flow from the air handler/coil where the drain is in the NEGATIVE (return) air flow. If you fail to trap it properly the unit will suck air up the drain, displacing the water until it either overflows in the unit or releases with a huge gush. The vent after the trap is to prevent a double trap scenario where multiple units are tied together or the condensate line has sags in it. It also serves as a handy clean out. Drains in the POSITIVE air flow require additional corrective action. Per the IMC (International Mechanical Code); "307.2.4 Traps. Condensate drains shall be trapped as required by the *equipment* or *appliance* manufacturer." Recommend an HVAC service professional review and designate whether or not a trap/vent is proper for your system.

No Drain Lines Installed at the Wall/Window HVAC Units Drain Hole
A condensate Drain Line/Pipe from the catch pan is a drain line that drains water from the catch pan. The catch pan and drain is a secondary back up to the condensate draining system that protects the condensate overflow from damaging interior substrates in the event of the main drain from the handler clogs or is backing up. When the main clogs, typical handler units have a secondary drain that overflows to the catch pan and thus, the catch pan drain is needed to circumvent that water to the exterior of the building. If the unit backs up condensate and it overflows into the pan without a drain, it will ultimately overflow and cause water damages. Fortunately, this is a relatively easy fix and can be performed by your HVAC technician at the next servicing and is recommended as soon as possible.

No Condensate Drain Line Observed from the Catch Pan under the Handler Unit to the Exterior
A condensate Drain Line/Pipe from the catch pan is a drain line that drains water from the catch pan. The catch pan and drain is a secondary back up to the condensate draining system that protects the condensate overflow from damaging interior substrates in the event of the main drain from the handler clogs or is backing up. When the main clogs, typical handler units have a secondary drain that overflows to the catch pan and thus, the catch pan drain is needed to circumvent that water to the exterior of the building. If the unit backs up condensate and it overflows into the pan without a drain, it will ultimately overflow and cause water damages. Fortunately, this is a relatively easy fix and can be performed by your HVAC technician at the next servicing.

Structural Framing/Support of the Handler Unit is Improper
Structural Framing/Support of the Handler Unit is improper and may allow damage to the unit if not fixed. Recommend a licensed contractor assess further and reframe as needed to local/state codes.

Central A/C Coolant Lines - Metal Box Conduit Cover Needs Cover to Defer Rodent Intrusion
HVAC coolant lines at the metal box conduit cover located is not properly filled to prevent rodent intrusion. The metal box out should be filled with an exterior rated polyurethane foam or better/as directed by a licensed contractor.

HVAC Coolant Lines Metal Box Conduit Cover is Loose at the Wall
This can allow rodent entry into the attic at the coolant line entry location. Recommend a licensed electrician resetting/fastening the cover and sealing all as is needed ASAP.

Central HVAC Exterior Unit Observed Appears Undersized
When the exterior unit is undersized, it does not have the capacity to move refrigerant fast enough to get the indoor coil cool enough. This results in higher electric bills and premature failures within the system. It is beyond the scope of a general home or building inspection to further diagnose the HVAC system. Recommend a licensed HVAC technician assess the system further and repair all where needed.

Central HVAC Interior Unit Observed Appears Undersized
When the interior unit is undersized, it can generally only vary 1/2ton and would be ok as long as it has a TXV to regulate the flow of the refrigerant. This could not be confirmed as it is beyond the scope of a general home or building inspection. Recommend a licensed HVAC technician assess further and repair where/if needed.

Central HVAC Exterior Unit Observed Appears Oversized
When the exterior unit is oversized, it cannot generally exceed ½ ton and would typically require an accumulator device outside so the excess refrigerant has some place to be stored. This is because the TXV limits the flow to the capacity of the indoor coil. If it does not have a TXV and an accumulator installed, it will result in low efficiency resulting in high electric bills and have premature compressor failure by making the compressor sluggish as it forces the lubricating oil out of the compressor, restricting both outdoor and indoor coils.

Door to Handler Unit Closet Space Needs to be Air Sealed
To ensure optimal efficiency and filtration, it is recommended to enforce the door jamb with function weather stripping aligning the door to defer air intrusion, providing an adequate air seal, allowing the return air to come from the hinged filter access only. Recommend a proper weather strip be installed at the base for proper air sealing.

Exposed Thermostat Wires Observed Spliced but not Sealed from the Elements at the Exterior
Many HVAC technicians, when installing the exterior unit to a central system, fail to properly cover the thermostat wires, either from negligent practice or because the wire is a little short of the panel and cover. Even if the wires are somewhat covered, when the area is inflicted with a heavy storm, the wires tend to come in contact with steady moisture. This will cause fluidic capillary action which causes water to enter the wires sheathing and leads back up the wire. Most copper will incur a copper oxide that can inhibit current. Recommend sealing all wire nuts with liquid tape after inspection and cleaning, if any, by a licensed technician.

Exterior Condensing Unit Coil Fins Observed Damaged Intermittently
The coil fins are constructed closely and are very thin. The fins are designed to expel heat energy from the coils through the convection process. The large fan mounted at the top of the unit, forces air through all of these coil

fins and coils, transferring heat energy from the coils to the fins by conduction and then to the air from the fan by convection. When the fins are damaged, it can severely damper the efficiency of this process, can wear the unit faster and ultimately, can increase energy bills considerably. Recommend a state licensed HVAC contractor review further and repair/replace as recommended by a licensed HVAC contractor.

Handler Unit; Particulates and Suspected Microbes on Wires Observed
This is caused by lack of routine servicing. Excess dust and particulate build up can accumulate on the wires within the handler unit. It is recommended to have the unit serviced bi-annually to all serviceable parts and treat any particulates on wires, blower blades, evaporator coils etc. to reduce the possibilities of culture of fungi that can grow in a neglected unit. If left to accumulate, a result, the unit strains more and runs longer, wearing the motors out and costing you higher bills. Additionally, the presents of some fungi microbes on the interior wires circumferential surface as presently observed can cause other areas to become contaminated as the air cycles them. If the unit has not been treated in some time, some or all of these things can occur. Fortunately, this is a routine issue and is easily remedied with an average minimal cost. Always get various servicing quotes and credentials from all technicians before servicing. Service ASAP.

No Exhaust Flue Observed connected to the Heating Furnace
Per the IMC (International Mechanical Code); "502.1 General. An exhaust system shall be provided, maintained and operated as specifically required by this section and for all occupied areas where machines, vats, tanks, furnaces, forges, salamanders and other *appliances, equipment* and processes in such areas produce or throw off dust or particles sufficiently light to float in the air, or which emit heat, odors, fumes, spray, gas or smoke, in such quantities so as to be irritating or injurious to health or safety."

Service Hatch to the Handler in the Attic Appears Insufficient
Access to the handler unit was insufficient. Per The 2015 IMC (International Mechanical Code); "306.3 Appliances in attics. Attics containing appliances shall be provided with an opening and unobstructed passageway large enough to allow removal of the largest *appliance*. The passageway shall not be less than 30 inches (762 mm) high and 22 inches (559 mm) wide and not more than 20 feet (6096 mm) in length measured along the centerline of the passageway from the opening to the *appliance*. The passageway shall have continuous solid flooring not less than 24 inches (610 mm) wide. A level service space not less than 30 inches (762 mm) deep and 30 inches (762 mm) wide shall be present at the front or service side of the *appliance*. The clear access opening dimensions shall be a minimum of 20 inches by 30 inches (508mmby 762 mm), and large enough to allow removal of the largest *appliance*." Recommend a licensed contractor assess the hatch further and repair as needed.

No Service Hatch to the Handler in the Attic Observed
Access to the handler unit was not observed. This can be a safety hazard. Without proper access to the unit to service it or in case of an emergency, a whole host of issues may arise. Without proper inspection of the unit, backflows, equipment failures microbial and particulate build up etc. cannot be addressed prior to the unit malfunctioning. This can lead to interior water damage, electrical shorts if the unit wiring has deficiencies or worse. Per The 2015 IMC (International Mechanical Code); "306.3 Appliances in attics. Attics containing appliances shall be provided with an opening and unobstructed passageway large enough to allow removal of the largest *appliance*. The passageway shall not be less than 30 inches (762 mm) high and 22 inches (559 mm) wide and not more than 20 feet (6096 mm) in length measured along the centerline of the passageway from the opening to the *appliance*. The passageway shall have continuous solid flooring not less than 24 inches (610 mm) wide. A level service space not less than 30 inches (762 mm) deep and 30 inches (762 mm) wide shall be present at the front or service side of the *appliance*. The clear access opening dimensions shall be a minimum of 20 inches by 30 inches (508mmby 762 mm), and large enough to allow removal of the largest *appliance*." Recommend a licensed contractor assess the area further and repair as needed.

No Ducting Sleeve Observed at the Coolant Line Running Through the Concrete Floor
Per the IMC, International Mechanical Code 2012; "SECTION 1107 REFRIGERANT PIPING 1107.2 Piping location. Refrigerant piping that crosses an open space that affords passageway in any building shall be not less than 7 feet 3 inches (2210 mm) above the floor unless the piping is located against the ceiling of such space. Refrigerant piping shall not be placed in any elevator, dumbwaiter or other shaft containing a moving object or in any shaft that has openings to living quarters or to means of egress. Refrigerant piping shall not be installed in an enclosed public stairway, stair landing or means of egress. 1107.2.1 Piping in concrete floors. Refrigerant piping installed in concrete floors shall be encased in pipe ducts. The piping shall be isolated and supported to prevent damaging vibration, stress and corrosion. 1107.2.1 Piping in concrete floors. Refrigerant piping installed

in concrete floors shall be encased in pipe ducts. The piping shall be isolated and supported to prevent damaging vibration, stress and corrosion. Recommend a licensed contractor repair to code as is needed.

Condensate Drain Line Observed Terminating at and on the Exterior Wall

Direct and consistent condensate water dripping on the exterior substrates, causes algae's and funguses to grow, potentially damaging the material surfaces etc. Recommend a licensed HVAC technician review the line further and install an extension and P-Trap if needed.

HVAC Ducting

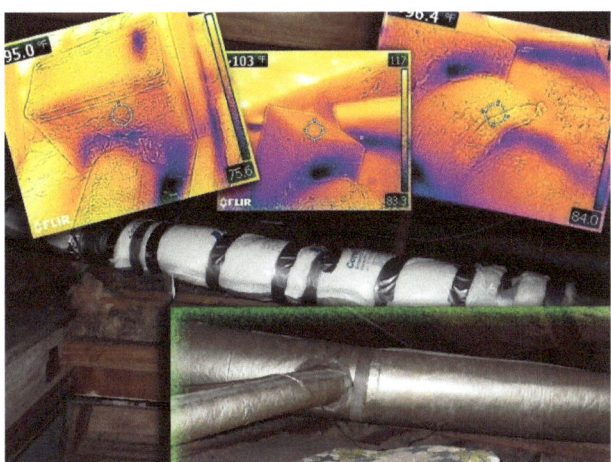

Replacement of HVAC equipment post 2009, no Mastic Observed on Collars/Joints within the Ducting System

Most state code requirements for HVAC mechanical and ducting, reflect the International Mechanical Code. Equipment sizing is no longer exempted for existing buildings. Existing equipment that need not meet minimum code efficiencies; shall be returned to the conditions of its listing. Per the IMC; "SECTION 312 HEATING AND COOLING LOAD CALCULATIONS 312.1 Load calculations. Heating and cooling system design loads for the purpose of sizing systems, appliances and *equipment* shall be determined in accordance with the procedures described in the *ASHRAE/ACCA* Standard 183. Alternatively, design loads shall be determined by an *approved* equivalent computation procedure, using the design parameters specified in Chapter 3 of the *International Energy Conservation Code*." With total replacement of HVAC evaporators and condensing units, all accessible (> 30 inches clearance) joints and seams in the air distribution system shall be inspected and sealed where needed using reinforced mastic or code approved equivalent. Signed certification by the contractor attached to air handler is required.

Exceptions: 1) Ducts in conditioned space 2) Joints or seams that are already sealed with fabric and mastic 3) If system is tested and repaired as necessary per the IMC (International Mechanical Code, Existing Ducting) Recommend the installation company review the system and tape/mastic all collars and joints per the state/local code as is needed.

Interior Handler Return/Distribution Seal at the Duct/Wall Abutment was not Properly Sealed

Various exposures to the wall/attic were observed and can allow unfiltered air into the building as well as rodents if they enter the attic. Improper duct taping/Mastic at the concerning areas was observed with air seal breaches throughout. The Wall/ceiling around the ducting need to be fully taped/sealed and mastic applied at all corners and openings. Air follows the path of least resistance. Filters can catch a lot of airborne particulates and if used properly can help maintain the serviceability of the unit, however, handler units are not entirely air tight and may draw negative static pressure. If the system pulls more than it can allow through the filter or if there are openings large enough, air will enter the handler around the filter area instead of through it. Key rule to note is air when forced, follows the path of least resistance. The suction of air, regardless of where it enters the handler, can ultimately be drawn from the cracks and openings into the wall and ceiling area, drawing in unfiltered and unconditioned air. Recommend a licensed HVAC technician seal all duct joints/collars as needed.

Loose Seal Observed at a Ducting Collar

Loose ducting collar was observed. Recommend a licensed HVAC technician repair as needed to prevent "sweating" at the joint or unfiltered air to enter the ducting system.

No Filter Observed at the Hinged Air Filter Grill
Filters are key integral components required for the handler to operate and function most efficiently. Filters do just what is implied by their name, they filter the air and inhibit most dust and airborne pathogen particulate from passing. If excess dust is allowed to pass the filter or return, it settles on the material surfaces and coil fins within the handler. The evaporator coil within the handler system assists with dehumidifying the building as the air passing the coil releases the moisture molecules held within the hotter air on to the coil. If dust builds up on this surface, the water and dust/particulate create a sludge of nutrient for molds/fungi to culture. For this reason and to provide higher efficiency to the system, it is highly recommended to install new air filters per each hinged grill and replace them as directed. Recommend allergen and pathogen inhibitive corrugated filters or better as needed.

No Service Hatch to the Attic Observed. Could Not Inspect Ducting
Without proper access to the ducting for servicing and inspecting it or in case of an emergency, a whole host of issues may arise. Without proper inspection of the ducting, loose tape joints, improper junctions, leaking collars, rodent damage or a many other variable may occur. This can allow unconditioned or filtered air from the attic to enter the system, potentially allowing microbial and particulate build up etc. within the system that cannot be addressed. This can lead to interior water damage, sweating, sic home or worse. Per The 2015 IMC (International Mechanical Code); "306.3 Appliances in attics. Attics containing appliances shall be provided with an opening and unobstructed passageway large enough to allow removal of the largest *appliance*. The passageway shall not be less than 30 inches (762 mm) high and 22 inches (559 mm) wide....The clear access opening dimensions shall be a minimum of 20 inches by 30 inches (508mmby 762 mm), and large enough to allow removal of the largest *appliance*." This code is in reference to the handler or other appliance that may have been stored in the attic. Since this isn't the case here, it is a reflection for the purpose of recommendation to readily access and service the ducting when needed. Recommend a licensed contractor assess the hatch further and repair as needed.

Handler Return/Distribution Ducting Enclosures Not Properly Sealed at the Air Handler
Various improper duct taping areas and methodology was observed with air seal breaches throughout. The ducting and enclosures need to be fully taped/sealed and mastic applied at all corners and openings. Air follows the path of least resistance. Filters can catch a lot of airborne particulates and if used properly can help maintain the serviceability of the unit, however, handler units are not entirely air tight and may draw negative static pressure. If the system pulls more than it can allow through the filter or if there are openings large enough, air will enter the handler around the filter area instead of through it. Key rule to note is air when forced, follows the path of least resistance. The suction of air, regardless of where it enters the handler, can ultimately be drawn from the cracks and openings through the wall and ceiling area, drawing in unfiltered and unconditioned air. Seal As Needed.

Distribution Ducting Not Properly Mastic Sealed at the Abutting Joints/Collars
Handler Return/Distribution Ducting was observed insufficiently sealed at the abutting joints and collars. In most states, newer sealing methodology requires that all ducting joints/collars in the system be resealed when the HVAC mechanical system is changed out but the ducting is left. This was not observed. The Ducting and Enclosures Need to be fully taped/sealed and mastic applied at all corners and openings. Air follows the path of least resistance. Filters can catch a lot of airborne particulates and if used properly can help maintain the serviceability of the unit, however, handler units are not entirely air tight and may draw negative static pressure. If the system pulls more than it can allow through the filter or if there are openings large enough, air will enter the handler around the filter area instead of through it. Key rule to note is air when forced, follows the path of least resistance. The suction of air, regardless of where it enters the handler, can ultimately be drawn from the cracks and openings into the wall and ceiling area, drawing in unfiltered and unconditioned air. Recommend a licensed HVAC technician seal all duct joints/collars as needed.

No Service Hatch to the Attic System to Inspect Ducting
Per The 2015 IMC (International Mechanical Code); "SECTION 306 ACCESS AND SERVICE SPACE 306.1 Access for maintenance and replacement. Appliances shall be accessible for inspection, service, repair and replacement without disabling the function of a fire-resistance-rated assembly or removing permanent construction, other appliances, venting systems or any other piping or ducts not connected to the *appliance* being inspected, serviced, repaired or replaced. A level working space at least 30 inches deep and 30 inches wide (762 mm by 762 mm) shall be provided in front of the control side to service an *appliance*." Recommend a licensed contractor assess the area further and repair as needed.

Return is Located Adjacent to an Egress Door
This area is particularly hot. When the door is not weatherized and especially if the door is hollow core/interior rated, thermal bridging and hot air intrusion is most abundant at these locations. The hot air rises, enters the return and thereby sends unconditioned air to the handler. In the summer, this can cause the unit to run longer to compensate for the returns placement. Recommend a licensed HVAC technician relocate the return where best suited and/or adding additional returns at the room(s) to prefer air pressures if needed and afford more compensatory conditioned air into the system, offsetting the amount of air pulled at the door.

Handler in Closet; Louvered Door. Filter Door Fasteners Missing at the Handler Filter Hatch
Filters are key integral components required for the handler to operate and function most efficiently. Filters do just what is implied by their name, they filter the air and inhibit most dust and airborne pathogen particulate from passing. If excess dust is allowed to pass the filter or return, it settles on the material surfaces and coil fins within the handler. The evaporator coil within the handler system assists with dehumidifying the building as the air passing the coil releases the moisture molecules held within the hotter air on to the coil. If dust builds up on this surface, the water and dust/particulate create sludge of nutrient for molds/fungi to culture. For this reason and to provide higher efficiency to the system, it is highly recommended to install fasteners, a new hatch or seal the entire interior of the handler closet and install a solid door to the closet with a hinged grill. Recommend allergen and pathogen inhibitive corrugated filters or better as needed. Recommend a licensed HVAC contractor assess the area further and repair as needed.

Filter Door Fasteners Missing at the Handler Filter Hatch
Filters are key integral components required for the handler to operate and function most efficiently. Filters do just what is implied by their name, they filter the air and inhibit most dust and airborne pathogen particulate from passing. If excess dust is allowed to pass the filter or return, it settles on the material surfaces and coil fins within the handler. The evaporator coil within the handler system assists with dehumidifying the building as the air passing the coil releases the moisture molecules held within the hotter air on to the coil. If dust builds up on this surface, the water and dust/particulate create sludge of nutrient for molds/fungi to culture. For this reason and to provide higher efficiency to the system, it is highly recommended to install fasteners or a new hatch. Recommend allergen and pathogen inhibitive corrugated filters or better as needed. Recommend a licensed HVAC contractor assess the area further and repair as needed.

Rodent Damage Observed at the Ducting in the Attic
Recommend a licensed pest control contractor assess the building for pests and exterminate as needed. Recommend a licensed HVAC technician repair as needed all damaged or leaking ducting to prevent "sweating" at the damaged location, joint or have unfiltered air enter the ducting system.

Recommend Installing a Pleated Air Filtration System to the HVAC System
The Pleated Filter is many times more efficient, effective, and cost-effective than the 'throwaway' fiberglass Furnace Filter or a mesh type reusable filter. An alarming percentage of HVAC professionals and Building Operators continue to promote and continue to use 'throwaway' Panel Filters as their primary HVAC air filtration. Recommend installing a pleated air filtration system for best results in maintaining the whole HVAC system compared to the standard norm. Recommend a licensed HVAC technician preform all work as needed.

Recommend Installing a New Pleated Air Filter in the System
The Pleated Filter is many times more efficient, effective, and cost-effective than the 'throwaway' fiberglass furnace filter or a mesh type reusable filter. An alarming percentage of HVAC professionals and building operators continue to promote and continue to use 'throwaway' panel filters as their primary HVAC air filtration. Recommend installing a new pleated air filter for best results in maintaining the system compared to the standard norm. Recommend a licensed HVAC technician preform all work as needed. Note: If the present filter is left in, the system can ware as it tries to push air through the constricted air filter. This can wear the system as a whole and cause the system to run more frequently, costing a lot more on your electric bills in general.

Exhaust Systems

Exhaust Vent Terminates in the Attic
Exhaust vent was observed terminating in the attic space. This will send hot moist air into the attic, potentially causing microbial growths on the attic substrates, insect or rodent intrusion etcetera. Recommend a state licensed mechanical contractor repair as is needed.

Gas Water Heater Vent Straps/Fasteners were Observed Loose
Recommend a state licensed contractor refasten per the NFPA and/or to all state/local code requirements to prevent damage to the vent and potential fire hazards.

Draft Hood Loose/Displaced at the Water Heater Abutment
Recommend a licensed plumbing and mechanical contractor replace/repair the draft hood to assist in stabilizing the vent and to provide proper back draft protection for the water heater unit as is needed.

No Barometric Damper Observed at the Gas Water Heater Flue Pipe
Why a Barometric Damper or Draft Regulator Is Needed; During oil burner operation, also on some gas fired equipment, combustion air moves into the burner are and combustion chamber as combustion air. As combustion continues, a mix of air and combustion gases continues onwards, moving out of the combustion chamber, up through the boiler or furnace heat exchanger, through the flue vent connector called the "stack pipe or flue pipe" and on into the chimney where these gases are finally vented outside, usually above the building roof. The force with which this air or combustion gas moves is the "draft" inside of the heating appliance. Too much draft increases heating appliance operating cost by venting heat out through the chimney instead of transferring the heat into the building where it was wanted. Too much draft can also increase chimney temperatures to an unsafe level. Too little draft can result in incomplete combustion, soot-clogging of heating equipment, a dangerous condition. Additionally, more dangerous heating appliance malfunctions can occur such as oil burner puff backs and in some cases dangerous production of carbon monoxide gas that leaks into the building (a potentially fatal problem). Recommend a licensed plumbing and mechanical contractor assess the area further and repair all as needed.

Flue Collar Observed not Attached Properly to the Exhaust Flue for the Gas Fired Water Heater
This can allow deadly scentless carbon monoxide to accumulate within the room housing the heater and can further back into the building through breaches in the air seals of the door(s), walls and ceiling where applicable.

PVC Flue Observed In Use for the Gas Heater Exhaust
The piping manufacturer recommends that inquiries about the suitability of plastic piping systems for venting combustion gases should be directed to the manufacturer of the water or space heating equipment being installed. As stated in the International Code Council's International Fuel Gas Code 503.4.1.1: **Plastic pipe and fittings used to vent appliances shall be installed in accordance with the appliance manufacturer's**

installation instructions. Furthermore, several of the ASTM standards applicable to PVC plastic pipe and fittings that this company manufactures their pipe to include the following note: This standard specification for PVC pipe does not include requirements for pipe and fittings intended to be used to vent combustion gases. Generally, for a new condensing water heater or boiler, the stack temperature will be about 20 degrees higher than the water temperature. The design and efficiency of the unit, along with several other factors, including water quality, will affect the stack temperature. If a water heater is set to store water at 140 F to minimize Legionella bacteria growth, the flue gas temperature will be about 160 F when the heater is new. The PVC Flue is used for venting the water heater exhaust, though legal if recommended by the manufacturer. As scale builds up and the heater efficiency falls off, the flue gas temperatures can easily increase to over 350 degrees F. Even if someone had their water heater set at 120 F, with scaling, the flue gas temperatures can rise well above 300 F. Boiler thermostats or burner controls are generally limited to 200 F, commercial water heater thermostats or burner controls to 180 F and residential water heater burner controls to 160 F, and all can overshoot by several degrees. As scale builds up on the heating surfaces, the scale insulates the flue gases from the hot water in the system, causing the flue gas temperatures to increase. For safety, though not required, it is recommended to re-pipe the PVC exhaust flue with a steel type for this vent.

Dryer Vent, Vents under the Building in the Crawl Space
Hot humid air that is projected into the crawl space can cause microbial growths on the wood sub floor, swell or delaminate edges of surface flooring above the vent, add lint allergens to concentrate under the building that may act as a beacon for pests. Recommend a licensed contractor redirect and install new exhaust pipe to the exterior of the building per the state and local code requirements.

No Exhaust Flue Observed Connected to the Heating Furnace
Per the IMC (International Mechanical Code); "502.1 General. An exhaust system shall be provided, maintained and operated as specifically required by this section and for all occupied areas where machines, vats, tanks, furnaces, forges, salamanders and other *appliances, equipment* and processes in such areas produce or throw off dust or particles sufficiently light to float in the air, or which emit heat, odors, fumes, spray, gas or smoke, in such quantities so as to be irritating or injurious to health or safety."

No Barometric Damper Observed at the Gas Water Heater Flue Pipe
Why a Barometric Damper or Draft Regulator Is Needed; During oil burner operation, also on some gas fired equipment, combustion air moves into the burner are and combustion chamber as combustion air. As combustion continues, a mix of air and combustion gases continues onwards, moving out of the combustion chamber, up through the boiler or furnace heat exchanger, through the flue vent connector called the "stack pipe or flue pipe" and on into the chimney where these gases are finally vented outside, usually above the building roof. The force with which this air or combustion gas moves is the "draft" inside of the heating appliance. Too much draft increases heating appliance operating cost by venting heat out through the chimney instead of transferring the heat into the building where it was wanted. Too much draft can also increase chimney temperatures to an unsafe level. Too little draft can result in incomplete combustion, soot-clogging of heating equipment, a dangerous condition. Additionally, more dangerous heating appliance malfunctions can occur such as oil burner puff backs and in some cases dangerous production of carbon monoxide gas that leaks into the building (a potentially fatal problem). Recommend a licensed plumbing and mechanical contractor assess the area further and repair all as needed.

Clothes Dryer Exhaust Expels into the Interior/Garage
Per The IRC/IBC 2012; "CHAPTER 15 EXHAUST SYSTEMS CLOTHES DRYER EXHAUST, [Subsection] MI502.1 General. Clothes dryers shall be exhausted in accordance with the manufacturer's instructions. M1502.2 Independent exhaust systems. Dryer exhaust systems shall be independent of all other systems and shall convey the moisture to the outdoors. Exception: This section shall not apply to the listed and labeled condensing (ductless) clothes dryers." Recommend a licensed mechanical/building contractor assess the area further and repair all as needed.

Dryer Vent Observed Expels into the Attic Space
Hot humid air filled with lint particulates project into the attic, providing nutrience for microbial growth when the humidity concentrated at the exhaust pipe elevates moisture levels in neighboring substrates etc. Per the IRC,IBC 2012; "CHAPTER 15 EXHAUST SYSTEMS MI501.1 Outdoor discharge. The air removed by every mechanical exhaust system shall be discharged to the outdoors in accordance with Section MI506.2. Air shall not be exhausted into an attic, soffit, ridge vent or crawl space." Recommend a licensed contractor assess the areas further, repair if needed and install the exhaust vent roof termination hood or other approved apparatus as is needed.

Chimney Flue Appeared Displaced at the Time of the Inspection
A loose flue can expel combustible gases and heat into areas not rated to handle such elements and can cause a fire or carbon monoxide to enter the home etc. In accordance with NFPA 31. 801.18.2; "Flue passageways. The flue gas passageway shall be free of obstructions and combustible deposits and shall be cleaned if previously used for venting a solid or liquid fuel-burning appliance or fireplace. The flue liner, chimney inner wall or vent inner wall shall be continuous and shall be free of cracks, gaps, perforations or other damage or deterioration which would allow the escape of combustion products, including gases, moisture and creosote." Recommend a licensed contractor assess the area further and repair all as needed.

Masonry Chimney Airspace Clearance/Fire Protection. No Liner Observed
As per the NFPA; 801.13. 801.18.4 Clearances. Chimneys and vents shall have airspace clearance to combustibles in accordance with the International Building Code and the chimney or vent manufacturer's installation instructions. Exception: Masonry chimneys without the required airspace clearances shall be permitted to be used if lined or relined with a chimney lining system listed for use in chimneys with reduced clearances in accordance with UL 1777. The chimney clearance shall be not less than permitted by the terms of the chimney liner listing and the manufacturer's instructions.

Chimney and Fireplace Appear to have Extensive Ware
Recommend replacing or rebuilding the fireplace to meet current code. Repair/Replace per State/Local codes and the NFPA; "801.18 Existing chimneys and vents. Where an *appliance* is permanently disconnected from an existing *chimney* or vent, or where an *appliance* is connected to an existing *chimney* or vent during the process of a new installation, the *chimney* or vent shall comply with Sections 801.18.1 through 801.18.4. 801.18.1 Size. The *chimney* or vent shall be resized as necessary to control flue gas condensation in the interior of the *chimney* or vent and to provide the *appliance* or *appliances* served with the required draft. For the venting of oil-fired *appliances* to masonry chimneys, the resizing shall be in accordance with NFPA 31. 801.18.2 Flue passageways. The flue gas passageway shall be free of obstructions and combustible deposits and shall be cleaned if previously used for venting a solid or liquid fuel-burning *appliance* or fireplace. The flue liner, *chimney* inner wall or vent inner wall shall be continuous and shall be free of cracks, gaps, perforations or other damage or deterioration which would allow the escape of *combustion* products, including gases, moisture and creosote. Where an oil-fired *appliance* is connected to an existing masonry *chimney,* such *chimney* flue shall be repaired or relined in accordance with NFPA 31. 801.18.3 Cleanout. Masonry chimneys shall be provided with a cleanout opening complying with Section 801.13. 801.18.4 Clearances. Chimneys and vents shall have airspace *clearance* to combustibles in accordance with the *International Building Code* and the *chimney* or vent manufacturer's installation instructions. Exception: Masonry chimneys without the required airspace *clearances* shall be permitted to be used if lined or relined with a *chimney* lining system *listed* for use in chimneys with reduced *clearances* in accordance with UL 1777. The *chimney clearance* shall be not less than permitted by the terms of the *chimney* liner listing and the manufacturer's instructions. 801.18.4.1 Fire blocking. Noncombustible fire blocking shall be provided in accordance with the International Building Code." *SOURCE: International Mechanical Code.*

Kitchen Exhaust Vent Terminates in the Attic
The exhaust vent for the kitchen is crucial, when installed, to be installed correctly. Incorrect installations, where heat and food exhausts expel in the attic, can allow humidity build up and combustible resins to accumulate on the substrates in the attic amongst other concerns. As per the International Mechanical Code; SECTION 505 DOMESTIC KITCHEN EXHAUST EQUIPMENT 505.1 Domestic systems. Where domestic range hoods and domestic appliances equipped with downdraft exhaust are located within dwelling units, such hoods and appliances shall discharge to the outdoors through sheet metal ducts.

No Heat Exhaust Vent Observed in the Bathroom
Recommend a licensed electrician/mechanical contractor review the area further and install a heat exhaust vent for the bathroom to help prevent humidity build up in the room when in use, causing sweating on the walls and ceiling.

Main Service

Occupied; Basic System Remarks Passing Inspection with GFCI Outlets

Basic Breaker Service Panel Comments Accessible
The service panel's dead front (service panel cover) was removed to inspect the wiring, breakers and grounding system. The panel and its component appeared to be in serviceable condition at the time of the inspection. Recommend an annual/routine inspection by a licensed inspector or electrician to ensure no defects are apparent.

Basic Fuse Service Panel Comments Accessible
The service panel's dead front (service panel cover) was removed to inspect the wiring, fuses and grounding system. The panel and its component appeared to be in serviceable condition at the time of the inspection, however, the fuse box is older and considered antiquated. Many insurance companies will not insure buildings with fuse panels because of their age and the known methods of jerry rigging the fuse sockets make them susceptible to tampering. Recommend a licensed electrician replace/repair as needed.

Main Breaker Suspected to be Undersized for the Load Requirement
Main breaker observed is rated 60 amps. This maximum ampacity of this breaker is typically undersized for the load capacity required for most state and local codes for dwellings, commercial buildings and most small to large apartment units. Additionally, most insurance companies require the main load/breaker ampacity to be a minimum of 100 amp. Recommend a state licensed contractor review the breaker and panel further and upgrade the load capacity/breaker as needed.

Extension Cords Used Throughout the Building
Extension cords observed throughout the building supplementing standard branch circuits and receptacles. This is a direct fire hazard and likely violates numerous codes per the NEC, state and local. It is highly recommended to have a licensed electrician review the area further and repair as is needed.

Stab-Lok Service/Distribution Panel is a Defective Panel Type and should be Replaced ASAP
Federal Pacific Electric (FPE) sold millions of panels between the 1950's and 1980's. Testing by the Consumer Product Safety Commission has shown these breakers to have an unacceptably high rate of failure, which creates a safety hazard. Testing has proven that virtually every panel installed in the United States contains defective breakers. FPE falsified their UL testing, making their UL listing void. Approximately 1 out of 3 breakers are defective. If a breaker fails to trip when it should, the wires in the home that are supposed to be protected can start on fire. Seeing known failure signs would be dead giveaways that there is a problem, but to truly know if the breaker would trip when it needs to, each breaker would need to actually be tested. This testing can be more expensive than having the entire panel replaced. Due to the known defects and limitations to testing, it is

recommended to have a licensed electrician review further for additional defects and replace the panel as is needed.

Occupied with GFCI Outlets
A representative amount of all outlets/receptacles were tested in the building. Accessible outlets were tested with a meter to check for proper voltage. All outlets observed were generating voltage optimally. Additionally, aside of any aforementioned deficiencies, all observed receptacles were tested for grounding and were found to be properly grounded. The service panel's dead front was removed to inspect the interior wiring. All wiring appeared properly gauged, fastened and operable at time of inspection. The bonding, if visible and grounding systems appeared to be serviceable and proper. The GFCI outlets were all tested and were functioning as designed at time of inspection. Aside of any deficiencies addressed within the body of this report, the overall condition of the electrical system was good/serviceable condition.

Occupied; Basic System Remarks Passing Inspection without GFCI Receptacles
A representative amount of outlets were tested in the building. Being that the building was occupied at the time of the inspection, various outlets could not be tested due to furniture obstructing the accessibility of the outlets. Where accessible, circuits were tested with a meter to check for proper voltage. All standard 110 branch circuits were generating voltage at optimally. All inspected outlets, where applicable, were tested for grounding and were found to be in serviceable condition. Aside of any aforementioned deficiencies addressed, all visible wiring was in good condition. The service panels' dead front was removed to inspect the interior wiring. All wiring was properly gauged, appeared to be properly fastened and operable at time of inspection. The bonding and grounding systems were serviceable and proper. Recommend installing GFCI receptacles at all water exposure locations i.e. kitchen, bathrooms, exterior. Aside of the aforementioned deficiencies, overall condition of the electrical system was serviceable.

Unoccupied Basic Passing Inspection with GFCI Receptacles
A representative amount of all outlets were tested in the building. All accessible outlets were tested with a meter to check for proper voltage. All outlets were generating voltage optimally. Additionally, accessible outlets inspected were tested for grounding and were found to be properly grounded. All visible wiring was in good condition aside of any noted deficiencies. The service panel's dead front was removed to inspect the interior wiring. All wiring was properly gauged, appeared to be properly fastened and operable at time of inspection. The bonding and grounding systems were serviceable and proper where visible. The GFCI receptacles were all tested and were functioning as designed at time of inspection. Overall condition of the electrical system was good/serviceable condition aside of any noted deficiencies.

Unoccupied Basic Passing Inspection without GFCI Receptacles
A representative amount of all outlets were tested in the building. All accessible outlets were tested with a meter to check for proper voltage. All outlets were generating voltage optimally. Also, all outlets were tested for grounding and were found to be properly grounded aside of any noted deficiencies. All visible wiring was in good condition aside of any aforementioned deficiencies. The service panel's dead front cover was removed to inspect the interior wiring. All wiring was properly gauged and appeared to be properly fastened at time of inspection. The bonding and grounding systems appeared serviceable and proper where visible. No GFCI receptacles installed. Recommend installing GFCI receptacles at all water exposures i.e. kitchen, bathrooms, exterior. Overall condition of the electrical system was good/serviceable condition aside of the aforementioned deficiencies.

Loose Breakers/Breakers Not Seated Properly
Loose or improper breakers may not contact the bus bar correctly and can lead to damage, shock, fire or worse. This occurs when circuit breakers get old, are of a non-compatible breaker type, correct breaker but not seated correctly and/or general corrosion fatigues the metal. The electricity makes a poor connection between the buss and the breaker. This poor connection causes sparks and heat that damages the panel.

Solid Strand Aluminum Wiring Observed
During the mid-1960 and early 1970's, single strand aluminum wiring was used extensively in residential electrical distribution. However, problems including the risk of electrical fires soon led to changes in the way aluminum conductors were manufactured. Aluminum wiring is still used in many industrial facilities, and even with these changes, evidence suggests there are still inherent problems with the use of single strand aluminum in electrical applications. In 1973, shortly after its establishment, the U.S. Consumer Product Safety Commission (CPSC) began investigating injuries and deaths resulting from electrically ignited house fires. Its research showed that "buildings wired with aluminum wire manufactured before 1972 were 55 times more likely to have

one or more connections reach 'Fire Hazard Conditions' than are buildings wired with copper." Prior to 1972, aluminum conductors were made of many different types of alloys. The aluminum typically being used at that time had very large coefficients of thermal expansion. This meant that devices made from this substance would expand and contract a great deal over small temperature increments. The single strand aluminum also had a high frequency of bending and crimp failures. It is highly recommended to have a licensed electrician rewire all solid strand branch circuits given the general known deficiencies.

Various Brand Breakers Observed in the Service Panel
Several different manufacturers of certain circuit breakers in a most panels is a violation. Some of them MAY be "listed" for use in that panel but a licensed electrician needs to check the listing label inside the door and reference further to deduce what the acceptable circuit breaker manufacturers are and the specific type numbers that are acceptable. Just because they fit, it does not make them correct. Loose or improper breakers may not contact the bus bar correctly and can lead to damage, fire, shock or worse. This occurs when circuit breakers get old, incorrect breakers are installed, breakers are not seated correctly or general corrosion fatigues the metal. The electricity makes a poor connection between the buss and the breaker. This poor connection causes sparks and heat that damages the panel.

Panel is Loose at the Wall
The electrical panel must be fastened correctly to the wall and be abutting a solid wall surface amongst other NEC requirements. Recommend a licensed electrician assess the area further and repair as is needed.

Double Taps in Service Panel
Double tapped wiring is ok if the circuit breaker is designed for two wires. If a circuit breaker is designed for two wires, it will say so right on the circuit breaker, and the terminal of the circuit breaker will be designed to hold two wires in place. To my knowledge, the only manufacturers that make circuit breakers that can be double tapped are Square D and Cutler Hammer but not all of their circuit breakers can be double tapped. If the circuit breaker isn't designed to hold two wires, the wires could come loose at some point in the future, even if they feel very tight today. Loose wires can lead to overheating, arcing, and possibly a fire. Recommend a licensed electrician repair as needed all deficiency and any other unobserved issues that may be noted during remediation.

Exposed Spliced Wire Junction Observed with Excess Sheathing Stripped
Wires that are junctional, where the wire sheathing is cut back to much, exposing the bare wire so that it is visible beyond the junction wire nuts, can allow these areas to contact each other and can short, causing arches. This is a direct fire hazard and repair is highly recommended. Recommend a licensed electrical contractor assess the area further and repair as needed.

Exposed Wires Observed in the Service Panel
Exposed wires observed at the time of the inspection. Loose wires can accidentally tap live wires during service panel servicing, inspection or from pests such as lizards (southern U.S), frogs, wasps, snakes, and rats' etcetera. Pests are routinely found to cause irreparable damage to service panels when there is a large enough orifice for the invader to enter. It is best practice to preempt future issues whenever possible and in this case, fastening loose wires, positioning them away from contact with breakers/bus bars and encasing all wires ends with wire caps. This can greatly reduce the risk of fire and other damage, shock or worse. Recommend a licensed electrician assess the area further and repair all as needed.

Overcrowding at Service Panel Abutting Screw Fasteners Area for the Panel Cover
Wires observed in the service panel to be encroaching/abutting the service panel's dead front cover screw fastener location. When engaging a screw it is far more likely to damage the PVC sheathing to the wires outer wall, causing an arch, energizing the panel and possibly causing a fire or damage to the unit.

Panel is not Fastened Evenly at the Wall
The electrical panel must be fastened correctly to the wall and be abutting a solid wall surface amongst other NEC, state or local requirements. Recommend a licensed electrician assess the area further and repair as is needed.

Conduit/Armored Cable Leading to the Panel is not Properly Braced
All conduit and armored cable raceways, should be fastened to the wall with proper C clamp fasteners intermittently as per the NEC code or better and/or as recommended by a licensed electrician, per NEC code. Recommend a licensed electrician assess the area further and repair per the NEC guidelines as is needed.

Service Mast Leading to the Panel is not Properly Braced
The service mast should be fastened to the wall with proper C clamp fasteners intermittently as per the NEC code or better as recommended by a licensed electrician. Recommend a licensed electrician repair per the NEC guidelines as needed.

Panel Punch Outs Are Missing
The punch outs to a service/distribution panel are pre pressed and semi cut circles in the metal sides, base or top of the panel that allow wires and conduit to enter the box. Punch outs should not be removed unless they will be closed from the elements and/or insect and pest intrusion free. When punch outs are removed but not enclosed, wasps, ants, mice, rats, snakes etc. can enter the panel and in many occasions, have proven to be very costly to the panel and the property owners as a result. When pests contact the main bus bar, they may cause a conduction on a circuit not rated and accidental fires and equipment damage can occur. It is highly recommended to have a licensed electrician install punch out caps on these locations.

Service Lateral is Loose Leading to the Panel and is not Properly Braced
The service lateral should be fastened to the wall with proper C clamp fasteners intermittently as per the NEC code or better as recommended by a licensed electrician. Recommend a licensed electrician repair per the NEC guidelines as is needed.

Stranded Wire at Grounding Bus Observed with Multiple Crimps/Cuts
Stranded/Multi Strand wires are rated for a general ampacity or flow of electricity on that specific circuit. Typically, the circuit the wire is a part of requires a thickness of the stranded wire observed. Electricity works for this example, like a flowing stream of water down a pipe, we can only draw as much as the pipe will allow. With electricity, when you try to run a circuit at its normal to maximum capacity, only now there are broken/severed strands. It acts like a damn not rated to withstand the pending current. At first, things appear ok, until too much demand is required or there is a surge. Arcing is a leader in causing residential building fires. Repairing wires cut, broken and crimped is generally a fairly easy repair for a well skilled and state licensed electrical contractor. It is highly recommended to have a state licensed electrical contractor repair the deficiency as is needed.

Circuits Entering the Panel are not Properly Secured. Fasteners are Missing
The punch outs to a service/distribution panel are pre pressed and semi cut circles in the metal sides, base or top of the panel that allow wires armored cable and conduit to enter the box. Punch outs should not be removed unless they will be closed from the elements and/or insect and pest intrusion free. Additionally, all circuits entering through the walls of the panel need to be fastened/secured to the panel so no accidental loosening of wires at the breakers and common/grounding bus pars can loosen and no unforeseen contacts with other circuits can occur. It is highly recommended to have a licensed electrician repair all per NEC guidelines as is needed.

Stranded Wire at the Wire/Breaker Abutment Observed with Multiple Crimps/Cuts
Stranded/Multi Strand wires are rated for a general ampacity or flow of electricity on that specific circuit. Typically, the circuit the wire is a part of, requires a thickness of the stranded wire observed. Electricity works for this example, like a flowing stream of water down a pipe, we can only draw as much as the pipe will allow. With electricity, when you try to run a circuit at its normal to maximum capacity, only now there are broken/severed strands. It acts like a damn not rated to withstand the pending current. At first, things appear ok, until too much demand is required or there is a surge. Arcing is a leader in causing residential building fires. Repairing wires cut, broken and crimped is generally a fairly easy repair for a well skilled and state licensed electrical contractor. It is highly recommended to have a state licensed electrical contractor repair the deficiency as is needed.

Stranded Wire at the Main Breaker/Wire Abutment Observed with Multiple Crimps/Cuts
Stranded/Multi Strand wires are rated for a general ampacity or flow of electricity on that specific circuit. Typically, the circuit the wire is a part of, requires a thickness of the stranded wire observed. Electricity works for this example, like a flowing stream of water down a pipe, we can only draw as much as the pipe will allow. With electricity, when you try to run a circuit at its normal to maximum capacity, only now there are broken/severed strands. It acts like a damn not rated to withstand the pending current. At first, things appear ok, until too much demand is required or there is a surge. Arcing is a leader in causing residential building fires. Repairing wires cut, broken and crimped is generally a fairly easy repair for a well skilled and state licensed electrical contractor. It is highly recommended to have a state licensed electrical contractor repair the deficiency as is needed.

Spliced Stranded Wire Observed within the Panel with Multiple Crimps/Cuts
Stranded/Multi Strand wires are rated for a general ampacity or flow of electricity on that specific circuit. Typically, the circuit the wire is a part of, requires a thickness of the stranded wire observed. Electricity works for this example, like a flowing stream of water down a pipe, we can only draw as much as the pipe will allow. With electricity, when you try to run a circuit at its normal to maximum capacity, only now there are broken/severed strands. It acts like a damn not rated to withstand the pending current. At first, things appear ok, until too much demand is required or there is a surge. Arcing is a leader in causing residential building fires. Repairing wires cut, broken and crimped is generally a fairly easy repair for a well skilled and state licensed electrical contractor. It is highly recommended to have a state licensed electrical contractor repair the deficiency as is needed.

Panel is of a Known Defective Type and is recommended to be Replace ASAP
The present service/distribution panel is of a known defective panel type. While there may be no visible signs of defects, there can be stealth failures and damage is often already present but not visible without disassembly which is NOT recommended as the hazards are only increased by messing with the equipment. It is recommended to have the panel replaced as soon as possible by a state licensed electrician.

Distribution Service

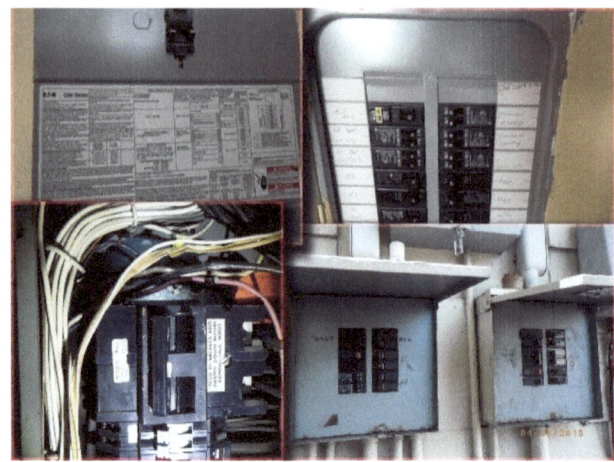

Solid Strand Aluminum Wiring Observed
During the mid-1960 and early 1970's, single strand aluminum wiring was used extensively in residential electrical distribution. However, problems including the risk of electrical fires soon led to changes in the way aluminum conductors were manufactured. Aluminum wiring is still used in many industrial facilities, and even with these changes, evidence suggests there are still inherent problems with the use of aluminum in electrical applications. In 1973, shortly after its establishment, the U.S. Consumer Product Safety Commission (CPSC) began investigating injuries and deaths resulting from electrically ignited house fires. Its research showed that "buildings wired with aluminum wire manufactured before 1972 were 55 times more likely to have one or more connections reach 'Fire Hazard Conditions' than are structures wired with copper." Prior to 1972, aluminum conductors were made of many different types of alloys. The single strand aluminum typically being used at that time had very large coefficients of thermal expansion. This meant that devices made from this substance would expand and contract a great deal over small temperature increments. The aluminum also had a high frequency of bending and creep failures. It is highly recommended to have a licensed electrician rewire all solid/single strand branch circuits given the general known deficiencies.

Various Brand Breakers Observed in the Distribution Panel
Several different manufacturers of circuit breakers is a violation of code for many panel types. Some of them MAY be "listed" for use in this panel type, but a licensed electrician needs to check the listing label inside the door and reference further to deduce what the acceptable circuit breaker manufacturers are and the specific type numbers that are acceptable. Just because they fit, it does not make them correct. Loose or improper breakers may not contact the bus bar correctly and can lead to damage, fire, shock or worse. This occurs when circuit breakers get old, incorrect breakers are installed, breakers are not seated correctly or general corrosion fatigues the metal. As a result, electricity can make a poor connection between the buss and the breaker. This poor connection causes sparks and heat that damages the panel. Recommend a licensed electrician review further and repair as needed per NEC guidelines.

Circuits Entering the Panel are not Properly Secured. Fasteners are missing
The punch outs to a service/distribution panel are pre pressed and semi cut circles in the metal sides, base or top of the panel that allow wires armored cable and conduit to enter the box. Punch outs should not be removed unless they will be closed from the elements and/or insect and pest intrusion free. Additionally, all circuits entering through the walls of the panel need to be fastened/secured to the panel so no accidental loosening of wires at the breakers and common/grounding bus pars can loosen and no unforeseen contacts with other circuits can occur. It is highly recommended to have a licensed electrician repair all per NEC guidelines as is needed.

Loose Breakers/Breakers Not Seated Properly
Loose or improper breakers may not contact the bus bar correctly and can lead to damage and fire or worse. This occurs when circuit breakers get old, incorrect breakers are installed, breakers are not seated correctly and/or general corrosion fatigues the metal. The electricity makes a poor connection between the buss and the breaker. This poor connection causes sparks and heat that damages the panel.

Double Taps in Distribution Panel
Double tapped wiring is ok if the circuit breaker is designed for two wires. If a circuit breaker is designed for two wires, it will say so right on the circuit breaker and the terminal of the circuit breaker will be designed to hold two wires in place. To my knowledge, the only manufacturers that make circuit breakers that can be double tapped are Square D and Cutler Hammer but not all of their circuit breakers can be double tapped. If the circuit breaker isn't designed to hold two wires, the wires could come loose at some point in the future, even if they feel very tight today. Loose wires can lead to overheating, arcing, and possibly a fire. Recommend a licensed electrician repair as needed the aforementioned deficiency and any other unobserved issues that may arise during remediation.

Exposed Spliced Wires Junction Observed with Excess Sheathing Stripped
Wires that are junctional, where the wire sheathing is cut back too much, exposing the bare wire so that it is visible beyond the junction wire nuts, can allow these areas to contact each other and can short causing arcing. This is a direct fire hazard and repair is highly recommended.

Stranded Wire at Grounding Bus Observed with Multiple Crimps/Cuts
Stranded/Multi Strand wires are rated for a general ampacity or flow of electricity on that specific circuit. Typically, the circuit the wire is a part of, requires a thickness of the stranded wire observed. Electricity works for this example, like a flowing stream of water down a pipe, we can only draw as much as the pipe will allow. With electricity, when you try to run a circuit at its normal to maximum capacity, only now there are broken/severed strands. It acts like a damn not rated to withstand the pending current. At first, things appear ok, until too much demand is required or there is a surge. Arcing is a leader in causing building fires. Repairing wires cut, broken and crimped is generally a fairly easy repair for a well skilled and state licensed electrical contractor. It is highly recommended to have a state licensed electrical contractor repair the deficiency as is needed.

Stranded Wire at the Breaker/Wire Abutment Observed with Multiple Crimps/Cuts
Stranded/Multi Strand wires are rated for a general ampacity or flow of electricity on that specific circuit. Typically, the circuit the wire is a part of requires a thickness of the stranded wire observed. Electricity works for this example, like a flowing stream of water down a pipe, we can only draw as much as the pipe will allow. With electricity, when you try to run a circuit at its normal to maximum capacity, only now there are broken/severed strands, it acts like a damn not rated to withstand the pending current. At first, things appear ok, until too much demand is required or there is a surge. Arcing is a leader in causing residential building fires. Repairing wires cut, broken and crimped is generally a fairly easy repair for a well skilled and state licensed electrical contractor. It is highly recommended to have a state licensed electrical residential contractor repair the deficiency as is needed.

Spliced Stranded Wire Observed Within the Panel with Multiple Crimps/Cuts
Stranded/Multi Strand wires are rated for a general ampacity or flow of electricity on that specific circuit. Typically, the circuit the wire is a part of, requires a thickness of the stranded wire observed. Electricity works for this example, like a flowing stream of water down a pipe, we can only draw as much as the pipe will allow. With electricity, when you try to run a circuit at its normal to maximum capacity, only now there are broken/severed strands. It acts like a damn not rated to withstand the pending current. At first, things appear ok, until too much demand is required or there is a surge. Arcing is a leader in causing building fires. Repairing wires cut; broken and crimped is generally a fairly easy repair for a well skilled and state licensed electrical contractor. It is highly recommended to have a state licensed electrical residential contractor repair the deficiency as is needed.

Conduit/Armored Cable Leading to the Panel is not Properly Braced
All conduit and armored cable raceways, should be fastened to the wall with proper C clamp fasteners intermittently as per the NEC code or better or as recommended by a licensed electrician per NEC code. Recommend a licensed electrician repair as is needed.

Double Taps in Distribution Panel
Double tapped wiring is ok if the circuit breaker is designed for two wires. If a circuit breaker is designed for two wires, it will say so right on the circuit breaker, and the terminal of the circuit breaker will be designed to hold two

wires in place. To my knowledge, the only manufacturers that make circuit breakers that can be double tapped are Square D and Cutler Hammer but not all of their circuit breakers can be double tapped. If the circuit breaker isn't designed to hold two wires, the wires could come loose at some point in the future, even if they feel very tight today. Loose wires can lead to overheating, arcing, and possibly a fire. Recommend a licensed electrician repair as needed the aforementioned deficiency and any other unobserved issues that may arise during remediation.

Exposed Wires Observed in the Distribution Panel
Exposed wires observed at the time of the inspection. Loose wires can accidentally tap live wires during service panel servicing, inspection or from pests such as lizards (southern U.S), frogs, wasps, snakes, and rat's etcetera. Pests are routinely found to cause irreparable damage to distribution panels when there is a large enough orifice for the invader to enter. It is best practice to preempt future issues whenever possible and in this case, fastening loose wires or positioning them away from contact with breakers/bus bars and encasing all wires ends with wire caps can greatly reduce the risk of fire and other damage, shock or worse. Recommend a licensed electrical contractor assess the area further and repair as needed.

Overcrowding at the Distribution Panel Abutting Screw Fasteners Area for the Dead Front Cover
Wires observed in the distribution panel to be encroaching/abutting the service panel's dead front cover screw fastener location. When engaging a screw it is far more likely to damage the PVC sheathing to the wires outer wall, causing an arcing, energizing the panel and possibly causing a fire or damage to the unit. Recommend a licensed electrical contractor assess the area further and repair as needed.

Panel is Loose at the Wall
The electrical panel must be fastened correctly to the wall and be abutting a solid wall surface amongst other NEC requirements. Recommend a licensed electrician repair as is needed.

Panel Is Not Fastened Evenly at the Wall
The electrical panel must be fastened correctly to the wall and be abutting a solid wall surface amongst other NEC requirements. Recommend a licensed electrician repair as is needed.

Panel Punch Outs Are Missing
The punch outs to a service/distribution panel are pre pressed and semi cut circles in the metal sides, base or top of the panel that allow wires conduit to enter the box. Punch outs should not be removed unless they will be closed from the elements and/or insect and pest intrusion free. When punch outs are removed but not enclosed, wasps, ants, mice, rats, snakes etc. can enter the panel and in many occasions have proven to be very costly to the panel and the property owners as a result. When pests contact the main bus bar they may cause a conduction on a circuit not rated and accidental fires and equipment damage can occur. It is highly recommended to have punch out caps on these locations ASAP. Recommend a licensed electrical contractor assess the area further and repair all as needed.

Circuits Entering the Panel are not Properly Secured. Fasteners are missing
The punch outs to a service/distribution panel are pre pressed and semi cut circles in the metal sides, base or top of the panel that allow wires armored cable and conduit to enter the box. Punch outs should not be removed unless they will be closed from the elements and/or insect and pest intrusion free. Additionally, all circuits entering through the walls of the panel need to be fastened/secured to the panel so no accidental loosening of wires at the breakers and common/grounding bus pars can loosen and no unforeseen contacts with other circuits can occur. It is highly recommended to have a licensed electrician repair all per NEC guidelines as is needed.

Branch Circuits Deficiencies

No Anti-Tip Bracket Observed at the Range/Oven
Anti-tip brackets are metal devices designed to prevent freestanding ranges from tipping. The intent is to prevent them from tipping over or onto a child or a pet. They are normally attached to a back/rear leg of the range and screwed into the wall that is behind the range. They are included in all installation kits for modern stand-alone range/ovens. A range that is not equipped with an anti-tip device may tip over if enough weight is applied to its open door, such as that from a large turkey or ham, or even a small child. A falling range can crush, scald, or burn anyone caught beneath. If you wish to install a bracket, it is recommended to have it installed by a professional contractor. The part can be purchased at most hardware stores or ordered from a manufacturer. Some manufacturers have been known to send their customers anti-tip brackets for free. Recommend having an anti-tip bracket installed as soon as possible.

Range/Oven Receptacle was Observed Unmounted and Lying on the Floor
Recommend a state licensed electrician repair the deficiency per NEC and state code requirements as is needed to prevent damage to the receptacle, shock or fire.

Loose Gang Box Observed at the Master Bathroom Sink Counter Back Splash
A gang box is the box to which houses, secures and retains the receptacle/switch in the wall cavity. The receptacle or switch is screw fastened to the box with wires running through the knockout locations to and from the box. A gang box is either installed during construction or renovation of the wall cavity permanently secured to a stud with nails/screws or it is installed after the wall was erected using the gypsum/wall board as the substrate to brace, using 2 screw tightening arms that clamp fasten to the wall. The latter manner, the clamp mechanisms, can come loose if not secured right or not tight enough. It is estimated this is the case but could not be determined at the time of the inspection. Recommend a licensed electrician examine the area further and repair as needed.

No GFCI Receptacles Observed
No GFCI or ground fault circuit interrupter receptacles observed. Recommend installing GFCI protected receptacles for receptacles within 6 feet of any water exposure.

No GFCI Receptacles Observed in the Bathrooms
Per the NEC; "Bathroom receptacles must be GFCI-protected [210.8(A)(1)]. In bathrooms, install at least one 15A or 20A, 125V receptacle within 3 ft. of the outside edge of each basin [210.52(D)]. Locate it on a wall or partition adjacent to the basin counter surface or on the side or face of the basin cabinet not more than 12 in. below the countertop. Receptacle outlet assemblies listed for this specific use may be installed in the countertop [210.52(D)]". Recommend a licensed electrical contractor install GFCI protected receptacles for receptacles within 6 feet of any water exposure, ensuring the required type/number of receptacles are installed to meet new code per most states and most localities.

Grounding Observed. Two Prong Polarized Outlets throughout the Building
Two prong polarized outlets were observed throughout the building. Outlets are antiquated and should be changed out to meet newer code standards. The branch circuits for the structure appeared to have grounding; however, at the time the structure was constructed, the receptacles had no third prong contact to provide a true ground. So in lieu of a proper ground, installers applied a false ground, supplying minimal protections, hooking the ground to the metal gang boxes. Recommend a licensed electrical contractor assess the area further and install 3 prong outlets, re-securing the ground wires from the gang boxes to the receptacles grounding screws.

Loose Receptacle(s) Contact(s)
The gap between the metal contacts causes electrical arcing. This may cause a slight sizzling or hissing noise. It does, however, create a high resistance connection which heats the material surfaces and can cause the receptacle outlet, outlet face and/or the plug blades to melt. If left alone, the outlet can get hot enough to start a fire. It is highly recommended to change all receptacles with loose contacts to updated receptacle equipment.

Ducted Kitchen Exhaust was Inoperable at the Time of the Inspection
You need a range hood to keep your kitchens air clean and healthy. A ducted hood actually moves the polluted air to the outside, getting rid of all forms of air pollution caused by cooking. Fresh air is drawn in from the outside, keeping the kitchen air clean, and preventing cooking odors and even grease particles from spreading throughout the house.

Insufficient Outlets at the Kitchen Peninsular Counter/Cabinet
Per the NEC; "210.52(C)(3) Peninsular Counter Spaces. At least one receptacle outlet shall be installed at each peninsular counter space with a long dimension of 600 mm (24 in.) or greater and a short dimension of 300 mm (12in.) or greater. A peninsular countertop is measured from the connecting edge. Additionally, 210.52(C)(5) requires that the receptacle be not more than 12" below the countertop and shall not be located where the countertop extends more than 6" beyond the base. Note: If the peninsula is divided by a range or sink then 210.52(C)(4) requires that any space larger than 12 x 24 inches have an outlet." Recommend a licensed electrical contractor assess the area further and repair as needed.

Insufficient Outlets Observed in the Kitchen
In every dwelling unit, receptacles must be installed in every kitchen, family room, dining room, living room, parlor, library, den, sunroom, bedroom, recreation room, or similar room or area. Per the NEC "Following the rules of 210.52(A)(1) thru (A)(3) [210.52(A)] Any wall space 2 ft. or more in width must have a receptacle installed so that no point measured horizontally along the floor line is more than 6 ft. from a receptacle outlet. You can't count floor receptacles that are more than 18 in. out from the wall [210.52(A)(3)] or those installed for kitchen countertop surface requirements [210.52(A)(4)]. The two or more 20A, 120V small-appliance branch circuits serving the kitchen, dining room, and similar areas [210.11(C)(1)] must serve all walls, floor and countertop receptacles [210.52(B)(1) and (2)] and the receptacle for refrigeration equipment. These circuits may not supply the outlets for luminaires or appliances, however, exceptions allow the small appliance circuits to serve clocks and gas-fired ranges, ovens, or counter-mounted cooking units [210.52(B)(2)]. You can supply the refrigeration equipment receptacle from an individual branch circuit rated 15A or greater [210.52(B)(1) Ex 2]. Kitchen countertop receptacles, as required by 210.52(C), must be supplied by at least two 20A, 120V small-appliance branch circuits [210.11(C)(1)]. Either can supply receptacle outlets in the same kitchen [210.52(B)(1)]. Compare any planned circuits against 210.52(A), (B), and (C) and Figure 210.52". Recommend a licensed electrical contractor assess the area further and repair all as needed.

Can Lighting Appears Antiquated? Thermal Leaks/Bridging Suspected
The can lighting appeared antiquated with suspected air and thermal leaks/infiltrations, recommend having a licensed electrician replace the can lighting and seal the abutting wall/gypsum board per the 2012 IRC/IBC; "N1102.4.4 (R402.4.4) Recessed lighting. Recessed luminaires installed in the building thermal envelope shall be sealed to limit air leakage between conditioned and unconditioned spaces. All recessed luminaires shall be IC-rated and labeled as having an air leakage rate not more than 2.0 cfm (0.944 L/s) when tested in accordance with ASTM E 283 at a 1.57 psf (75 Pa) pressure differential. All recessed luminaires shall be sealed with a gasket or caulk between the housing and the interior wall or ceiling covering."

Reverse Neutral/Reverse Polarity Observed when the Outlets Tested
Most electrical devices are designed so that their "on-off" switch interrupts electrical power at the point of entry into the appliance or device circuitry or components. If you switch the hot and neutral wires that may not quite be the case, and parts of the device may potentially remain energized even when the electrical device switch is OFF. No electrical current may flow, but it could flow if someone touches the wrong part of the device. Damage

may be caused in other circumstances as well, as we describe next. Reversed polarity on an electrical outlet is dangerous. If you accidentally reverse these wires, the device you plug in to the receptacle may "work", but it is unsafe and risks a short circuit, shock, or fire. The hot/live black wire (or red wire) should connect to the brass-colored screw terminals on the electrical receptacle, usually marked BLACK or HOT. The "neutral" white wire should be connected to the silver-colored screw terminals on the electrical receptacle, usually marked NEUTRAL or WHITE. It is highly recommended to have a licensed electrical contractor assess the area further and repair any reverse neutral receptacles ASAP.

Jacuzzi Tub Access Panel is Grouted Shut
In accordance with NEC (National Electric Code) all motors and electrical equipment pertaining to the tub need to be "Readily Accessible". Because many potential faults can occur, immediate access to the power and other equipment is needed. The code is as follows: NEC DEFINITIONS; "Readily Accessible Capable of being reached quickly for operation, renewal or inspection without requiring those concerned to use a tool, to climb over, remove obstacles or other. Accessible (as applied to wiring methods). Capable of being removed or exposed without damaging the building structure or finish or not permanently closed in by the structure or finish of the building. Accessible (as applied to equipment) admitting close approach; not guarded by locked doors, elevation, or other effective means. NEC 110.3(B) All electrical equipment shall be installed and used in accordance with the listing requirements and manufacturer's instructions. 680.73 Accessibility. Electrical equipment for hydro massage bathtubs must be capable of being removed or exposed without damaging the building structure or finish. Where the hydro massage bathtub is cord-and plug-connected with the supply receptacle accessible only through an access opening, the receptacle must face toward the opening and be within 1 ft. of the opening. Article 430.14(A) states that, "motors shall be located so that adequate ventilation is provided and so that maintenance can be readily accomplished." 314.29 Boxes, Conduit Bodies, and Handhole Enclosures to Be Accessible. Boxes, conduit bodies, and handhole enclosures shall be installed so that the wiring contained in them can be rendered accessible without removing any part of the building NEC 400.8 Uses Not Permitted Flexible cords and cables shall not be used for the following: (5) Where concealed by walls, floors, or ceilings or located above suspended or dropped ceilings 430.102 Disconnect Means Location (B) Motor Disconnect. A disconnecting means must be located in sight from the motor location and the driven machinery location. 430.107 Readily Accessible. The disconnecting means shall be readily accessible". Recommend a licensed contractor assess the area further and repair to allow the hatch to be vented and accessed as needed.

Jacuzzi Tub Access Panel Was Not Observed
In accordance with NEC (National Electric Code) all motors and electrical equipment pertaining to the tub need to be "Readily Accessible". Because many potential faults can occur, immediate access to the power and other equipment is needed. The code is as follows: NEC DEFINITIONS; "Readily Accessible Capable of being reached quickly for operation, renewal or inspection without requiring those concerned to use a tool, to climb over, remove obstacles or other. Accessible (as applied to wiring methods). Capable of being removed or exposed without damaging the building structure or finish or not permanently closed in by the structure or finish of the building. Accessible (as applied to equipment) admitting close approach; not guarded by locked doors, elevation, or other effective means. NEC 110.3(B) All electrical equipment shall be installed and used in accordance with the listing requirements and manufacturer's instructions. 680.73 Accessibility. Electrical equipment for hydro massage bathtubs must be capable of being removed or exposed without damaging the building structure or finish. Where the hydro massage bathtub is cord-and plug-connected with the supply receptacle accessible only through an access opening, the receptacle must face toward the opening and be within 1 ft. of the opening. Article 430.14(A) states that, "motors shall be located so that adequate ventilation is provided and so that maintenance can be readily accomplished." 314.29 Boxes, Conduit Bodies, and Handhole Enclosures to Be Accessible. Boxes, conduit bodies, and handhole enclosures shall be installed so that the wiring contained in them can be rendered accessible without removing any part of the building NEC 400.8 Uses Not Permitted Flexible cords and cables shall not be used for the following: (5) Where concealed by walls, floors, or ceilings or located above suspended or dropped ceilings 430.102 Disconnect Means Location (B) Motor Disconnect. A disconnecting means must be located in sight from the motor location and the driven machinery location. 430.107 Readily Accessible. The disconnecting means shall be readily accessible". Recommend a licensed electrical contractor assess further and repair as needed.

Exterior Grade UF Branch Circuit Wire Observed Exposed at Grade
The exterior grade wire was observed exposed to the elements at grade/ground level. This can allow the wire to be damaged by pets, pests, children, lawn equipment U.V. radiation etc. and as well pose a safety hazard. A few considerations regarding exterior wiring are as follows; Exterior UF wire is permissible for use to the exterior of the home in most locations of the US, however, its intended purpose is to be buried. Depending on local

code, UF is allowed underground typically at a min 18" and above ground in some areas but can waver depending on locations. Conduit is recommended above ground. If it's down low it may be considered subject to damage. Thin wall metal conduit cannot be used underground in most locations within the US. Electrical PVC conduit is recommended for the above ground portion. If you use UF underground, you need conduit to provide protection where it emerges from the ground. Most codes will allow the heavier schedule PVC. Recommend individual THWN wires in the conduit. UF in a complete conduit run is not recommended and likely not permitted to code. Also, regular Romex is not recommended and likely prohibited in wet locations even if in conduit. The circuit will need GFCI protection, if not present. Check local codes, some don't allow UF. Most will allow PVC, some require rigid heavy wall steel. Ultimately though, PVC conduit wins for its flexibility, since you can pull multiple wires through without snags etc. NOTE: You cannot run normal indoor NM cable in buried conduit. Buried conduit is a wet location. You must run wet rated wire for your region. You cannot run THHN wire for buried conduit in most locations either. Most codes and the NEC states to use THWN, although most wire is dual rated. Recommend a licensed electrician bury the wire to code as needed.

Interior Flooring

Drywood Termite Frass/Damage Suspected at the Floors and Sills
Termite frass/damage was suspected at and within the interior intermittent at the floors and sills. Dry wood termites swarm in the evening and at night during the warmer months of the year. It is very hard to find where they are coming from because they live so deeply in the lumber. Dry wood termite colonies are small colonies only about 3,000 termites. When the colony reaches about 3,000 termites, then will swarm to start a colony elsewhere. They need very little moisture and are often found in the attic wood framing, wall studs, door casings and window frames. Dry wood termites obtain moisture from the water produced by the digestion of cellulose, no matter how old the wood is. Spot treatments, such as orange oil applications, use insecticides applied to control known dry wood termite colonies, such as those found in a door casing, windowsills or pieces of furniture. For newer buildings, this is the recommended treatment by honest pest control servicemen and is fairly nominal in price. Advantages to dry wood alternative treatments are: The structure does not have to be unoccupied during treatment, just the immediate work area. There is a residual effect to the termiticide, if re-infestation occurs and the insects come in contact with the treated area, the transfer effect will start again and the colony will be eliminated. Most important, this method uses material chemicals very low in mammalian toxicity.

Floor Tile Suspected to have been Applied Over Tile
The floor tile appears to have been applied over another layer of tile. It is unknown as to the coarse nature of the tiles surface, however, tile is not made to be applied this way. The mortar cannot be sure to fully adhere to the underlying substrate, the underlying tile, causing tiles to come loose over time. This in trade, causes the grout to chip, tiles to break, water to enter the cracks and trap potentially causing noxious microbial growths if unseen and neglected or unknown. Further, the tiles installation instructions generally do not allow for installations over current tile and call for a course and unified base flooring such as cement, cement board or seam sealed plywood etc. Recommend a state licensed tile installation and remediation contractor assess further and repair as needed.

Various Staining Observed Throughout the Carpeting
Carpet appears to be at the end of its known life expectancy and is recommended to be replaced by a licensed flooring contractor.

Loose Floor Boards Observed
Loose floor boards can occur for various reasons including insufficient nailing or nail length/type, improper nailing methodology, loose or corroded nails or fasteners. Recommend a licensed contractor assess the area further and repair as needed.

Subfloor Particle Board Decking Suspected to be Fractured/ Punctured
The floor deck is a particle board and was/is known for these fracture types. Particle board was thought to be an equivalent to OSB or ply wood but proved defective at times in floor decking applications. The problem is,

particle board is just glue and sawdust, and it absorbs liquid like a sponge. When it absorbs liquid, it swells. Recommend a licensed subflooring contractor assess the area further and repair/replace as needed.

Subfloor Particle Board Subfloor Decking Suspected to be Loose
The floor deck is a particle board and was/is known for these fracture types. Particle board was thought to be an equivalent to OSB or ply wood but proved defective at times in floor decking applications. The problem is, particle board is just glue and sawdust, and it absorbs liquid like a sponge. When it absorbs liquid, it swells. Recommend a licensed subflooring contractor assess the area further and repair/replace as needed.

Laminate Flooring Observed Buckling
Laminate flooring, generally, is not constructed to withstand excess water or mopping with direct water exposures. Heavy moisture can cause buckling/swelling at the laminate abutting/interlocking joints. In most laminate flooring types, when the flooring does swell at the joints, it does not usually retake its form as is known to occur in hard wood flooring.

Cracked/Loose Tiles Observed on Wood Subfloor
Cracked/loose tiles often occur on wood subfloors from excessive live load applied to a particularly softer region on the floor. Often, softer regions may occur due to insufficient joist spanning or insufficient wood subfloor deck thicknesses. Additionally, improper mortar mixes, insufficient mortar or application methodology may also contribute to tile cracks. It cannot be determined fully what the cause is during a general building inspection.

Cracked/Loose Tiles Observed on Slab Floor
Cracked/loose tiles often occur on from excess live load applied to an improperly laid tile or tiles over weaker/improperly mixed mortar. Insufficient mortar or application methodology may also contribute to tile cracks. It cannot be determined fully what the cause is during a general building inspection and is recommended to have a licensed flooring contractor assess the area further and repair as needed.

Tile Grouting Joints appear to be filled with a Mortar or Thin Set, Not Grout
For tile flooring, grout is used at the abutting joints. Mortar and thin set are applications used under the tile. Mortar is to adhere the tile and thin set is typically used to level an off even slab floor. Both mortar and thin set are not designed for the tile joints and severely hinders the removal process, should you ever decide to apply new flooring. Recommend a licensed tile repair and installation contractor assess the area further and repair as needed.

Mobile Homes

Subfloor Particle Board Decking Suspected to be Fractured/Punctured
The floor deck is a particle board and was/is known for these fracture types. Particle board was thought to be an equivalent to OSB or ply wood but proved defective at times in floor decking applications. Turns out, particle board is not good for many things construction related. The problem is, particle board is just glue and sawdust, and it absorbs liquid like a sponge (it also doesn't hold nails well due to expansion/retraction). When it absorbs liquid, it swells. In many mobile home framing applications/methodology, the floor decking is continuous, under interior walls. It is highly recommended to have a state licensed building contractor assess the area further to attain a best practice repair method.

Walls

Chinese Drywall Suspected
As stated in "CHINESE DRYWALL Q&A BY GARY ROSEN, PH.D.: After 2005 builders no longer wanted to use imported Chinese drywall but there was still stock and it is alleged that some of the stock was mixed with US boards. Extensive use of Chinese drywall happened at the end of 2004 and 2005 during the period of peak U.S. drywall shortages. But houses built after this period could still have some of the left over Chinese drywall. All of the problem Chinese drywall contains a high degree of organic contaminants. The BNBM Chinese drywall and US (USG, National, GP, French (LaFarge) and Norwegian (NorGyp) drywall do not. The material, either the gypsum core and/or the paper face, emits Sulphur gases that have a rotten egg odor that is detectable by the nose at very, very low levels. According to Knauf in a letter dated: November 29, 2006: Chemical analysis of the bulk plasterboard indicates that it contains a naturally-occurring iron disulfide mineral (e.g., pyrite). According to Knauf, chemical analyses suggest that this mineral appears to be the source of the sulfur-containing (smelly) compounds emitted from this product... Heat and moisture/ humidity activate the chemical reaction that releases the Sulphur gases... In single family homes the wall cavities are connected to the open/ventilated attics. When the attics get hot and humid in the summer, this hot and humid air enters the home's wall cavities and reacts with the Sulphur compounds in the (unpainted on the inside of the wall) drywall and causes the smells. In high rise buildings wall cavities are not connected to any sources of outside (moist/hot) air so the problem Chinese drywall does not appear to smell in high rises or the smell is significantly reduced compared to when in single family homes...Based on our studies we believe that the problem Chinese drywall (not BNBM) does not meet ASTM standards and is not structurally sound. We believe that the material continues to disintegrate and weaken quite possibly due to the high levels of organic contaminants. We believe that over time the problem Chinese drywall on ceilings may collapse. Such collapse would be covered under most home owner (HO-3) policies and may actually be a blessing in disguise for home owners. AC supply ducting in the attic that causes condensation problems over problem Chinese ceiling drywall could accelerate the ceiling." Due to the many unknowns without proper testing, it is highly recommended to have a licensed contractor specializing in drywall testing, assess the area further and repair if/where needed.

Wall Tile Suspected to have been Applied Over Tile
The wall tile appears to have been applied over another layer of tile. It is unknown as to the coarse nature of the tiles surface, however, tile is not made to be applied this way. The mortar cannot be sure to fully adhere to the underlying substrate, the tile, causing tiles to come loose over time. This is exacerbated by gravity as the tile is applied vertically to the wall. This applied load will be a constant until the tiles may loosen or are disrupted and start to fall etc. This in trade, causes the grout to chip, tiles to break and if water is present, to enter the cracks and trap potentially causing noxious microbial growths if unseen and neglected/unknown. Further, the tiles installation instructions generally do not allow for installations over current tile and call for a course and unified base or rough finished substrate prescribed for most locations to code standards such as cement, cement board or seam sealed plywood etc. In some limited circumstances, green board may be used. Recommend a state licensed tile installation and remediation contractor assess further and repair as needed.

WL Elevated Moisture, Water Damage and Suspected Microbial Growth Observed

As stated by: The National Institutes of Health Moisture and Mold Remediation Standard Operating Procedures; "Wallboard: If the wallboard cannot be dried within 48 hours, measure twelve (12) inches above the water mark/damage and remove and discard wallboard below that point. Remove and discard damp insulation, and ventilate the wall cavity. In some cases it may be difficult to tell if the wallboard has been sufficiently dried. A moisture meter can be used to check for moisture. Use a moisture meter, check the affected area and compare the reading to a control reading in a non-affected area (see section titled "Response Equipment")." It is unknown the extent of time the wall has been holding elevated moisture, however, due to the current assessment, it is highly recommended to have a licensed mold remediation company assess this area further and repair all as needed.

Kitchen Cabinets have Observed Drywall Screws Installed Improperly

Drywall screws seem to be a DIY guys go to screw, since it is the most often used screw observed being used in pretty much any building project. Drywall screws however, are not rated to withstand loads beyond gypsum board typically. Additionally, drywall screws are not corrosion resistant and can start corroding early in their life especially in a kitchen. Recommend a licensed contractor assess the area further and reinstall all cabinets to code prior to use to prevent cabinet or wall damage and collapse of a wall mounted cabinet or shelf.

Bathroom Shower Wall has Wide Grout Joint(s) Abutting the Wall with Cracks/Compromises

It is suspected that the tile layout was not done prior to installing them. This may be indicative that the shower/bathroom was renovated by someone who may not have known or installed the materials to code. The shower pan and flashing materials are all covered and could not be assessed. The wide grout joint appears to have crack compromises within the grout. This is likely caused by shrinkage or may have occurred because the grout had a poor mix. To prevent water intrusion within the wall, at minimum, it is recommend having a licensed tub and tile installation and repair contractor assess the area further and repair all as needed.

Ceilings

Chinese Drywall Suspected
As stated in "CHINESE DRYWALL Q&A BY GARY ROSEN, PH.D.: After 2005 builders no longer wanted to use imported Chinese drywall but there was still stock and it is alleged that some of the stock was mixed with US boards. Extensive use of Chinese drywall happened at the end of 2004 and 2005 during the period of peak U.S. drywall shortages. But houses built after this period could still have some of the left over Chinese drywall. All of the problem Chinese drywall contains a high degree of organic contaminants. The BNBM Chinese drywall and US (USG, National, GP, French (LaFarge) and Norwegian (NorGyp) drywall do not. The material, either the gypsum core and/or the paper face, emits Sulphur gases that have a rotten egg odor that is detectable by the nose at very, very low levels. According to Knauf in a letter dated: November 29, 2006: Chemical analysis of the bulk plasterboard indicates that it contains a naturally-occurring iron disulfide mineral (e.g., pyrite). According to Knauf, chemical analyses suggest that this mineral appears to be the source of the sulfur-containing (smelly) compounds emitted from this product… Heat and moisture/ humidity activate the chemical reaction that releases the Sulphur gases… In single family homes the wall cavities are connected to the open/ventilated attics. When the attics get hot and humid in the summer, this hot and humid air enters the home's wall cavities and reacts with the Sulphur compounds in the (unpainted on the inside of the wall) drywall and causes the smells. In high rise buildings wall cavities are not connected to any sources of outside (moist/hot) air so the problem Chinese drywall does not appear to smell in high rises or the smell is significantly reduced compared to when in single family homes…Based on our studies we believe that the problem Chinese drywall (not BNBM) does not meet ASTM standards and is not structurally sound. We believe that the material continues to disintegrate and weaken quite possibly due to the high levels of organic contaminants. We believe that over time the problem Chinese drywall on ceilings may collapse. Such collapse would be covered under most home owner (HO-3) policies and may actually be a blessing in disguise for home owners. AC supply ducting in the attic that causes condensation problems over problem Chinese ceiling drywall could accelerate the ceiling." Due to the many unknowns without proper testing, it is highly recommended to have a licensed contractor specializing in drywall testing, assess the area further and repair if/where needed.

Thermal Leaks/Bridging Suspected at the Older Can Lights
The can lighting appeared antiquated with suspected air and thermal leaks/infiltrations, recommend having a licensed electrician replace the can lighting and seal the abutting wall/gypsum board per the 2012 IRC/IBC; "N1102.4.4 (R402.4.4) Recessed lighting. Recessed luminaires installed in the building thermal envelope shall be sealed to limit air leakage between conditioned and unconditioned spaces. All recessed luminaires shall be IC-rated and labeled as having an air leakage rate not more than 2.0 cfm (0.944 L/s) when tested in accordance with ASTM E 283 at a 1.57 psf (75 Pa) pressure differential. All recessed luminaires shall be sealed with a gasket or caulk between the housing and the interior wall or ceiling covering."

Garage Ceiling Fastening Observed Loose

Due to garage interiors commonly being unconditioned and the attic spaces overhead, typically lack insulation. Thermal bridging, thermal expansion and moisture born corrosion can all play in causing ceiling gypsum/drywall tape joints to loosen and fasteners to corrode. Prior to 2000 roughly, buildings garage ceiling boards were fastened to the ceiling wood joists with nails. Unfortunately, nails due not provide the equivalent dead load capacity long term. Nails can corrode around their shafts, causing their ability to carry the load to diminish, ultimately loosening at the ceiling from moisture and heat exposure inducing expansion/retraction. Per the 2012 IRC "TABLE R702.3.5 MINIMUM THICKNESS AND APPLICATION OF GYPSUM BOARD Subsection e. Type X gypsum board for garage ceilings beneath habitable rooms shall be installed perpendicular to the ceiling framing and shall be fastened at maximum 6 inches o.c. by minimum 17/s inches 6d coated nails or equivalent drywall screws." Recommend a licensed drywall installation contractor assess the area further and repair as needed.

Water Stains and Moisture Elevated and Suspected Molds on the Gypsum Board

Ceilings present a different set of circumstances than with walls that are aggravated by the horizontal orientation of the product. Insulation in the attic, when installed correctly is 8" thick typically. If water contacts the insulation from, say, a roof leak, prior to it contacting and leaking at the gypsum ceiling board, the insulation may become soaked, heavily weighted and trap water for an extended period of time. Gypsum board derives most of its rigidity from the tensile strength of its surfacing papers. Severe or prolonged exposure to elevated moisture levels will cause the paper fiber to loosen or expand, allowing the weight of the product to weigh down and a permanent deformation (sag) will occur when the area dries. There is little that can be done to correct a set-sag in a ceiling other than replacing the ceilings sagging/sections with new products. One of the most perplexing problems to deal with is the growth of suspected molds and mildew under various moisture conditions and elevations. Mold and mildew usually occur in areas of extended dampness, moisture migration, poor air circulation and temperatures that reach above 65 degrees Fahrenheit. In the south east region of the US, humidity is abundant. These water stains and suspected molds were visibly observed only and NO lab testing was performed to corroborate any suspicions by the inspector. It is highly recommended to have a licensed mold remediation company assess the area further and treat/replace as needed.

Older Existing Construction-Ingress to the Home from the Garage Leads Directly Into a Room

This is a bad idea for a number of reasons, the biggest and most obvious is carbon monoxide poisoning at a lethal dose. Per the 2012 IRC/IBC; "R302.5 Dwelling/garage opening/penetration protection. Openings and penetrations through the walls or ceilings separating the dwelling from the garage shall be in accordance with Sections R302.5.1 through R302.5.3. R302.5.1 Opening protection. Openings from a private garage directly into a room used for sleeping purposes shall not be permitted. Other openings between the garage 50 2012 INTERNATIONAL RESIDENTIAL CODE BUILDING PLANNING and residence shall be equipped with solid wood doors not less than 35 mm in thickness, solid or honeycomb-core steel doors not less than 35 mm thick, or 20 minute fire-rated doors, equipped with a self-closing device." Recommend a licensed contractor enclose the door/ingress into the bedroom, providing an air seal into the envelope of the home per code.

Water Stains on the Ceilings Gypsum Board, Moisture Levels Nominal

Ceilings present a different set of circumstances than with walls that are aggravated by the horizontal orientation of the product. Insulation in the attic, when installed correctly is 8" thick typically. If water contacts the insulation from, say, a roof leak, prior to it contacting and leaking at the gypsum ceiling board, the insulation may become soaked, heavily weighted and trap water for an extended period of time. Gypsum board derives most of its rigidity from the tensile strength of its surfacing papers. Severe or prolonged exposure to elevated moisture levels will cause the paper fiber to loosen or expand, allowing the weight of the product to weigh down and a permanent deformation (sag) will occur when the area dries. There is little that can be done to correct a set-sag in a ceiling other than replacing the ceilings sagging/sections with new products. One of the most perplexing problems to deal with is the growth of suspected molds and mildew under various moisture conditions and elevations. Mold and mildew usually occur in areas of extended dampness, moisture migration, poor air circulation and temperatures that reach above 65 degrees Fahrenheit. In the south east region of the US, humidity is abundant. These water stains were visibly observed only and NO lab testing was performed to corroborate any suspicions by the inspector. Moisture metering was performed on the readily available substrate and found to be at safe moisture levels. It is highly recommended to have a licensed mold remediation company assess the area further and treat/replace as needed.

Popcorn Ceiling Texture was Observed Peeling

Humidity and the formation of mildew are more common in bathrooms and kitchens but can happen in other locations of the home where the humidity is high, such as the garage. The interior living and bedrooms, if air conditioned, generally do not undergo this type of problem. Other reasons may cause the texture to peel such as attic humidity, direct water, improper priming etc. With high humidity, mildew may begin to form underneath the texture layer of a popcorn ceiling. The popcorn ceiling will become damp and no longer retains its adhesion to the drywall underneath. Peeling often is first apparent in corners. You may first notice stains or discoloration patterns forming before the ceiling begins to peel. In some instances popcorn ceiling can be patched and retextured. When humidity is a problem, paint the ceiling and walls of the area with a paint made especially for humid environments to decrease the risk of mildew occurring again. When drywall dust is the issue, you may need to scrape the entire popcorn texture off and retexture the entire area. Recommend a licensed interior drywall contractor assess the area further and repair as needed.

Popcorn Ceiling Peeling. Water Stains Observed. Suspect Roof Leak

Humidity and the formation of mildew are more common in bathrooms and kitchens but can happen in other locations of the home where the humidity is high, such as the garage. The interior living and bedrooms, if air conditioned, generally do not undergo this type of problem. Other reasons may cause the texture to peel such as attic humidity, direct water, improper priming etc. With high humidity, mildew may begin to form underneath the texture layer of a popcorn ceiling. The popcorn ceiling will become damp and no longer retains its adhesion to the drywall underneath. Peeling often is first apparent in corners. You may first notice stains or discoloration patterns forming before the ceiling begins to peel. It is suspected, that the roof is compromised within the region above the ceiling damage. Recommend a licensed roofing contractor and an interior drywall / mold remediation contractor assess the area further and repair as needed.

Popcorn Ceiling Peeling. Water Stains Observed. Suspect Plumbing Leak

Humidity and the formation of mildew are more common in bathrooms and kitchens but can happen in other locations of the home where the humidity is high, such as the garage. The interior living and bedrooms, if air-conditioned, generally do not undergo this type of problem. Other reasons may cause the texture to peel such as attic humidity, direct water, improper priming etc. With high humidity, mildew may begin to form underneath the texture layer of a popcorn ceiling. The popcorn ceiling will become damp and no longer retains its adhesion to the drywall underneath. Peeling often is first apparent in corners. You may first notice stains or discoloration patterns forming before the ceiling begins to peel. Often in two story homes, a water leak upstairs runs directly to the ceiling below it. Ceiling repair is often necessary due to the damage caused to the popcorn ceiling. Many popcorn ceilings or portions of them in the affected areas that were wet and have not begun to peel, once the leak is fixed and the ceiling dries, the texture will often loosen from its base. It is suspected, that the plumbing above the ceiling is compromised within the region above the ceiling damage. Recommend a licensed plumber and an interior drywall/mold remediation contractor assess the area further and repair as needed.

Popcorn Ceiling Peeling. Suspect Improper Treatment for Drywall Dust Prior

When a popcorn ceiling texture coating is applied directly on undusted drywall substrates, it may not adhere entirely to the drywall itself but instead, to a thin layer of dust. Drywall joint compound is used to connect joints of two pieces of drywall, which are then usually sanded smooth. The leftover dust should be wiped off using a damp rag. However, this step can be forgotten. Often the popcorn ceiling will peel up in strips directly around and on the affected drywall joints. In some instances popcorn ceiling can be patched and retextured. When humidity is a problem, paint the ceiling and walls of the area with a paint made especially for humid environments to decrease the risk of mildew occurring again. When drywall dust is the issue, you may need to scrape the entire popcorn texture off and retexture the entire area. The entire ceiling may not be stable and is highly recommended to have a licensed drywall and texture contractor assess the arera further and repair all as needed.

Smoke/Fire Detectors & Suppression Systems

Smoke Detectors Appear Antiquated and should be Replaced per NFPA Recommendations
The NFPA suggests changing your smoke detectors every 10 years. According to the National Fire Protection Association (NFPA), approximately two-thirds of U.S. household fire deaths result from fires in buildings with: No smoke alarms and Working smoke alarms with old or missing batteries. Whether it's a residential dwelling or in a commercial building, the selection and maintenance of an early fire warning system is critical to save lives and minimize property loss. Most, if not, all insurance companies require a smoke or fire detection system for residential dwellings in order to obtain insurance. Smoke alarms should be placed on each level of your building and outside of each sleeping area, where applicable. If bedroom doors close, additional alarms should be installed inside the bedrooms as well. Since smoke rises, the smoke detectors should be on the ceiling at least four inches away from the nearest wall and away from drafts from windows or air ducts/registers. As always, make sure to follow manufacturer's installation instructions and verify all codes and compliance with your local authority. That could include your building inspector, fire marshal or insurance bureau. There are two broad types of fire alarm systems; heat detectors and smoke alarms. Knowing the differences between the various types of fire alarms and suppression systems available is key to matching the appropriate product to the application. Recommend a licensed specialist review the area further provide an adequate smoke/CO_2 detection system as is needed.

Various Missing Smoke Detectors Observed in the Multi Unit Building
For NFPA new construction guidelines and as may be required by local codes; NFPA 30.3.4.5 Smoke Alarms. "Smoke alarms shall be installed in accordance with 9.6.2.10 in every sleeping area, outside every sleeping area in the immediate vicinity of the bedrooms, and on all levels of the dwelling unit, including basements." Recommend licensed contractor asses the areas further and install per NFPA, state and local codes as needed.

No Deficiencies Observed at the Time of the Inspection
Smoke detectors were tested and serviceable at the time of the inspection. NOTE: According to the National Fire Protection Association (NFPA), approximately two-thirds of U.S. household fire deaths result from fires in buildings with: No smoke alarms and Working smoke alarms with old or missing batteries. Whether it's a residential dwelling or in a commercial building, the selection and maintenance of an early fire warning system is critical to save lives and minimize property loss. Most, if not, all insurance companies require a smoke or fire detection system for residential dwellings in order to obtain insurance. Smoke alarms should be placed on each level of your building and outside of each sleeping area. If bedroom doors close, additional alarms should be installed inside the bedrooms as well. Since smoke rises, the smoke detectors should be on the ceiling at least four inches away from the nearest wall and away from drafts from windows or air ducts/registers. As always,

make sure to follow manufacturer's installation instructions and verify all codes and compliance with your local authority. That could include your building inspector, fire marshal or insurance bureau. There are two broad types of fire alarm systems; heat detectors and smoke alarms. Knowing the differences between the various types of fire alarms and suppression systems available is key to matching the appropriate product to the application.

No Fire Extinguishers Observed
Almost all fires are small in their early stage and can be put out quickly if the proper fire extinguisher is available, and the person discovering the fire has been trained to use the fire extinguisher at hand. The requirements for portable fire extinguishers in general industry are governed by OSHA regulation 29 CFR 1910.157. 1910.157(c)(1): The employer shall provide portable fire extinguishers and shall mount, locate and identify them so that they are readily accessible to employees without subjecting the employees to possible injury. Rules for apartment buildings and condos vary. For residential single family dwellings, no general requirement is typical, however, certain localities may require specific rules that require them. It is highly recommended to have portable fire extinguishers installed per OSHA and NFPA recommendations.

No Fire Extinguishers Observed at the Common Areas to the Multi Unit Building
Per the NFPA; "A portable fire extinguisher can save lives and property by putting out a small fire or containing it until the fire department arrives; but portable extinguishers have limitations. Because fire grows and spreads so rapidly, the number one priority for residents is to get out safely. Safety tips: Use a portable fire extinguisher when the fire is confined to a small area, such as a wastebasket, and is not growing; everyone has exited the building; the fire department has been called or is being called; and the room is not filled with smoke. To operate a fire extinguisher, remember the word PASS: **P**ull the pin. Hold the extinguisher with the nozzle pointing away from you, and release the locking mechanism. **A**im low. Point the extinguisher at the base of the fire. **S**queeze the lever slowly and evenly. **S**weep the nozzle from side-to-side. For the home, select a multi-purpose extinguisher (can be used on all types of home fires) that is large enough to put out a small fire, but not so heavy as to be difficult to handle. Choose a fire extinguisher that carries the label of an independent testing laboratory. Read the instructions that come with the fire extinguisher and become familiar with its parts and operation before a fire breaks out. Local fire departments or fire equipment distributors often offer hands-on fire extinguisher trainings. Install fire extinguishers close to an exit and keep your back to a clear exit when you use the device so you can make an easy escape if the fire cannot be controlled. If the room fills with smoke, leave immediately. Know when to go. Fire extinguishers are one element of a fire response plan, but the primary element is safe escape. Every household should have a home fire escape plan and working smoke alarms. Source: http://www.nfpa.org/safety-information/for-consumers/fire-and-safety-equipment/fire-extinguishers

No Smoke Detectors Observed in the Multi Unit Building
This is a known fire hazard. Most insurance companies require fire protection systems to be installed. Minimally, For NFPA new construction guidelines and as may be required by local codes; NFPA 30.3.4.5 Smoke Alarms. "Smoke alarms shall be installed in accordance with 9.6.2.10 in every sleeping area, outside every sleeping area in the immediate vicinity of the bedrooms, and on all levels of the dwelling unit, including basements." Recommend a licensed contractor asses the areas further and install per NFPA, state and local codes as needed.

No Smoke Detectors Observed within the Building
Per the NFPA, "In 2009-2013, smoke alarms sounded in more than half (53%) of the home fires reported to U.S. fire departments. Also, three of every five home fire deaths resulted from fires in homes with no smoke alarms (38%) or no working smoke alarms (21%). Finally, no smoke alarms were present in almost two out of every five (38%) home fire deaths." **Source:** NFPA's "Smoke Alarms in U.S. Home Fires" report, September 2015. Recommend installing smoke alarms in accordance with NFPA 72, by a licensed fire protection technician as is needed.

No Fire Extinguishers Observed In/On the Building at the Time of the Inspection
Per the NFPA, Published on August 22, 2012 "A portable fire extinguisher can save lives and property by putting out a small fire or containing it until the fire department arrives; but portable extinguishers have limitations. Because fire grows and spreads so rapidly, the number one priority for residents is to get out safely. Safety tips; 1. Use a portable fire extinguisher when the fire is confined to a small area, such as a wastebasket, and is not growing; everyone has exited the building; the fire department has been called or is being called; and the room is not filled with smoke. 2. To operate a fire extinguisher, remember the word PASS: **P**ull the pin. Hold the extinguisher with the nozzle pointing away from you, and release the locking mechanism. **A**im low. Point the extinguisher at the base of the fire. **S**queeze the lever slowly and evenly. **S**weep the nozzle from side-to-side.

For the home, select a multi-purpose extinguisher (can be used on all types of home fires) that is large enough to put out a small fire, but not so heavy as to be difficult to handle. Choose a fire extinguisher that carries the label of an independent testing laboratory. Read the instructions that come with the fire extinguisher and become familiar with its parts and operation before a fire breaks out. Local fire departments or fire equipment distributors often offer hands-on fire extinguisher trainings. Install fire extinguishers close to an exit and keep your back to a clear exit when you use the device so you can make an easy escape if the fire cannot be controlled. If the room fills with smoke, leave immediately. Know when to go. Fire extinguishers are one element of a fire response plan, but the primary element is safe escape. Every household should have a home fire escape plan and working smoke alarms. *NFPA does not test, label or approve any products." Source:* http://www.nfpa.org/safety-information/for-consumers/fire-and-safety-equipment/fire-extinguishers

No Carbon Monoxide Detectors Observed

Per the NFPA; "Although the popularity of carbon monoxide (CO) alarms has been growing in recent years, it cannot be assumed that everyone is familiar with the hazards of carbon monoxide poisoning in the home. Often called the invisible killer, carbon monoxide is an odorless, colorless gas created when fuels (such as gasoline, wood, coal, natural gas, propane, oil, and methane) burn incompletely. In the home, heating and cooking equipment that burn fuel are potential sources of carbon monoxide. Vehicles or generators running in an attached garage can also produce dangerous levels of carbon monoxide. **Facts and Figures:** The dangers of CO exposure depend on a number of variables, including the victim's health and activity level. Infants, pregnant women, and people with physical conditions that limit their body's ability to use oxygen (i.e. emphysema, asthma, heart disease) can be more severely affected by lower concentrations of CO than healthy adults would be. A person can be poisoned by a small amount of CO over a longer period of time or by a large amount of CO over a shorter amount of time. In 2010, U.S. fire departments responded to an estimated 80,100 non-fire CO incidents in which carbon monoxide was found, or an average of nine such calls per hour. The number of incidents increased 96 percent from 40,900 incidents reported in 2003. This increase is most likely due to the increased use of CO detectors, which alert people to the presence of CO." **Source:** Non-Fire Carbon Monoxide Incidents," by Ben Evarts, March 2012. **Related NFPA report** "Deaths and Injuries due to Non-Fire Exposure to Gases" report by John R. Hall, Jr., September 2013.

Recommend a licensed fire protection contractor assess the areas further and install as directed per the NFPA requirements.

Smoke Detectors were Antiquated and Inoperable within the Building

Per the NFPA, "In 2009-2013, smoke alarms sounded in more than half (53%) of the home fires reported to U.S. fire departments. Also, three of every five home fire deaths resulted from fires in homes with no smoke alarms (38%) or no working smoke alarms (21%). Finally, no smoke alarms were present in almost two out of every five (38%) home fire deaths." **Source:** NFPA's "Smoke Alarms in U.S. Home Fires" report, September 2015. Recommend installing smoke alarms in accordance with NFPA 72, by a licensed fire protection technician as is needed.

Insufficient Smoke Detectors Observed within the Building

Per the NFPA, "In 2009-2013, smoke alarms sounded in more than half (53%) of the home fires reported to U.S. fire departments. Also, three of every five home fire deaths resulted from fires in homes with no smoke alarms (38%) or no working smoke alarms (21%). Finally, no smoke alarms were present in almost two out of every five (38%) home fire deaths." **Source:** NFPA's "Smoke Alarms in U.S. Home Fires" report, September 2015. Recommend installing smoke alarms in accordance with NFPA 72, by a licensed fire protection technician as is needed.

Garage

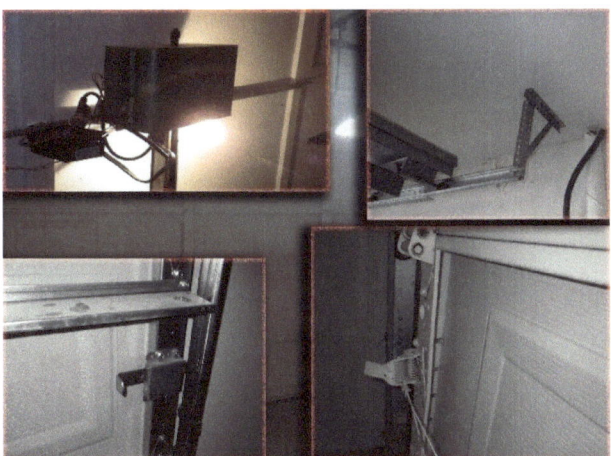

Concrete Slab; Cubicle/Moisture Cracking from Weathering Observed
The cracks appear to be from weathering of the concrete. Additionally, a bad concrete batch or too much water in the initial pouring, may have been applied. Cubicle and Web Cracks will form and progress many times in a web fashion if they and the concrete surrounding them are not treated. Where cracks are larger, expansion joint sealant is recommended. For cubicle cracking resulting in wide gaps of 1/8th inch or more, major repairs or complete replacement may be required. Recommend the use of concrete sealants NOT mortar/concrete unless recommended by a state licensed contractor. Recommend a licensed contractor assess the concrete further and repair all as needed.

Garage Door Buck, Wood Jams Lag Bolted to the Wall Improperly, Missing Fasteners at the Top
The wood buck is installed typically using lag bolts/screws intermittent in accordance with current code. The most common area where channeling/garage door tension occurs is at the top tension pulleys/torsion bars so fasteners for the wood bracing is vital at this location. Fasteners were observed missing at the time of the inspection. Recommend a licensed garage door service contractor assess the area further and repair as needed.

Automatic Door Torsion Spring is Broke, Visible on the Torsion Tube
Torsion spring appears compromised and will not lift the door. Recommend a licensed technician inspect and repair/replace the spring(s) as needed.

Sensor Guards Not Present on the Garage Door
Sensor guards are vital in residential buildings and buildings where small children, animals and elderly will be present. Sensor guards stop the door from closing and reverse the draw chain to lift the door, potentially saving the life and/or preventing injury. Recommend a state licensed technician repair as needed.

New Construction; Improper Ceiling Fastening Methodology Observed
Per the 2012 IRC "TABLE R702.3.5 MINIMUM THICKNESS AND APPLICATION OF GYPSUM BOARD Subsection e. Type X gypsum board for garage ceilings beneath habitable rooms shall be installed perpendicular to the ceiling framing and shall be fastened at maximum 6 inches o.c. by minimum 17/s inches 6d coated nails or equivalent drywall screws." Recommend a licensed drywall installation contractor assess the area further and repair as needed.

Moisture and Basic Settlement Cracks Suspected on the Ceiling at Tape Joints
The exterior and interior walls and ceilings undergo ebbs and flows of contraction and expansion every day. Depending on the space, the heat and humidity content, pressures, outside/inside humidity and amount of time enduring the conditions, buildings walls may crack just because of this expansion as well as from varying temperatures of neighboring components. This is called "thermal bridging" because in heat and/or humid

conditions, expansion generally occurs more, but at different rates for each component. Recommend a licensed contractor assess the area further and repair as needed.

Garage Door/Panel Observed with Suspected Vehicle Damage
Suspect vehicular damage. Door panel(s) were observed damaged. Recommend a licensed garage door repair and installation contractor assess the area further and repair as needed.

New Construction; Improper/Loose Ceiling Fasters/Tape Joints Observed
Per the 2012 IRC "TABLE R702.3.5 MINIMUM THICKNESS AND APPLICATION OF GYPSUM BOARD Subsection e. Type X gypsum board for garage ceilings beneath habitable rooms shall be installed perpendicular to the ceiling framing and shall be fastened at maximum 6 inches o.c. by minimum 17/s inches 6d coated nails or equivalent drywall screws." Loose ceiling boards can fall, causing serious injury or worse. Recommend a licensed drywall installation contractor assess the area further and repair as needed.

Ceiling Fastening Observed Loose
Due to garage interiors commonly being unconditioned and the attic spaces overhead, typically lack insulation. Thermal bridging, thermal expansion and moisture born corrosion can all play in causing ceiling gypsum/drywall tape joints to loosen and fasteners to corrode. Prior to 2000 roughly, buildings garage ceiling boards were fastened to the ceiling wood joists with nails. Unfortunately, nails due not provide the equivalent dead load capacity long term. Nails can corrode around their shafts, causing their ability to carry the load to diminish, ultimately loosening at the ceiling from moisture and heat exposure inducing expansion/retraction. Per the 2012 IRC "TABLE R702.3.5 MINIMUM THICKNESS AND APPLICATION OF GYPSUM BOARD Subsection e. Type X gypsum board for garage ceilings beneath habitable rooms shall be installed perpendicular to the ceiling framing and shall be fastened at maximum 6 inches o.c. by minimum 17/s inches 6d coated nails or equivalent drywall screws." Recommend a licensed drywall installation contractor assess the area further and repair as needed.

Center Crack in Poured Concrete. No Control Joints Observed
Common Hairline Cracks Observed. As natural settlement is replaced by artificial compounding of the excavated areas, it is more often after pouring, that the natural settlement occurs. This may have been exacerbated by vehicle loading. Additionally, there was no control joints observed in the garage. Sectioned control joints are longer than 10' feet in length before an expansion joint on the opposing horizontal/vertical lengths. Cracks will form where shrinkage occurs and settlement will usually exploit them. Filling cracks with an expansion joint sealant is recommended.

Common Cracks Observed in Garage Poured Concrete Slab
Common Hairline Cracks Observed. As natural settlement is replaced by artificial compounding of the excavated areas, it is more often after pouring, that the natural settlement occurs. This may have been exacerbated by vehicle loading as well as when the sectioned joints are longer than 10' feet in length before an expansion joint on the opposing horizontal/vertical lengths. Cracks will form where shrinkage occurs and settlement will usually exploit them. Filling cracks with an expansion joint sealant can reduce soil shift at the location.

Base Wall Seal Compromised; Foundation Protrudes Past Siding
It was not confirmed that there was any permitting for the renovation / installation, so it is not confirmed that proper flashing was used at the base of the wall. Framing of the enclosed area is not generally discernible as the material items are covered and may not have the structural support needed to sustain maximum wind load in the event of a high wind storm. Structural ties, wiring, flashing and vapor barriers are all covered, if present, behind the walls and cannot be determined. As long as the foundation or masonry skirting wall protrude beyond the exterior wall/siding you will have moisture wicking up. The paint and stucco sealant compromises are apparent and water is able to enter. This can/may be rotting the underlying wood. Even with a moisture breach, the protruding foundation might allow rain to splash up and keep the bottom of your cladding wet. Getting copper used to form gutters, a contractor may form a custom apron and counter flashing or better. If a pitch was added into the apron flashing, such as a 45 +/degree angle toward the base past the foundation extending several inches down the foundation face, like drip edge flashing at the base. Aluminum or copper will probably be best. Recommend a licensed contractor assess further and repair as needed/recommended to local/state codes.

Fireplaces

Backdraft
When a fire place or wood stove chimney is functioning normally, a hot fire initiates an updraft that forces the transfer of waste gases from the fire location, up through it. Those gasses then disperse into the outside air. At times, a draft can develop that moves in the downward direction, filling the house with smoke and noxious gases. Such a backdraft can result from a fire that is not burning hot enough. Because hot air rises, this results in zones of different pressures within a structure. The pressure is generally lower in cooler areas, typical in lower areas of the building and higher where warm air collects more abundant, typical to the highest points of the building. The pressure in the lower zones can be lower than atmospheric pressure, so if the fireplace or woodstove is located at one of these zones, the chimney may have a permanent downdraft and may require modification. Neutralize the air pressure by opening a window in the fireplace room to eliminate this backdraft. Obstructions in the chimney that restrict the flow of air can also prevent a proper updraft from forming. The result is the fire smolders and backdrafts smoke into the room. The obstructions can be caused by creosote build-up, indicating a chimney cleaning is needed. Backdrafts also occur when a chimney is too low. Larger flue size requires a taller chimney. Additionally, obstructions at the chimney opening such as overhanging branches or adjacent buildings can interfere with a proper updraft. The solution again is to raise the chimney. Additional issues may apply. Other possible conditions may be present. In all cases, it is recommended to have a licensed Chimney/Fireplace Service and Repair Contractor to repair all as needed BEFORE use, as backdrafts can be deadly.

Heavy Creosote Observed in the Flue
This is a common issue that occurs as a byproduct of burning wood, especially wet wood. Some of the byproduct adheres to the side walls of the flue, firebox, smoke chamber etc. This resin build up can cause ignition at the buildup and potentially cause a fire within the flue or worse. Recommend basic cleaning of the unit to prevent additional deficiencies. Recommend a licensed contractor assess the area further and service as needed.

Heavy Creosote Resin Observed in the Firebox, Flue and Smoke Chamber
This is a common issue that occurs as a byproduct of burning wood, especially wet wood. Some of the byproduct adheres to the side walls of the flue, firebox, smoke chamber etc. This resin build up can cause ignition at the buildup and potentially cause a fire within the flue or worse. Recommend basic cleaning of the unit to prevent additional deficiencies. Recommend a licensed contractor assess the area further and service as needed.

Refractory Panel has Observed Serviceable Hairline Cracks
Refractory panel(s) appears to have hairline crack(s). These are commonly caused by individuals unknowingly using the poker stick a bit too harshly, hitting the back or side panels repetitively. Over time, the repeated hits coupled with the heat of the fires may stress the panel at the hit site, causing hairline cracks. These cracks were

observed to be serviceable but should be monitored and all wood handling tools should be used with care. Cracks that exceed 1/16th inch or a dimes thickness should be considered irreparable and should be replaced.

Refractory Panel has Observed Cracks
Refractory panel(s) appears to have crack(s). These are commonly caused by individuals unknowingly using the poker stick a bit too harshly, hitting the back or side panels repetitively. Over time, the repeated hits coupled with the heat of the fires may stress the panel at the hit site, causing hairline cracks. These cracks were observed to be greater than a 1/16th of an inch. Cracks that exceed 1/16th inch or a dimes thickness should be considered irreparable and should be replaced. Recommend a licensed contractor specializing in fireplace and chimney repair, assess the area further and repair all as is needed.

Chimney Pointing Observed to be Eroding
Recommend a licensed chimney repair specialist, assess the area further and repoint as needed.

Refractory Brick in the Firebox Appears Loose, Points Damage Observed
Recommend a licensed fireplace and chimney repair contractor assess the area further and repair as is needed to defer potential embers from falling into the crevasses, causing an uncontrolled fire should the embers contact a combustible surface.

Efflorescence Observed in the Firebox
Efflorescence often occurs on masonry, particularly brick, when water moves through a wall and brings out salts to the surface that are not commonly bound as part of the concrete. As the water evaporates, the salts are left behind. The salts appear as white, fluffy deposits that can usually be simply brushed off by hand. The resulting white deposits are referred to as efflorescence. Efflorescence is sometimes referred to as salt-petering. Since primary efflorescence brings out salts that are not ordinarily part of the cement stone, it is not a structural concern but, rather, an aesthetic concern. For prefab chimneys and fireplaces, this is usually a flashing compromise of a sort. For masonry/brick chimneys, this can be indicative of water resistance failures within the exterior walls brick/sealer but may also be due to flashing compromises. Recommend a licensed chimney service and repair contractor assess the area further and repair as needed.

Chimney Flue Appeared Displaced at the Time of the Inspection
A loose flue can expel combustible gases and heat into areas not rated to handle such elements and can cause a fire or carbon monoxide to enter the home etc. In accordance with NFPA 31. 801.18.2; "Flue passageways. The flue gas passageway shall be free of obstructions and combustible deposits and shall be cleaned if previously used for venting a solid or liquid fuel-burning *appliance* or fireplace. The flue liner, *chimney* inner wall or vent inner wall shall be continuous and shall be free of cracks, gaps, perforations or other damage or deterioration which would allow the escape of *combustion* products, including gases, moisture and creosote." Recommend a licensed contractor assess the area further and repair all as needed.

Masonry Chimney Airspace Clearance/Fire Protection. No Liner Observed
As per the NFPA; 801.13. 801.18.4 Clearances. Chimneys and vents shall have airspace clearance to combustibles in accordance with the International Building Code and the chimney or vent manufacturer's installation instructions. Exception: Masonry chimneys without the required airspace clearances shall be permitted to be used if lined or relined with a chimney lining system listed for use in chimneys with reduced clearances in accordance with UL 1777. The chimney clearance shall be not less than permitted by the terms of the chimney liner listing and the manufacturer's instructions.

Chimney and Fireplace Appear to have Extensive Ware
Recommend replacing or rebuilding the fireplace to meet current code. Repair/Replace per State/Local codes and the NFPA; "801.18 Existing chimneys and vents. Where an *appliance* is permanently disconnected from an existing *chimney* or vent, or where an *appliance* is connected to an existing *chimney* or vent during the process of a new installation, the *chimney* or vent shall comply with Sections 801.18.1 through 801.18.4. 801.18.1 Size. The *chimney* or vent shall be resized as necessary to control flue gas condensation in the interior of the *chimney* or vent and to provide the *appliance* or *appliances* served with the required draft. For the venting of oil-fired *appliances* to masonry chimneys, the resizing shall be in accordance with NFPA 31. 801.18.2 Flue passageways. The flue gas passageway shall be free of obstructions and combustible deposits and shall be cleaned if previously used for venting a solid or liquid fuel-burning *appliance* or fireplace. The flue liner, *chimney* inner wall or vent inner wall shall be continuous and shall be free of cracks, gaps, perforations or other damage or deterioration which would allow the escape of *combustion* products, including gases, moisture and creosote. Where an oil-fired *appliance* is connected to an existing masonry *chimney*, such *chimney* flue shall be repaired

or relined in accordance with NFPA 31. 801.18.3 Cleanout. Masonry chimneys shall be provided with a cleanout opening complying with Section 801.13. 801.18.4 Clearances. Chimneys and vents shall have airspace *clearance* to combustibles in accordance with the *International Building Code* and the *chimney* or vent manufacturer's installation instructions. Exception: Masonry chimneys without the required airspace *clearances* shall be permitted to be used if lined or relined with a *chimney* lining system *listed* for use in chimneys with reduced *clearances* in accordance with UL 1777. The *chimney clearance* shall be not less than permitted by the terms of the *chimney* liner listing and the manufacturer's instructions. 801.18.4.1 Fire blocking. Noncombustible fire blocking shall be provided in accordance with the International Building Code.*" SOURCE: International Mechanical Code.*

Chimney Cap appears Loose
Recommend a licensed building contractor assess the area further and refasten as is needed.

Chimney Suspected to Terminate too Close to the Roof/Slope
A variation on a "too short" metal or masonry chimney is a chimney that may loot tall enough to some folks but which lacks the adequate clearance from the roof top, a neighboring wall of an additional elevation to the building, from a neighboring roof slope etc. As per the ICC; "2113.9 Termination. Chimneys shall extend at least 2 feet (610 mm) higher than any portion of the building within 10 feet (3048 mm), but shall not be less than 3 feet (914 mm) above the highest point where the chimney passes through the roof." "More restrictive termination requirements are specified for medium and high-heat appliances." For a picture reference, see "Figure 2113.9 MINIMUM TERMINATION OF CHIMNEYS". Recommend a licensed contractor assess the area in depth and repair all as needed to code standards.

Masonry Chimney Liner Was Not Observed at the Time of the Inspection
The chimney liner forms the flue sleeve or passageway. The liner is the conduit for all combustion gases and particulates to escape the home. The liner is required per code, to withstand high temperatures and corrosive chemicals. It also acts as a protection for the masonry chimney walls and allows the chimney to properly vent the gases from the building. A mismatch between the type of flue liner and the type of chimney can result in a hazardous operating condition. Per the ICC/International Code Council; "2113.11 Flue lining (material). Masonry chimneys shall be lined. The lining material shall be appropriate for the type of appliance connected, according to the terms of the appliance listing and the manufacturer's instructions." Recommend a licensed contractor assess the area in depth and repair all as needed.

Masonry Chimney Liner was Observed Heavily Corroded at the Time of the Inspection
The chimney liner forms the flue sleeve or passageway. The liner is the conduit for all combustion gases and particulates to escape the home. The liner is required per code, to withstand high temperatures and corrosive chemicals. It also acts as a protection for the masonry chimney walls and allows the chimney to properly vent the gases from the building. Under the present condition, using the fire place may result in a hazardous operating condition. Per the ICC/International Code Council; "2113.11 Flue lining (material). Masonry chimneys shall be lined. The lining material shall be appropriate for the type of appliance connected, according to the terms of the appliance listing and the manufacturer's instructions." Recommend a licensed contractor assess the area in depth and repair all as needed.

Exhaust

Dryer Vent Not Observed at the Exterior/Roof of the Building
No dryer vent was readily observable at the time of the inspection. Per the ICC; "M1502.3 Duct termination. Exhaust ducts shall terminate on the outside of the building. Exhaust duct terminations shall be in accordance with the dryer manufacturer's installation instructions. If the manufacturer's instructions do not specify a termination location, the exhaust duct shall terminate not less than 3 feet (914 mm) in any direction from openings into buildings. Exhaust duct terminations shall be equipped with a backdraft damper. Screens shall not be installed at the duct termination." Recommend a licensed contractor asses the area further and repair if needed.

References

ICC (International Code Council);
IMC, International Mechanical Code 2009-2015
IPC, International Plumbing Code 2009-2015
NFPA, National Fire Protection Agency 2002-2013
NEC, National Electric Code 2005-2015
NIH, National Institute of Health
EPA, Environmental Protection Agency
Wikipedia
Webster's Dictionary
Inspectapedia.com
InterNACHI, International Association of Certified Home Inspectors
ACI, American Concrete Institute
Gypsum Association

Daniel Zevetchin References

- Field Inspector since 1998
- Licensed through the International Association of Certified Home Inspectors since 2008
- FL Licensed Home Inspector since 2010
- FL Licensed All Lines Adjuster since 2013
- Sponsored for Residential/Building Contractors license 2008